A COMMENTARY
ON THE BOOK OF
LEVITICUS

A COMMENTARY ON THE BOOK OF LEVITICUS

ANDREW BONAR

BAKER BOOK HOUSE
Grand Rapids, Michigan

Reprinted 1978 by Baker Book House
from the edition issued in 1852
by James Nisbet and Company

ISBN: 0-8010-0730-5

First printing, June 1978
Second printing, April 1979

PREFACE

Some years ago, while perusing the Book of Leviticus in the course of his daily study of the Scriptures, the author was arrested amid the shadows of a past dispensation, and led to write short notes as he went along. Not long after, another perusal of this inspired book—conducted in a similar way, and with much prayer for the teaching of the Spirit of truth—refreshed his own soul yet more, and led him on to inquire what others had gleaned in the same field. Some friends who, in this age of activity and bustle, find time to delight themselves in the law of the Lord, saw the notes, and urged their publication.

There are few critical difficulties in the book; its chief obscurity arises from its enigmatical ceremonies. The author fears he may not always have succeeded in discovering the precise view of truth intended to be exhibited in these symbolic rites; but he has made the attempt, not thinking it irreverent to examine both sides of the veil, now that it has been rent. The Holy Spirit surely wishes us to inquire into what He has written; and the unhealthy tone of many true Christians may be accounted for by the too plain fact that they do not meditate much on the whole counsel of God. Experience, as well as the Word itself (Ps. i. 2, 3), might lead us to value very highly the habit of deeply pondering the discoveries of the mind of God given in all parts of Scripture, even the darkest.

Throughout this Commentary, the truth that saves, and the truth that sanctifies, is set before the reader in a variety of aspects, according as each typical rite seemed to suggest. It may thus be useful to all classes of persons. And what, if even some of the house of Israel may have their eye attracted to the Saviour, while giving heed to the signification of those ceremonies which to their fathers were sign-posts (אותות, Ps. lxxiv. 9) in the way of life?

COLLACE, *May* 5, 1846.

PREFACE TO THE THIRD EDITION

A FEW corrections have been made, and a few additional remarks introduced, in this edition. The subjects of the Book of Scripture briefly expounded in these pages are all of a vital nature, though the form in which they were presented by Moses is obsolete. A writer of the middle ages, Hildebert, suggests much by these few lines:

> " Quis locus Auroræ postquam Sol venit ad ortum ?
> Quisne locus votis teneat cum navita portum ?
> Lex Aurora fuit; bos et capra vota fuere;
> *Crux* Sol, *Crux* portus. Hæc omnia præteriere.
> *Crux* clausit templum, *Crux* solvit ænigmata legis.
> Sub *Cruce* cessat ephod, et deficit unctio regis."

CONTENTS

COMMENTARY ON LEVITICUS

THE NATURE OF THE BOOK

THERE is no book, in the whole compass of that inspired Volume which the Holy Ghost has given us, that contains more of the very words of God than *Leviticus*. It is God that is the direct speaker in almost every page; his gracious words are recorded in the form wherein they were uttered. This consideration cannot fail to send us to the study of it with singular interest and attention.

It has been called "*Leviticus*," because its typical institutions, in all their variety, were committed to the care of *the tribe of Levi*, or to the priests, who were of that tribe. The Greek translators of the Pentateuch devised that name. The Talmud, for similar reasons, calls it תּוֹרַת הַכֹּהֲנִים, "the law of the priests." But Jewish writers in general are content with a simpler title; they take the first words of the book as the name, calling it וַיִּקְרָא, "Vayikra," *q. d.* the book that begins with the words, "And the Lord called."

It carries within itself the seal of its Divine origin. As an internal proof of its author being Divine, some have been content to allege the prophecy contained in chap. xxvi., the fulfilment of which is spread before the eyes of all the earth. But if, in addition to this, we find every chapter throughout presenting views of doctrine and practice that exactly dovetail into the unfigurative statements of the New Testament, surely we shall then acknowledge that it bears the impress of the Divine mind from beginning to end.

The Gospel of the grace of God, with all that follows in its train, may be found in Leviticus. This is the glorious attraction of the book to every reader who feels himself a sinner. The New Testament has about forty references to its various ordinances.

The rites here detailed were typical; and every type was designed and intended by God to bear resemblance to some spiritual truth. The likeness between type and antitype is never accidental. The very excellency of these rites consists in their being chosen by God for the end of shadowing forth "good things to come" (Heb. x. 1). As it is not a mere accidental resemblance to the Lord's body and blood that obtains in the bread and wine used in the Lord's supper, but on the contrary, a likeness that made the symbols suitable to be selected for that end; so is it in the case of every Levitical type. Much of our satisfaction and edification in tracing the correspondence between type and antitype will depend on the firmness with which we hold this principle.

If it be asked why a typical mode of shewing forth truth was adopted to such an extent in those early days, it may be difficult to give a precise answer. It is plain, such a method of instruction may answer many purposes.

It may not only meet the end of simplifying the truth, it may also open the mind to comprehend more, while it deepens present impressions of things known. The existence of a type does not always argue that the thing typified is obscurely seen, or imperfectly known. On the contrary, there was a type in the garden of Eden—the tree of life,—while life, in all its meaning, was fully comprehended by Adam. In all probability, there will be typical objects in the millennial age; for there is to be a river which shall flow from Jerusalem to water the valley of Shittim (Joel iii. 18), the same of which Ezekiel (xlvii. 1) and Zechariah (xiv. 8) speak. This river is said to be for the healing of the Dead Sea, while on its banks grow majestic trees, whose leaves are for the healing of the nations. No doubt a spiritual significance lies hid in these visible signs; the visible symbol seems to be a broad seal and sign of the peculiar truth manifested in these days, viz. the overflowing stream of the Holy Spirit (who shall be poured out at Jerusalem on the house of David first), winding its course over earth to convey saving health to all nations. Certain it is that types do not necessarily imply that the antitype is dimly known. The Lord may use them as he uses Gospel ordinances at present, to convey light to us, and leave more indelible impressions. A German writer (Hahn) has said, "Types were institutions intended to deepen, expand, and ennoble the circle of thoughts and desires, and thus heighten the moral and spiritual wants, as well as the intelligence and susceptibility of the chosen people."* And not less truly is this point touched upon by the Reformer Tyndale, in

---

* Southey says of Laud: "He began his dying address in that state of *calm but deepest feeling*, when the mind seeks for fancies, types, and dim similitudes, and extracts from them consolation and strength."—(*Book of the Church.*)

his *Prologue into the Third Book of Moses :*—"Though sacrifices and ceremonies can be no ground or foundation to build upon—that is, though we can prove nought with them—yet, when we have once found out Christ and his mysteries, then we may borrow figures, that is to say, allegories, similitudes, and examples, *to open Christ, and the secrets of God hid in Christ, even unto the quick;* and can declare them more lively and sensibly with them than with all the words of the world. For similitudes have more virtue and power with them than bare words, and lead a man's understanding further into the pith and marrow and spiritual understanding of the thing, than all the words that can be imagined." Again he says, "Allegories *prove* nothing; but the very use of allegories is to declare and open a text, that it may be better perceived and understood. . . . . There is not a better, more vehement, or mightier thing to make a man understand withal, than an allegory. For allegories make a man quick-witted, and print wisdom in him, and make it to abide, when bare words go but in at the one ear and out at the other."

The Epistle to the Hebrews lays down the principles upon which we are to interpret Leviticus. The specimens there given of types applied furnish a model for our guidance in other cases ; and the writer's manner of address in that Epistle leads us to suppose that it was no new thing for an Israelite thus to understand the ritual of Moses. No doubt old Simeon (Luke ii. 25) frequented the temple daily in order to read in its rites the future development of a suffering Saviour, as well as to pray and worship. Anna the prophetess did the same; for all these knew that they prophesied of the grace that was to come to us, and therefore inquired and searched diligently (1 Pet. i. 10). Had Aaron, or some other holy priest of his line, been "carried away in the spirit," and shewn the accomplishment of all that these rites pre-figured, how joyful ever after would have been his daily service in the sanctuary! When shewn the great Antitype, and that each one of these shadows pictured something in the person or work of that Redeemer, then, ever after, to handle the vessels of the sanctuary would be rich food to his soul. It would be "feeding beside the still waters, and in green pastures." For the bondage of these elements did not consist in sprinkling the blood, washing in the laver, waving the wave-shoulder, or the like; but in doing all this without perceiving the truth thereby exhibited. Probably to a true Israelite, taught of God, there would be no more of bondage in handling these material ele-ments, than there is at this day to a true believer in handling the symbolic bread and wine through which he " discerns the body and blood of the Lord." It would be an Israelite's hope every morning, as he left the "dwell-ings of Jacob," to see "in the gates of Zion," more of the Lamb of God, while gazing on the morning sacrifice. " I will compass thine altar, O Lord, that I may publish with the voice of thanksgiving, and tell of all thy wondrous works" (Ps. xxvi. 6, 7). And, as the sun declined, he would seek to have his soul again anointed, after a busy day's vexations, by beholding the evening lamb.

Tyndale says, that while there is " a star-light of Christ" in all the ceremonies, there is in some so truly " the light of the broad day," that he cannot but believe that God had shewed Moses the secrets of Christ and the very manner of his death beforehand. At all events, it was what they did see of Christ through this medium that so endeared to them the tabernacle and temple-courts. It was the very home of their souls. " How amiable are thy tabernacles, O Lord of hosts! My soul longeth, yea, even fainteth for the courts of the Lord!" (Ps. lxxxiv. 1, 2.) And it is thus we can understand how those thousands (or rather, tens of thousands) who believed were all "zealous of the law" (Acts xxi. 20). The Christian elders of Jerusalem, including James and other apostles, lent their sanction to their zeal in some degree; and Paul himself saw nothing necessarily sinful in it. For it was all well, if they used the law only as "their schoolmaster to bring them to Christ" (Gal. iii. 24). It must have been thus that Paul himself employed his thoughts while "purifying himself" in the temple, and engaging in the other ordinances regarding vows (Acts xxi. 26). His thoughts would be on the Antitype; and possibly the actual performing of these rites by a fully enlightened soul might lead to some distinct views of truth contained in them, which would have escaped the observation of a mere spectator. And, if we may throw out a conjecture on a subject where Millennarians and Anti-millennarians are alike at sea—is it not possible that some such end as this may be answered by the temple which Ezekiel foretells as yet to be built? (chap. xl., &c.) Believing nations may frequent that temple in order to get understanding in these types and shadows. They may go up to the mountain of the Lord's house, to be there taught his ways (Isa. ii. 3). In that temple they may learn how not one tittle of the law has failed. As they look on the sons of Zadok ministering in that peculiar sanctuary, they may learn portions of truth with new impressiveness and fulness. Indeed, the very fact that the order of arrangement in Ezekiel entirely differs from the order observed in either tabernacle or temple, and that the edifice itself is reared on a plan varying from every former sanctuary, is sufficient to suggest the idea that it is meant to cast light on former types and shadows. Many Levitical rites appear to us unmeaning ; but they would not do so if presented in a new relation. As it is said of the rigid features of a marble statue, that they may be made to move and vary their expression so as even to smile, when a skilful hand knows how to move a bright light before it ; so may it be with these apparently lifeless figures, in the light of that bright millennial day. At all events, it is probably then that this much-neglected book of Leviticus shall be fully appreciated. Israel—the good olive-tree—shall again yield its fatness to the nations round (Rom. xi. 17). Their ancient ritual may then be more fully understood, and blessed truth found beaming forth from long obscurity. When Jesus, the High Priest, comes forth from the Holiest, there may be here fountains of living water to which he shall lead us—Himself seen to be the glorious Antitype, the Alpha and the Omega !

But let us proceed to the contents of this book. It will be found that it contains a full system of truth, exhibiting sin and the sinner, grace and the Saviour, comprehending, also, details of duty, and openings into the ages to come — whatever, in short, bears upon a sinner's walk with a reconciled God, and his conversation in this present evil world. Our heavenly Father has condescended to teach his children by most expressive pictures ; and, even in this, much of his love appears.

The one great principle of interpretation which we keep before us, is apostolic practice. This is the key we have used. We find the sacred writers adduce the likeness that exists between the thing that was typified and the type itself, and resting satisfied there. So we lay down this as our great rule,—there must be obvious resemblance. And next, we search into these types, in the belief that Christ is the centre-truth of Revelation; and surely no principle is more obviously true? The body or substance of the law is Christ (Col. ii. 17), and types are a series of shadows projected from Christ "the body." It is this Messiah that has been, from the beginning, the chief object to be unveiled to the view of men; and in the fact that New Testament light has risen, lies our advantage in searching what these things signify. Mr M'Cheyne, of Dundee, thus expressed himself, on one occasion, regarding this point, in a letter to a friend:— "Suppose," said he, "that one to whom you were a stranger was wrapt in a thick veil, so that you could not discern his features; still, if the lineaments were pointed out to you through the folds, you could form some idea of the beauty and form of the veiled one. But suppose that one whom you know and love—whose features you have often studied face to face—were to be veiled up in this way, how easily you would discern the features and form of this beloved one! Just so, *the Jews* looked upon a veiled Saviour, whom they had never seen unveiled. *We*, under the New Testament, look upon an unveiled Saviour; and, going back on the Old, we can see, far better than the Jews could, the features and form of Jesus the Beloved, under that veil. . In Isaac offered (Gen. xxii.), in the scape-goat (Lev. xvi.), in the shadow of the great rock (Isa. xxxii. 2), in the apple-tree (Song ii. 2), what exquisite pictures there are seen of Jesus! and how much more plainly we can see the meaning than believers of old!" To the same purpose John Bunyan writes. He represents Mansoul, in his *Holy War*, as feasting at the Prince's table, and then getting riddles set before them. "These riddles were made upon the King

Shaddai, and Immanuel his son, and upon his wars and doings with Mansoul. . . . . And when they read in the scheme where the riddles were writ, and *looked in the face of the Prince*, things looked so like, the one to the other, that Mansoul could not forbear but say, ' *This* is *the Lamb! This* is *the Sacrifice! This* is *the Rock! This* is the *Red Cow! This* is *the Door!* and *This* is *the Way!*' "

The space of a month was occupied in delivering the various ordinances of this book to Moses. This is proved from Exod. xl. 17, compared with Numb. i. 1. It is the revelations of that one memorable month that are now to form the subject of our study. Witsius (*De Mysterio Tab.*) has remarked, that God took only six days to creation, but spent forty days with Moses in directing him to make the tabernacle —because the *work of grace* is more glorious than the work of creation. And so we find *the law* from Sinai occupying three days at most, while these rules that exhibited the love and grace of God are spread over many weeks.

CHAPTER I

The Burnt-Offering

"Behold the Lamb of God, which taketh away the sin of the world!"—
John i. 29

THE TABERNACLE was that tent whose two apartments, separated by the veil, formed the *Holy Place*, and the *Most Holy*. This "tabernacle" was God's dwelling-place on earth; where he met with men,—the token of his returning to man after the fall. It was here that "the voice of the Lord God" was often heard, as in Eden, in the cool of the day.

> Ver. 1. *And the Lord called unto Moses, and spake unto him out of the tabernacle of the congregation, saying,*—

The cloud that guided Israel* had descended on the tabernacle; and while this pillar stood over it, the glory of the Lord filled the Holy of holies within (Exod. xl. 34). Rays of this glory were streaming out all around, perhaps like the light that shone from Christ's form " on the holy mount," through his raiment, till the whole hill shone. Out of the midst of this " excellent glory" (2 Pet. i. 17) came the voice of the Lord. He called on Moses as at the bush; and having fixed the undivided

---

* In Exod. xl. 34–38, we have the general history of this cloud; not the narrative of its motions on a particular occasion.

attention of Moses on him that spake, Jehovah utters his
mind.   What love is here!   The heart of our God, in
the midst of all his own joy, yearning to pour itself out
to man!

The date of these laws is probably a few days after
the tabernacle had been set up.   They are given not from
Sinai, though at its foot (see chap. xxvii. 34); but from
over the mercy-seat, from between the cherubim, where
the glory had so lately found a resting-place.   Perhaps
this intimated that all these institutions about to be
given bear on the same great subject, viz. *Atonement
and its effects.*   Sinai and its law a few weeks before,
with the dark apostasy in the matter of the golden calf,
had lately taught them the necessity of reconciliation,
and made their conscience thirst for that living water.
And it is given here.   The first clause of this book
declares a reconciled God—" *The Lord called to Moses,*"
as a man to his friend.

> Ver. 2. *Speak unto the children of Israel, and say unto them, If
> any man of you bring an offering unto the Lord, ye shall bring
> your offering* * *of the cattle, even of the herd and of the flock.*

When the Lord said, "*Speak to the children of Israel,*"
instead of himself addressing them, it taught the people
their need of a Mediator.   It was as if he had said,
These things are addressed to sinners who cannot see my
face or hear my voice, except through a daysman.

The offerings first spoken of are those that are to be
wholly consumed—types of complete exhaustion of wrath.
In these cases, everything about the animal was consumed,
sinews, horns, bones, hoof, the wool on the sheep's head,
and the hair on the goat's beard—(Willet).   Hence they

---

* The Septuagint render this " προσοισετε τα δωρα ὑμῶν."   Hence, perhaps, Heb. viii. 3, " gifts and sacrifices."

were called *whole burnt-offerings* (ὁλοκαυτώματα). God prescribes the symbols of atonement, even as he fixed on the ransom itself. It is a sovereign God that sinners are dealing with ; and in so doing, he fixed on the *herd and the flock*, as the only class of cattle (בְּהֵמָה), or four-footed beasts, that he would accept. If we are to inquire into a reason for this beyond his mere sovereignty, there are two that readily present themselves as every way probable. First, oxen, sheep, and goats (the herd and flock) are easily got by men, being at their hand. He did not wish to make them go in pursuit of beasts for offering, for salvation is brought to our hand by our God. Second, the characteristics of these animals fit them to be convenient types of various truths relating to sacrifice. The ox taken from feeding by the river-side, or the sheep from its quiet pastures,—perhaps from among the lilies of Sharon,—was an emblem of the Redeemer leaving the joy and blessedness of his Father's presence, where he had been ever " by the streams that make glad the city of God." Another reason has been assigned,* viz. all these were *horned* animals. Whether in the East such were reckoned more valuable than other animals we cannot say. It is, at least, worthy of notice, that the horn, which is the symbol of power and honour, is found in them all.

> Ver. 3. *If his offering be a burnt-sacrifice of the herd, let him offer a male without blemish: he shall offer it of his own voluntary will, at the door of the tabernacle of the congregation, before the Lord.*

" A male," representing the second Adam, "without blemish." Christ, by his one offering, makes his Church spotless (Eph. v. 27), and, therefore, he was to be so

* See Guild's *Moses Unveiled.*

himself. Of course, therefore, the type of him must be so. In the peace-offerings it was different: for these typified rather *the effects* of Christ's atonement on the receiver than *himself atoning;* and the animal, in that case, might have some defect or blemish, even as *the effects* of his work may be imperfectly experienced by the sinner, though the work itself is perfect. But whatever speaks of Christ himself must speak of perfection. *"Before the Lord"* is an expression ever recurring: it is remarkable that it should occur so often. But perhaps it was because the Lord meant thus to insert a Divine safeguard against the Socinian idea, that sacrifice chiefly had reference *to the offerer*, not *to God.* Every sacrifice is brought before "the great Inhabitant of the sanctuary." So also this expression guards us against Popish error, as if ministers of Christ are priests in the same sense as the line of Aaron. No; ministers of Christ *approach men* in behalf of God, who sends them as ambassadors, but these priests *approached God* in behalf of guilty men. *"He shall offer it of his own voluntary will."** The Gospel warrant is, "Whosoever will, let him come." There must be a willing soul; none but a soul made willing in the day of his power pays any regard to atonement. The Lord allows *all that are willing*, to come to the atoning provision. "Are you *thirsty* for the living God? for yonder altar's sacrifice?" might some son of Aaron say to a fearful soul. The fearful conscience replies, "I cannot well tell if I be really *thirsty* for him." "But are you, then, *willing* to go to yonder altar?" "Yes, I am." "Then you may come; for

---

* Some translate this, "*He shall offer it in order to be accepted.*" I do not think this meaning can be proved to be the true one, although the Septuagint generally renders the expression, "δεκτον έναντι Κύριου;" and the Oxford MS. here has, "δεκτον αὐτῷ ἐξιλασθαι ἐναντι Κυριου."

read Leviticus i. 3, and see that it is neither riches nor poverty, moral attainment nor deep experience, but simply a conscience willing to be bathed in atonement, that is spoken of by the God of Israel."

Come then with the sacrifice to *"the door of the tabernacle."* The *altar* was near the door of the tabernacle; it faced it. It was the first object that met the eye of a worshipper coming in. The priest met him there, and led the offerer with his sacrifice on to the altar. The presenting any sacrifice there was a type of the worshipper's object being to get admission into the presence of God by entrance at that door ("access," Eph. ii. 18). Thus the offerer walked silently and with holy awe to the door of the tabernacle, and there met his God.

As a type of Christ, it would declare Christ's willing offering of himself—" Lo, I come; " and how he was, in the fulness of time, led silently as a lamb to the slaughter. For we are to distinguish between the presentation of Christ *before* he went forth, and the presentation of himself *after* all was done.

> Ver. 4. *And he shall put his hand upon the head of the burnt-offering; and it shall be accepted for him, to make atonement for him.*

This action of the offerer gives us a view of *faith*. The offerer puts his hand on the same head whereon the Lord's hand was laid, and thereby agrees to all that is implied in his choosing that offering. God and the believing soul meet at the same point, and are satisfied by the same display of the Divine attributes.—" *He shall put his hand.*"* It is yet more forcible in the

* We make no reference, here nor elsewhere, to Jewish traditions as to the manner in which the thing was done, and the words used. It is strange that Ainsworth, Patrick, Outram, and others, should waste so much time in this

Hebrew—"He shall *lean* his hand" (וְסָמַךְ), the very word used in Psalm lxxxviii. 7, "Thy wrath leaneth hard upon me." We lean our soul on the same person on whom Jehovah leant his wrath.

When the worshipper had thus simply left his sins, conveyed by the laying on of his hand upon the sacrifice, he stands aside. This is all his part. The treatment of the victim is the Lord's part. The happy Israelite who saw this truth might go home, saying, "I have put my hand on its head; it shall be accepted as an atonement." Faith in the Lord's testimony was the ground of an Israelite's peace of conscience,—nothing of it rested on his own frame of mind, character, or conduct.

> Ver. 5. *And he shall kill the bullock before the Lord; and the priests, Aaron's sons, shall bring the blood, and sprinkle the blood round about upon the altar that is by the door of the tabernacle of the congregation.*

It is interesting to notice here, that Outram, Witsius, and others, seem to have proved that, in patriarchal ages, every man might offer his own sacrifice. Heads of families, and heads of a tribe or nation, often acted for those under them; but the idea that the *first-born* were the *only* priests is without foundation. The patriarchal age was taught that every man must take Christ for himself personally. In the Mosaic economy, however, this is altered. There is another truth to be shewn forth. Any one (2 Chron. xxx. 17) might kill the animal—any common Levite, or even the offerer himself —for there may be many executioners of God's wrath. Earth and hell were used in executing the Father's pur-

department. Are these traditions anything more than human fancy—often, too, of a somewhat modern date? Augustine judged well when he said, " *Quid scriptura voluerit, non quod illi opinati fuerint, inquirendum.*"

pose toward the Prince of Life. But there is only one appointed way for dispensing mercy; and therefore only priests must engage in the act that signified the bestowal of pardon.

The animal is "killed" in the presence of the Lord. And now, what an awfully solemn sight! The priest "*brings forward the blood.*" As he bears it onward, in one of the bowls of the altar, all gaze upon the warm crimson blood! *It is the life!* So that when the blood is thus brought forward, the *life* of the sacrifice is brought before God! It is as if the living soul of the sinner were carried, in its utter helplessness and in all its filthiness, and laid down before the Holy One!

The blood was then "*sprinkled round about upon the altar.*" The life being taken away, the sinner's naked soul is exhibited! He deserves this stroke of death— death in the Lord's presence, as a satisfaction to his holiness! As the blood that covered the door on the night of the Passover represented the inmates' life as already taken, so the blood on the altar and its sides signified that the offerer's life was forfeited and taken. It was thus that Jesus "poured out his soul unto death" for us.

It was, further, "*round about,*" as well as "upon," the altar. This held it up on all sides to view; and the voice from the altar now is, "Look unto me, and be ye saved, all the ends of the earth." All within the camp might look and live; for this sacrifice represents Christ's dying as the only way for any, and the sufficient way for all.

The altar mentioned here was the "*altar of brass;*" not the "*golden* altar," which stood in the Holy Place.*

Ver. 6. *And he shall flay the burnt-offering, and cut it into his pieces.*

* See some remarks on *the brass* of this altar in a note, chap. xiv. 5.

Here, again, any one might act, as well as the priest;
for any of God's creatures may be the executioners of his
wrath. "*He shall flay.*"—The skin torn from off the
slain animal may intimate the complete exposure of the
victim, uncovered, and laid open to the piercing eye of
the beholder. But specially, it seems to shew that there
is no covering of inherent righteousness on the person of
the sinner. While the skin was unwounded, the inward
parts were safe from the knife; thus, so long as man had
personal *righteousness interposing*, no knife could pierce
his soul. But the taking away of the victim's skin
shewed that the sinner had no such protection in God's
view; even as the bringing of such skins to Adam and
Eve, after the fall, shewed that God saw them destitute
of every covering, and had, in his mercy, provided clothing for them by means of sacrifice.

The "*cutting it into pieces*" would at last leave the
sacrifice a mangled mass of flesh and bones. Entire dislocation of every joint, and separation of every limb and
member, was the process. By this the excruciating torment due to the sinner seems signified. God's sword—
his Abraham's knife—spares not the sacrifice; but uses
its sharpness and strength to pierce and destroy to the
uttermost. The slashing sword of wrath leaves nothing
to the guilty; but, as "one woe is past, behold, another
woe cometh quickly." Yet it is "*into his pieces.*"
There was an order observed—a regularity and deliberate systematic procedure. So will it be in the damna-
tion of hell; every pang will be weighed by perfect holiness, every stroke deliberated upon ere it is inflicted.
And, in truth, this deliberate infliction is the most awful
feature of justice. It leaves the sufferer hopeless. The
stroke is awfully relentless, determined, righteous! Such,

too, were the Saviour's sufferings. Every part and pore
of his frame was thus mangled ; every member of his
body, every feeling of his soul. There was not an action
of his life, or desire in his heart, but was combined with
woe ; and all so just, that from the cross he lifts his
eyes to his Father, and looking on him as he had ever
done, cries, " But thou art holy !" (Ps. xxii. 3.)

Ver. 7. *And the sons* of Aaron the priest shall put fire upon
the altar, and lay the wood in order upon the fire.*

This verse is well illustrated by Heb. ix. 14, " Who,
through the eternal Spirit, offered himself without spot
to God." Christ was prepared, in his human nature, by
the Holy Spirit. The Father prepared the fire of wrath,
filled the vial with that wrath, and then poured it out.
The Holy Spirit, as Heb. ix. 14 declares, set all things in
order, in Christ's human nature, ready for the vial being
poured out. At the moment when the fire came down
and consumed him, love to God and man was at its
highest pitch in his soul—obedience, holy regard for the
Divine law, hatred of sin, love to man.

The wood, taken by itself, is not a type of anything ;
but it must be taken thus :—the *laying the wood in
order preparatory to the fire coming.* In this view it
represents what we have just said.

The fire was from that *fire* which descended from the
cloudy pillar. It was, therefore, divinely intended to
shew " *the wrath of God revealed from heaven*" against
all ungodliness of men. Indeed, the fire from the bosom
of that cloud was no less than a type of *wrath from the*

* We sometimes see mistakes committed in representations of tabernacle
scenes. *Levites* are made to act as priests, and *Levites* are exhibited blowing
the silver trumpets. But all this was the duty of *Aaron's sons alone.* True ;
they were Levites, but they were the priestly family among the Levites. Priests
are Levites, but all Levites are not priests.

bosom of God against him who lay in his bosom (see chap. vi. 9, and ix. 24).

> Ver. 8. *And the priests, Aaron's sons, shall lay the parts, the head, and the fat, in order upon the wood that is on the fire which is upon the altar.*

The *fat* did, of course, help the flame to consume the *head*, notwithstanding the gushing stream of blood. But what is the type? *The head* was that whereon the offerer leant his hand, conveying to it his load of guilt. *The fat* (פָּדֶר) is a word that occurs only thrice, viz. here, and ver. 12, and chap. viii. 20. Some understand it to be the *midriff*; others, the fat separated from the rest of the flesh; but there is no way of arriving at the certain import. The type, however, is obvious. The *head* and this *fat* are two pieces—one *outward*, the other *inward*; thus representing the whole *inner and outer man*. Christ's whole manhood, *body and soul*, was placed on the altar, in the fire, and endured the wrath of God. There could be no type of his *soul* otherwise than by selecting some inward part to signify it; and that is done here by the "*fat.*" It is on the *fat*, too, that the fire specially kindles. It is at the man's heart, feelings, and desires that God expresses his indignation most fully. It is the *heart* that is desperately wicked. It is the carnal mind that is enmity against God.*

> Ver. 9. *But his inwards and his legs shall he wash in water: and the priest shall burn all on the altar, to be a burnt-sacrifice, an offering made by fire, of a sweet savour unto the Lord.*

Answerable to the "*head* and *fat*" of the former

---

* The North American Indians long practised sacrifice; and D. Brainerd, in his *Journal*, tells us of a great sacrifice where " they burnt the fat of the inwards in the fire, and sometimes raised the flame to a prodigious height."

verse, as parts representing the *inward* and *outward,* we
have here the *legs and the intestines.*   The legs and intestines may be supposed to be selected to mark outward
and inward defilement—man's polluted nature needing
to be washed in water.   But why wash these in water, if
they are to be burnt ?   Because here is a *sacrifice for
others*—"the just for the unjust"—Christ taking our
place.   Now, lest anything should seem to indicate personal defilement in him, these portions are washed in
water, and then presented.   Christ's body and soul, all
his person, and all his acts, were holy.   His walk was
holy, and his inmost affections holy.

Such was the sacrifice on which the fire came!   See
Isaac on the wood! but the knife has pierced this Isaac!
—in symbol, the original and immutable sentence, " *Thou
shalt die.*"   Here is *death;* and it has come in such a
manner as not to leave a vestige of the victim's former
aspect.   The victim is all disfigured, and has become a
mass of disjointed bones and mangled flesh, because thus
shall it be in the case of the lost in hell.   The lost sinner's
former joy, and even all his relics of comfort, are gone
for ever—no lover or friend would ever be able to recognise that lost one.   Even as it was with Jesus when
he took the position of the lost; his visage seemed to
every eye more marred than any man, and his form more
than the sons of men.   But lo! as if even all this were
not expressive enough, that mangled mass is committed
to the flames, and in the consuming flame, every remaining mark of its former state disappears.   All is ashes.
So complete is the doom of the lost—as testified on this
altar, and fulfilled by Jesus when he took the sinner's
place.   That smoke attests that God's righteousness is
fully satisfied in the suffering victim.   His blood—his

soul—is poured out! and the flame of Divine wrath burns
up the suffering one!   The smoke ascends—"*a sweet
savour to the Lord.*"   He points to it, and shews therein
his holy name honoured, and his law magnified.   It is
sweet to Jehovah to behold this sight in a fallen world.
It reminds him, so to speak, of that Sabbath-rest over
the first creation (Gen. ii. 2); only this is deeper rest, as
being rest after trouble.   This "sweet savour" is literally
"*savour of rest*" (רִיחַ נִיחוֹחַ); as if the savour stayed his
wrath and calmed his soul.   So Eph. v. 2.   And at the
view of that ascending smoke, more joyful hallelujahs are
sung than will be heard over the smoke of the pit (Rev.
xix. 3).   For here *love* has free scope as well as *righteousness*.   What a rest will the millennial and heavenly rest
be, when, in addition to other elements, it has in it this
element of perfect satisfaction—"He *shall rest in his
love!*" (Zeph. iii. 17.)

Such, then, is the "*ox and bullock that has horns and
hoofs*" (Ps. lxix. 31); and such, too, the meaning of the
offering.   The Antitype set forth in Psalm lxix. has magnified the name of the Lord, and set aside the type.

> Ver. 10. *And if his offering be of the flocks, namely, of the sheep,
> or of the goats, for a burnt-sacrifice; he shall bring it a male
> without blemish.*

It appears that wealthier men generally selected *oxen*
as their offering;* and men less able took· *sheep* or goats;
while ver. 14 shews that those yet poorer brought *doves*.
God thus left the sacrifice open alike to the *rich*, the
middle classes, and the labouring *poor*.   For in Jesus
Christ there is neither Greek nor Jew, barbarian nor
Scythian, bond nor free; he is within reach of all alike.

---

* That is, *oxen* were always *part* of their sacrifice.   Thus Numb. vii. and
1 Chron. xxix. 21.

Our High Priest welcomes sinners under the wide name, "*Him that cometh*" (John vi. 37); the advancing foot-steps of a sinner to his altar, whether he be great or small, is a sweet sound in our Aaron's ear.

Here is specially included the offering of *the lamb*. Morning and evening this was done by the priest for all Israel. " He was led as a lamb to the slaughter"* (Isa. liii. 7). Every day that picture was exhibited to Israel.

> Ver. 11. *And he shall kill it on the side of the altar northward before the Lord: and the priests, Aaron's sons, shall sprinkle his blood round about upon the altar.*

There is a peculiarity here which does not occur in the sacrifices of the herd, namely, it is to be killed on *the north side* of the altar. One obvious reason seems to be this : there was a necessity, for the sake of order, that there should be a separate place for killing *the oxen* and *the sheep*. No quarter of the heavens was sacred; and since, at other times, the sacrifice was presented on the east side, a variety like this answered the purpose of proclaiming that Jesus is offered to any soul in any na-tion, east or north, *i.e.* from east to west, north to south, his death is presented to the view of all, to be believed by men as soon as they see it. " Look unto me, and be ye saved, *all the ends* of the earth."†

> Ver. 12, 13. *And he shall cut it into his pieces, with his head and his fat; and the priest shall lay them in order on the wood*

---

* An old writer asks, why Christ is called so often " *the Lamb* of God," and not " *the ox*, or *the ram*, of God." The reply is, because these were not offered " every day," whereas *the lamb* was a daily offering, and therefore fitted to proclaim Christ's blood as always ready for use.

† Some have tried without success to discover a deeper meaning in the " *north*," and have suggested that the omission of it in Ps. lxxv. 6 strengthens this idea. But in that passage " *south*" also is omitted, the Hebrew being מִמִּדְבָּר, " *from the desert*," referring to the caravans, which, amid all their rare commodities, never brought the gift spoken of.

*that is on the fire which is upon the altar. But he shall wash
the inwards and the legs with water; and the priest shall bring
it all, and burn it upon the altar: it is a burnt-sacrifice, an
offering made by fire, of a sweet savour unto the Lord.*

The sheep or goat is not commanded to be *"flayed,"*
as ver. 6 commands as to the *ox* or *bullock;* perhaps
because *flaying* signified the defencelessness of the victim
left without a covering. Now, the *sheep* or *goat* is, by its
very nature, defenceless enough. Our attention, therefore,
in this type, is rather fixed on the complete stroke of the
knife, that separates all into its pieces ready for the fire.
When the Lord said, "Awake, O sword, against my
Shepherd" (Zech. xiii. 7), the Saviour was smitten to
the very soul, and wrath came down on him like fire.

In ver. 13, the words, *"and shall bring it all near,"*
intimate the solemn care with which the priest advanced
to the spot and lighted the wood, attending to every
point, although his offering was one of the *flock,* and not
of the *herd.* This clause seems intended to put equal
honour on the offering of the *flock* as on that of the
herd, for the *Antitype* is all that gives either of them
any importance.

The other particulars are the same as those mentioned
in verses 7-9.

How simple the rules laid down for ordering his
favourite type—*the lamb!* But let us not fail to notice
that *the use made of the lamb* is what we are chiefly
called to observe—not *the lamb itself* in particular; as if
to shew that it is not *Christ's meek nature,* but *Christ,*
the meek and lowly one, *in his connexion with the altar,*
that we ought to be reminded of by the name "*Lamb.*"
If it had been his character only, or chiefly, that was
referred to in that name—"Lamb of God," there would

have been no propriety in typifying him by the "ox" and the "goat." But if the *manner of his death* and the intention of his sufferings were mainly referred to, then all is appropriate.

BURNT-OFFERING OF FOWLS

Ver. 14. *And if the burnt-sacrifice for his offering to the Lord be of fowls, then shall he bring his offering of turtle-doves, or of young pigeons.*

In John ii. 14, we find this third class of offerings referred to, along with the other two,—*oxen, sheep,* and *doves.*

From chap. v. 7, we learn that the poorer class were to bring this sort of sacrifice. "To the poor the Gospel is preached;" and ministers must be as solicitous for the salvation of the poor as of the rich.

The dove or pigeon was to be a male; for the Hebrew word for "young pigeons" is בְּנֵי יוֹנָה, "sons of the dove." Thus it was fitter to represent Christ. And of the winged tribes, none were ever taken for sacrifice, except the dove and the turtle-dove. These abounded in the Holy Land, so that the poorest could get them easily.* They were fitted, also, to be emblems of Jesus, just as was *the lamb.* He is undefiled and holy, full of love and tenderness; therefore *the dove* is his type. And as the *dove* at the Deluge brought the message of peace, and as the turtle-dove is the known emblem of peace, because its voice is heard from the *olive-tree* (itself the

* In the course of my ordinary visits in the country, I one day sat down to converse with a poor illiterate believer, at whose board a beautiful tame pigeon used to feed. I opened the Bible at this passage, and shewed this type of a suffering Saviour. It seemed to be specially blessed—she long remembered this type of Jesus: and in this simple incident, there seemed to me discernible something of the wisdom and goodness that so provided for the poor of Israel.

type of peace), in quiet, calm security, so, on this ground more specially, they are the better types of Jesus. The previous suffering of the offered dove, or turtle, represents Christ suffering ere he enters into peace, and becomes the peace-maker. Taken from his Father's bosom, he comes to suffer. The dove, "by the rivers of water" (Song v. 12), in peace and joy, is caught, and wrung to death on the altar. The olive-groves must be searched, and the turtle-dove taken from its own happy, peaceful olive-tree. It is then violently brought to the altar, and left lifeless there! Thus it was with Jesus. But from this suffering and death of the Peaceful One results *"peace on earth." "He is our peace"* (Eph. ii. 14). He breathes out on us nothing less than his own peace—*"My peace I give unto you"* (John xiv. 27). And soon, too, as the grand and wide result of all, "the voice of the turtle (the herald of spring and of storms past) shall be heard in our land" (Song ii. 12); and the deluge of fire being passed, this dove shall bring its olive-branch to announce to the new earth that wrath is for ever turned away. Christ, who died to make peace, shall reign in peace, over a peaceful earth, which his own blood has made the dwelling of righteousness.

He of whom these things are spoken, when on earth, shewed, from such Scriptures as these, that he needed to suffer unto death. "Thus it is written, and thus it behoved Christ to suffer" (Luke xxiv. 46), said Jesus, while shewing the things written in the law of Moses concerning himself.

> Ver. 15. *And the priest shall bring it unto the altar, and wring off his head, and burn it on the altar; and the blood thereof shall be wrung out at the side of the altar.*

The method of putting the dove to death must be

regulated by the nature of the victim; hence, here it is by "*wringing off his head.*" But this arrangement is the better fitted to exhibit another feature in the death of Jesus, viz. the awful violence done to one so pure, so tender, and so lovely. We shrink back from the terrible harshness of the act, whether it be plunging the knife into the neck of the innocent lamb, or wringing off the head of the tender dove. But, on this very account, the circumstances are the better figure of the death of Jesus. "He had done no violence, neither was any deceit in his mouth; yet it pleased the Lord to bruise him."

After this, "*the blood* was to be wrung out" (נִמְצָה, squeezed or pressed out) over the side of the altar, till it ran in a crimson stream down the altar's side, in view of all. Then it collects at the foot of the altar; and there is a cry, like that from the souls under the altar in Rev. vi. 9, *against the cause of this blood-shedding*, viz. sin. A testimony against sin ascends up into the ears of the Lord of Sabaoth. But his blood speaketh better things than the blood of Abel, or the cry of the martyred ones; for the response to this cry of blood is not vengeance, but *pardon to man*.

It was the priest who performed this apparently harsh and cruel act, for the *Father* bruised Jesus, and the priest acts in his name.

> Ver. 16. *And he shall pluck away his crop with his feathers, and cast it beside the altar, on the east part, by the place of the ashes.*

The crop, containing the food, seems to be considered unclean, because an emblem of man's appetites. Now, as there was nothing of man's sinful appetites in the Holy One, there must be nothing even in the type, that might lead us to suppose that he was otherwise than perfectly

holy.   Hence "*the crop*" is removed.   "*The feathers*,"
also, are removed, because they are a covering to the
dove; and it must be left quite unsheltered when the
drops of the storm fall thick and heavy upon it.   These
are to be cast to "the *place of ashes*," out of sight of
God; and thus the dove is offered, in a state of purity
and of unprotectedness, on the altar.

> Ver. 17. *And he shall cleave it with the wings thereof, but shall
> not divide it asunder: and the priest shall burn it upon the
> altar, upon the wood that is upon the fire: it is a burnt-
> sacrifice, an offering made by fire, of a sweet savour unto the
> Lord.*

"The cleaving" (שִׁסַּע) implies such a separation as is
not complete.   It is only *dislocation*, but not *disruption*
of the parts, as is also explained in the clause, "*but shall
not divide it asunder*."   In this we see another typical
circumstance.   It is like that in the case of the paschal
lamb—"A bone of him shall not be broken."   At the
same time, this type gives us, in addition, a reference to
the Saviour's racked frame on the cross, when he said,
"*All my bones* are out of joint" (Ps. xxii. 14).   All this
seems intended to declare that Jesus, in his death, was
whole, though broken,—"*sin for us*," but "*no sin in him*."

"*With the wings thereof*," to shew nothing left what-
soever that could be means of escape—total weakness.
Jesus said, as he suffered, "I am poured out like water"
(Ps. xxii. 14).

And this sacrifice is "of a *sweet savour* to the Lord."
It satisfies the Father well—so much so, that we find his
redeemed ones called by the name that refers us back to
the sacrifice.   For example—the Church is called "*the
dove*" (Song ii. 14).   So—"Deliver not the soul of thy
turtle-dove into the hands of the enemy" (Ps. lxxiv. 19).

Just as both Christ and his Church are called "*the lily*," in Song ii. 1, 2; and both his voice and theirs is "like the voice of many waters" in the book of Revelation (comp. Rev. i. 15; xiv. 2; xix. 6). If the Church says, "Behold, thou art fair, my beloved (דּוֹדִי), yea, pleasant" (Song i. 16), it is in response to Christ, who had said, "Behold, thou art fair, my love (רַעְיָתִי); behold, thou art fair." So truly one is Christ and his people, they are in a manner identified! "Lord, thou art my righteousness, and I am thy sin; thou hast taken from me what was mine, and given me what was thine." "'Ω τῆς γλυκείας ἀνταλλαγῆς! ὦ τῆς ἀνεξιχνιαστου δημιουργιας! ὦ τῶν ἀπροσδοκήτων εὐεργεσιῶν!"—(*Epist. ad Diognet.* 9.) "Oh, sweet exchange! Oh, unsearchable device! Oh, benefits beyond all expectation!"

And now, looking back on this chapter, let us briefly notice that the rudimental sketch of these offerings, and the mode of their presentation, will be found *at the gate of Eden.* Some have sought for their origin* in Egyptian ceremonies, at one time imitated, at another purposely opposed. But this is altogether erroneous.

Davison refuses to admit that *sacrifice* in the patriarchal time was identical in meaning with *sacrifice* in the Mosaic dispensation—admitting that, if that identity could be made out, the Divine origin of sacrifice would be proved.† Now, is there one text in all the Bible to shew that *sacrifice* (which Davison gladly admits had in it *the atoning principle* in the institutions of Moses) ever has more than one meaning? As well might we ask evidence to prove that "to *call on the name of the Lord*" in the

---

* *Vide* Spencer, &c.
† On *The Origin and Intention of Primitive Sacrifice.*

days of Enos was quite a different act from *"calling on the name of the Lord"* in the days of the Psalmist; or that *"righteousness"* in Abraham's day (Gen. xv. 6) was different from *"righteousness"* in Paul's days (Rom. iv. 3). Just as we believe the *Hiddekel* and *Euphrates* of Genesis ii. are the same as the Hiddekel and Euphrates of later history; and *the cherubim* of Genesis iii. the same as those in the tabernacle; and the *"sweet savour"* of Genesis viii. 21 the same as that in Leviticus i. 9 and Ephesians v. 2; so do we regard the *intention of sacrifice* as always the same throughout Scripture. There would therefore be need, not of proof to establish this principle, but of *argument to refute* it. Ours is the obvious and common-sense principle. All these ordinances were parts of the one telescope, through which men saw the Star of Bethlehem from afar. In Mosaic rites, the telescope was drawn out farther than at Eden, and the focus at which the grand object could be best seen was more nearly found. But the *gate of Eden* presents us with the same truths in a more rudimental form.

Some have traced the outlines of the Mosaic ritual at the gate of Eden in the following manner:—Within the gate stood *the cherubim*, occupying the hallowed spot where the Tree of Life waved its branches. This resembled the *Holy of holies;* and the veil that prevented the approach of any from without was the *flaming sword*, flashing its sheets of fire on every side. But opposite to this sword, at some distance, we see *an altar*, where our first parents shed the blood of sacrifice—shewing in type how the barred-up way of access to the Tree of Life was to be opened by the blood of the woman's bruised seed. On this *altar* bloody and unbloody offerings were appointed to be presented in their season. And when we find *clean* and *unclean* noticed (Gen. viii. 20), and in Abraham's case (Gen. xv. 9, 10), the heifer and goat, the turtle and the pigeon, and also "commandments, statutes, and laws" (parallel to Lev. xxvi. 46), we cannot but believe that these fuller institutions in Leviticus are just the expansion of what *Adam* first received. The Levitical dispensation is the acorn of Eden grown to a full oak. If so, then may we say, that the child Jesus, wrapped in his swaddling-clothes, was, in these ceremonies, laid down at the gate of Eden!

CHAPTER II

The Meat-Offering

" I beseech you therefore, brethren, by the mercies of God, that ye present your bodies a living sacrifice, holy, acceptable unto God."—
Rom. xii. 1

*" The things which were sent from you, an odour of a sweet smell, a sacrifice acceptable, well-pleasing to God."—*Phil. iv. 18

Ver. 1. *And when any will offer a meat-offering unto the Lord, his offering shall be of fine flour; and he shall pour oil upon it, and put frankincense thereon.*

In Daniel ix. 27, "He shall cause the *sacrifice* and *oblation* to cease," there seems to be reference made to the two great divisions, *sacrifices with, and sacrifices without, blood.* For the words are more exactly, "He shall cause sacrifice and *meat-offering* (מִנְחָה) to cease." So also in 1 Sam. iii. 14, and Ps. xl. 6. We have now come to this second class of offerings.

The meat-offering (so called by our translators because the greater part of it was used for food) represents the offerer's *person and property*, his body and his possessions.* When he had by the burnt-offering obtained full

---

* Ainsworth gives in substance the same meaning of the type, when he says that it signified " the sanctification of persons and actions, and the acceptation of them." Patrick is evidently far wrong when he speaks of these meat-offerings as a merciful provision for those who could not afford to offer animal sacrifices.

acceptance for his soul, he comes next to give up his whole substance to the Lord who has redeemed him. The mercies of God constrain him to give up all he has to the Lord. The *meat-offering* was generally, or rather always, presented along with some animal sacrifice, in order to shew the connexion between pardon of sin and devotion to the Lord. The moment we are pardoned, all we are, and all we have, becomes the property of Christ. "Ye are not your own, for ye are bought with a price" (1 Cor. vi. 19). Our Redeemer and kinsman buys first Ruth, the Moabitess herself, and next, he claims also the field and inheritance. Joseph, who saves our life, buys up our bodies and our substance.

A type that was to represent this dedication of *body and property* behoved to be one that had no *blood* therein; for blood is the life or *soul*, which has been already offered.

This distinction may have existed as early as the days of Adam. When God instituted animal sacrifice to represent the atonement by death, he probably also instituted this other sort; the fact of this latter existing, and its meaning and use being definitely understood, would tend to confirm the exclusive use of animal sacrifice when *atonement* was to be shewn forth. Cain's offering of *first-fruits* might have been acceptable as a *meat-offering*, if it had been founded upon the slain lamb, and had followed as a consequence from that sacrifice.* But the statement in Heb. xi. 4 lets us know that Cain had not faith in the seed of the woman; therefore his offering

---

* In this view Ambrose (*De Incarnat. Dom. Sacram.*, cap. i.) is not wrong:— "Nihil invenio quod in specie munerum reprehendam, nisi quod et Cain munera sua displicuisse cognovit, et Dominus dixit, Si recte offeras, recte autem non dividas, peccâsti. Ubi igitur est crimen? Ubi culpa? Non in oblatione muneris, sed in oblationis affectu."

was hateful to God. Cain's attempt was virtually this,—
to present himself and his property to God, as if they had
been under no curse that needed *blood* first of all to wash
them. He sought to be accepted by his *holiness*, and so
overthrew *salvation by Christ.* Acts of charity, substituted for Christ's work, as a means of pacifying the conscience, make up precisely this sin of Cain. Nor are
they less mistaken who think, by self-denial, and by doing
good to others in their life and conduct, to obtain favour,
and be accepted with God. This is offering the meat-
offering ere the man has been cleansed by the burnt-
offering. It is putting *sanctification* before *justification.**
And there is a tendency to this error in those books
which recommend anxious souls, that are not yet come to
Christ, to draw up a form of self-dedication, and solemnly
give themselves to the Lord. These counsellors are in
danger of leading souls past the *blood of the Lamb,*
and of putting the *meat-offering* too hastily into their
hands.

This meat-offering was presented daily, along with the
morning and evening sacrifice, teaching us to give all we
have to the Lord's use, not by irregular impulse on particular exigencies, but *daily.*

In Isaiah lxvi. 20, the words, "They shall bring all
your brethren an *offering* (מִנְחָה) to the Lord," are very
appropriate when we keep in mind that this is the

---

* An instance of such-like self-righteousness we find among the early Fathers.
Ephraim Syrus seems never to have found the blood-sprinkled way, but to have
travelled onward to eternity over a road strewn with the palm-branches of good
feelings and deeds of self-denial, and watered with tears at every step. His
wretched scheme of peace may be gathered from such congratulations as these:
—"Μακαρίζω ὑμᾶς, ὦ γνήσιοι, ὅτι ὀρθῇ πολιτείᾳ φίλους ἑαυτοὺς ἐποιήσατε
τῷ Θεῷ."—(Λογος A.) He counts those friends of his happy because he thinks
"they have made themselves acceptable to God by their manner of life." The
same remark replies to the writings of Thomas-à-Kempis.

typical meaning of the meat-offering—these *persons* are
the meat-offering.   Perhaps, also, in 1 Samuel xxvi. 19,
"If the Lord have stirred thee up against me, let him
accept a *meat-offering*" (מִנְחָה), there may be reference
to this species of offering, representing the person and all
he possessed.   At the same time, the word מִנְחָה, when
not contrasted or conjoined with the sacrifice, is often
used as a generic term for any offering.*

But we have still to call attention to the chief application of this type.   It shews forth *Christ himself*.   And
indeed, this should have been noticed first of all, had it
not been for the sake of first establishing the precise
point of view in which this type sets forth its object.
We are to consider it as representing *Christ himself, in
all his work of obedience*—soul and body.   He is the
"fine wheat," pure, unspotted; yet also "baked," &c.,
because subjected to every various suffering.   The burnt-
offering being presented and consumed, Christ's glorious
obedience in his human nature, and *all that belonged to
him*, was accepted, as well as his sacrifice; for he and
all that is his was ever set apart for, and accepted by
the Father.   "Lord, truly I am thy servant" (Ps. cxvi.
16).   And if it represent Christ, it includes his Church.
Christ, and his body the Church, are presented to the
Father, and accepted.   Christ, and *all his possessions* in
heaven and earth, whether possessions of dominion or
possessions in the souls of men and angels, were all presented to, and accepted by the Father.   And Christ
delights thus to honour the Father.   He will delight to

---

* And so the Septuagint sometimes render it by θυσία, and sometimes by
προσφορὰ.   In Ezek. xlv. 15, where it occurs, the meaning would have been
brought out more exactly by rendering the clause thus:—"One lamb out of the
flock, from the pastures of Israel, for an *offering* (a *Mincha*, as in Gen. iv. 4),
even for burnt-offerings and for peace-offerings."

deliver up even the kingdom to the Father (1 Cor. xv. 24). What an example for each of his people! Let us behold our pattern, and give up ourselves, body and soul and substance, to the glory of our God.

Let us now examine the chapter in detail.

The *meat-offering* must be of *fine flour*,—the fine wheat of Palestine, not the coarser קֶמַח, "*meal*," but the fine סֹלֶת, bolted and sifted well. It must in all cases be not less than the tenth of an ephah (chap. v. 11); in most cases far more (see Numb. vii. 13). It was taken from the best of their fields, and cleansed from the bran by passing through the sieve. The rich seem to have offered it in the shape of pure fine flour, white as snow, heaping it up, probably, as in Numb. vii. 13, on a silver charger, or in a silver bowl, in princely manner. It thus formed a type, beautiful and pleasant to the eye, of the man's *self and substance* dedicated to God, when now made pure by the blood of sacrifice that had removed his sin. For if forgiven, then a blessing rested upon his basket and his store, on the fruit of his body, and the fruit of his ground, the fruit of his cattle, and the increase of his kine (see Deut. xxviii. 3–6). Even as Jesus, when raised from the tomb, was henceforth no more under the curse of sin, but was blessed in body, for his body was no longer weary or feeble; and blessed in company, for no longer was he numbered among transgressors; and blessed in all his inheritance, for "all power was given him in heaven and in earth."

The *oil* poured on the fine flour denoted *setting apart*. It was oil that was used by Jacob at Bethel in setting apart his stone pillow to commemorate his vision; and every priest and king was thus set apart for his office. Oil, used on these occasions, is elsewhere appropriated to

mean *the Spirit's operation*—the Spirit setting apart
whom he pleases for any office.

The *frankincense,* fragrant in its smell, denoted the
acceptableness of the offering. As a flower or plant—
the rose of Sharon or the balm of Gilead—would induce
any passing traveller to stoop down over them, and regale
himself with their fragrance, so the testimony borne by
Christ's work to the character of Godhead brings the
Father to bend over any to whom it is imparted, and to
rest over him in his love. The Lord Jesus says to his
Church, in Song iv. 6, "Until the day break, and the
shadows flee away, I will get me to the mountain of
myrrh, and the hill of frankincense." This spot must be
the Father's right hand. In like manner, then, it ought
to be the holy purpose of believing souls who are looking for Christ, to dwell so entirely amid the Redeemer's
merits, that, like the maidens of king Ahasuerus (Esther
ii. 12), they shall be fragrant with the sweet odours,
and with these alone, when the Bridegroom comes.

When Christ presented his human person and all he
had, he was indeed *fragrant* to the Father, and the oil
of the Spirit was on him above his fellows (see Isa. lxi. 1;
Ps. xlv. 7; Heb. ix. 14).

And equally complete in him is every believer also.
Like Jesus, each believer is God's wheat—his fine flour.
He is clothed in the fine linen, white and clean, and
stands by Christ's side, in the likeness of Christ. Even
now is he able to say, "As he is (at the Father's right
hand), so are we in this world"—as completely righteous,
as really accepted (1 John iv. 17).

> Ver. 2. *And he shall bring it to Aaron's sons the priests: and
> he shall take thereout his handful of the flour thereof, and of
> the oil thereof, with all the frankincense thereof; and the priest*

*shall burn the memorial of it upon the altar, to be an offering
made by fire, of a sweet savour unto the Lord.*

One of Aaron's sons was to take a handful out of what
was brought, a handful of flour, and a proportional quantity of the oil. Along with this he was to take " *all
the frankincense,*" because all was needed to express the
complete acceptance. This is " *the memorial of the
meat-offering* "*—a part for the whole. In dedication
of our body and property, we need not go through every
article in detail, but we take some part as a specimen
and an earnest of all the rest.

In Acts x. 4, Cornelius's "prayers and alms" are called
" a memorial." These alms and prayers were a specimen
of the whole man's dedication. He was a believer, like
old Simeon, already accepted, and this *meat-offering* of
his, the dedication of self and substance, expressed by
prayers and alms, was acknowledged on the part of God
by the gift of more light and liberty.

> Ver. 3. *And the remnant of the meat-offering shall be Aaron's
> and his sons'; it is a thing most holy of the offerings of the
> Lord made by fire.*

The offering is declared " *most holy.*" And to shew
that *the mass* was so, as well as the *handful,* the remnant
is given to Aaron's sons to feast upon. Even Aaron, who
bore on his mitre " Holiness to the Lord," could safely
eat of it.

---

* Isaiah (lxvi. 3) refers first to the *burnt-offering,* speaking of slaying the lamb
and the ox; and then in the next clause, to the *meat-offering,* speaking of him
that " *offers a* מִנְחָה *and maketh a frankincense-memorial* " מַזְכִּיר לְבֹנָה.
Milton has, without authority, blended these two together in his description of
Abel's offering, *Paradise Lost,* xi.

> "* * * * * A shepherd next,
> More meek, came with the firstlings of his flock
> Choicest and best; then, sacrificing laid
> The inwards and the fat, *with incense strew'd,*
> On the cleft wood."

In this manner we are assured of the true and thorough
acceptance of our dedicated things, when once we are
forgiven.   How complete is the assurance we have of the
acceptance of Christ and all that are his!   Nay, even of
their substance.   There is a blessing "on their basket
and on their store."   So completely is its curse removed,
that under the tree in the plains of Mamre, angels,
and the Lord of angels, eat of Abraham's bread and his
fatted calf!

But the declaration, "It is a thing most holy," teaches
us how we should regard every member of our body as
belonging to God ; and everything we possess.   " *Ye are
not your own.*"   "*It is most holy.*"   How little do we feel
it to be so!

> Ver. 4. *And if thou bring an oblation of a meat-offering baken in
> the oven, it shall be unleavened cakes of fine flour mingled with
> oil, or unleavened wafers anointed with oil.*

A part of the type of the *fine flour*, already noticed,
may be that *Christ* was *ground* by sore agony, and
endured unutterable anguish when *bruised* for us.   And
so *the wine* of the *drink-offering*, afterwards noticed,
would imply a reference to the wine-press, out of which
he came.   And in like manner, the *oven* here mentioned,
and the other articles exposed to the fire, would contain
a reference to his enduring the fierce flame of wrath.*

But admitting this use of the emblems to be doubtful,
we find a certain and obvious meaning in the *diversities of
form* in which the *meat-offering* appears.   As in chap. i.
we saw that God, for the sake of the less wealthy, took
a lamb or a dove, when a more costly sacrifice would have

---

* Willet quotes Pellicanus, who applies these varieties in the preparation of
the meat-offering to the manifold nature of afflictions : " Nunc Clibanus, nunc
Patilla, nunc Craticula dici possunt :" a true remark, whether contained here or
not.

been beyond the reach of the offerer; so it is here : for
the sake of different ranks in society, the *meat-offering*
has a form in which any one may be able to present it.
If he is rich, let him bring his fine flour from the finest of
the wheat.   If he is not able to do this, let him bring " *a
meat-offering baken in the oven.*"   If he cannot afford
this, having no oven, then let him bring somewhat " *baken
in the fire-plate,*" or pan.   If even this is not in his power,
he will at least possess *a frying-pan,* and let him bring
what it prepares.   God excuses none, of whatever rank,
from dedicating themselves and their substance to him.
The widow has two mites to cast into the Lord's treasury.
In 1 Chron. xxiii. 29, this gradation seems referred to
when it is said, " For that which is baked in the pan,
and for that which is fried, and for all manner of measure
and size."

The oven was a utensil which was generally possessed
by all in the middle ranks of life.   If they have this, let
them prepare in it " cakes" (חַלּוֹת), of a larger size, and
" wafers" (רְקִיקִים), cakes of a smaller size, and bring
these as their meat-offering.   The larger cakes must have
" oil *mingled through them ;*" the smaller and thinner must
have oil *on* them.   In both cases, the oil *that sets apart*
must not be wanting.   Nay, where it is possible, it must
form part, as it were, of the substance, by being mingled
with it.

And there must be no *leaven ;* for leaven indicates
corruption at work.   If we give grudgingly, with restless,
impatient, tumultuous, anxious feelings, we are offering
with *leaven.*   We must dedicate *self and substance* in
Christ's spirit—" *Not my will,* but thine be done."

Ver. 5. *And if thy oblation be a meat-offering, baken in a pan, it
shall be of fine flour unleavened, mingled with oil.*

This is another form in which it may be presented, if the man be yet poorer than the last mentioned; if he use the "*fire-plate*" in his house, and not "*the oven*." The only article of furniture absolutely necessary for preparing food seems to have been the "frying-pan" of verse 7. Anything more than that indicated comfort and ease. The "cakes" and "wafers" of last verse evidently intimated a moderate degree of luxury. And this man also possessed some degree of independence in his circumstances. Perhaps he occupied the station of a tradesman, if not somewhat above that. He, too, must dedicate all to the Lord.

> Ver. 6. *Thou shalt part it in pieces, and pour oil thereon: it is a meat-offering.*

This division into pieces may shew that *every part* of our substance is to be given up. We must allow God to divide and choose and appropriate as he pleases. And then, *each part* must be "*anointed with oil;*" set apart by the priest's hand. Both *the whole*, as a whole, and every part of it, must be given up to the Lord.

> Ver. 7. *And if thy oblation be a meat-offering baken in the frying-pan, it shall be made of fine flour with oil.*

The shallow frying-pan (a shallow vessel of earth, used to this day by the Arabs, and called *Tagen*) indicated poverty, if the man had this and no other culinary utensil. It was used in boiling, and therefore was indispensable. He, too, must offer what he has. God is willing to have him and his; he does not despise the poor. Nay, by attending to different classes of men, he finds out opportunities of some new exhibition of his wisdom and grace.

Here the opportunity is afforded of enforcing the lesson,

that whatever is wanting, *oil* must not be wanting : the Spirit must set apart whatever is really dedicated.

> Ver. 8. *And thou shalt bring the meat-offering that is made of these things unto the Lord: and when it is presented unto the priest, he shall bring it unto the altar.*

A poor worshipper might be apt to be discouraged when he witnessed the more costly gifts of others : therefore the Lord kindly condescends to assure his heart by specially inserting here these directions to the priest, viz. that he must take the humblest meat-offering, and present it on the altar. The priest might be ready to neglect so poor an offering ; but here he is warned, " When the offerer presents it, the priest shall bring it." Our Master was ever more tender-hearted than his disciples. The disciples rebuked those who brought little children to him ; but Jesus said, " Suffer them to come." *Jehovah*, God of Israel, is *Jesus*, the Son of man !

> Ver. 9. *And the priest shall take from the meat-offering a memorial thereof, and shall burn it upon the altar: it is an offering made by fire, of a sweet savour unto the Lord.*

The memorial is what was directed to be taken, ver. 2. And this is to be done as much in this poorer offering as when it was fine flour. There is no virtue in the size or in the quality of the thing.

The "*sweet savour*" reminds us of Paul's words to the Philippians, when they had, though poor, given him what they could spare of their substance: " I have received of Epaphroditus the things which were sent from you, an odour of a sweet smell" (Phil. iv. 18). Jesus in heaven smells this sweet savour, and will reward it at the day of his appearing.

> Ver. 10. *And that which is left of the meat-offering shall be*

*Aaron's and his sons'; it is a thing most holy of the offerings
of the Lord made by fire.*

It is most holy (see ver. 3 again), and it is taken from
the fire-offerings of the Lord, expressing complete appropriation by the Lord, of the things offered to him.   He
takes what we offer; it is not a mere compliment.   We
may not say, "*I give myself to the Lord*," and then do as
we please.   The Lord takes us at our word.   We are no
more our own, nor is our body ours, nor our members,
nor our money, nor our health, nor our talents, nor our
reputation, nor our affections, nor our relations, nor our
very life itself.   All is the Lord's—in his treasury—
"among the offerings made by fire," that ascend up to
heaven in the smoke of the altar.

Then follow some general rules in regard to the general
subject of meat-offerings.

Ver. 11. *No meat-offering, which ye shall bring unto the Lord,
shall be made with leaven: for ye shall burn no leaven, nor
any honey, in any offering of the Lord made by fire.*

Leaven indicates *corruption*, and is the very opposite
of *salt*, which preserves (ver. 13), and which must never
be wanting.   *Honey* includes all that is sweet, like the
honey* of grapes, figs, and the reed or calamus (which grew
on the banks of the waters of Merom), and it is forbidden
both because it turns to sourness, and leads to fermen-
tation, and perhaps also because it is a luxury; and the
Lord desires nothing of earthly sweetness.   His offerings
must have neither corruption nor carnal sweetness.   We
must, like Christ, be the Lord's; holy and separate from the
world, not pleasing ourselves.   In chap. xxiii. 17, there is

---

* Jarchi says, כל מתיק פרי —"all sweetness of fruit,"—sweet things obtained
from any fruit.   Honey was reckoned corrupting, because it ferments.   The
Chaldee uses מבדיש in the sense of fermenting, a word derived from דְּבַשׁ,
"honey."—(*Rosenmüller.*)

a special lesson taught by *the presence of leaven* in the two loaves of the first-fruits; it is altogether unlike this case.

> Ver. 12. *As for the oblation of the first-fruits, ye shall offer them unto the Lord; but they shall not be burnt on the altar for a sweet savour.*

The first ripe fruits of any sort are meant. These, when offered, were typical of presenting the person's self and substance, and hence are included in the subject of *meat-offering.* But they are not to be brought to the altar, because they shew us *Christ in a peculiar aspect;* and that aspect seems to be *Christ glorified*, or raised up, after suffering. Hence there is no burning of any part of them, for the suffering is done. The Holy Spirit takes truth in portions, and seems sometimes to turn our eye away from one portion of truth on purpose to let us see better some other portion, by keeping our attention for a time fixed on that alone.

> Ver. 13. *And every oblation of thy meat-offering shalt thou season with salt; neither shalt thou suffer the salt of the covenant of thy God to be lacking from thy meat-offering: with all thine offerings thou shalt offer salt.*

This *salt* indicates *corruption removed and prevented;* and in the case of the meat-offering, it is as if to say, *Thy body and thy substance are become healthy now;* they shall not rot. They are not like those of the ungodly in James v. 2, " Your riches are corrupted." There is a blessing on thy body and thy estate. And next it intimates the *friendship* (of which salt was a well-known emblem) now existing between God and the man. God can sup with man, and man with God (Rev. iii. 18). There is a covenant between him and God, even in regard to the beasts of the field (Job v. 23), and fowls of heaven (Hos. ii. 18). The friendship of God extends to

his people's property; and to assure us of this he appoints
the salt in *the meat-offering*—the offering that especially
typified their substance.   How comforting to labouring
men! how cheering to care-worn merchants—if they dedicate themselves to God, he is interested in their property
as much as they themselves are!   "Who is a God like
unto thee!"   But more; "*with all thine offerings thou shalt
offer salt,*" declared that the sweet savour of these sacrifices was not momentary and passing, but enduring and
eternal.   By this declaration he sprinkles every sacrifice
with the salt of his unchanging satisfaction.   And "the
covenant by sacrifice" (Ps. l. 5) is thus confirmed on the
part of God: he declares that he on his part will be
faithful.

> Ver. 14. *And if thou offer a meat-offering of thy first-fruits unto
> the Lord, thou shalt offer, for the meat-offering of thy first-
> fruits, green ears of corn dried by the fire, even corn beaten
> out of full ears.*

These are voluntary meat-offerings, and they differ
from those of verse 12.   The sense is, "If thou wishest
to make a common meat-offering out of these first-fruits,
it shall be done in the following manner."   A peculiar
typical circumstance attends these.   These are "*ears of
corn,*" a figure of Christ (John xii. 24); and "*ears of the
best kind,*" for so the Hebrew (כַּרְמֶל) intimates.   They
are "*dried by the fire,*" to represent Jesus feeling the
wrath of his Father, as when he said, "My strength is
dried up," *i.e.* the whole force of my being is dried up
(Ps. xxii. 15); "I am withered like grass" (Ps. cii. 4).
O how affecting a picture of the Man of sorrows!   How
like the very life!   The best ears of the finest corn in
the plains of Israel are plucked while yet green; and
instead of being left to ripen in the cool breeze, and

under a genial sun, are withered up by the scorching fire.
It was thus that the only pure humanity that ever walked
on the plains of earth was wasted away in three-and-
thirty years by the heat of wrath he had never deserved.
While obeying night and day, with all his soul and
strength, the burning wrath of God was drying up his
frame.   " *Beaten out of full ears*," represents the bruises
and strokes whereby he was prepared for the altar.
" Though he were a Son, yet learned he obedience by the
things which he suffered" (Heb. ii. 10).   It is after this
preparation that he is a perfect meat-offering, fully devoted, body and substance, to the Lord.

In all this he is "*First-fruits*," intimating that many
more shall follow.   *He* the first-fruits, then all that are
his in like manner.   We must be conformed to Jesus in
all things; and here it is taught us that we must be conformed to him in self-dedication—self-renunciation.   We
must please the Father; as he left us an example, saying,
" I do always those things that please him" (John viii.
29), even under the blackest sky.

> Ver. 15. *And thou shalt put oil upon it, and lay frankincense
> thereon: it is a meat-offering.*
> Ver. 16. *And the priest shall burn the memorial of it, part of the
> beaten corn thereof, and part of the oil thereof,* with all the
> frankincense thereof: it is an offering made by fire unto the
> Lord.*

The smoke and the fragrance ascend to heaven.   All is
accepted—Christ first, then each of his people.   He
passed through suffering, fire, and flame—then was
accepted.   They, being reckoned one with him, are
treated as if they had done so too.   Whatever sufferings
are left to them are not atoning, but only sanctifying.

* עַל, " una cum," says Rosenmüller.

THE DRINK-OFFERING.

Some one might here ask, *Why is there no mention of the wine-offering or drink-offering?* It is rather remarkable that the drink-offering should be omitted in the midst of so full a setting forth of tabernacle rites. It is often joined with burnt-offerings and meat-offerings, as in Ezek. xlv. 17. But properly speaking, the *drink-offering* was not a part of any sacrifice; though it was never offered by itself alone. It was a rite superadded, to express the worshipper's hearty concurrence in all that he saw done at the altar. Hence, it could be deferred till a convenient time arrived. It appears from Numbers xv. 2, 4, that it was not to be observed till they came to Canaan, and had reached the plentiful vineyards of Sorek and Engedi.

But we may notice, in passing, the object and meaning of this ordinance. It was " strong wine poured unto the Lord" (Numb. xxviii. 7). *Wine* is the representation of joy, and hence it was an expression, on the offerer's part, of his cheerful and hearty acquiescence in all that was done at the altar. He saw the lamb slain—a type of atoning blood for his guilty soul; he saw the meat-offering presented—a type of entire dedication to the Lord; and, therefore, when he lifted up the cup of wine, and poured it forth before the Lord at the altar, over the ashes of the sacrifice, and the memorial of the meat-offering, his so doing was equivalent to his saying, " In all this I do heartily acquiesce. I welcome atoning blood to my guilty soul, and I give up my redeemed soul to him that has atoned for me. Amen, Amen!"

It is to this drink-offering that reference is made in Judges ix. 13, where wine is said to " *cheer God and*

man." It is not to wine used at table for convivial purposes that allusion is there made, but to wine used at the
altar.   There it did truly gladden God and man.   Like
the water of the well of Bethlehem poured out by David,
it expressed the heart poured out.   *The Lord rejoiceth* to
see a sinner accept the offered atonement.   Is not the
shepherd's heart glad when he finds the lost sheep?   Does
not the father weep for very joy as he sees his prodigal
return, and fall upon his neck?   And likewise the Lord
rejoiced to see a ransomed sinner giving himself up to his
God, as he rejoiced over Abraham when he did not withhold even Isaac.   " He taketh pleasure in them that fear
him."   On the other hand, the sinner himself was glad
as he poured out the wine; for there is " joy and peace
in believing," in accepting the offered Saviour.   Nor less
so in giving up all to the Lord; for he that giveth up
" houses and lands" for Christ's sake, receives a hundred-
fold more in this present life.   Is it not, then, true, that
" wine made glad the heart of God and man?"   Might
not the vine that grew in Israel's land say, " *Should I
leave my wine, that cheereth God and man?*"   The *olive*,
in the same manner, could say, "Should I leave my
fatness, wherewith by me they *honour God and man?*"
(Judges ix. 9;) because olive-oil supplied the tabernacle
lamps, as well as lighted up the halls of princes; and
some part of a hin of oil—the special symbol of consecration—must accompany every *meat-offering* (Numb.
xv. 5, 6).

If it be here asked, Did our Lord fulfil the type of
the drink-offering?   We say, Yes; by the entire willingness he ever felt, to suffer, and to obey for us.   Even on
the night wherein he was betrayed, *he sang, and gave
God praise that he must die.*   And perhaps there is

more meaning in the words of Luke xxii. 20 than is
generally noticed. "This *cup* is the New Testament in
my blood." This wine-cup not only *exhibits* the blood
that seals the New Covenant, but *exhibits it as the wine
that may cheer our souls.* The blood of the grape of the
True Vine gladdens God and man.

But returning to the immediate subject of the chapter
before us, let us sum it up by briefly quoting Hannah's
offering (1 Sam. i. 24) when Samuel was weaned. We
find there *three bullocks.* This is the *burnt-offering*—a
bullock for herself, and for her husband, and for her
child; and as if to express her belief that her child
needed atoning blood, she offers· a bullock for him as
well as for herself, nay (ver. 25), expressly offers it at
the moment of presenting him. Next, we find the *ephah
of flour.* This is the *meat-offering.* It expressed the
dedication of themselves, and all they had, to God. An
ephah contained ten omers or ten deals, and three of
these was the usual quantity that went to each meat-
offering (Numb. xv. 9, 12) on such an occasion as this.
But here, no doubt, their meat-offering had more than
three omers, just in order to shew overflowing love.
The *bottle of wine,* last of all, was intended for the
drink-offering; and as an ephah of flour was far more
than was required by law, even for so many persons
(Numb. xv. 9), so no doubt this bottle of wine was more
than full measure, and was poured out before the Lord
to express the entire cheerfulness wherewith all this was
done by the parties concerned. It was after all this
(1 Sam. i. 28, and ii. 1) that they filled the tabernacle
with the voice of adoration and praise, and then returned
rejoicing to Ramah.

That this mode of worshipping the Lord was not

infrequent in Israel may appear, further, from 1 Sam. x. 3. The three worshippers whom Saul met "going up to God to Bethel," along Tabor plain, were carrying, 1. *A kid;* one for each, to be a burnt-offering; 2. *A loaf of bread,* or large *cake;* one for each, to be a meat-offering; 3. *A bottle of wine;* one for all, as in Samuel's case.

"Happy are the people that are in such a case; yea, happy the people whose God is the Lord!" Happy the people where again and again some thankful worshipper is saying, "What shall I render to the Lord for all his benefits towards me? I will take the *cup of salvation,* and call upon the name of the Lord" (Ps. cxvi. 13). The *drink-offering of wine,* poured out before the Lord over the peace-offering that some Israelite had brought in the way of thanks for benefits received (as Numb. xv. 3 directs), this is "the *cup of salvation.*" And from time to time the courts of the Lord's house are enlivened by the happy countenance of some grateful worshipper, who smiles with delight as the priest pours out for him the sparkling wine of Lebanon or Sorek. Nor is it less true that the Lord himself rejoices—his heart is "cheered;" he rests in his love, making his love the very canopy over all.

CHAPTER III

The Peace-Offerings

" Therefore, being justified by faith, we have peace with God, through our Lord Jesus Christ; by whom also we have access by faith into this grace wherein we stand."—Rom. v. 1, 2

Ver. 1. *And if his oblation be a sacrifice of peace-offering; if he offer it of the herd, whether it be a male or female, he shall offer it without blemish before the Lord.*

THE PEACE-OFFERING* is introduced to our notice without any formal statement of the connexion between it and the preceding offerings. That there is a connexion is taken for granted, and the prophet Amos (v. 22) refers to this understood order when he says, " Though ye offer me *burnt-offerings*, and your *meat-offerings*, I will not accept them ; neither will I regard the *peace-offerings* of your fat beasts." The connexion is simply this: a justified soul, devoted to the Lord in all things, spontaneously engages in acts of praise and exercises of fellowship. The Lord takes for granted that such a soul, having free access to him now, will make abundant use of that access. Often will this now redeemed sinner look up and sing,

---

* In Hebrew the word is always plural, except in Amos v. 22. It is in every other place שְׁלָמִים, perhaps equivalent to " *things pertaining to peace* "—things that spoke of peace, viz. the divided pieces of the sacrifice, some parts burnt on the altar, some feasted upon by the priest, some by the offerer. Various sorts of blessing, included in the word *peace*, were thus set forth.

"O Lord, truly I am thy servant; I am thy servant,
and the son of thine handmaid: thou hast loosed my
bonds. I will *offer to thee the sacrifice of thanksgiving,*
and will call upon the name of the Lord" (Ps. cxvi. 16).

The animal might be a *female.*   In this offering *the
effects* of atonement are represented more than *the manner*
of it; and therefore there is no particular restriction to
males.*   Just as we afterwards find that part of the
animal was to be *feasted upon,* and not all to be burned,
as in the whole burnt-offering; because here the object
principally intended is to shew Christ's offering *conveying
blessing to the offerer.*   It is true, that in the peace-offering
presented by the priest himself, and in that presented at
the season of first-fruits, there is an injunction that it be
a *male* that is offered; but the reason in these cases may
be, that on occasions which were more than ordinarily
solemn, there was a special intention to exhibit something
of the *manner,* as well as the *effects,* of Christ's sacrifice
—*Himself,* as well as what he accomplished, was to be
shewn.

It must be "*without blemish;*" for it represents "the
holy child Jesus;" "altogether lovely;" "who knew no
sin"—the Head of a Church that is to be "without spot,
or wrinkle, or any such thing."

> Ver. 2. *And he shall lay his hand upon the head of his offering,
> and kill it at the door of the tabernacle of the congregation:
> and Aaron's sons, the priests, shall sprinkle the blood upon the
> altar round about.*

The offerer's hand, resting on the head of the animal,
was equivalent to his pointing to Christ as the source of
his blessings; *q. d.* "The chastisement of my peace is

---

* So, a *kid* might be taken as well as a *lamb* for the Passover (Exod. xiii. 5)
Attention was directed to the *use made* of the blood; not to the kind of animal

laid upon him ; therefore I am come this day, laden with
benefits, to give thanks while I enjoy the blessing" (see
above, chap. i. 5).   And let us again notice the words,
"*kill it at the door of the tabernacle.*"   We cannot cross
the threshold of his Father's house, and enter his many
mansions, except by his peace-speaking blood.   "*Being
justified by faith, we have peace—we have access into his
grace*" (Rom. v. 1, 2).

> Ver. 3, 4. *And he shall offer of the sacrifice of the peace-offering
> an offering made by fire unto the Lord; the fat that covereth
> the inwards, and all the fat that is upon the inwards, and the
> two kidneys, and the fat that is on them, which is by the flanks,
> and the caul above the liver, with the kidneys, it shall he take
> away.*

From a comparison of Exod. xxix. 13, it becomes plain
that *all* the pieces here mentioned were to be removed
from the animal, and burnt by themselves.   "*It shall he
take*" is equivalent to "*this—all this shall he take.*"

They were not to burn the whole animal, but only
these portions.   Thése portions were like "*the memorial*"
(chap. ii. 2) in the case of the meat-offering.   And the
parts chosen for this end are the richest parts, *the fat—*
the fat *within,* and the fat that might be said to be *without*
(ver. 9), in the case of the lamb.

Peculiar care is to be given to take out all *the fat that
was within,* "*the fat that covers the inwards,*" or intestines ;
next, "*the kidneys,*" which are composed of the richest
substance, richer than even fat ;* then "*the fat in which
the kidneys*" are imbedded, and which *is* "*on the loins*"
(flanks), *i.e.* the inner fat muscles of the loins which had

---

* Hence Deut. xxii. 14, "*the fat of the kidneys of wheat,*" is used to express the highest degree of richness in the wheat.   Patrick quotes Aristotle *de
Animal.*, iii. 9, "ἔχουσι δὲ νεφροὶ μάλιστα τῶν σπλαγχνῶν πιμελήν."

the collops of fat (Job xv. 27) ; and "*the caul* (יֹתֶרֶת)
above the liver and above the kidneys" (see the margin
and the original Hebrew).   It is not easy to ascertain the
meaning of "*the caul*," some making it one of the lobes
of the liver (Gesenius, from the Septuagint) ; others the
midriff; and others the *gall-bladder*.   It is every way
likely that it was some fat part near the liver and
kidneys.

Now, observe that all these portions of the animal are
the richest; and also deeply seated, near the heart.   In
an offering of thanks and fellowship, nothing was more
appropriate than to enjoin that the pieces presented
should be those seated *deep within*.   We approach a
reconciled God, to hold fellowship with him as Adam did
in Eden in the cool of the day; or rather as those before
the throne do in their holy worship.   We come to praise,
to glorify, to enjoy our God.   What, then, can we bring
but the *most inward* feelings, all of *the richest kind*, and
all from the depth of the soul.   Our reins (Heb. כְּלָיוֹת,
same as "kidneys") must yield their desires, in all abundance, to the God that trieth the "heart and reins" (Ps.
vii. 9).   Our loins were before "filled with pain" (Isa.
xxi. 3), because sin's "loathsome disease" spread through
them (Ps. xxxviii. 7) ; therefore now we consecrate their
strength, using it all for him, "the effectual working of
whose power" has set us free.   Yea, whatever can be
found anywhere in or about our heart and reins, we yield
it all to him who "poured out his soul unto death."   This
is communion with God.

Such was the rich offering of his soul which Jesus made
as our peace-offering, when "by the eternal Spirit he
offered himself to God."   Every deep affection, every
emotion, all that love could feel, all that desire could

yearn over, was presented by him to the Father in that
hour when he became "our peace" (Eph. ii. 14).

And all these feelings were at the moment tried and
tested by *the fire* which blazed around them.   The just
wrath of God seemed to spurn and thrust down each
heartfelt emotion ; yet all remained unchanged and
undiminished, and were poured into the mould of the
Father's heart by that very heat of wrath.

We, as reconciled, are to pour out these same feelings
in all their fulness, but under the kindly influence of love.
The heat of love, not the fire of wrath, is to melt our
souls and pour forth our feelings.

> Ver. 5. *And Aaron's sons shall burn it on the altar upon the
> burnt-sacrifice, which is upon the wood that is on the fire : it
> is an offering made by fire of a sweet savour unto the Lord.*

Here the Septuagint have " ὀσμη εὐωδιας Κυριῳ," the
terms employed by Paul in Eph. v. 2—" θυσια εἰς ὀσμην
εὐωδιας."

The parts thus prepared, the fat parts, are to be put
on the altar ; but not at random, anywhere on the altar.
A particular mode is fixed upon.   They are to be put
" *on the sacrifice that is upon the wood which feeds the
flame*" of the altar.   *The daily sacrifice* is referred to,
which typified the atonement in all its fulness.   Upon
this, therefore, must the pieces of the peace-offerings be
laid.   Our daily acts of communion with God, our daily
praise, our daily thanksgiving, must be founded afresh on
the work of Jesus.   " *By him* therefore let us offer the
sacrifice of praise to God *continually*" (Heb. xiii. 15).

> Ver. 6. *And if his offering, for a sacrifice of peace-offering unto the
> Lord, be of the flock, male or female, he shall offer it without
> blemish.*

The Father's delight in his Son seems plainly exhibited

in the ever-recurring direction—"*without blemish.*" The eye of God rested with infinite complacency on the spotlessness of Jesus. "Behold my servant whom I have chosen, mine elect (*q.d.* my chosen Lamb), in whom my soul delighteth." It is an expression that teaches us by its frequent repetition, both the holy delight which the Father had in "the holy child Jesus," and the delight he will have in his unblemished Church. It is a holy God that speaks; it is the author of the holy law. The lawgiver is he who prescribes the type of a fulfilled and satisfied law. We recognise the God and Father of our Lord and Saviour "just, while he justifies." It is truly pleasant, unspeakably precious, to see God's thorough demand for spotlessness; for thus we are assured, that beyond all doubt, our reconciliation is solid. It is full reconciliation to a God who is fully satisfied.

> Ver. 7, 8. *If he offer a lamb for his offering, then shall he offer it before the Lord. And he shall lay his hand upon the head of his offering, and kill it before the tabernacle of the congregation: and Aaron's sons shall sprinkle the blood thereof round about upon the altar.*

The lamb is as fully acknowledged as the offering from the herd—the bullock or heifer; for it is not the thing itself, but what it represented, that has value in it. One of the ends answered by permitting a gradation in the value of the things sacrificed, was this; it turned attention to the *Antitype*, instead of the *type itself*—to *the Lamb of God*, instead of the value of the mere animal.

> Ver. 9, 10. *And he shall offer, of the sacrifice of the peace-offering, an offering made by fire unto the Lord; the fat thereof, and the whole rump, it shall he take off hard by the back-bone; and the fat that covereth the inwards, and all the fat that is upon the inwards, and the two kidneys, and the fat*

*that is upon them, which is by the flanks, and the caul above
the liver, with the kidneys, it shall he take away.*

The only difference here, from ver. 3, 4, is, that here
we have, in addition to the other pieces already noticed,
"*the rump*," or *tail* (אַלְיָה). In Syrian sheep, this ˉwas
a part of the animal which the shepherd reckoned very
valuable; it is large,* and, being composed of a substance
between fat and marrow, is not inferior in taste and
quality to marrow. Still the richest portions are claimed
for the altar. Every rich thought, every rich emotion,
every intense feeling, was devoted by Christ for us, and
is to be now sent back by us to him. And it is said,
"*the tail he shall remove close by the back-bone*," *q.d.*
take it entire and complete—leaving nothing behind.

Perhaps we are entitled to consider the Psalmist as
referring to this offering in Ps. lxiii. 5, "*My soul shall
be satisfied as with marrow and fatness*"—here is the
reference to the pieces presented—*q.d.* My soul shall
be satisfied, as if I had received all that is intimated by
the rich pieces of the peace-offering. And so also, when
Isaiah says (lv. 2), "*Eat ye that which is good, and let
your soul delight itself in fatness*," *q.d.* Come to the great
peace-offering, and take the richest portions, even those
selected for God! Enjoy the very love wherewith the
Father loveth the Son!

Ver. 11. *And the priest shall burn it upon the altar: it is the food
of the offering made by fire unto the Lord.*

Instead of saying, "It is a sweet savour," we have
here another expression, equally significant. "*It is the
food, the sacrifice made by fire.*" It is called "food," or
"bread," because God is now regarded as a Father feast-

---

* This is so well known that writers usually refer us to Aristotle *de Animal.*,
viii. 28, where he says, " Οὐρας ἔχει το πλατος πηχεως."

ing his prodigal children who have returned home, or as
a friend entertaining guests.   Hence Ezekiel xliv. 7, "Ye
offer my *bread*, the fat and the blood;" and hence *the
altar* is called "*the table* of the Lord" (Mal. i. 7; also
Lev. xxi. 22). This represents God as one at table
with his people; they feast together.   He is no more
their foe.   If it was the chief aggravation of Judas's sin,
"*He that eateth bread with me hath lifted up his heel
against me;*" then it is impossible for God to be otherwise than an eternal friend, "an everlasting Father," to
those whom he invites home.   In this view we see the
keenness of the reproach in Mal. i. 7, 12, and in Ezek.
xliv. 7. They treated the privilege of children and
friends with contempt; God, in his most kindly aspect,
was despised and scorned.

> Ver. 12, 13. *And if his offering be a goat, then he shall offer it
> before the Lord.   And he shall lay his hand upon the head of
> it, and kill it before the tabernacle of the congregation: and
> the sons of Aaron shall sprinkle the blood thereof upon the
> altar round about.   And he shall offer thereof his offering,
> even an offering made by fire unto the Lord.*

The *goat* stands here in the same relation to the
peace-offering from the herd, as did the *turtle-dove and
pigeon* to the bullock of the whole burnt-sacrifice.   The
poorer sort might bring the goat; when he could not
bring the blood of bulls, he brought the blood of goats.
And thus, still, they were prevented from attaching importance to the mere type.

The *goat* represents Jesus as one taken out of the
flock for the salvation of the rest.   Let us suppose we
saw "a flock of goats appearing from Mount Gilead"
(Song vi. 5).   The lion from Bashan rushes upon this
flock; *one* is seized, and is soon within the jaws of the

lion! This prey is enough; the lion is satisfied, and retires; the flock is saved by the death of one. This incidental substitution does not, indeed, shew forth the manner of our Substitute's suffering; but it is an illustration of the fact, that *one* dying saved the *whole flock.* The *goat* is one of a class that goes in flocks in Palestine, and so are fitted to represent Christ and his people. And, perhaps, the fact of an animal like the *goat* being selected to be among the types of Christ, was intended to prevent the error of those who would place the value of Christ's undertaking in his *character* alone. They say, "Behold his meekness—he is the Lamb of God!" Well, all that is true; it is implied in his being "without blemish." But that cannot be the true point to which our eye is intended to be directed by the types; for what, then, becomes of the *goat?* They may tell us of the meekness of the lamb, and patience of the bullock, and tenderness of the turtle-dove; but the *goat*, what is to be said of it? Surely it is not without a special providence that the *goat* is inserted, where, if the order of chap. i. had been followed, we would have had a *turtle-dove?* The reason is, to let us see that the main thing to be noticed in these types is the *atonement* which they represented. Observe the stroke that falls on the victim, the fire that consumes the victim, the blood that must flow from the victim, whether it be a bullock, a lamb, a turtle-dove, or a goat.

The Socinian view of Christ's death is thus contradicted by these various types; and our eye is intently fixed on the *atoning character* of the animal, more than on anything in its nature.

While other types do exhibit the character and nature of the Saviour, it was fitting that one type, such as this

of the goat, should thus guard us against the idea that
that in itself was *atonement*.

> Ver. 14–16. *The fat that covereth the inwards, and all the*
> *fat that is upon the inwards, and the two kidneys, and the*
> *fat that is upon them, which is by the flanks, and the caul*
> *above the liver, with the kidneys, it shall he take away. And*
> *the priest shall burn them upon the altar: it is the food of the*
> *offering made by fire, for a sweet savour.*

This offered *goat* is as fully accepted, as a peace-
offering, as was the lamb or bullock; for *the atoning*
aspect of the type is just as complete in this case as in
any other. "It is food—an offering made by fire"—as
ver. 11.

> Ver. 17. *All the fat is the Lord's. It shall be a perpetual*
> *statute for your generations, throughout all your dwellings,*
> *that ye eat neither fat nor blood.*

Some think "*the fat*" is *the fat of beasts used in sacri-*
fice (chap. vii. 25). But, perhaps, it was *the fat of all*
beasts used " in *their dwellings.*" Those parts mentioned
as sacrificial must always be set aside. But the fat of
other parts of the animal (the fat that was part of the
flesh) was used, and reckoned a luxury; see Neh. viii. 10
—"Eat the fat." This is the most probable explanation.
There may be a reproof intended in Ezek. xxxiv. 3, "Ye
eat the fat," as if they even took the forbidden portions.
"*Blood*," because *the life*—the sign of atonement—must
not be eaten. It is the solemn type of the poured-out
soul.

Thus in the *dwellings* of Israel there was something to
keep them in daily remembrance of the Great Sacrifice.
Their deep and awful reverence must be felt at home as
well as in the sanctuary. Their homes are made a *sanc-*
tuary thereby, as they set apart *the fat and the blood* at

their tables! And thus they live as redeemed men, realising their dependence on the blood of Jesus, and delighting to cast the crown at his feet in every new remembrance of his work.

Few ordinances were more blessed than these Peace-offerings. Yet, like the Lord's Supper with us, often were they turned to sin. The lascivious woman in Prov. vii. 14, comes forth saying, "I have *peace-offerings* with me; this day have I paid my vows." She had actually gone up among the devoutest class of worshippers to pre-sent a thank-offering, and had stood at the altar as one at peace with God. Having now received from the priest those pieces of the sacrifice that were to be feasted upon, lo! she hurries to her dwelling, and prepares a banquet of lewdness. She quiets her conscience by constraining herself to spend some of her time and some of her sub-stance in his sanctuary. She deceives her fellow-creatures, too, and maintains a character for religion; and then she rushes back to sin without remorse. Is there nothing of this in our land? What means Christmas-mirth, after pretended observance of Christ's being born? What means the sudden worldliness of so many on the day fol-lowing their approach to the Lord's Table? What means the worldly talk and levity of a Sabbath afternoon, or evening, after worship is done?

Contrast with this the true worshipper, as he appears in Psalm lxvi. He has received mercies, and is truly thankful. He comes up to the sanctuary with his offer-ings, saying—

"I will go into thy house with burnt-offerings; I will pay thee my vows, which my lips have uttered, and my mouth hath spoken, when I was in trouble" (ver. 13, 14).

In the "burnt-offerings," we see his approach to the altar with the common and general sacrifice; and next, in his "*paying vows*," we see he has brought his *peace-offerings* with him. Again, therefore, he says at the altar—

" I will offer unto thee burnt-sacrifices of fatlings " (ver. 15).

This is the general offering, brought from the best of his flock and herd. Then follow *the peace-offerings*—

" With the incense (קְטֹרֶת, *fuming smoke*) of rams ; I will offer bullocks with goats. Selah."

Having brought his offerings, he is in no haste to depart, notwithstanding; for his heart is full. Ere, therefore, he leaves the sanctuary, he utters the language of a soul at peace with God—

" Come and hear, all ye that fear God, and I will declare what he hath done for my soul. I cried unto him with my mouth, and he was extolled with my tongue. If I regard iniquity in my heart, the Lord will not hear me : but verily God hath heard me ; he hath attended to the voice of my prayer. Blessed be God, which hath not turned away my prayer, nor his mercy from me !"

This, truly, is one whom "*the very God of peace*" has sanctified, and whose whole spirit, and body, and soul, he will preserve blameless unto the coming of the Lord Jesus Christ (1 Thess. v. 23).

CHAPTER IV

The Sin-Offering

" Little children, these things write I unto you, that ye sin not. And if any man sin, we have an advocate with the Father, Jesus Christ the righteous: and he is the propitiation for our sins; and not for ours only, but also for the sins of the whole world."—1 John ii. 1, 2

WERE a scorpion on our brow, prepared to thrust in its deadly sting, while we were unconscious of any danger, surely the friend would deserve our thanks who saw the black scorpion there, and cried aloud to us to sweep it off. Such is a *sin of ignorance;* and God, who is "a God of knowledge," is the gracious friend. In this character he appears here.

> Ver. 1, 2. *And the Lord spake unto Moses, saying, Speak unto the children of Israel, saying, If a soul shall sin through ignorance against any of the commandments of the Lord, concerning things which ought not to be done, and shall do against any of them :—*

The former chapters of this book have been in substance like the first chapter of John's first Epistle. We have been shewn in type that life eternal which was manifested to us in Christ the great Atonement. Next, we were shewn that the Lord had a claim on all that is ours, and therefore must we give up ourselves and all

that is ours to him.   This done, we walk in fellowship
with him.

These things having been written to us, in the first
three chapters, to the end "that we sin not"—that we
may not live like the dark world around us, but may be
drawn to him who draws us with his cords of love—the
Lord now speaks again to "the children of Israel"—his
"little children." He points out what is to be done
when they come to the knowledge of sin of which they
were not aware before.   The cases are understood to be
things committed, not mere *omissions* of duty; and how
saddening to find that we grieve the Lord in so many
hidden ways!   We have a heart as prone to sin, as the
body is to weariness.

The *sin through ignorance* (שְׁגָגָה) is the same that
David prays against in Ps. xix. 12, "Who can understand his *errors* (שְׁגִיאוֹת)? cleanse thou me from secret
things!" These are not sins of omission, but acts committed by a person when, at the time, he did not suppose
that what he did was sin.*   Although he did the thing
deliberately, yet he did not perceive the *sin* of it.   So
deceitful is sin, we may be committing that abominable
thing which cast angels into an immediate and an eternal
hell, and yet at the moment be totally unaware!   Want
of knowledge of the truth, and too little tenderness of
conscience, hide it from us.   Hardness of heart and a
corrupt nature cause us to sin unperceived.   But here
again the form of the Son of man appears! *Jehovah,*
God of Israel, institutes sacrifice for *sins of ignorance,*
and thereby discovers the same compassionate and con-

---

* Josh. xx. 3, "Who killeth any person *in ignorance* (בִּשְׁגָגָה) and did not
know," *i. e.* did not know that his action would have had that effect (comp.
Deut. xix. 4).

siderate heart that appears in our High Priest, "*who can have compassion on* THE IGNORANT!" (Heb. v. 2.) Amidst the types of this Tabernacle we recognise the presence of Jesus—it is his voice that shakes the curtains and speaks in the ear of Moses—"*If a soul shall sin through igno-rance!*" The same yesterday, to-day, and for ever!

THE PRIEST'S SIN

Ver. 3, 4. *If the priest that is anointed do sin according to. the sin of the people; then let him bring, for his sin which he hath sinned, a young bullock without blemish unto the Lord for a sin-offering. And he shall bring the bullock unto the door of the tabernacle of the congregation before the Lord; and shall lay his hand upon the bullock's head, and kill the bullock before the Lord.*

The *anointed* priest must mean the *High Priest*, for he only was anointed. In ver. 5, the Septuagint have so understood it, for they give " ὁ ἱερευς ὁ Χριστος ὁ τετελειω-μενος." Now, the first case is that of *the anointed priest* sinning. "The law maketh men high priests that have infirmity" (Heb. vii. 28). This sin the priest may have committed in his public services, in the execution of his office. Being invested with office, his sins are peculiarly aggravated, and peculiarly dangerous—their effect upon others may be incalculable. The words, "*according to the sin of the people*" (לְאַשְׁמַת.הָעָם) are more properly rendered, "so *as to cause the people to sin*,"—he sins *to the* sinning of the people. (Τοῦ τον λαον ἁμαρτεῖν.—Septuagint. "*Delinquere faciens populum.*"—Vulg.) The Old Testament ministry involved awful responsibilities, as well as the New. The personal holiness of the priest is pro-vided for by this consideration, that if he, because of de-ficient wisdom, or because he had not faithfully sought

help from the sanctuary, were guilty of some mistake in
the service, or polluted some of the holy vessels, his sin
would injure thousands of souls. It might destroy the
comfort of thousands; it might misrepresent the way of
acceptance to thousands, and thereby ruin their souls.
It left the sanctuary-door open to Satan. And, on the
other hand, in such circumstances, surely the people would
learn to pray for the ministering priest, and to feel, that
after all, he was no more than an instrument used by
God for their sakes. There seems thus to have been, in
all ages, the flow of the same sympathies through Christ's
body, the Church. The Church has been ever "com-
pacted by that which every joint supplieth." But let us
proceed.

Hitherto we have seen *atonement* made by sacrifice,
but now we are to see *imputation of sin*. *Atonement* is
effected by *imputation of sin* to another. The priest's
sin is to be brought to the altar. He is to bring "*a bullock.*" This is the very same kind of offering as when the
whole congregation sin. As the most bulky and most
expensive form of sacrifice was *the bullock,* the priest
must take this form of sacrifice, in order to make more
obvious to the eye his concern for his sin. He spares no
cost in bringing his sin to the altar; and the people
learn from.him to spare no cost in bringing their sins to
the atoning blood.

The *type,* applied to our Surety, may be this—that
when Christ, our Anointed Priest, took upon him our sin
as his own, he had to offer exactly what we would have
had to do ourselves, had we been reckoned with in our
own persons. If there be sin found upon the priest,
then his offering must be no less than the whole congregation's.

Ver. 5, 6. *And the priest that is anointed shall take of the bullock's blood, and bring it to the tabernacle of the congregation. And the priest shall dip his finger in the blood, and
sprinkle of the blood seven times before the Lord, before the
veil of the sanctuary.*

The "*seven times,*" throughout all Scripture, intimates
a *perfect and complete* action.* The blood is to be
thoroughly exhibited before the Lord—life openly exhibited as taken to honour the law that had been violated.
It is not, at this time, taken *within* the veil, for that
would require the priest to enter the Holy of holies—a
thing permitted only once a year. But it is taken very
near the mercy-seat—it is taken "*before* the veil," while
the Lord, that dwelt between the cherubim, bent down
to listen to the cry that came up from the sin-atoning
blood.

Was the blood sprinkled *on* the veil? Some say not,
but only on the floor, *close to* the veil. The floor of the
Holy Place was dyed in blood; a threshold of blood
was formed, over which the high priest must pass on the
day of atonement, when he entered into the Most Holy,
drawing aside the veil. It is *blood* that opens our way
into the presence of God; it is the voice of atoning blood
that prevails with him who dwells within. Others, however, with more probability, think the blood was sprinkled *on the veil.*† It might intimate that atonement was

* The "*seven times*" of some passages, and the "*once*" of others (Heb. x.
10; 1 Pet. iii. 18), intimate the same thing, viz. so completely done that no
more is needed. It is the *one action in seven parts*, for the satisfaction of all
who see it done. And so the "*One Spirit*," and the "*Seven Spirits*." The
Pythagoreans learned from the Hebrews to account this number very important
in religious acts.

† The Hebrew is doubtful; אֵת פְּנֵי פָרְכֶת is put at the close of the sentence.
Most probably it is so put, in order to define what "*before the Lord*" meant.
The Septuagint is "κατὰ τὸ καταπέτασμα." But Aben Ezra has יזה על פרכת,
"he shall sprinkle on the veil."

yet to rend that veil; and, as that beautiful veil represented the Saviour's holy humanity (Heb. x. 20), O
how expressive was the continual repetition of this
blood-sprinkling seven times! As often as the priest
offered a sin-offering, the veil was wet again with blood
which dropt on the floor. Is this Christ bathed in the
blood of atonement? Yes; "through that veil" the way
was opened to us—through the flesh of Jesus—through
the body that for us was drenched in the sweat of blood.

> Ver. 7. *And the priest shall put some of the blood upon the horns
> of the altar of sweet incense before the Lord, which is in the
> tabernacle of the congregation; and shall pour all the blood
> of the bullock at the bottom of the altar of the burnt-offering,
> which is at the door of the tabernacle of the congregation.*

The priest retires a few steps from before the veil.
Having gazed solemnly on the seven times sprinkled
blood, in the light of the golden candlestick, he is
directed to another act. He is to approach the golden
altar—that altar whereon sweet incense was presented.
Incense, being fragrant, represented that which is pleasing,
and which has in it acceptability; and when offered
along with prayer, praise, or any feeling of the soul,
exhibited a type of the merits of the Surety enveloping
his people's services. The *horns* of this altar (said to have
been of a pyramidical shape) represented the power and
strength that lay in this mode of approaching Jehovah.
The horn is the recognised symbol of power. *Incense
ascending between the four horns* was symbolical of
praise, prayer, or any service presented to God, ascending with *all-prevailing merit*. And *blood*, placed on
these horns,* exhibited the strong appeal to God made

---

* There is no *incense* burnt on this altar on this occasion, "in order to teach
us," says an old writer, "not to confide in our *prayers* for pardon."

by atonement. A strong appeal to God is made by the
blood thus placed on the horns of the golden altar. It
is like the voice in Rev. ix. 13.

We have seen that the priest first of all sprinkled the
blood on the floor, close to the veil, or on the veil, whence
it fell in drops to the ground, so that a cry was heard
ascending from the Holy Place itself. And then he
sprinkled it on the *four horns of the altar of intercession*,
that an appeal of unbroken strength might go up into the
ears of the Lord from the very place of strong crying.
He knew that it spoke better things than the blood of
Abel. When the anointed priest was thus engaged, was
he not a type of Jesus in the act of expiating his people's
guilt? Probably the priest knelt, and then prostrated
himself on the ground, as he sprinkled the blood before
the veil; and it would be with many tears, and strong
crying from the depths of his soul, that he touched the
altar's horns—a type of Jesus in the garden, when he
fell on his face, and, being in an agony, prayed more
earnestly, and "offered up supplications, with strong
crying and tears, to him that was able to save him from
death" (Heb. v. 7). Although in this case, the priest's
sense of guilt was personal, and therefore was deep and
piercing, yet when Jesus took on him our sins, he, too,
felt them, and felt them as if they had been his own. He
cried, "*Mine iniquities* have taken hold upon me!" (Ps.
xl. 12.) Identifying himself with us, his soul grieved
immeasurably for the sin he bore, and his tears dropt on
the awful burden which he took up, as sincerely as if it
had been altogether his own.

At length the priest comes from the Holy Place—leaving
it, however, filled with the cry of blood—a cry for pardon!
—and proceeds to the altar of burnt-offering, directly

opposite the door. There he pours out the rest of the blood, at the foot of the altar,* his eye looking straight toward the Holy Place. Within and without the Holy Place, the voice of atonement was now heard ascending from the blood. What a sermon was thus preached to the people! Atonement is the essence of it—atonement needed for even one sin, and applied as soon as the sin was known. There is no trifling with God. What a ransom for the soul is given!—*life*—the *life* of the Seed of the Woman! What care to present it—what earnestness! The Holy Place is filled with its cry, and the courts without also; and the priest's soul is intently engaged in this one awful matter! The people, perceiving the whole transaction, must have felt it singularly powerful, first, for conviction—" *Whosoever shall keep the whole law, and yet offend in one point, he is guilty of all* " (James ii. 10); and, secondly, for invitation—" *To-day, if ye will hear his voice, harden not your hearts.*"

> Ver. 8–10. *And he shall take off from it all the fat of the bullock for the sin-offering; the fat that covereth the inwards, and all the fat that is upon the inwards, and the two kidneys, and the fat that is upon them, which is by the flanks, and the caul above the liver, with the kidneys, it shall he take away, as it was taken off from the bullock of the sacrifice of peace-offerings; and the priest shall burn them upon the altar of the burnt-offering.*

The same ceremonies as were used in the peace-offerings are *intentionally* introduced here (see iii. 10). The object seems to be, to shew the offerer that he *is now accepted.* It is not in vain that he has sprinkled the blood on the floor of the Holy Place and its altar of incense, and poured out what of the blood remained, in sight of

---

* It is said, that in Jerusalem, there was an underground canal at the altar in the temple, by which the blood was carried off to the brook Cedron.—*Patrick.*

all the people.   God gives this sign of reconciliation, viz.
at this stage of his offering, the sacrifice is treated as a
peace-offering.   The voice of peace now breathes over the
sacrifice, and through the courts, as much as if a voice had
said, "It is a savour of rest."

> Ver. 11, 12. *And the skin of the bullock, and all his flesh, with
> his head, and with his legs, and his inwards, and his dung,
> even the whole bullock shall he carry forth without the camp
> unto a clean place, where the ashes are poured out, and burn
> him on the wood with fire: where the ashes are poured out
> shall he be burnt.*

But that the priest, and all present, might go home
with an awful conviction of the heinousness even of forgiven sin, other things remained to be done.   We are not
to forget sin, because it has been atoned for; and we are
not to think lightly of sin, because it is washed away.
Our God wishes his people to retain a deep and lively
sense of their guilt, even when forgiven.   Hence the concluding ceremonies in the case of the priest's sin.

The very *skin* of the bullock is to be burnt—thus
expressing more complete destruction than even in the
case of the whole burnt-offering.   Here is the holy law
exacting the last mite; for *the skin* is taken, and the
whole flesh, the *head* and *legs* (i. 8), the *intestines,* and the
very dung—"*even the whole bullock!*"   Unsparing justice,
that is, unspotted justice!   And yet more.   As if the
altar were too near God's presence to express fully that
part of the sinner's desert which consists in suffering
torment far off from God, all this is to be done "*without
the camp*"—a distance, it is calculated, of four miles from
the Holy Place.   In all sacrifices, indeed, this separation
from God is represented in some degree by the *ashes*
being carried away out of the camp; but, to call attention

still more to this special truth, we are here shewn the
bullock burnt on the wood, " *without the camp, where the
ashes were wont to be poured out.*" It was *over* the very
ashes that lay poured out there; for, in the last clause of
the verse, the preposition עַל is used. " The *clean place*"
is defined to be this place of ashes. It was clean, because,
when reduced to ashes by consuming fire, all guilt was
away from the victim, as intimated in Ps. xx. 3, " *Let him
turn thy burnt-sacrifice to ashes*" (יְדַשְׁנֶה), the word used
here also.

At this part of the ceremonies, there was meant to be
exhibited a type of hell. This burning afar off, away
from the Holy Place, yet seen by the whole congregation,
was a terrible glance at that truth—" They shall be tormented with fire and brimstone in the presence of the
holy angels, and in presence of the Lamb; and the smoke
of their torment ascendeth up for ever and ever" (Rev.
xiv. 10).

It is plain, also, that God took the opportunity which
this offering afforded, or rather shaped this part of the
rites belonging to the offering, in order to shew somewhat
more of Christ's death.

In every sacrifice which was of a *public* nature, or for
a *public person*, the animal was carried without the camp,
as we may see in chap. xvi. 27, on the day of atonement.
The reason of this was that, in these cases, Christ's *public*
sacrifice, as offered to the whole world, and every creature,
and as fulfilling the law's demands to the last mite, was
to be especially prefigured. It is carried " *without the
camp*," as Jesus was crucified outside of the gates of
Jerusalem (Heb. xiii. 12), that it might be in sight of all
the camp, as Christ's one offering is held up to all the
world, to be used by whosoever will. Next, suffering far

off from the Holy Place, with his Father's face hidden, and all the fire of wrath in his soul and on his body, Jesus farther fulfilled this type in regard to the entire satisfaction demanded by the law. And, inasmuch as he suffered at Jerusalem, where the ashes of the sacrifices were poured out, he may be said to have fulfilled the type of the "clean place." For we see him, *over these remnants of typical sacrifice, offering up the one true and perfect offering.* But it was *Calvary* that was specially a "*place of ashes,*" inasmuch as there the demands of justice were wont to be satisfied, and the bones of victims to human law cast out. *Joseph's new tomb,* hewn out of the very rock of Calvary, is the exact counterpart to the "*clean place,*" at the very spot where the ashes of so many dead men were to be found all around.

What a view of hell does the suffering Saviour give! The face-covering between him and his Father— the criminal's veil hung over him for three hours, the three hours of darkness—away from the Holy Place— driven from the mercy-seat, and beyond the bounds of the holy city—an outcast, a forsaken soul, a spectacle to all that passed by—wrath to the uttermost within, and his person, even to the eye, more marred than any man, while his cry, "My God! my God! why hast thou forsaken me?" ascended up as the smoke of the sacrifice, to heaven, shewing the heat of the unutterable agony, and testifying the unswerving exactness of the holy law. What a contrast to his Coming again without sin, and entering Jerusalem again with the voice of the archangel, in all his glory, bringing with him those whom he redeemed by that death on Calvary!

In one respect his people are to imitate the view of him shewn in this type. As he went forth to witness for

God's holy law—went forth without the gate, a spectacle
to all the earth ; so they, redeemed by him, are to go
forth to witness of that death and redemption which he
has accomplished (Heb. xiii. 12).   We are to " go forth
unto him ;" we are to be constantly, as it were, viewing
that spectacle of united love and justice, looking to his
cross ; though in so doing we make ourselves objects of
amazement and contempt to the world, who contemn those
whom they see going forth to stand by the side of the
Crucified One.

THE CONGREGATION'S SIN.

Ver. 13. *And if the whole congregation of Israel sin through*
ignorance, and the thing be hid from the eyes of the assembly,
and they have done somewhat against any of the command-
ments of the Lord, concerning things which should not be done,
and are guilty ;—

The moral law was sometimes broken by the nation at
large ; as in the matter of the golden calf, and the murmuring at the report of the spies.   It is thought by Rashi
that a sin like this occurred when " the Sanhedrim did
not instruct the people in regard to some ceremonial
observance."   Admitting that such cases occurred, yet it
is important to notice, that even if the people were led
into sin by their priest, they are not excused : they are
guilty, and suffer the consequences.*   The prophet Hosea
(iv. 6–9) shews that people are not freed from sin or
punishment in such cases.

This, however, is but one way whereby the congregation are led into sin.   Often it happened that a man made
little use of his knowledge, and so ate holy things, as we

---

* The proper rendering of " *are guilty,*" אָשֵׁמוּ, is, in this place, " *are suffer-*
ing the penalty."   As in Ps. xxxiv. 21, 22, " shall be desolate ;" and Isa.
xxiv. 6.

find, chap. xxii. 14 ; and the whole people, in 1 Sam. xiv. 33, ate of the blood.   Though they had not despised the priest, nor refused the law at his lips, yet they might let the word slip from their mind; as in Heb. ii. 1, we are told may still occur.

We all know that it is possible for a child of God to be cherishing unawares some idol, or indulging, like Eli, a too easy temper.   Or he may be rash in his words, and frowning in his looks, where Jesus would only have looked on in grief.   He may be cherishing pride like Hezekiah (Isa. xxxix.), or exhibiting blind zeal as the sons of Zebe-dee.   He may be unawares substituting labour for fellow-ship with God, working without love, and suffering without faith in exercise.   Prejudice against particular doctrines may be his secret sin ; or wrong motives may be in-fluencing him to do right actions.   He may contrive to retain the look of greenness when the sap is gone.   Even a whole community of believers may be pervaded by some such sin.

But more specially, a whole church may be in the state of the congregation referred to here.   It may be deny-ing some great truth in theory or in practice.   Thus, it may make light of the duty which kings and magistrates owe to Christ ; as is done by some churches.   It may be suffering " that woman Jezebel to teach and to seduce" (Rev. ii. 20).   It may be admitting some civil element into the management of its spiritual affairs, as is done in many Protestant Churches.   It may be shutting its eyes to some great truth, or winking at some heresy.   It may teach error in doctrine ; or it may have left its first love. It may have allowed discipline to have become lax and corrupt, as, alas ! is too generally true of all the Churches of the Reformation.

These secret sins may be keeping God from blessing the whole people, though he blesses individuals. Somewhere amid these sources is to be found the origin of much of our inefficiency and unprofitableness. *Ai* cannot be taken because of the accursed thing in the camp. The mariners cannot make out the voyage to Tarshish with Jonah on board.

Israel was thus led to constant self-examination and close attention to the revealed will of God.

> Ver. 14. *When the sin, which they have sinned against it, is known, then the congregation shall offer a young bullock for the sin, and bring him before the tabernacle of the congregation.*

Their offering is the same as the priest's, because of their mutual relation. The people's sin is not overlooked, but is judged with as much severity as the priest's. Every man must bear his own burden; and God is jealously holy.

> Ver. 15. *And the elders of the congregation shall lay their hands upon the head of the bullock before the Lord; and the bullock shall be killed before the Lord.*

The elders, in the name of the people, convey the guilt of the people to the head of the victim. It was this class of men—*the elders*—that put Jesus to death, with the priests. Now here we see that *their* act was a national act—strictly national—since they were representatives of all Israel. And their cry, "*His blood be on us*," joining with the multitude, was a national rejection of Jesus. Ah, had they then joined to put their hands on him as the acknowledged sacrifice, they might have remained to this day!

The guilt of the whole people was thus made to meet in one point, viz. on the bullock. It is to a scene like

this that Isaiah (liii. 6) refers—" The Lord made the
iniquity of us all to meet on him" (הִפְגִּיעַ בּוֹ).

> Ver. 16–20. *And the priest that is anointed shall bring of the
> bullock's blood to the tabernacle of the congregation; and the
> priest shall dip his finger in some of the blood, and sprinkle
> it seven times before the Lord, even before the veil. And
> he shall put some of the blood upon the horns of the altar
> which is before the Lord, that is in the tabernacle of the con-
> gregation, and shall pour out all the blood at the bottom of
> the altar of the burnt-offering, which is at the door of the
> tabernacle of the congregation. And he shall take all his
> fat from him, and burn it upon the altar. And he shall do
> with the bullock as he did with the bullock for a sin-offering,
> so shall he do with this: and the priest shall make an atone-
> ment for them, and it shall be forgiven them.*

The expression, ver. 20, is to be understood, " He shall
do in this case *as he has done already*," in the case of a
bullock for sin-offering, viz. ver. 3. The declaration, " *It
shall be forgiven*," seems inserted here because otherwise
there is not here, as in the last case, any particular exhibition of *peace*, as in ver. 8–10. This declaration, therefore, is made, that pardon may be assuredly known.

> Ver. 21. *And he shall carry forth the bullock without the camp,
> and burn him as he burned the first bullock: it is a sin-offering
> for the congregation.*

It is remarkable, that *after* the declaration of *forgiveness*, these other ceremonies take place. They are intended, no doubt, to impress a horror of sin on the soul,
even after it is forgiven. The forgiven man is most capable of seeing the horror of sin ; and therefore the people
are first pardoned, and then led out to see the last mite
exacted without the camp. See the same order observed,
and for the same reason, we suppose, at ver. 11, 12.
None but a pardoned man could have uttered Paul's cry,

" O wretched man that I am ; who shall deliver me from the body of this death ?" (Rom. vii. 24.)

The identity of Christ and his people, also, is taught by *their* offering being burnt exactly in all respects as the *priest's*, whose offering more especially typified Jesus.

THE RULER'S SIN

Ver. 22, 23. When a ruler hath sinned, and done somewhat through ignorance against any of the commandments of the Lord his God, concerning things which should not be done, and is guilty; or if his sin, wherein he hath sinned, come to his knowledge; he shall bring his offering, a kid of the goats, a male without blemish.

" If a ruler has sinned . . . . and is *suffering the penalty*," as in ver. 13.   The ruler may sin ignorantly, and be led to know his sin by some *suffering*, like Abimelech, in Gen. xx. 3–17 ; or it might be by some friend's reproof, or by new circumstances occurring.   So ver. 27.

The *ruler* is such a one as those *princes* (נְשִׂיאִים) of the tribes in Numb. vii.   It includes all civil magistrates.   His high responsibility is here shewn just as in Prov. xxix. 12, " If a ruler hearken to lies, all his servants will be wicked."

It is said, " *The Lord his God;*" as if to call attention to the duty of publicly recognising the Lord, and of *rulers* having the Lord as their own God.   A ruler is specially bound to be a man of God.   This is taken for granted here, " *The Lord his God.*"   No casting off of Messiah's cords here.   He that ruleth over men must be as the Just One, " ruling in the fear of God."

" *A kid of the goats*" is his sin-offering.   It is a different victim from that offered by the priest or congregation, in order to shew that God definitely marks sin.   And yet still the essence of atonement is the same, the blood of a

victim that dies.   Priest or prince must alike be atoned
for by blood.   The *"male without blemish"* is the spotless Saviour, the Son of man.

> Ver. 24, 25. *And he shall lay his hand upon the head of the*
> *goat, and kill it in the place where they kill the burnt-offering*
> *before the Lord: it is a sin-offering.   And the priest shall*
> *take of the blood of the sin-offering with his finger, and put it*
> *upon the horns of the altar of burnt-offering, and shall pour*
> *out his blood at the bottom of the altar of burnt-offering.*

It seems intentionally twice stated here, that the *altar*
of burnt-offering was to be the place where his sin-
offering was to be presented;—it is to be killed where
the usual sacrifices for that altar are killed, and its blood
is to be sprinkled there.   The reason may be this:—
The *altar of incense* in the Holy Place was peculiarly the
scene of the priest's intercession, and of the people's
prayers as *a congregation.*   The sins in *holy things*
pointed inward, toward the Holy Place.   On the other
hand, a ruler's sins pointed toward the camp.   Hence,
the blood that atones for his sin is sprinkled on the horns
of that altar where it would be publicly observed.   The
cry of the blood on the four horns,—the *strong* cry,
based on *all-prevailing* atonement,—was to ascend within
hearing, as it were, of all his subjects, inasmuch as his
sins affected the welfare of the nation.

> Ver. 26.   *And he shall burn all his fat upon the altar, as the*
> *fat of the sacrifice of peace-offerings: and the priest shall*
> *make an atonement for him as concerning his sin, and it shall*
> *be forgiven him.*

The last clause may be intended to draw attention to
the fact, that in this instance the atonement is because of
this particular sin, and not simply because he is a sinner

in nature and by common actual transgressions. The opportunity is here embraced of impressing on us the need of atonement for particular sins,—for every sin by itself ; and for those little-regarded sins which we apologise for by saying, " I did not know of it." Jonathan's sin in taking a little honey (1 Sam. xiv. 39, 43), and Abimelech's sin (Gen. xx. 6), shew how jealous God is of even what *appears* sin, especially in public persons.

SINS OF INDIVIDUALS

Ver. 27, 28. *And if any one of the common people sin through ignorance, while he doeth somewhat against any of the commandments of the Lord, concerning things which ought not to be done, and be guilty* (see ver. 13)*; or if his sin, which he hath sinned, come to his knowledge: then he shall bring his offering, a kid of the goats, a female without blemish, for his sin which he hath sinned.*

" *A female* " is here offered. Each kind of sin is thus definitely noticed, and each sinner's case treated by itself. But why is it a *female*, since Christ is typified by these offerings ?—It is not easy to say. Perhaps it was intended by God, that by occasionally taking *female* sacrifices, Israel should be kept from ever once supposing that atonement was not intended equally for the daughters of Zion. The circumstance that a *female kid* is here fixed upon served to take off the impression that the *male* intimated only the atonement of the *men* of Israel. Though, however, its being male or female is of use for other lessons, it is not the chief point to be noticed ; the point to be observed is, that the blood is an *atonement*. The subsidiary ideas are not to be dwelt upon always ; but everywhere the principle of *atonement by blood* is to be kept in the sinner's view.

" *For his sin which he hath sinned.*" Lest the man

should think that the sin was trifling, because he was a common man, and not a ruler, this emphatic notice is taken of his sin :—

> Ver. 29–31. *And he shall lay his hand upon the head of the sin-offering, and slay the sin-offering in the place of the burnt-offering. And the priest shall take of the blood thereof, with his finger, and put it upon the horns of the altar of burnt-offering, and shall pour out all the blood thereof at the bottom of the altar. And he shall take away all the fat thereof, as the fat is taken away from off the sacrifice of peace-offerings; and the priest shall burn it upon the altar for a sweet savour unto the Lord; and the priest shall make an atonement for him, and it shall be forgiven him.*

The clause, "*for a sweet savour unto the Lord,*" occurs here, though omitted in the three preceding cases. The reason may be to shew the worshipper, that though he was a common man, and not a ruler, yet still as much attention is paid to him as to the others. The offering which *he* presents is a sweet savour, as much as *Noah's.* The full acceptance and full favour shewn to every believer alike is immeasurably sweet. One family! all alike accepted! and all alike kept as the apple of his eye! And thus this sin, that unawares was troubling him, is away. And when even one sin, and that a sin of ignorance, is completely removed, who can tell how much light may flow into our now cleansed souls? A new window is opened,—a new eye—when the scale has fallen from it.

> Ver. 32–34. *And if he bring a lamb for a sin-offering, he shall bring it a female without blemish. And he shall lay his hand upon the head of the sin-offering, and slay it for a sin-offering in the place where they kill the burnt-offering. And the priest shall take of the blood of the sin-offering with his finger, and put it upon the horns of the altar of burnt-*

offering, and shall pour out all the blood thereof at the bottom of the altar.

It might sometimes not be easy to bring a kid. If so, let a lamb be taken. Only, blood must be shed. The poor man's lamb is specially noticed and fully received as the richer man's offering. *" Like precious faith"* is the common property of all God's family—*" One Lord, one faith."*

> Ver. 35. *And he shall take away all the fat thereof, as the fat of the lamb is taken away from the sacrifice of the peace-offerings; and the priest shall burn them upon the altar, according to the offerings made by fire unto the Lord: and the priest shall make an atonement for his sin that he hath committed, and it shall be forgiven him.*

The expression, *" according to* the offerings made by fire," should be *" in addition to* (עַל) the offerings,"—the daily sacrifice, morning and evening,—or, *" upon the* offerings," *i.e.* over the very remnants of the daily sacrifice. It is exactly like chap. iii. 5. We are there taught that particular sins must be cast upon the one great Atonement; and the cases that occur in this chapter of special guilt are just specific applications of the great truth taught in the daily sacrifice.

Israel was taught that their different offerings were all of one nature in the main with the general burnt-offering;—one Saviour only was prefigured, and one atonement. These sin-offerings, presented *" upon the daily sacrifice,"* resemble tributary streams pouring in their waters into one great ocean. " Christ *once* suffered for sins, the Just for the unjust, to bring us unto God" (1 Pet. iii. 18).* O how anxious is our God to purge

---

* In Numb. xxii. 26, another direction is given, viz. in a case where the nation had for a time forsaken the law of Moses. This happened under several

us from every stain! The priest's hyssop is introduced
into every corner of the building, that we may be altogether pure. Well may we join the seraphim in their
song, " Holy, holy, holy, is the Lord of hosts."

Some have regarded the offences for which satisfaction
is made in this chapter as offences of a national kind—
offences against *the Theocracy*, by which an Israelite forfeited the favour of Jehovah as his Theocratic Ruler, and
was for a time cut off from his protection. Even when
taken in this limited view, how significant are *the sacrifices!* The offender comes confessing his sin, and bringing
a victim to suffer in his stead. The animal is slain in his
room; the man is forgiven, and retains his standing as a
protected Israelite—remaining under the shadow of the
Guardian Cloud. The *sacrifice* never failed to produce
this effect; but nothing else than the sacrifice ever did—
"Without shedding of blood there is no remission." This
principle of the Divine government was engraven on the
hearts of Israel, viz. whosoever is pardoned any offence
must be pardoned by means of another's death. " The
great multitude" of the saved are all pardoned by one
of infinite worth having died for them all (see 2 Cor.
v. 14).

idolatrous kings, such as Manasseh. Ignorance became the sin of the next
generation. Perhaps, Josiah's alarm at the hearing of the law found in the
temple is the kind of case there intended. In ver. 27-29, individuals are taught
to seek personal pardon besides.

CHAPTER V

Sin-offering for Sins of Inadvertency

" Brethren, if a man be overtaken in a fault, ye which are spiritual,
restore such an one in the spirit of meekness."*—Gal. vi. 3

> Ver. 1. *And if a soul sin, and hear the voice of swearing, and
> is a witness, whether he hath seen or known of it; if he do
> not utter it, then he shall bear his iniquity.*

THE meaning is, "If a person sin in this respect," viz.
that he hear the oath of adjuration administered by the
judge, and is able to tell, having either seen or otherwise
known the matter about which he is to testify: if such a
man do not tell all he knows, he shall be reckoned guilty
of a sin.

"The *voice of swearing*" undoubtedly means here the
adjuration of a judge to a prisoner. The term (אָלָה)
employed here is the same as that used in 1 Sam. xiv. 24,
"Saul had adjured (וַיֹּאֶל) the people;" and in 1 Kings viii.
31, "If an adjuration be laid upon him," adjuring him to
speak out the truth; and Judges xvii. 2, "The eleven
hundred shekels of silver that were taken from thee,
about which thou didst *adjure;*" and Prov. xxix. 24, "He
heareth an adjuration, and yet telleth not." The judge,
in a court of justice, was permitted to elicit information

---

* " Overtaken," is προληφθῃ, hurried into sin ere he is well aware (Bretschneider). " Fault," is παραπτωμα, transgression, sin.

from the witness by solemnly charging him to answer and tell all he knew, under penalty of a curse from God, if he did not reveal the whole truth. It was in those circumstances that our Lord was placed before the High Priest (Matt. xxvi. 63). He was then, surely, in the depths of humiliation! For now he is called upon, under threatening of the curse of his own Father, to break that strange silence, and tell all he knows—"*I adjure thee by the living God, that thou tell us whether thou be the Christ, the Son of God.*" And then it was that the Lamb of God no longer kept himself dumb; but, bowing to the solemn force of this adjuration, shewed the same meekness in replying as before he had done in keeping silence. From the depth of his humiliation he pointed upward to the throne, and declared himself Son of God, and Judge of quick and dead.

The sins mentioned in this chapter are chiefly sins arising from negligence—sins which might have been avoided, had the person been more careful.

The case of the *witness*, in ver. 1, is one where the person omitted to tell particulars which he could have told, or else, through carelessness, mis-stated some things. Let us learn the breadth of God's holy law! Not a tittle fails. Let us learn the Holy Spirit's keen observation of sin in us. Let us learn to be jealous over ourselves, and seek to be of "quick discernment in the fear of the Lord." Much sin is committed by *omissions*. Duties *partially* done have in them the guilt of Ananias and Sapphira.

Ver. 2. *Or if a soul touch any unclean thing, whether it be a carcase of an unclean beast, or a carcase of unclean cattle, or the carcase of unclean creeping things, and if it be hidden from him; he also shall be unclean, and guilty.*

These, as well as ver. 3, are cases where *others* could see the pollution, though the man himself might be unaware of it at the time. They were, therefore, cases of a public injury in some degree. Through inadvertency a man might touch a carcase* of an unclean "beast" (חַיָּה), the term used for the sort of animals most commonly met with in every-day work. These are noticed first, as it was most likely they would oftenest meet with them. Then "cattle" in the fields or forests. Lastly, "creeping things," such as the weasel, the mouse, or the lizard (xi. 30). Thus there is a gradation, greater, middle, and smallest; as if to say to us, that any degree of pollution is offensive to a pure and holy God. A true Israelite ought to keep completely free from all that defiles, however trifling, in the eye of the world. Whatever sin God's eye resteth on, that is the sin which the man of God abhors. The man after God's own heart prays, "Cleanse thou me from secret faults" (Ps. xix. 12). And, in reference to its being "*hidden*," yet still chargeable upon the sinner, he exclaims, "Thou hast set our iniquities before thee, *our secret sins* in the light of thy countenance" (Ps. xc. 8).

Here, too, we learn that "sin is the *transgression of the law*" (1 John iii. 4). It is not merely when we act contrary *to the dictates of conscience* that we sin; we may often be sinning when conscience never upbraids us. The most part of a sinner's life is spent without any check on the part of conscience—that being dead and corrupt, fallen and depraved, responding to the man's lusts, rather than to the will of God. Hence it is said here, that though

---

* Were *dead bodies* reckoned unclean on the ground that they are the fruit of *sin?* The sting of *death* is, as it were, sunk into them; and so *sin* is proved to be there.

"*it be hidden from him,*" he shall be unclean. He is guilty, though his conscience did not warn him of the guilt contracted.

Awful truth! We know not what we do! When the Book is opened and read, what 'a record of *unfelt guilt!* "*Had they known,* they would not have crucified the Lord of glory;" but yet their act was the blackest of sins. Who can tell what pages there may be in the Book of Remembrance?*

> Ver. 3. *Or if he touch the uncleanness of man, whatsoever uncleanness it be that a man shall be defiled withal, and it be hid from him; when he knoweth of it, then he shall be guilty.*

This last clause is equivalent to "If it be hid from him, *though he afterward* come to know it." "*The uncleanness of a man*" is such as *the leprosy* or a *running issue* caused.

Again the lesson is enforced, that unconscious as our depraved souls may be of the presence of sin, sin may have polluted us, and separated between us and God. We are guarded against the deceitfulness of sin. We need to be told of sin by others. Our coming afterwards to know our sin, may often be by means of our brethren's reproofs, and their quicker discernment of evil. Hence it is written, "Exhort one another daily, while it is called To-day, lest any of you be hardened through the deceitfulness of sin" (Heb. iii. 13).

> Ver. 4. *Or if a soul swear, pronouncing with his lips to do evil, or to do good, whatsoever it be that a man shall pronounce with an oath, and it be hid from him; when he knoweth of it, then he shall be guilty in one of these.*

---

* Francis Quarles truly, though quaintly, says of a sin of ignorance,—
> "It is a hideous mist that wets amain,
> Though it appear not in the form of rain."

More literally, " If a person swear, *blabbing with his lips*"—rashly uttering his vow.   The careless way of doing even what is right is here condemned.   Inconsiderateness is a heinous crime, for the man is appealing to God; and especially so when the thing vowed is evil. The case of man inadvertently swearing to do evil, is a case like *Jephthah's.   Jephthah* meant good, but it turned out to be evil of a flagrant nature.   The clause, " And it be hid from him," is equivalent to " And did not rightly understand the thing about which he swore."   There is a solemn lesson taught us in regard to the mode of doing even right things.   Approach the Holy One with fear and reverence.   But alas! how plentiful is the flow of hidden sin committed in our dedications to God, or in resolutions to be his, expressed to him in prayer and praise.   Even in saying or writing " God willing" (D.V.), this secret sin may be oftentimes chargeable upon our unconscious souls.

" *In one of these*," *i.e.* any of the cases mentioned—the adjuration; touching the dead body, or other uncleanness; and rash vows.

> Ver. 5, 6. *And it shall be, when he shall be guilty in one of these things, that he shall confess that he hath sinned in that thing.   And he shall bring his trespass-offering unto the Lord, for his sin which he hath sinned, a female from the flock, a lamb, or a kid of the goats, for a sin-offering; and the priest shall make an atonement for him concerning his sin.*

The first thing that strikes us here as very noticeable is the injunction, " *He shall confess that he hath sinned.*" Abarbinel, on the sixteenth chapter, says, that confession necessarily accompanied every sacrifice for sin.   But we have not met this duty before, in the express form of a command, because hitherto the sins brought to the altar were open and admitted sins.* But here the sins are "*hidden;*" and therefore the offerer must openly confess them, that so God may be honoured—" That thou mightest be justified when thou speakest, and be clear when thou judgest" (Psalm li. 4). This is the end of confession; it vindicates God, proclaiming him just in the penalty he inflicts. We see this in *Achan's* case, when Joshua said, " My son, give, I pray thee, glory to the Lord God of Israel, and make confession unto him, and tell me now what thou hast done; hide it not from me" (Josh. vii. 19). It is thus that, when we truly *confess,* we become witnesses for God—we testify that *we* have come to see the sin and its evil, which he declared that his pure eye saw. The original uses a word for *confess,* which in another form means to *praise* (הִתְוַדָּה and הוֹדָה); and in the New Testament as well as the Old, the two acts are often reckoned the same.† The tribute to the holiness of the Lord, paid in confession, is *praise* to his name. *We* decrease; *he* increases.

"*He shall bring his trespass-offering.*" Some suppose that there were on this occasion, first the *trespass*-offering, and then a sin-offering. But not so: it ought to be rendered, " He shall bring his offering;" the word אָשָׁם being used not as a specific term, but as a general term for any offering on account of sin. And it is thus that it is used by Isaiah (liii. 10), " When thou shalt make his soul an *offering for sin*" (תָּשִׂים אָשָׁם נַפְשׁוֹ).

The offering is to be " *a female from the flock.*" It

---

* There is no doubt but that the laying on of the hand on the animal's head involved confession of sin. So common was confession, that John the Baptist's practice of insisting on confession of sin from all that came to his baptism excited no opposition. They were thus naturally led to understand what he meant by telling them to lay their sins on the " Coming One."

† See the same use of ἐξομολογοῦμαι.

is a less glaring sin than some others, such as chap. iv.
1–27, and therefore a *female*, and a *young one*, is taken.
And either a *female kid*, or a *female lamb*, may be chosen;
the object being to fix the offerer's attention upon the
blood shed for his sin, and not upon any quality in the
victim, as might have been the result, had only the *lamb*
been allowed.   His *sin and its atonement* is all that must
engage the offerer.

> Ver. 7. *And if he be not able to bring a lamb, then he shall bring,*
> *for his trespass which he hath committed, two turtle-doves, or*
> *two young pigeons, unto the Lord; one for a sin-offering, and*
> *the other for a burnt-offering.*

Here, again, we see the God of Israel manifesting
himself to be that very Saviour who "preached glad
tidings to the poor."   The two doves are allowed for
their sake.

But why *two?*   Is this not equivalent to an intimation that *one* turtle-dove or pigeon would not represent
the Saviour?   Is this not attaching importance to the
mere material of the sacrifice?   The answer to these
questions leads us to a very interesting view of the
Lord's tender regard to the feelings of the poor of his
people.

There is no importance attached to the mere number,
considered in itself; for in chap. i. 15, there was only
one turtle-dove sacrificed; and it was sufficient as a
type, and equivalent to the one bullock or lamb.   But
here and elsewhere, where *two* doves are offered, there is
a special reason why two are chosen.   The one is always
for a *sin-offering*, and the other for a *burnt-offering*.
Now, in the *sin-offering*, when it was a lamb or the like,
there were portions left for the use of the priest, after
the sacrifice was offered; and these portions, received

and feasted on by the priest, were equivalent to a declaration of the complete removal of the sin, since the priest himself could thus fearlessly use them. But there was no room for this being done when a turtle-dove was offered. There were no portions for the priest to feast upon. Hence, in order that the poor worshipper might not lose this consoling part of the type, he is told to offer a second turtle-dove as a *burnt-offering*. And in this latter offering, the Lord himself directly receives all, and pronounces all to be a " *sweet savour* " (chap. i. 17); so that the poor saint gets even a more hearty assurance of his offering being accepted, than does another who only gets this assurance by means of the priest's receiving his portion to feast upon, and seeing the priest's household feast thereon.

> Ver. 8, 9. *And he shall bring them unto the priest, who shall offer that which is for the sin-offering first, and wring off his head from his neck, but shall not divide it asunder. And he shall sprinkle of the blood of the sin-offering upon the side of the altar; and the rest of the blood shall be wrung out at the bottom of the altar.*

There is some difference in the ceremony observed here in slaying the turtle-dove from that of chap. i. 14. The head is to be wrung off, yet so as not to separate it from the body. It would hang down upon the lifeless body, the blood also dropping upon its white clean plumage. Was it meant to be a type of Jesus bowing his head as he gave up the ghost? His head, bleeding with the thorns that had crowned him, dropped upon his bosom as the sting of death entered his holy frame.

There may be a farther type. The Passover lamb, of which not a bone was broken, prefigured Jesus as one " not a bone of whose body should be broken;" and yet, at the same time, it prefigured the complete keeping and safety of Christ's body the Church; as it is written, in Psalm xxxiv. 20, " He keepeth all his bones; not one of them is broken." So also here; the bowing of the Saviour's head seems prefigured—not too small a circumstance for an Evangelist to record, and for the Father to remember, regarding the well-beloved Son ; but there may also be herein a type of the glorious truth, that *Christ* and his *body the Church* cannot be separated. The head and the body must be left undivided.

In chapter i. 15, there is no mention of the *sprinkling of any of the blood upon the altar.* But here some of it is first *sprinkled* on the side of the altar, then the rest *wrung out* at the bottom. The sprinkling on the altar's side was quite sufficient to declare *life taken ;* and as the second dove would have its blood *wrung out over the side* of the altar, there was a fitness in making this difference. At the same time, it shews us how *sprinkling a part* or *pouring out the whole,* express equally the same truth; just as in baptism, the symbol is equally significant, whether the water be sprinkled on the person or the person plunged into the water.

> Ver. 10. *And he shall offer the second for a burnt-offering, according to the manner; and the priest shall make an atonement for him, for his sin which he hath sinned, and it shall be forgiven him.*

"Thus shall the priest make an atonement for him [cleansing him] from the sin which he hath sinned."* The poor saint has full and ample testimony given to the completeness of his offering. The one great ocean— "Christ ONCE suffered"—"one sacrifice" (Heb. x. 12)

---

* This seems to be the force of מֵחַטָּאתוֹ here and ver. 6. It is a *constructio prægnans,* as in ver. 16, חָטָא מִן.

makes the bullock appear as insignificant as the turtle-dove. The waves of the sea cover every shallow pool.

> Ver. 11. *But if he be not able to bring two turtle-doves, or two young pigeons; then he that sinned shall bring for his offering the tenth part of an ephah of fine flour for a sin-offering: he shall put no oil upon it, neither shall he put any frankincense thereon; for it is a sin-offering.*

The Lord descends even to the poorest of all, those who had no lamb to spare. He provides for the *Lazaruses* of Israel, and the widows who have but two mites remaining, in the very spirit of love wherein Jesus spoke of them. It is Jesus who, as Jehovah, arranges these types for the comfort of his afflicted people.

The *burnt-offering* was never allowed to be of any inanimate thing. For in that great type of the Saviour, *blood* must flow. It must exhibit *life taken,* and the sentence, "Thou *shalt surely die,*" executed. The sacrifice which was the groundwork of all the rest must exhibit *death.* But this point being settled and established, any danger of misapprehension is removed. Whatever may afterwards be the varieties permitted in the forms of offering, yet at the threshold the necessity for the shedding of blood in order to remission must be declared and testified (Heb. ix. 22). But now there is here a permission granted—a permission which cannot be misunderstood, since its application is limited to this one particular class of persons, and for special reasons—a permission to bring an *offering of fine flour,* when the man is too poor to bring two turtle-doves or young pigeons. This meat-offering is expressly spoken of as not the strict and proper offering, but merely a substitute for that better kind.*

---

* Socinians in vain try to make a handle of this case; for if ever there was an instance where it could be said, "*Exceptio probat regulam,*" it is here.

And, as remarked by Magee, the poor man would look forward to the day of atonement to complete what this was a substitute for.   He is then to take a handful of the fine wheat of the land of his Israel.   A few ears of the wheat of that land would furnish enough; and every Israelite had some family inheritance.   An *omer*, or the *tenth part of an ephah*, is the quantity; just the very quantity of manna that sufficed for each day's support.   Probably the poor man, who needed to bring his offering for a *sin committed*, was thus taught to give up just his food for that day—fasting before the Lord.

As in the Jealousy-offering (Numb. v.), no oil or frankincense must be put upon it; for the very intention of it is to present to the Lord the *person and substance* of the offerer (see chap. ii. 1) as altogether defiled—a mass of sin!

No doubt this new kind of sin-offering is intentionally permitted, in order to shew some things that the *animal* sacrifice could not have shewn forth.   It exhibits not the soul only (that is taken for granted when the body and substance are devoted), but all that belongs to the person —his body and his property—as needing to be redeemed by sacrifice, since it has become polluted.   All is forfeited —no frankincense of sweet savour on it, no oil of consecration.

Ver. 12, 13. *Then shall he bring it to the priest, and the priest shall take his handful of it, even a memorial thereof, and burn it on the altar, according to the offerings made by fire unto the Lord: it is a sin-offering.   And the priest shall make an atonement for him, as touching his sin that he hath sinned in one of these, and it shall be forgiven him: and the remnant shall be the priest's, as a meat-offering.*

The memorial of this mass of sin is consumed in the

fire of wrath; but the priest takes his portion, in order
to shew that the sin is cleansed out from the mass.

Shall it not be thus at the resurrection morning? The
body now cleansed, and *earth itself* purged by fire? Then
is *man* fully redeemed; his soul, his body, his inheritance
or possessions. No sin left to bring in a secret curse! no
Gibeonite-blood lying hid in its bosom to bring on sudden
and unthought-of woes. No Achan-treasure in the tent-
floor, provoking the eyes of the Lord's glory.

In looking back on this chapter concerning sins of
inadvertency, how awful is the view it presents of the
Lord's jealousy! "His eyes are as a flame of fire;" and
he "judges not according to the hearing of the ear," but
according to the truth that remains untold. How great
the provocation that his own saints give to him daily, by
touching the unclean, and by other almost imperceptible
movements of the heart towards evil. "Woe is me! I
am undone; for I am a man of unclean lips, and I
dwell among a people of unclean lips!" In such cases
we need to take for ourselves the counsel that Cain rejected when the Lord said, "If thou doest well (sinnest
not) shalt thou not be accepted? and if thou doest not
well (sinnest), a sin-offering lieth at thy door" (חַטָּאת
רֹבֵץ) (Gen. iv. 7). How ancient is the grace of God!
How old is that gracious saying, "These things write I
unto you, that *ye sin not*; and if *any man sin*, we have
an advocate with the Father, Jesus Christ the righteous;
and he is the propitiation for our sins."

In these ancient days, there was the same grace exhibited to the sinner as there is under the New Testament. God held out forgiveness, full and immediate, in
order to allure the sinner, without delay, back to fellow-

ship with himself. And as now, so then, many abused this grace. They used it not to cleanse their conscience, but to lull it asleep. Of these Solomon is supposed to complain,* in Prov. xiii. 6, " *Wickedness perverteth the sin-offering*" (תְּסַלֵּף חַטָּאת). Nevertheless, the truth of God stood sure; " *righteousness preserved the perfect.*"

---

* See Faber *on Sacrifice.*

CHAPTER V—CHAPTER VI

𝕿𝖍𝖊 𝕿𝖗𝖊𝖘𝖕𝖆𝖘𝖘-𝕺𝖋𝖋𝖊𝖗𝖎𝖓𝖌

" *Whatsoever things are true, whatsoever things are honest, whatsoever things are just, whatsoever things are pure, whatsoever things are lovely, whatsoever things are of good report , . . . think on these things . . . . and the God of peace shall be with you.*"—Phil. iv. 8, 9

Ver. 14. *And the Lord spake unto Moses, saying, If a soul commit a trespass,—*

MANY of the best writers, such as Outram, come to no definite conclusion as to the difference between the *sin-offering* and the *trespass-offering*. But we are satisfied, on the whole, that the *trespass-offering* (אָשָׁם) was offered in cases where the sin was more private, and confined to the individual's knowledge. The sin was known only to the man himself; and hence it was less hurtful in its effects. We have seen that chapter v. 6 is no contradiction to this especial use of the word, as אָשָׁם was originally as general in its sense as חָטָא ; and in Isaiah liii. 10, either it is used in that same general way, or, if meant to be more special, the sense will be, " When thou shalt make his soul *an offering for sins which no one ever saw him commit;* for he had done no violence, nor was deceit in his mouth."

The *sin-offering*, being of a more public nature, was on that account more fitted to be the usual type of Christ's offering. It was both public and definite.

The *trespass-offering* was always a *ram*. It was thus fitted to remind Israel of Abraham's offering Isaac, when the *ram* was substituted. The blood of it was always put "*on the sides*" of the altar; not on the horns, as in the case of the sin-offering, where the offering was more of a public nature, and needed to be held up to all.

The cases here are—

1. Fraud toward God in respect to things in his worship.

2. Fraud towards man. The instances given are specimens of wrong done by the trespasser to the first and second tables of the law.

Perhaps it was too much for a frail mortal to hear the Lord speak long. There was a short interval between the last revelation of the will of the Lord, and this that followed it. Silence reigned through the Holy Place; and under the beams of the bright cloud of glory, Moses would sit down, and trace on his tablets the directions just received. And now the voice of the Lord spoke again—the same voice that afterwards said to John in Patmos, "Write the things which thou hast seen, and the things which are, and the things which shall be hereafter." It then declared of each church of Asia, "*I know thy works.*" It is the voice of the same holy and jealous, yet gracious and tender Priest, the same true and faithful Witness. The voice said—

Ver. 15. *If a soul commit a trespass, and sin through ignorance, in the holy things of the Lord; then he shall bring for his trespass unto the Lord a ram without blemish out of the flocks, with thy estimation by shekels of silver, after the shekel of the sanctuary, for a trespass-offering.*

That we may see the sort of sins meant here, let us refer to a special case. The class of sins here is *transgressions in regard to the holy things of the Lord*. Now, in Ecclesiastes v. 6, we have such a case. "Suffer not thy mouth to cause thy flesh to sin ; neither say thou before the angel, that it was an error (שְׁגָגָה, as here) : wherefore should God be angry at thy voice, and destroy the work of thine hands?" The wish to be spoken well of, and to become eminent for piety in the eyes of the people and priest, led this man, while attending public worship in the temple, to vow with his lips more than he could, or more than he really wished to give. By this rash vow, he came under the sin mentioned in this chapter, ver. 4. But this is not all. When the priest* came (see 1 Sam. ii. 13) to take his share of the offering according to the law, the man was tempted to deny that he had vowed so much ; and thus he fell into the sin of *trespass*, mentioned in ver. 15 of this chapter, inasmuch as he withholds what he promised to the house of God. God will destroy his prosperity, unless such a man forthwith bring the trespass-offering. Similar cases might be given ; thus, if a man eat the first-fruits (Exod. xxxiv. 26), or shear the first-born sheep (Deut. xv. 19)—(Ainsworth), he is to bring "*a ram without blemish out of the flock.*" He is to choose one of the most valuable of his flock, a type of him who was "chosen out of the people," "one that was mighty" (Ps. lxxxix. 19). It was to be costly ; it must not be of an inferior sort, but (Deut. xxxii. 14) of that sort which were "rams of the breed of Bashan." The priest is to estimate the value according to the standard of the sanc-

---

* The *angel* or messenger seems to be the *priest himself*. So he is called in Malachi ii. 7. And if so, is it not with a reference to the *jealous angel* in Exod. xxxii. 34? The priest is his representative, presiding over the temple.

tuary. Probably we are hereby taught the costliness of the Redeemer's offering.

Consider the "*estimation.*" It was not every offering that would answer the great end; it must be a costly, precious offering—the precious blood of the Son of God (2 Pet. i. 19). Who can tell how high it was estimated in the sanctuary above, where not one spot of sin ever found a rest in the most secret heart of one ministering spirit? The question is asked, Is this *one offering* sufficient for the sinner? The Holy One applies the test of his law, and measures it by his own holy nature, and finds it such that he declares, "I am well pleased;" "I lay in Zion a tried stone;" "He hath magnified the law, and made it honourable."

But, 2. Was it such as reached the case of others? Yes; it was meant for others. He who wrought it out was a surety. His body was "prepared" for the sake of others. His eye ran down with tears for others. The words such as never man spake, were for others. "He suffered, the Just for the unjust."

3. But may I use it? Yes, not only you *may*, but you *must* use it, or perish.

> Ver. 16. *And he shall make amends for the harm that he hath done in the holy thing, and shall add the fifth part thereto, and give it unto the priest: and the priest shall make an atonement for him with the ram of the trespass-offering, and it shall be forgiven him.*

The trespasser is to be no gainer by defrauding God's house. He is to suffer, even in temporal things, as a punishment for his sin. He is to bring, in addition to the thing of which he defrauded God, money to the extent of one-fifth of the value of the thing. This was given to the priest as the head of the people in things of

God, and representative of God in holy duties. It was
to be a *double tithe* because of the attempt to defraud
God.* We shall never be gainers by stinting our time
and service in the worship of God. What we withdraw
from him, he will withdraw from us in another way.
Besides, the very fact of cherishing such an idea in our
minds will cause the Lord to veil his grace and glory
from our view until we have anew sought him by the
blood of Jesus. And in the meantime, the sorrow and
darkness of our heart will teach us that it is a bitter
thing to depart from the Lord.

But there is something in this part of the ordinance
far more significant still. It seems to exhibit the require-
ments of God in order to a true atonement. Atonement
must consist—

1. Of *restitution of the principal*—restoring all that
was lost. The injury done is to be made up by the person submitting to give back every item he took away.

2. Of *the addition of more.* There must be also a
making up of the wrong done, by the person suffering
loss, as a recompence for the evil. In these two pro-
visions, do we not see set forth in symbol the great fact
that God in atonement must get back all the honour that
his law lost for a time by man's fraud; and also must
have the honour of his law vindicated by the payment of an amount of suffering? The *active* obedience
of Christ gave the one; his *passive* obedience provided
the other.

These principles being thus set forth and agreed to, the
ram was brought forward, wherein was exhibited the *per-*

---

* The tithe regularly paid was an acknowledgment that God had a right to
the things tithed; and this double tithe was an acknowledgment, that in consequence of this attempt to defraud him, his right must be *doubly* acknowledged.

son that was to be the giver of atonement.   A ram "out of the flock," even as Christ was " one chosen out of the people" (Ps. lxxxix. 19).

> Ver. 17. *And if a soul sin, and commit any of these things which are forbidden to be done by the commandments of the Lord; though he wist it not, yet is he guilty, and shall bear his iniquity.*

This is a remarkable passage in proof of the awful sin that may be committed through ignorance—" *Though he wist it not, yet is he guilty.*"   Knowledge was within his reach in this case; for the things spoken of are matters connected with sanctuary worship.   It is even such a case as Paul's, whose ignorance was no excuse for his sin, since he might have inquired and known.*

The cases referred to here are evidently those wherein *holy things, or things connected with worship*, were neglected or defectively performed.   It is that class of cases wherein—it may be through ignorance—the Lord was defrauded of what was due in his worship.

> Ver. 18, 19. *And he shall bring a ram without blemish out of the flock, with thy estimation, for a trespass-offering, unto the priest: and the priest shall make an atonement for him concerning his ignorance wherein he erred, and wist it not; and it shall be forgiven him.   It is a trespass-offering: he hath certainly trespassed against the Lord.*

How emphatic is the rehearsal of his sin—" Atonement for him concerning his ignorance wherein he erred, and wist it not;" and again, " He hath certainly trespassed against the Lord;" though men would have been ready to treat it as a light matter !

* Evidently, in 1 Tim. i. 13, we are to read thus : "Putting me into the ministry, who was before a blasphemer, and a persecutor, and injurious, though I obtained mercy.   For I did all this ignorantly in unbelief," *q.d.* for my ignorance and unbelief (both equally inexcusable) led me to these excesses.

Israel was thus shut up to the solemn duty of inquiring
into the Lord's revealed will. By treating ignorance as a
sin of such magnitude, the Lord made provision among
his people for securing a thorough and continual search
into his mind and will; and thus, no doubt, family
instruction was universal in every tent in the wilderness,
and the nation were an intelligent as well as a peculiar
people.

(CHAP. VI. 1–7)

Ver. 1. And the Lord spake unto Moses, saying,—

There was silence again in the Holy Place, until Moses
had recorded the above precepts bearing on Jehovah's
own special worship. And when these trespasses against
the first table of the law had been declared and marked,
the voice of the Lord was again heard. We may recognise the same voice that spoke on that mountain of Galilee;
for here is the same principle of broad, holy exactness in
applying the law as in Matt. v. The mind of the Father
and of his Son is one and the same as to the extent of
the law, even as it is alike in love to the transgressor.

*Ver. 2, 3. If a soul sin, and commit a trespass against the Lord,
and lie unto his neighbour in that which was delivered him to
keep, or in fellowship, or in a thing taken away by violence, or
hath deceived his neighbour; or hath found that which was lost,
and lieth concerning it, and sweareth falsely; in any of all
these that a man doeth, sinning therein:—*

Here is a specimen selected of the common forms in
which defrauding others may occur. There is first a
temptation mentioned, to which friends are exposed with
one another in private intercourse. A man asks his
friend to keep something for him; or, in the wider accep-

tation of the original term (פִּקָּדוֹן), gives a neighbour a
trust to manage for him of any kind, or commits to his
care for the time, any article.   The LXX. have used the
word "παραθηκη," which, in 2 Tim. i. 12, is rendered,
" *What I have committed to him.*"   Anything lent to
another is included; a tool, like the prophet's borrowed
axe (2 Kings vi. 5), or a sum of money left in a neighbour's keeping (Exod. xxii. 7); in short, any " stuff"
(Exod. xxii. 7), or articles (כֵּלִים).   A lent book, or borrowed umbrella, would come under this law; and how
few have the sincere honesty of that son of the prophets,
in 2 Kings vi. 5, vexed because the thing injured in their
hands was a borrowed thing!—" Alas! my master, for it
was borrowed!"   The Lord expects, in such case, complete disinterestedness; the man is to do to others as he
would have others do to him.   Any denial of having
received the thing, any appropriation of it to himself, any
carelessness in the keeping of it, is a *trespass* in the eye
of God.   You have wronged God in wronging your
neighbour.

The case of "*fellowship*," or partnership, refers to the
transactions of public life ; not, however, to openly un-
lawful acts, but to acts lawful in appearance, while selfish
in reality.   This points specially to business transactions,
where there ought to be the utmost disinterestedness, one
partner giving more scrupulous attention to the interests
of the other than to his own, mortifying his jealous self-
love by his regard to his partner's concerns.   This is the
generous morality of the God of Israel.   The same head
would include the conscientious observances of government
regulations or commercial laws, as to taxes on goods.
These regulations being understood principles on which
trade is carried on, are really of the nature of " fellow-

ship." So also bargains in trade ; though not many are
so jealous as Abraham in Gen. xxiii., to avoid even the
appearance of wronging others. Most are as Prov. xx. 14.

"*A thing taken by violence*," includes cases of oppres-
sion or hardship, where mere power deals with weakness.
Such was Naboth's case (1 Kings xxi. 2); such was Isaac's
(Gen. xxvi. 4).

"*Or hath deceived his neighbour.*" The word עָשַׁק is
rightly rendered, in the Septuagint, ἠδίκησε. It speaks of
another form of oppression—"hath deceitfully oppressed."
There are cases of strong, but secret terror, as when a
landlord uses his pecuniary superiority to constrain a
tenant's vote, or force a dependant to attend a particular
place of worship. It exists, too, where a mistress thought-
lessly gives too much work to her servants, or where a
farmer exacts unceasing labour, from morning to night,
at the hands of his ploughmen, or where a shopkeeper's
business is carried on at such a rate that his apprentices
have no calm rest of body or soul. In another shape, a
Jew was guilty of this trespass if, in using the permission
(Deut. xxiii. 24, 25) to pluck grapes, or ears of corn, as
he passed his neighbour's grounds, he took more than he
would have done had he been in his own vineyard or
corn fields.

"*Or hath found that which was lost, and lieth concerning it.*" Unconcerned at the anxiety it may have given
to the loser, the man refuses to part with what he has
found. This is surely selfishness in the extreme. But it
is so, also, if the finder is not willing to hear of an owner,
glad only at his own advantage, and saying, "The owner
may never miss it—God has thrown it into my hands."
The Lord teaches us not to build up our joy on the loss
or sorrow of others.

Such is the kind care of the God of Israel. Is he not still "The Eagle" over them, stirring up her nest, and fluttering over her young? He teaches his family to be full of love—superiors, inferiors, equals. He would infuse the holy feelings of heaven into the camp of Israel. Truly, society regulated by the Lord is blessed society, for his own love flows through it all, and is the very joints and bands. Hence it is that a sin against a neighbour, in one of these points, is a "*trespass against the Lord*" (ver. 1). The *selfish* man is an unholy man, altogether unlike God. Yet earth is full of such. When men are happy themselves, they take no thought of others' misery. When at ease, they disregard the pain of others. Some even relieve distress out of subtle selfishness, seeking thereby to be free to indulge themselves with less compunction. Not so the Lord. The eternal Son comes forth from the bosom of the Blessed, and, for the sake of the vilest, dives into the depths of misery. "He restored what he took not away," and "delivered him that without cause was his enemy." And in proportion as we feel much of this love of God to us, we shall feel much love to him, and to our brother also (1 John iv. 20).

> Ver. 4, 5. *Then it shall be, because he hath sinned, and is guilty, that he shall restore that which he took violently away, or the thing which he hath deceitfully gotten, or that which was delivered him to keep, or the lost thing which he found, or all that about which he hath sworn falsely; he shall even restore it in the principal, and shall add the fifth part more thereto, and give it unto him to whom it appertaineth, in the day of his trespass-offering.*

Patrick renders ver. 4, "If he sin and acknowledge his guilt;" for if his case were one where witnesses convicted him, then Exod. xxii. 7-9 held good. The case of

Zaccheus, on the day of his coming to Jesus ("the day of his trespass-offering" surely), illustrates this restitution as an attendant upon forgiveness. When the Lord forgave him, the same Lord also inclined him to restore what he had unjustly taken, and to give back far more than he had taken.

The fifth part is given, in addition to the principal, just as in the case of holy things being fraudulently withheld. It is a *double tithe* (two-tenths), and so is equivalent to a *double acknowledgment* of the person's right to the thing, of which he had been, for a time, unjustly deprived. See chap. v. 15, 16.

No doubt this exceeding jealousy on the part of God in maintaining the rights of men, and exhibiting such strict equity, was intended to display to the world what his own holy character is. The most impartial and extensive justice is here exhibited. And his demand for restitution shews that the Lord will maintain his violated rights to the uttermost. It further proves, that while he requires (as John proclaimed, Luke iii. 8, 10–14) repentance and amendment, still it is not these that in any degree satisfy the Lord; for there is, in addition to the restoring of the principal, a new demand by the law, for the very act of attempting to defraud it—one-fifth part beyond the former demand! Thus was Israel prepared for an awful enforcement of Divine claims in the person of Immanuel; and thus were they shewn what must be the infinite merit of him who should be able to restore all that had been taken away from his God!

Ver. 6, 7. *And he shall bring his trespass-offering unto the Lord, a ram without blemish out of the flock, with thy estimation, for a trespass-offering unto the priest: and the priest shall make an atonement for him before the Lord; and it shall be for-*

given him, for any thing of all that he hath done, in trespassing therein.

"*For any of all the things*"—thus proclaiming that "the blood of Jesus cleanseth from all sin." The case of *presumptuous* sins is not referred to here, for these involved a disregard, in the offender, to the very offerings that could exhibit pardon to his conscience. But this section ends with the proclamation of free forgiveness from all manner of sin. The Lord would thus at once allure the sinner from his transgression, and lead him to the immediate joy of reconciliation. It is the surest and speediest way to lead him out of his former path of guilt. "There is forgiveness with thee, that thou mayest be feared."

With Israel, as with us, there were many who saw no meaning or reason in God's appointments. Want of true conviction of sin made them despise these types, while the godly, who felt their loins filled with a grievous disease, found therein their daily refreshment. This is the true sense of Prov. xiv. 9, when properly rendered—"*Fools make a mock of the trespass-offering, but with the righteous it is in esteem.*" The Septuagint seem to have had a glimpse of this meaning, for they use "καθαρισμὸς" for אָשָׁם, and they render רָצוֹן, "δεκτός." The godly cherished these typical delineations of atonement, while the careless, earthly-minded Israelite saw nothing in them to desire. None go to the hiding-place who fear no storm. The stream flows by unheeded when the traveller on its banks is not thirsty. The whole will not use the physician. Sense of sin renders Jesus precious to the soul. How Peter loved the risen Saviour, who relieved him of the load of his denial! A sight of wrath to come gives a new aspect to every spiritual thing. In Egypt, a sight of the destroying angel's sword would make Israel prize the blood. Ishmael might have mocked at the ram caught in the thicket; but not so Isaac, who had been bound with the cords of death. It is only "fools" that will "mock at the trespass-offering;" with the righteous it is held in unspeakable esteem. Their song is, "Thanks be unto God for his unspeakable gift!"

Special Rules for the Priests who minister at the Altar of God.

"God .. hath reconciled us to himself by Jesus Christ, and hath given to us the ministry of reconciliation. For he hath made him to be sin for us, who knew no sin; that we might be made the righteousness of God in him."—2 Cor. v. 18, 21

REGARDING THE WHOLE BURNT-OFFERING.

Ver. 8, 9. *And the Lord spake unto Moses, saying, Command Aaron and his sons, saying, This is the law of the burnt-offering: It is the burnt-offering, because of the burning upon the altar all night unto the morning, and the fire of the altar shall be burning in it.*

THE ground traversed over in chapters i., ii., iii., iv., v., is now re-traversed, but for a quite different object. Supplemental directions to the priests, in regard to their part in the offering of the sacrifices, is the object in view. But this gives opportunity for the typifying of some most important truths.

"*The law of the burnt-offering,*" or of things to be observed in offering it, is first stated. Perhaps, in ver. 9, we should read the parenthesis thus—" As for the burnt-offering, it is to be burning* on the altar all night until the morning; and the fire of the altar must be kept burning on it." However, retaining our rendering, we have the fact, that the fire must be kept burning the whole night long.

The Holy One speaks again from the Holy Place. He now tells some of the more awful thoughts of his soul. His words reveal views of sin and righteousness that appear overwhelmingly awful to men. His eternal justice, flaming forth against all iniquity, is declared to Israel in the *fire* of the altar. This fire is never to be extinguished; "for every one of his righteous judgments endureth for ever" (Ps. cxix. 160). It burns all night long—an emblem of the sleeplessness of hell, where "they have no rest, day nor night"—and of the ever-watchful eye of righteousness that looks down on this earth.

Perhaps it was intended to exhibit two things :—

1. "The smoke of their torment ascendeth up for ever and ever . . . . . tormented with fire and brimstone in presence of the holy angels, and in the presence of the Lamb" (Rev. xiv. 10, compared with ver. 18). The whole camp saw this fire, burning in the open court all night long. "So shall you perish," might an Israelitish father say to his children, taking them to his tent door, and pointing them, in the gloom and silence of night, to the altar, "So shall you perish, and be for ever in the flames, unless you repent!"

2. It exhibited, also, the way of escape. See, there is a victim on the altar, on which these flames feed! Here is Christ in our room. His suffering, seen and accepted

---

* Horsley renders עַל מוֹקְדָה, "upon the burning fuel;" and others to the same effect. See Ainsworth. Hengstenberg, on Ps. cii. 3, understands the word, "the *whole heap of fuel.*"

by the Father, was held forth continually to the faith of Israel, night and day. And upon that type, the pledge and token of the real sacrifice, did the eye of the Father delight to rest night and day. It pleased him well to see his justice and his love thus met together there. And the man of Israel, who understood the type, slept in peace, sustained by this truth, which the straggling rays from the altar gleamed into his tent.

> Ver. 10. *And the priest shall put on his linen garment, and his linen breeches shall he put upon his flesh, and take up the ashes which the fire hath consumed with the burnt-offering on the altar, and he shall put them beside the altar.*

The linen* garment is a type of purity, as we see in the book of Revelation (xix. 8). The priest is the emblem of the Redeemer in his perfect purity coming to the work of atonement. The word for garment† means a suit of clothes. It takes in the linen breeches, as well as all the other parts of the priest's dress. His whole suit is to be the garb of purity. It is not *glory* that is set forth; these are not the "golden garments." It is holy humanity; it is Jesus in humiliation, but without one stain of sin. There is a special reason for the direction as to the linen breeches. It is meant to denote the completeness of the purity that clothes him; it clothes him to his very skin, and "covers the flesh of his nakedness" (Exod. xxviii. 42). It was not only our unrighteousness, and our corrupt nature, that Jesus was free from; but also from that other part of our original sin, which consists in *the imputed guilt of Adam*. The linen breeches that "covered the nakedness" of the priest, lead us back at once to our first parents' sin, when

---

* The word is בַּד, not שֵׁשׁ. The latter is a finer sort, supposed to be silk.

† מַד, the ‎י‎ in which, in the opinion of Ewald, is merely the sign of the Status Constr., as in חָיְתוֹ.

they were naked and ashamed in the garden, after the
Fall. Here we see *this sin* also covered. He who comes
to atone for all our sins has himself freedom from all—
completely pure.

"*He shall take up the ashes which the fire has consumed,*" *i.e.* the ashes *of that which the fire has consumed*,
viz. the wood. By the figure which grammarians call
ellipsis, or breviloquence, "*ashes*" is used for the material out of which *ashes* came; as Isaiah (xlvii. 2) speaks of
grinding "*meal.*"—(Ainsworth.) The wood was under-
neath the burnt-offering.* This being done, the ashes
were to be placed by themselves, for a little time, "*beside
the altar.*" All eyes would thus see them and take notice
of them, before they were carried out into a clean place.

Probably there were two reasons for this action.

1. The fire was thus kept clear and bright, the ashes
being removed. God thereby taught them that he was
not careless as to this matter, but required that the type
of his justice should be kept full and unobscured.

2. The *ashes* were shewn for the purpose of making it
manifest that the flame had not spared the victim, but
had turned it into ashes. It was not a mere threatening
when the angels foretold that Sodom and Gomorrah were
to be destroyed for their sin ; their doom (2 Pet. ii. 6) is
declared to have come on them, "turning them to ashes."
So here, all that was threatened is fulfilled. There the
ashes lie ; any eye may see them. The vengeance has
been accomplished ! The sacrifice is turned into ashes!
Justice has found its object! The lightning has struck

---

* Another rendering is, " The ashes of the fire that has consumed the burnt-
offering on the altar."—(*Horsley.*) But this requires a transposition of the words.
May it not be, " He shall take up the ashes when the fire consumes the burnt-
offering on the altar ? "

the lightning-rod, and is now passed! View Ps. xx. 4 in
this light—" Remember all thy offerings, and accept"—
turn to ashes—" thy burnt-sacrifice." The Lord's arrows
are not pointless; he performs all his threatenings, for he
is holy. " O Lord God of hosts, who is a strong Lord like
unto thee ? or to thy faithfulness round about thee" (Ps.
lxxxix. 8).

> Ver. 11. *And he shall put off his garments, and put on other gar-
> ments, and carry forth the ashes without the camp unto a clean
> place.*

The priest, coming out of the sanctuary, lays aside
these linen garments, and goes forth out of the camp in
another dress. These linen garments are now reckoned
polluted ; the sin he carried in with him cleaves to them.
In another linen dress, therefore—another priestly suit *
—he goes on to the spot where the ashes were to be left,
as memorials of the curse having come on the victim.
May this be intended to shew that Christ, specially at his
death, was to be " numbered with the transgressors?" He
seemed to die as one who had no holiness, no righteousness, no innocence—" *He made his grave with the wicked.*"
But, casting off this appearance of being a transgressor, as
he cries, " It is finished," he is carried to a clean spot.
His surety-character appeared—he is buried in Joseph's
tomb.†

---

* Some think this must have been a dress of meaner materials than the linen,
to represent sin cleaving to him. But where do we ever read of such ?

† Some propose to change the rendering of Isa. liii. 9, in order to bring out
explicitly the fact that Christ *died* among *transgressors*, but was *buried* with
the *rich*. But is there any ground for this proposed change ? Whether the original admits of it, is doubtful ; for few Jews will be satisfied with the rendering
of במתיו, " his *tomb*." It is obviously far better to keep the present rendering—

" *He made his grave with the wicked* (plural),
    And with the rich (singular) *in his death*," *i. e.* when he died.

" *Unto a clean place*," as in chap. iv. 12. In after days this clean place may have been some spot beyond the walls of Jerusalem. In Jer. xxxi. 40, "the valley *of the ashes*" is mentioned—a place which was used for this purpose, and may have been at the very Calvary where the Great Sacrifice was offered, and its ashes laid.

Ver. 12. *And the fire upon the altar shall be burning in it* [*i. e.* on the bosom of the altar]; *it shall not be put out: and the priest shall burn wood on it every morning, and lay the burnt-offering in order upon it; and he shall burn thereon the fat of the peace-offerings.*

Formerly, the fact was mentioned of the fire never being allowed to go out. Here there is mention made of the manner in which it was kept burning. The wood

At the hour of his death, behold the providence of God! A rich man, one of the most honourable and esteemed in Jerusalem, a member of Sanhedrim, and a disciple, unexpectedly appears at Calvary. This was Joseph of Arimathea, without exception the most singularly noble character introduced to us in the Gospels. This rich man had been *driven into concealment* by the plots formed against him by the Jews, on account of his defending Jesus in the Sanhedrim openly (Luke xxiii. 51). This is what John says (chap. xix. 38)—" Being a disciple," " κεκρυμμένος δὲ διὰ τὸν φόβον τῶν 'Ιουδαίων"—not " SECRETLY," for it is, not " κεκρυμμένως" (though even the *adverb* might mean, as in the Septuagint of Jer. xiii. 17, " *in secret places*"), but " *secreted*," or forced to hide by reason of their plots. He was the very contrast to timid Nicodemus, bold and unreserved. Behold! then, this man suddenly returns to the city; and finding that all is over, he boldly seeks the body of Jesus, his beloved Master. And next, he and Nicodemus—two rich men, but the one all boldness, the other nervously timid—lay the body in its silent tomb. And where is the tomb? " In *the place where he was crucified*" (John xix. 41); that is, at the very spot where criminals were put to death, and where they used to be buried. Extraordinary as it may appear, *this very spot* was the spot where *Joseph's new tomb* was hewn out of a rock! The stony sides of the tomb—the new tomb—" *the clean place*," where Jesus was laid—were part of the malefactor's hill. His dead body is " *with the rich man and with the wicked* " in the hour of his death! His grave is the property of a rich man; and yet the rocks which form the partition between his tomb and that of the other Calvary malefactors, are themselves part of Golgotha. Is there not here a fulfilment of Isaiah's words to the letter, and that in a way so unlikely, that no eye could have foreseen it but His, who fore-ordained the whole?

was to be supplied constantly in sufficient measure, and
the sacrifice laid thereon. There is an object for the
Divine justice to seize upon; and this victim must be
shewn every morning, exposed to that intolerable flame.
Christ bears the vehement heat of Jehovah's altar—the
reality of wrath.

There is no "*putting out*" of this fire.* "The *fire is
not quenched*," is Christ's own expression; perhaps in
reference to this type (Mark ix. 44). There will be no
putting out of these flames in eternity—no waters to
quench them—no interference of God's mercy to end
them. The company of their ungodly friends will not
"put out" any of the torments of the damned; nor shall
any intellectual efforts "put them out," by diverting
men's thoughts from their deserved doom. Christ's
agony is the proof of this. If ever God would have
"put out" one flame, it would have been in his case.
Yet he withheld no suffering—"all his waves" were
against him; he laid him in "the lowest pit."

Perhaps "*burn the fat of the peace-offerings*" is introduced here to shew how the flame was to be fed. The
fat must feed it till it blazes bright and strong, casting its
light through the darkness, in view of all the camp. It
was an awful view of Divine justice; it figured out the
tremendous fierceness of almighty wrath. Yet inasmuch
as it is "*the fat of peace-offerings*," a discerning, believing
worshipper may find the elements of peace even here.

---

* In Song viii. 6, "vehement flame" is most generally understood to be "the
flame of Jehovah" (לַהֲבָת יָהּ). The love of Jesus is seen in proportion as we see
the heat of the wrath which he bore for us. "Love is strong as death—like the
flame of Jehovah," *i. e.* on the altar. How great was the sin of Ahaz (2 Chron.
xxviii. 24) when he shut up the temple! There was this ingredient in his guilt:
he was attempting to extinguish the perpetual fire on the altar, as if thereby to hide
from his view the type of God's justice and a coming hell—a sin-avenging God.

The peace-offering on which that flame has fed declared
his reconciliation; so that he can read the assurance of
his acceptance even in these flames! Justice fully satisfied, and yet the worshipper standing in peace, is the
truth taught us by the blazing flame of this altar. "*Our
God is a consuming fire.*"

> Ver. 13. *The fire shall ever be burning upon the altar; it shall
> never go out.*

Throughout, we are emphatically shewn that this fire
has no end. We are reminded of John's words, "The
wrath of God *abideth* on him" (John iii. 36), and Christ's
thrice-repeated declaration, "Where their worm dieth
not, and their fire is not quenched" (Mark ix.) The
word for "go out" is the same that elsewhere is rendered
"*quenched*" (תִכְבֶּה). The *eternal* justice of Jehovah
shall never cease to find fuel in hell; and never shall it
cease to find satisfaction in the Altar of the Great High
Priest. Hence we see that an *everlasting* righteousness
was what we needed (Dan. ix. 24). "*Eternal* redemption" is what has been obtained for us (Heb. ix. 12).

REGARDING THE MEAT-OFFERING

> Ver. 14. *And this is the law of the meat-offering: The sons of Aaron
> shall offer it before the Lord, before the altar.*

The duties of the priest are dwelt upon here. The
officiating priest shall take the meat-offering from the
worshipper, and shall present it. He shall do this
solemnly, coming up "*before the altar,*" *i. e.* in front of
it, in sight of all the people who stand by. For thus the
dedication of all that the man has—body and property,
as well as soul—is publicly declared. All are witnesses
that now he is not his own.

Ver. 15. *And he shall take of it his handful, of the flour of the meat-offering, and of the oil thereof, and all the frankincense which is upon the meat-offering, and shall burn it upon the altar for a sweet savour, even the memorial of it, unto the Lord.*

When the *memorial* (see chap. ii. 2) was taken and burnt, the offerer saw a sight that refreshed his soul. He saw the altar smoking, and felt the air breathing with his accepted gift—" a savour of rest." It was on such occasions as these that the priests exhibited salvation and its results so fully to the comfort of the worshippers, that " the saints shouted for joy" (Ps. cxxxii. 16).

Ver. 16. *And the remainder thereof shall Aaron and his sons eat: with unleavened bread shall it be eaten in the holy place; in the court of the tabernacle of the congregation they shall eat it.*

It ought to be rendered, "Unleavened shall it be eaten;" * that is, the remainder which Aaron and his sons received as their part, shall be eaten in the form of unleavened bread. There must not be anything in it that would intimate sin or corruption ; for since the memorial has been offered, the remainder is reckoned pure, so pure that it may be put into the hands of the priests as food, and eaten on holy ground. It may present to us the fact, that when *Jesus* was once offered as a "sweet savour of rest," then *what remained*, viz. his body the Church, was pure, and might be freely admitted to holy ground—to heaven, and to all heavenly employments.

The "*holy place*" here, is the *court of the tabernacle* (ver. 26), where the altar and laver stood. It is "holy" on the same principle that Peter calls the hill of transfiguration "the holy mount" (2 Pet. i. 18) ; and because the same God was present there who made the place "holy

---

* ἄζυμα βρωθησεται (Sept.)—Eaten as unleavened.   " Comedet absque fermento" (Vulg.)

ground" to Moses at the bush (Exod. iii. 5). There is a passage in Numbers (xviii. 10) where the court seems to be called "most holy"—"In the most holy place shalt thou eat it"—unless we render the words (as Horsley proposes), "Among the most holy *things* thou shalt eat it." Patrick's explanation of it, by a reference to the holy chambers in Ezekiel xlii., is altogether out of the question. It seems to be simply the holiness arising from the Lord's presence, hallowing the courts where such offerings were made, that is meant.

In Leviticus xxiv. 9, and elsewhere, it is again called "the holy place." And no wonder; for it was "*at the door* of the tabernacle" (vii. 31)—in other words, opposite the altar, which was the prominent object in the view of all in the courts, but specially of any at the entrance. To this, allusion is made in Isa. lxii. 9, when thank-offerings of corn and wine are spoken of as feasted on "*in the courts of my holiness.*"

> Ver. 17. *It shall not be baken with leaven. I have given it unto them for their portion of my offerings made by fire: it is most holy, as is the sin-offering, and as the trespass-offering.*

They are directed not to use it as they might do bread at their own dwellings: "There must be no *leaven* in it, for it is a gift to them from me. Let it, then, derive its sweetness and relish to their taste from the consideration that it is my gift to them." This is truly like Hannah, Samuel's mother: when, rejoicing after her son's birth, she sings, not of her joy in her first-born, but of her joy in him who gave her the rich gift—"My heart rejoiceth *in the Lord; mine horn is exalted in the Lord"* (1 Sam. ii. 1). There is here, also, a cheering notice of the full communion that subsists between God and his people—"*I* have given it for THEIR portion, out of MY offerings." As if

there was an intercommunity of goods—of blessings—
between God and his people. He and they alike feast
upon the same holiness and purity, found in the Righteous One.

Ministers, and indeed all God's people, are here taught
not to consider the smallest service or offering as unim-
portant. Lest these "cakes," and "flour," and "baken
things" should be treated slightly, the Lord as solemnly
declared, "It is most holy, as is the sin-offering, and as
the trespass-offering."

> Ver. 18. *All the males among the children of Aaron shall eat of it.
> It shall be a statute for ever in your generations concerning the
> offerings of the Lord made by fire: every one that toucheth them
> shall be holy.*

While all the males of Aaron's line might eat thereof,
every one must remember in all generations to do so
with deep reverence; for "every one (or everything) that
toucheth them shall be holy." Any person or thing
touching them was to be reckoned as *set apart* to holy
purposes, to be treated accordingly. Garments, vessels,
or the like, must be then considered as on holy ground;
and, accordingly, must be washed in clean water, as an
emblem of setting apart from common use. *Persons*, too,
that came in contact, must wash themselves, being, like
Moses at the bush, suddenly drawn into God's presence,
where they must put off the shoe.

What a circle of deep awe was thus drawn round the
altar and its offerings! "God is greatly to be feared in
the assembly of his saints, and to be had in reverence
of all that are about him" (Ps. lxxxix. 7). Nothing is
more blissful than God's presence, yet nothing more solem-
nising. Bethel was "the gate of heaven," and yet "how
dreadful!" This is holy bliss; it is not as the world's joy.

Ver. 19, 20. *And the Lord spake unto Moses, saying, This is the offering of Aaron, and of his sons, which they shall offer unto the Lord in the day when he is anointed; the tenth part of an ephah of fine flour for a meat-offering perpetual, half of it in the morning, and half thereof at night.*

"*A meat-offering perpetual*" means, that this shall be *in all ages* the manner of the *priest's meat-offering*. The common priests and Aaron offered it at their first entering an office, that is, "the *day when he is anointed.*" They had been already told *what* to bring, in Exod. xxix. 2, but they are told *how* to bring it—what ceremonies to use in the bringing of it.

The priest's meat-offering was of "fine flour," in "cakes and wafers" (Exod. xxix. 2), and "baken in the pan" (ver. 21). It thus contained a reference to the *two* most common sorts of meat-offering mentioned in chap. ii. 1–6. It was neither the richest nor the poorest.

The omer, or tenth part of the ephah, is fixed on as the measure. It might remind them of the *omer of manna* which they used daily to gather; and the omer of it kept in the golden pot. When they remembered that manna, would not their hearts naturally feel their obligations to devote all their substance to him who gave them bread from heaven, and was still commanding the blessing on their fields and dwellings?

Ver. 21. *In a pan it shall be made with oil; and when it is baken, thou shalt bring it in: and the baken pieces of the meat-offering shalt thou offer for a sweet savour unto the Lord.*

They were to bring it ready-baken, that is, prepared in the form of cakes and wafers, as Exod. xxix. 2 directed, and as chap. ii. 5 appoints in regard to things baken in the pan.

The *oil*, and other particulars, have been noticed above. The bringing it to the altar, all ready, may have been

meant to teach the need of a fully-prepared offering—
nothing imperfect—if presented to the Lord for acceptance.

> Ver. 22, 23. *And the priest of his sons, that is anointed in his
> stead, shall offer it: it is a statute for ever unto the Lord: it
> shall be wholly burnt. For every meat-offering for the priest
> shall be wholly burnt: it shall not be eaten.*

The ministering high priest already in office presented
this offering of the sons of Aaron on the day of their
consecration.

It is particularly declared that it must be "*wholly
burnt*"—"*not eaten*"—because it was a priest's offering
(see ver. 30 also). This prefigured, no doubt, the truth
that Christ gave Himself, entirely and completely, as the
offering. This type refers to the Saviour alone, not to
his people. It is speaking only of the Head, not of the
members. He who was his people's priest, in giving
himself, gave himself wholly, soul and body, to the consuming flame. " Our God is a consuming fire:" and that
fire withered his spirit as he bore the curse. This meat-
offering was wholly burnt, because it is the meat-offering
of the priest, who is the type of Jesus.

REGARDING THE SIN-OFFERING

> Ver. 24, 25. *And the Lord spake unto Moses, saying, Speak un-
> to Aaron and to his sons, saying, This is the law of the sin-
> offering: In the place where the burnt-offering is killed shall
> the sin-offering be killed before the Lord: it is most holy.*

It must be brought solemnly before the Lord, like the
great burnt-offering, and killed on the same spot, on the
north side of the altar (i. 11). It is to one and the same
atonement that all these sacrifices refer.

" It is most holy." All sacrifices were to be regarded
with awful reverence. For it was as if the worshippers

were standing at the cross, where the Marys stood, and saw the Saviour die. Or like the heavenly host, when they saw the disembodied soul ("*the blood was the life*") of the Redeemer come in before the Father, at the moment the last mite was paid, and he had cried, "It is finished." Was there ever such an hour in heaven? or shall there ever be such an hour in earth or heaven? Even in the act of accepting the atonement made, how solemnly does the soul feel that receives it! See Isaiah, when the live coal touched his lips. What, then, must have been the hour when atonement itself was spread out complete? The hour when a lost sheep returns is solemn; but what is this to the hour when the Shepherd himself returned?

> Ver. 26. *The priest that offereth* it for sin shall eat it; in the holy place shall it be eaten, in the court of the tabernacle of the congregation.*

The Lord, who "by himself purged away sin," holds communion with the once sinful man. He accepts the offerer who presents this sacrifice. In Hosea iv. 8, this rite is referred to—"They eat up the *sin-offering* of my people" (חַטָּאת); and then "lift up their hearts to their iniquity." The degenerate priests one moment engaged in duty, and the next ran back to sin.

> Ver. 27, 28. *Whatsoever shall touch the flesh thereof shall be holy: and when there is sprinkled of the blood thereof upon any garment, thou shalt wash that whereon it was sprinkled in the holy place. But the earthen vessel wherein it is sodden shall be broken: and if it be sodden in a brasen pot, it shall be both scoured and rinsed in water.*

How awful is atoning blood! Even things without life, such as garments, are held in dreadful sacredness if

---

* הַכֹּהֵן הַמְחַטֵּא אֹתָהּ. May it be, "Who maketh it sin;" *i. e.* by thus offering it, he makes it a mass of sin? See this use of the word in chap. ix. 15.

this blood touch them.   No wonder, then, that this earth, on which fell the blood of the Son of God, has a sacredness in the eye of God.   It must be set apart for holy ends, since the blood of Jesus has wet its soil.   And as the earthen vessel, within which the sacrifice was offered, must be broken, and not used for any meaner end again ; so must our *Earth* be decomposed and new-moulded, for it must be kept for the use of him whose sacrifice was offered there.   And as the brazen *vessel* must be rinsed and scoured, so must this earth be freed from all that dims its beauty, and be set apart for holy ends.   It must be purified and reserved for holy purposes ; for the blood of Jesus has dropt upon it, and made it more sacred than any spot, except where he himself dwells.   "My holy mountain" (Isa. xi. 9), is the name it gets from himself, when he is telling how he means to cleanse it for his own use.

> Ver. 29, 30: *All the males among the priests shall eat thereof:*
> *it is most holy.   And no sin-offering, whereof any of the blood*
> *is brought into the tabernacle of the congregation, to reconcile*
> *withal in the holy place, shall be eaten; it shall be burnt in*
> *the fire.*

Again the sacredness of it is declared.   It seems as if nothing was so fitted to teach us holiness as complete atonement.   "He sitteth between the cherubim," says Ps. xcix. 1, looking down on the sprinkled blood ; therefore, "Let the earth be moved."

The sin-offerings are the class of sacrifices mentioned as "those *whereof any of the blood is brought into the tabernacle, to reconcile withal in the holy place.*"   Now, these will be found to be the same sin-offerings that were "*burnt without the camp*" (Heb. xiii. 11).   All of which specially and peculiarly prefigured the entireness of the

Saviour's work (see chap. iv. 12). On this account they are never to be eaten, but all consumed ; as observed in a similar case (ver. 23). On some occasions the Lord is pleased to exhibit parts of the truth separately, withdrawing our view, for the sake of deeper impressiveness, from all but one point at a time. This seems to be done here. We are here led to notice the entireness and completeness of the offering, apart from the results of restoring fellowship between the sinner and his God, which "eating" would have intimated. The transfer of the offerer's guilt to the victim was so complete that the victim is altogether polluted—all "*made sin.*" Hence nothing of it whatsoever must be used ; the fire must thoroughly consume it all. Thus we behold the debt and the gold that pays it, all told down on the floor of the holy place ! What a debt ! What a payment ! The last mite is there ! Behold the demands of a holy God ! And these all met and satisfied ! Behold the sacrifice and the fire !—and then the sacrifice "*wholly consumed !*" How fierce the heat of the flame ! How complete the consumption ! Thus terribly pure is the justice of the Lord in vindicating his holy law—that jealous God, who is " Holy, holy, holy !"

(Chap. VII)

REGARDING THE TRESPASS-OFFERING

Ver. 1, 2. Likewise this is the law of the trespass-offering: it is most holy. In the place where they kill the burnt-offering shall they kill the trespass-offering: and the blood thereof shall he sprinkle round about upon the altar.

So much had been said of the blood of the sin-offering, in chap. iv., that there was no need to call attention to that matter in giving directions to the priests regarding it. But there had been little said about the blood of the trespass-offering; and therefore it is specially noticed here. The blood must be "*sprinkled round about upon the altar.*" Surely Israel must have felt that their souls were reckoned very guilty by their God, since he spoke to them so continually in the language of *blood.* None but a heavy-laden sinner could relish this never-varying exhibition of blood to the eye of the worshipper. The pilgrims to Zion, in after days, must often, as they journeyed through the vale of Baca, have wondered what was to be seen and heard in the courts of the Lord's house, of which the worshippers sang, "*How amiable* are thy tabernacles, O Lord of hosts! My soul longeth, yea, even fainteth, for the courts of the Lord; my heart and my flesh crieth out for the living God. . . . Blessed are they that dwell in thy house!" (Ps. lxxxiv. 1, 2, 4.) And when they arrived, and saw in these courts *blood* on the altar, *blood* in the bowls of the altar, *blood* on its four horns, *blood* on its sides, *blood* meeting the eye at every turn, none but a deeply-convicted soul, none but a soul really alive to the guilt of a broken law, could enter into the song, and cry with the worshippers, "*How amiable!*" Even so with a preached Saviour at this day, and a sin-convinced soul!

> Ver. 3–6. *And he shall offer of it all the fat thereof; the rump, and the fat that covereth the inwards, and the two kidneys, and the fat that is on them,* which is by the flanks, and the caul that is above the liver, with the kidneys, it shall he take away. And the priest shall burn them upon the altar for an offering made by fire unto the Lord: it is a trespass-offering. Every male among the priests shall eat thereof: it shall be eaten in the holy place: it is most holy.*

* "The fat that is on them," and that, too, which is " on the flanks"—a construction similar to Ps. cxxxiii. 3, "The dew of Hermon, and also the dew that descendeth on the mountains of Zion."

These rites had been prescribed, in chaps. iii. and iv., in regard to other offerings, but had not been prescribed as belonging to the trespass-offering; and as the *priests* are specially instructed here, the specific directions come in appropriately here.

The Lord is not weary of repeating these types, both because of his wondrous love to the sinner, and his still more unfathomable love to him whom he holds out to fallen man in each of these figures—his Well-beloved.

Ver. 7. *As the sin-offering is, so is the trespass-offering: there is one law for them: the priest that maketh atonement therewith shall have it.*

" One law," not in regard to all the ceremonies used therein, but in regard to this special circumstance of the priest having the pieces left as his portion (see in chap. vi. 26). The design of this may have been to fix attention on one special result of atonement, viz. that he who is the means of making atonement has a claim on *all* that the offerer brings; thus shewing forth Christ's claim on his people for whom he atones—" Ye are not your own; for ye are bought with a price" (1 Cor. vi. 20).

GENERAL RULE REGARDING PORTIONS BELONGING TO THE PRIESTS

Ver. 8. *And the priest that offereth any man's burnt-offering, even the priest shall have to himself the skin of the burnt-offering which he hath offered.*

This general rule seems naturally to follow the special case just noticed in ver. 7. There we see "*the skin*" given to the priest, irresistibly reminding us of the *skins* that clothed Adam and Eve. If Jesus, at the gate of Eden, acting as our Priest, appointed sacrifice to be offered there, then he had a right to the *skins*, as priest;

and the use to which he appropriated them was *clothing Adam and Eve.*   He has clothing for the naked soul— " fine raiment" (Rev. iii. 18)—obtained from his own sacrifice.   Even at the gate of Eden he began to " counsel us to buy of him fine raiment, that we might be clothed." And this is his office still (Rev. iii. 18).

> Ver. 9, 10. *And all the meat-offering that is baken in the oven, and all that is dressed in the frying-pan and in the pan, shall be the priest's that offereth it.   And every meat-offering mingled with oil, and dry, shall all the sons of Aaron have, one as much as another.*

" *All the meat-offering*"—after the memorial was taken, of course (see chap. ii. 2, 9).   All the kinds of meat-offering are mentioned here—those prepared in the *oven, frying-pan,* and *pan.*   Then, in ver. 10, the *heap of fine flour* is meant by " every meat-offering mingled with oil, and *dry.*"   It is not baked, but *dry;* the oil being on it merely to consecrate it.

The meaning of this part of the type has already been noticed in chap. ii.

REGARDING PEACE-OFFERINGS

> Ver. 11. *And this is the law of the sacrifice of peace-offerings, which he shall offer unto the Lord.*

The Jews say that the peace-offerings for *thanksgiving* were brought on such occasions as Psalm cvii. mentions —on occasions of deliverance from danger in travelling the desert, or voyaging the sea, or captivity, or sickness. The words used in that psalm countenance the idea (ver. 22), " *And let them sacrifice the sacrifices of thanksgiving, and declare his works with rejoicing.*"   Peace-offerings brought on occasion of a *vow* were probably very similar, but with this difference, that *in the time of danger*—e. g.

a storm at sea, or simoom in the desert—they were promised or vowed to the Lord. Such *vowed peace-offerings*
go under the name of "*sacrifices of thanksgiving*," in
Ps. cxvi. 17, compared with verses 1, 14, 18.

Those called "*voluntary*" (נְדָבָה) were probably
brought just because the soul of the worshipper was, at
the time, overflowing with gratitude; there was not, in
this case, any peculiar event to call for them. They were
nearly allied to *praise*, in so far as both *these offerings*
("*free-will offerings*") and *praise* were dictated simply by
the fulness of the worshipper's heart. Hence the phraseology of Ps. cxix. 108, "Accept, I beseech thee, the free-
will offerings of my mouth." And Heb. xiii. 15, "By
him, therefore, let us offer the sacrifice of praise to God
continually, that is, the fruit of our lips, giving thanks to
his name."

> Ver. 12. *If he offer it for a thanksgiving, then he shall offer with*
> *the sacrifice of thanksgiving unleavened cakes mingled with oil,*
> *and unleavened wafers anointed with oil, and cakes mingled*
> *with oil, of fine flour, fried.*

The last clause means, "the cakes mingled with oil
shall be made of fine flour prepared." The second sort
of meat-offering is fixed upon as the kind to be brought
along with peace-offerings; because, perhaps, it was understood that the offerer was a man able to bring this, if he
could afford to bring a thanksgiving sacrifice. And the
meat-offering naturally accompanies an expression of
gratitude; for it is a binding of the offerer to the Lord,
himself and all he has, body and substance, as well as
soul. So, in Psalm cxvi., where the vows are paid by a
sacrifice of thanksgiving, we hear the offerer saying also,
in ver. 16, "O Lord, truly I am thy servant." What is
the meaning of the redeemed casting even their crowns

at Christ's feet? Is not this their expression of abounding
gratitude? They would fain have nothing of their own.
Let all be his.

> Ver. 13, 14. *Besides the cakes, he shall offer for his offering
> leavened bread with the sacrifice of thanksgiving of his peace-
> offerings. And of it he shall offer one out of the whole obla-
> tion for an heave-offering unto the Lord, and it shall be the
> priest's that sprinkleth the blood of the peace-offerings.*

Here is a remarkable appointment. "*Leavened bread*"
is to be offered. To understand this, we are to keep in
mind that this is a *peace-offering*, and therefore the offerer
is in a reconciled state toward God. His sins are all forgiven; there is peace between him and his God. But
this reconciliation does not declare that there is no corruption left remaining in the worshipper. Perfect pardon
does not imply perfect holiness. There is a remnant of
evil left. But here we see that remnant of evil brought
out before the Lord. The "*leavened cakes*" intimate the
corruption of the offerer; and God having graciously
accepted him, and delivered him from evils in the world
(for this is an offering of thanksgiving for special mercies),
he testifies his gratitude by bringing out what of corruption is found in his soul, that it may be removed. "Being
made free from sin, ye have your fruit unto holiness"
(Rom. vi. 22).

And to express yet more fully the intention of bringing
out this "*leavened bread,*" the 14th verse tells that it is to
be "*heaved to the Lord.*"* One cake of this bread that
is leavened is heaved up to the Lord; the priest lifts it up

---

* The word is תְּרוּמָה, and the "wave-offering" is תְּנוּפָה. Both words imply
the same action; but the former is the more comprehensive. The "wave-offering" is confined to lesser things, that could easily be lifted up. Neither term
implies anything as to a new *kind* of sacrifice, but only a new *mode* of presenting the sacrifice.

before the Lord, and, in the sight of all the congregation, waves it to the four quarters of the heavens, as a sign that he is giving it over to the Lord. Thus the grateful offerer presents to the Lord all he has, and spreads out his very corruptions to be dealt with as the Lord sees good. Was he not saying, while the priest thus waved the leavened cake to the four winds, "Search me, O God, and know my heart; try me, and know my thoughts; and see if there be any wicked way in me, and lead me in the way everlasting" (Ps. cxxxix. 23, 24). Patrick remarks that the *leavened bread* was not put upon the altar. It is held up in order to be removed.

> Ver. 15. *And the flesh of the sacrifice of his peace-offerings for thanksgiving shall be eaten the same day that it is offered; he shall not leave any of it until the morning.*

The priest that sprinkled the blood was to eat the pieces of this peace-offering the *same day* that it was offered. Some say that this rule prevented covetousness arising in the priests; no one had it in his power to hoard up. Others say that this rule was fitted to promote brotherly love; for he must call together his friends, in order to have it all finished. But these uses are only incidental. The true uses lie much nearer the surface. Israel might hereby be taught to offer thanksgiving while the benefit was still fresh and recent. Besides this, and most specially, the offerer who saw the priest cut it in pieces, and feast thereon, knew thereby that God had accepted his gift, and returned rejoicing to his dwelling, like David and his people, when their peace-offerings were ended, at the bringing up of the ark (2 Sam. vi. 17–19). The Lord took special notice of this free, spontaneous thank-offering, inasmuch as he commanded it to be immediately eaten, thus speedily assuring the worshipper of peace and acceptance. The love of our God is too full to be restrained from us one moment longer than is needful for the manifestation of his holiness.

> Ver 16, 17. *But if the sacrifice of his offering be a vow, or a voluntary offering, it shall be eaten the same day that he offereth his sacrifice; and on the morrow also the remainder of it shall be eaten. But the remainder of the flesh of the sacrifice on the third day shall be burnt with fire.*

This is the case of a peace-offering offered on occasions when the man had bound himself by a *vow* to present it; and those other occasions when he brought it *voluntarily*, that is, of his own thought, although nothing special had occurred to him to draw it forth. There is one particular in which this offering is to be dealt with differently from the first kind. The time within which it must be eaten is never extended beyond the *third* day; and if any portion remained so long as the third day, that part is to be forthwith brought out and burnt. Every precaution is taken that none of the portions should suffer the taint of corruption. The type refers to the incorruption of the Surety, after he had been offered as a sacrifice. When the third day came round, God completed his testimony to the acceptance of his Son's work, by forthwith raising him from the dead, ere corruption could begin. It seems to be implied here, that "*what remained*" was to be speedily consumed on the third day—perhaps as soon as morning dawned, in order to be the more exact type of the resurrection—"*early on the first day of the week.*"

> Ver. 18. *And if any of the flesh of the sacrifice of his peace-offerings be eaten at all on the third day, it shall not be accepted, neither shall it be imputed unto him that offereth it: it shall be an abomination, and the soul that eateth of it shall bear his iniquity.*

How strictly is the type guarded, that so there may be no misrepresentation of the Antitype! Lest possibly it should corrupt by the third day, it is never to be eaten then; for holy fellowship with God must be set forth by eating it pure. They must make haste, therefore, to eat it; they might eat it the very same day as it was offered (ver. 16). Why, then, delay? And to insure attention to this, the *offerer's* own interest is bound up with it; for here it is declared that *he* loses the whole comfort of his offering if any part should be left till the third day—"it shall not be imputed to him," *i. e.* not reckoned as a peace-offering at all. And if any one rashly persist in eating it, or eat it ignorantly, on that day, he is defiled and unclean.

How careful ought we to be to represent Christ's work to our people exactly as it is held forth in Scripture! How jealous ought we to be of any departure from the pattern shewn to us, since the Father is so jealous over even the figures and emblems of the doing and suffering of his beloved Son. We need all wisdom and prudence; our people need to implore such direction for us; and they, on their own part, need the Spirit of wisdom and revelation in the knowledge of Christ, in order to receive without mistake what is set before them.

> Ver. 19. *And the flesh that toucheth any unclean thing shall not be eaten; it shall be burnt with fire: and as for the flesh, all that be clean shall eat thereof.*

Here it is commanded, *first*, that the flesh be clean; *next*, that they be clean who eat it. The priests must keep off from the peace-offering the approach of anything unclean; and having thus guarded the flesh and kept it pure, they must take care that those who feast thereon be ceremonially clean. It is an *accepted work* that must form our food; and it must be fed upon by *accepted persons.* Hence the case of the Jews in John xviii. 28—they wished to eat the peace-offerings that accompanied the Passover, and therefore kept themselves from ceremonial defilement.

Here is again brought before us the jealous care of God. He must shew himself holy, even while he pours out his love. His unalterable righteousness and purity must be manifested at the tomb of Jesus, in the very hour when he is about to declare the Surety's work accepted, and access open for the sinner to the bosom of his God.

> Ver. 20, 21. *But the soul that eateth of the flesh of the sacrifice of peace-offerings that pertain unto the Lord, having his uncleanness upon him, even that soul shall be cut off from his people. Moreover, the soul that shall touch any unclean thing, as the uncleanness of man, or any unclean beast, or any abominable unclean thing, and eat of the flesh of the sacrifice of peace-offerings which pertain unto the Lord, even that soul shall be cut off from his people.*

This "*cutting off from his people*" seems to be, not death, but complete expulsion from all ordinances. The person was excommunicated, and left to the judgment of God. It seems, from chap. xxii. 4–9, that death was sometimes sent by God immediately, to ratify the act of the priests. The act was, in such cases, like breaking through the fence drawn round Mount Sinai, and coming in to gaze. The *source* of the sin, we should observe, is comparatively immaterial, if the fact of the sin be established. "Whether from man, beast, or thing," it mattered not, if *uncleanness* had been contracted. The Lord shews us that theories as to the *origin of evil*, and apologies drawn from the manner in which we were led astray, can have no effect in disproving the sin itself. It seems implied, also, that no man was to be allowed to plead that it happened accidentally, or was only a trivial matter; the enumeration of "*man, beast, thing*," is sweeping and decisive.

And now, we see the reference in Psalm xxii. 27— "*The meek shall eat, and be satisfied.*" The *meek* are they who bow to God's will, and follow his rules. They may freely eat when complying with his rules. In that Psalm, the food is Christ, our slain Lamb; of whom we may freely partake as often as we will, if only we comply with the rule to come to this feast on the simple warrant, " All things are ready." So to come is true *meekness.*

GENERAL LAWS REGARDING THE FAT AND THE BLOOD

Ver. 22, 23. *And the Lord spake unto Moses, saying, Speak unto the children of Israel, saying, Ye shall eat no manner of fat, of ox, or of sheep, or of goat.*

Probably the frequent occurrence of *fat* in the peace-offerings led to the introduction of this rule in this place; and the prohibition of *fat* was naturally connected with that regarding *blood* in ver. 26.

These three, " *ox, sheep, goat,*" include all the classes of animals offered in sacrifice. And " *the fat* " forbidden is all those pieces elsewhere mentioned as sacrificial, devoted to the fire. On feast-days, we read of the people " eating the fat and drinking the sweet." In this case, the fat of sheep and oxen seems meant. But the pieces were not to be sacrificial pieces. Our rendering conveys too wide a prohibition; it ought to be rendered, " *Ye shall not eat any fat of ox,*" &c., viz. any of that spoken of in iii. 17.

What we give to the Lord must be wholly his. We must not give it to the Lord, and then again draw it back

for our own use. Holy things must be completely left at
the Lord's disposal, like the money laid at the apostles'
feet by Joses of Cyprus (Acts iv. 36).

> Ver. 24. *And the fat of the beast that dieth of itself, and the fat of*
> *that which is torn with beasts, may be used in any other use;*
> *but ye shall in no wise eat of it.*

They might use the fat of such torn beasts and such
diseased ones, for a blaze on their own hearth, or for
domestic purposes; but they must not use the sacrificial
portions for food, even when the animal cannot be brought
to the altar.

God's claim upon them must be kept ever in view.
These pieces are the Lord's in all cases; and had *they*
eaten pieces that were to be consumed on the altar, then
the type would be interfered with. These pieces being
set apart to signify the *inmost desires* given up to God,
man must never *feast* on them. They are no portion for
him. The strength of our desires and feelings is already
given away; we cannot spend it on any but God himself.

> Ver. 25. *For whosoever eateth the fat of the beast, of which men*
> *offer an offering made by fire unto the Lord, even the soul that*
> *eateth it shall be cut off from his people.*

The injunction is repeated, because the temptation
might occur very often in common life; and the penalty
is complete excommunication from the holy people. We
are thus taught the awful guilt of transgressing even the
smallest precept that comes from the mouth of the Lord.
It is a case like this, where there is no other reason for
the thing being binding but just this, viz. *the Lord has*
said it; it is such a case that best shews us the majesty
and glory of the Lord. He is such, that to deviate from
the slightest of his precepts is a sin that deserves cutting
off from the holy people. "O God, who is like unto thee?"

It is thus, too, that we arrive at a simple but very awful view of *sin itself*. The essence of its enormity is, *opposition to the will of the Holy One*. And as the smallest precept given forth by him, discovers the desires of his heart, so, to oppose this precept, is really to thwart the purpose and desire of the Lord's heart—the Lord's nature—his very Godhead.

We should view every precept as proceeding from the heart of him " who so loved us;" and in this light every precept will connect us with his love.

> Ver. 26, 27. *Moreover, ye shall eat no manner of blood, whether it be of fowl or of beast, in any of your dwellings. Whatsoever soul it be that eateth any manner of blood, even that soul shall be cut off from his people.*

Because *the blood* was set apart (see iii. 17) to represent *life poured out* as an atonement. How often was the stream of Calvary thus made to flow within their view! How often were weary Israelites thus refreshed "in their dwellings" by a sight of *blood set apart*, leading them to him who was to come and pour out his soul unto death!

RULES REGARDING THE PARTS OF THE PEACE-OFFERING, SPECIALLY THE BREAST AND THE SHOULDER

> Ver. 28, 29. *And the Lord spake unto Moses, saying, Speak unto the children of Israel, saying, He that offereth the sacrifice of his peace-offerings unto the Lord, shall bring his oblation unto the Lord of the sacrifice of his peace-offerings.*

The meaning is, " He that cometh to present a peace-offering *as his sacrifice*, shall, in so doing, bring the requisite parts."

Some new truths are here put before us in the peace-offering; and these truths are, all of them, comforting to the priest's heart. It is the priests who are specially addressed in the directions of this chapter, so that it was natural to bring in, at this point, what bore upon their comfort.

> Ver. 30, 31. *His own hands shall bring the offerings of the Lord made by fire; the fat, with the breast, it shall he bring, that the breast may be waved for a wave-offering before the Lord. And the priest shall burn the fat upon the altar; but the breast shall be Aaron's and his sons'.*

The offerer himself—"his own hands"—must bring the offering; for we must come to God in our own person, each of us for ourselves, and enter into fellowship with him for our own souls. Each of us, when reconciled, must bring to God "*the fat;*" all mentioned in chap. iii. 3, 4, typical of every deep-seated desire, every inward affection. And we bring, also, *the breast*, in connexion with *the fat*, intimating the heart's affections and sympathies. Aaron and his sons receive *the breast* as their portion, as if to declare that the reconciled worshipper, now at peace with God, had true sympathy with, and love towards, the priest, by whose instrumentality this blessing came to him. We are taught, in this manner, the worshipper's affectionate feelings to his officiating priest— similar, in kind, to the feeling that now subsists between a pastor whom the Spirit anoints to preach glad tidings to the meek, and the people who shout for joy at the voice. At the same time, it also taught the redeemed sinner's complete devotion of heart and mind to Jesus, his High Priest, who procures the peace, and gives the joy, of reconciliation.

The names of the twelve tribes on the precious stones that were placed both on the *shoulder* and on the *breast* of the high priest, seem to confirm and establish this view. For we seem to be taught the *affection* and the *power* of

the priest, in the engraved stones worn on the breast and
the shoulder.

The *waving* of it was an action designed to shew
publicly that the thing waved was given over to God.
The priest lifted it up, and probably moved it from east
to west, from north to south, as if to say that all ends of
the earth might be witnesses that this was now given up
to God.   The whole heart, open, full, entire, is devoted
to the Lord.

> Ver. 32, 33. *And the right shoulder shall ye give unto the priest
> for an heave-offering of the sacrifices of your peace-offerings.
> He among the sons of Aaron that offereth the blood of the
> peace-offerings, and the fat, shall have the right shoulder for
> his part.*

The *right shoulder*, as well as the breast, is presented;
for there must be *hand* and *heart* together in a full dedication to the Lord.   It is the *shoulder*, as being that
which bore the burden ; and the *right shoulder*, as that
had most strength to support a burden.   A true Israelite,
in the enjoyment of reconciliation, felt himself bound to
help the priest with heart and hand, because he was the
Lord's minister to him for good.   He would daily make
supplication for him, that his soul might be "satiated
with fatness" as he handled the types, and might never
grow weary in his work; that he might be able, also, to
tell a waiting people somewhat of the wonders he saw.
For, I suppose, the priest often spoke to the worshippers,
and directed their eye to the person of Him who was to
come—to Him whose glorious form was as yet hid amid
the drapery of the earthly sanctuary.

But, besides this, the true worshipper hereby presented
himself to the Great High Priest, saying, in a manner,
" Here is my person, soul and body; pour into my heart

all thy spirit, and put thy yoke upon my willing shoulder, for thou hast redeemed me."

And yet once more. It shewed forth Christ, our peace-offering,* presenting himself to the Father, heart and hand, to do the Father's will. In full *sympathy* with his Father's will, and full *co-operation* with him in one grand design of redemption, he presents himself as "*our Peace.*" And herein is the security of our peace, that he and the Father are one in counsel, purpose, love, and action.

Once more. These portions are given to the priests directly by the Lord, because the priests had no lot or inheritance assigned them in Israel. But this mode of providing for their wants was well fitted to keep them ever looking to the Lord alone, in having whom they could never want. For truly does Augustine say (Ps. lvi.), "*Quantum-libet sis avarus, sufficit tibi Deus.*"

> Ver. 34. *For the wave-breast and the heave-shoulder have I taken of the children of Israel from off the sacrifices of their peace-offerings, and have given them unto Aaron the priest, and unto his sons, by a statute for ever, from among the children of Israel.*

"*A statute for ever.*" To mark how reasonable it appeared in the Lord's eyes, he declares that this statute shall never be altered. So long as their polity continued,

---

* Some (see especially Edzardus, in Note 33, in his Latin translation and comment on the tract of the Gemara, "*De Idololatria*") try to find types of *The Cross*, in *the heaving* and *the waving* of these pieces. They think it is seen in waving them up and across. And they go to other similar ceremonies, such as anointing the four corners of the altar with oil—putting blood on the same—anointing Aaron and his sons with oil on *hands, feet,* and *ears*—putting blood on them in the same manner—the roasting of the Paschal Lamb on the spit (which the Jews say was always of wood)—the leaven cakes cut in pieces, *i. e. decussatæ in formam* X "—the position of the priest's hands when lifting them up to bless—and even the gratework of the inside of the altar. But this is fancy. The brazen serpent, and the "man hanged on the tree as accursed," are the only clear types of *the cross*. Ps. xxii. 15 is a prophecy, not a type.

this statute must remain in force.   The unalterable and necessary connexion between *reconciliation* and *self-dedication* may be held forth in this everlasting statute.   Indeed, nothing is so natural to the reconciled soul, enjoying the fellowship of the Father and the Son, as this complete giving up of heart and hand to him that "*offered the blood*" (ver. 33); for we should have noticed that these are the due of "*him who offered the blood,*" as if to keep our attention fixed on the fact, that it is the Redeemer's blood shed for us that has given him this right to all we are and all we can yield.

"*I have taken.*"   The Lord himself specially appoints this to be done, and speaks of his appointment as one that should be noticed and observed, as being important in his eyes.

GENERAL REMARKS ON THE PRECEDING RULES

Ver. 35, 36. *This is the portion* of the anointing of Aaron, and of the anointing of his sons, out of the offerings of the Lord made by fire, in the day when he presented them to minister unto the Lord in the priest's office; which the Lord commanded to be given them of the children of Israel, in the day that he anointed them, by a statute for ever throughout their generations.*

More literally, " *This is the anointing* of Aaron ;" *i. e.* this is what is involved in the anointing.   This is the lot and portion of the sons of Aaron, and of Aaron himself, the moment he is anointed.   These are the privileges and duties connected with their anointing.   Willett† notes

---

* מִשְׁחָה.   Rosenmüller proposes to adopt for this word the Arabic sense, "portion-measure;" and another critic finds in Ethiopic the word " *myshach,*" a feast, which might give a good sense here.   But the word מָשַׁח, "to anoint," with its derivatives, is a term belonging to the Tabernacle, and evidently applied specially to its usages.   An " ἅπαξ λεγομενον " would be out of place here.

† Hexapla on *Levit.*

that the *presenting* of Aaron and his sons was on the first day, and the *anointing* was on the eighth day.

It is characteristic of the Lord's way thus to state all the provision made for a duty or an office before the person actually enters upon that duty or office. Hence he tells the priests what shall be their work, and what their comforts under it, *before they are consecrated.* The details of consecration are in next chapter. It is like his way in other things, and like his way in the Gospel, where he first sets before the sinner the full provision made for him, in privilege and in duty; and thus, by exhibiting the easy yoke and the light burden, leads him to take on all gladly. Everywhere we trace the hand of the same God—the God and Father of our Lord and Saviour Jesus Christ.

Ver. 37. *This is the law of the burnt-offering, of the meat-offering, and of the sin-offering, and of the trespass-offering, and of the consecrations, and of the sacrifice of the peace offerings,—*

It may seem out of place to insert "*consecrations*" here. But probably the reason is this:—The directions given above, in regard to sin-offerings (chap. vi. 24) and trespass-offerings (chap. vii. 1) in general, were to be observed also in the case of these offerings being presented by the priests on the day of their consecration. Hence, by inserting the clause here, "this is the *law of the consecrations*," the priests were made aware that, in regard to themselves, there was to be no change in any of the rites observed in sin-offerings and trespass-offerings.

The Lord leaves no one's duty doubtful. His mind may be ascertained. "If it were not so, I would have told you" (John xiv. 2), may be held as a general rule.

Ver. 38. *Which the Lord commanded Moses in mount Sinai, in the day that he commanded the children of Israel to offer their oblations unto the Lord, in the wilderness of Sinai.*

This reminds us, again, that the mode of receiving atonement is revealed by God to the sinner. The *need of atonement* was made known by God on Sinai, when he so awfully alarmed the camp. Then, that there was forgiveness with him—atonement—was made known. And now, the mode of receiving and applying it has been made known—all by God himself. We, who are in this wilderness, are taught still by the same God in the same way. The law from Sinai awakens; then the Mediator's message to us, from the same Sinai, gives peace. Jesus, who had the law of God " within his heart " (Psalm xl. 8, "in the midst of his bowels"), not merely in his hands, like Moses, comes down from fellowship with the Father, to lead the sinner to the very communion he enjoyed himself. He leads us, by his blood, above all the clouds and thunders of the hill,* to see " the body of heaven in its clearness, with the pavement of sapphire-stone," and to the God of Israel himself, who is well pleased, and lays no hand but the hand of love on these " nobles of Israel" lifted up from the dunghill to take their place among the princes of his people. Here, then, let us eat and drink; on that very spot let us eat " hidden manna," and drink " the water of life."

It may be suitable here to inquire into the meaning of a phrase occurring not unfrequently, " *Sacrifices of righteousness*" (see Ps. iv. 5, and li. 19). The expression is taken from the book of Deuteronomy (chap. xxxiii. 19), and means *sacrifices presented in a right way.* What Malachi (iii. 3) speaks of as done בִּצְדָקָה,

* As typified more fully in Exod. xxiv.

" in righteousness," these other passages express by calling them " sacrifices of righteousness."   The form זִבְחֵי צֶדֶק, is phraseology quite authorised by מֹאזְנֵי צֶדֶק (Lev. xix. 36), " balances of righteousness," &c.

The passage in Ps. iv. 5 occurs in beautiful connexion. The context tells of the godly man set apart by the Lord as his peculiar treasure; and whenever this treasure is in peril, the Lord at once hastens to help (ver. 3). The man thus kept, is one who lives in holy awe—one who searches out the leaven, and spreads it out before God (ver. 4). In so doing, he is led to use the appointed sacrifices, and there he finds repose, resting as a pardoned man (ver. 5).

Not less beautiful is Ps. li. 16, 17, which speaks of another kind of sacrifice at first view—" *The sacrifices of God are a broken spirit.*"   David, newly forgiven, and wondering at the grace which cleansed him from foul adultery, and the crimson stains of murder and deceit, inquires, after all this, " What shall I render unto the Lord for all his benefits ?"   How shall I ever recompense such free love, such overflowing grace ?   This is evidently the secret train of feeling that led to ver. 16—" *For thou desirest not sacrifice,*" &c.   If mere gifts of lambs or oxen would sufficiently express my gratitude, then I would give them.   There is not a lamb in my flock, an ox in my stall, that I would spare.   But that is not what thou desirest as *a proof of true thankfulness.*   There is a better thank-offering still.   Let me walk softly all my days. Let me give thee " *a broken heart,*" *i. e.* let me cherish, all my days, that holy, tender frame of spirit that feels for thy honour, and loveth thee so intensely as to be broken-hearted when thou art wronged!

CHAPTER VIII

The Priesthood entering on their Office

*" The law maketh men high priests which have infirmity; but the word
of the oath, which was since the law, maketh the Son, who is consecrated
for evermore."*—Heb. vii. 28

THE *priesthood* in Israel had nothing in common with the
priesthood of *Papal Rome.* The priests are for the
people, not the people for the priests. The people are
first attended to; then the priests. Neither was there a
shadow of *Erastianism;* for the ruler, Moses, commanded
nothing to Aaron and his sons except what *the Lord
revealed,* and sent him to tell. And the Lord, in these
ordinances regarding the priesthood, gave a shadow of
the heavenly transactions between the Father and the
Son.—(Owen.)

> Ver. 1–3. *And the Lord spake unto Moses, saying, Take Aaron,
> and his sons with him, and the garments, and the anointing
> oil, and a bullock for the sin-offering, and two rams,
> and a basket of unleavened bread; and gather thou all the
> congregation together unto the door of the tabernacle of the
> congregation.*

As the sacrifices are ever leading us to the great *altar
of brass,* and as the continual washings that are mentioned in this chapter will be ever turning us to the *laver
of brass,* let us here, for a moment, fix our eye upon

them. The one shews us *pardon of sin* by Christ's death, the other shews us *purification of heart* by Christ's Spirit. Who is there that desires not these blessings, if he is an awakened man at all? Who, then, would not join Israel, going up to the feasts, in singing, "*How amiable are thy tabernacles, O Lord of hosts!*" (Ps. lxxxiv. 1.) Leave your sweet retreat under the fig-tree, Nathanael; leave your delicious vineyard, and your garden that blooms like another Eden, and come thou up to the courts of the tabernacle. A sin-convinced soul will find what it needs. Lo! that *altar*. Bathe thy conscience there; for the blood there sheweth the Saviour's death till he come! And next refresh thy cleansed conscience at the *laver;* for there the same Messiah holds forth to thee his Spirit. He that comes to the *altar* may go on to the *laver*. "He that believeth on me, out of him shall flow rivers of living water."

But why is there such a singular peculiarity in the construction of both altar and laver? The former was covered with the brass of the censers that had been held in the polluted hands of Korah, Dathan, and his company (Numb. xvi. ·38); and the latter was formed of the brass that was obtained from the mirrors of the women (Exod. xxxviii. 8) who worshipped at the tabernacle door, and had been used but too frequently to gratify the unholy feelings called forth by "the lust of the eye."

I. The brazen censers of Korah and his company contrasted very evidently with the *golden censer* of a true priest. The *gold* of the latter marked its heavenly character and use, as we see also in the gold of the candlestick, of the table, and of the mercy-seat, or in the golden streets and golden harps of New Jerusalem. But nevertheless, out of these polluted materials the Lord forms the altar where atonement for sin was to be made.* *Shittim-wood* (very durable and incorruptible) is spread over with plates of this brass. Is not this fitted to remind us that Christ had the " likeness of sinful flesh"— the shittim-wood being veiled and hid by the brass ? In the very nature that sinned so presumptuously the Lord Jesus appears; and, wearing that nature, presents in it his offering—only, in his person it was so pure that the " altar sanctified the gift." When he arose and ascended, he threw off this obscurity, and was "the *golden* altar."

II. The *laver*, made of the mirror brass, held pure water, which was the type of the Holy Spirit. In our very nature, which in our hands serves only the purposes of sin and vanity, the Redeemer exhibited purity—the very purity of the Holy Ghost, who dwelt in him without measure! He took the brass from the women of Israel (Exod. xxxviii. 8). He took our true nature from the womb of the Virgin; and, assuming it to himself, thereby made it holy. And so it became a holy vessel for the Spirit to fill. Here, then, is Jesus made unto us of God " *sanctification* " as well as " righteousness." And, in like manner, when the " *sea of brass* " appears in Solomon's temple, it seems to be still Christ, who was in the likeness of sinful flesh, the source of the world's holiness.

Perhaps we might take another view of the general arrangement of these courts. May we not say that there is something here to remind us of each person of the Godhead? In yonder *Holy of holies*, behind the veil, in light inaccessible, is the symbol of *the Father*. Then, at yonder gate, meeting the view of every inquirer, is the

---

* When in contrast with the *gold*, brass is a symbol of inferior nature; see Daniel's image. But when in contrast with *earth*, or crumbling dust, it may be a symbol of durability; see Zech. vi. 1.

Altar of Sacrifice, the symbol of *the Son*, who said, " Lo,
I come." And between, stands the laver of pure water,
the symbol of the *Holy Ghost*. The whole might be
called Ephesians ii. 18 written in sacred hieroglyphics—
" *Through him we both have access by one Spirit unto the
Father.*"

Now let us hasten forward to the scene before us.

We may view the scene all at once; its details are
given afterwards. God commands Aaron and his sons
to approach the altar, in sight of all the people, with all
the furniture of consecration. Let us see them walking
toward the altar, conscious of the awfully solemn situation in which they are placed. The deep thoughtfulness
of the father is reflected upon his four attending sons,
whose souls cannot but tremble when they see the trembling step of their aged father, though accustomed to
meet with God. Moses comes with them, bearing the
things needed for consecration. You see *the garments*
(Exod. xxviii. 2) of the priesthood, ready to cover their
persons, as the skins clothed Adam and Eve, in type of
imputed righteousness. Notice, also, the *anointing oil*
(Exod. xxx. 23), the sight of which reminds the priest of
their need of the Spirit of all grace. Close by, at their
side, stands the *bullock for a sin-offering*, on whose head
they are this day to lay their sins; and beside the bullock are *two rams*, one for the burnt-offering—such as
their father Abraham offered in room of his son Isaac—
the other for *consecration* (ver. 22). Thus they stand
in presence of types that all speak of their sin and their
poverty of soul; they cannot lift their eye without seeing
sin staring them in the face. And, to complete all, there
is a basket of *unleavened bread*, which they are to present as a type of their whole persons and substance being

devoted full and entire to God, without mixture of leaven. The whole congregation look on upon this spectacle in silence. It is the priesthood entering on their office! wherein they are to stand ever after, offering Israel's sacrifices, and bringing back the news of reconciliation.

Although not so personally interested, yet with a still deeper wonder and concern, the holy congregation of heaven stood round when the Son of God was about to enter on his priestly office, saying, " Sacrifice and offering thou wouldest not, but a body hast thou prepared for me. ... Lo! I come to do thy will, O God" (Heb. x. 5-7).

Moses acts here for God. Philo and some of the Jews call him *High Priest*,* because of his actings in regard to the tabernacle. But it is far better to regard him as somewhat like *Melchisedec*—king and mediator and prophet. , He is peculiar, however; for he is not " king and priest," but " king and mediator." So many types did it require to set forth Jesus.

> Ver. 4. *And Moses did as the Lord commanded him; and the assembly was gathered together unto the door of the tabernacle of the congregation.*

No sooner does Moses hear than he goes forth to obey; and no sooner do the people hear than they are seen gathering themselves at the door of the tabernacle. All Israel was interested in their priesthood, and should know how their priests were qualified for their office ; even as all earth should look on and see the qualifications of the Great High Priest, who gave *himself*, saying, " Lo! I come."

> Ver. 5, 6. *And Moses said unto the congregation, This is the thing which the Lord commanded to be done. And Moses brought Aaron and his sons, and washed them with water.*

---

* *See* Patrick.

Moses stood by the laver, and said, " This is the thing which the Lord commanded to be done." And so saying, he called Aaron and his sons to come near. He then laved the pure water upon them, to intimate that they must be clean and holy. And as the water used was water from the laver, the type signified that it was the Holy Ghost who was to give them this purity. After this day, they needed not to wash their bodies, but only their feet, when it happened that their feet were soiled during services, and their hands when they were soiled at the altar. Our Lord has been supposed to allude to this in John xiii. 10, " *He that is washed needeth not save to wash his feet, but is clean every whit.*" A man, after being in the bath, is clean; only his feet may be soiled on the floor as he steps along. So, a priest, after this washing of his person on the consecration-day, is clean; only he may need to wash his feet or hands again. Being publicly led by God to the full Spirit, and shewn the living waters, he has a right to return as often as his office may call for a renewal of the application. That cleansing water, or sanctification, needs to be used on all exigencies; and how appropriate, on entering on office, to shew him the full supply!

When our Lord used the words in John xiii. 8, he seems to say, " I am doing to you as was done to the priests; if I wash thee not, thou hast no part with me. I am thus, under a figure, preparing you for immediate duty, like priests in the temple. You are consecrated to me already; but often will you need to apply the water again to your feet." This is true of all believers, who are " priests unto God." *

* Others suppose that the allusion to the *bath* is the true one, and the cleansing is *pardon*. But at Passover time, temple-allusions were far more natural.

Ver. 7. *And he put upon him the coat, and girded him with the girdle, and clothed him with the robe, and put the ephod upon him, and he girded him with the curious girdle of the ephod, and bound it unto him therewith.*

Besides *purification*, the priests must be endowed with peculiar gifts and graces. Our Great High Priest must be not only "holy, harmless, undefiled, separate from sinners," but also furnished with extraordinary and complete endowments.

The *coat* and *girdle*, as well as *an ephod* and *a mitre*, of less costly material and less attractive form, were worn by all the sons of Aaron. In them we are taught, that any one who appears as priest at all must be *clothed* in righteousness, and *girt* for active obedience; and must have, in addition, a special covering for those *shoulders* which were to bear the weight of a people's guilt, and that *brow* which was to be lifted up in confession. But the *High Priest* was marked out more peculiarly still. He has as much as the other priests to mark him out; but he has more also—and it is *his* dress that is specially noticed here.

In speaking of these garments, it is right to classify them, or at least to have some idea of the system observed in the arrangement of them.

1. *The Ephod* is to be considered the original dress of a priest. By itself, and without any other mark, it was the distinguishing characteristic of one bearing a priestly office. Its simplest form was that of a robe, flung over the shoulders (ἐπωμίς, in the Sept.), made of linen. Perhaps its pattern was that significant clothing of sacrificial skins cast over Adam by God (Gen. iii. 21), to cover his sinful person. The significance of it was, *q. d.* they need to be covered who approach God. If seraphim cover

their feet and face before God, much more children of
men must approach with holy reverence. They must
have a hiding or covering for their sins. This seems to
be the plain object of *the ephod*. It is thus, accordingly,
that we find priests described very frequently, *e. g.*
1 Sam. ii. 28; xiv. 3; xxi. 9; xxii. 18; xxiii. 6; xxx. 7.
When David said, " *Bring hither the ephod*," the meaning
was, that the priest should put on his characteristic dress,
and inquire at God.   " *Having a priest over the house of
God, let us draw near*," would be the New Testament
language.   Hence we understand *Gideon's ephod* (Judg.
viii. 27).   It was well meant, though followed with evil
consequences.   The ephod was to shew the sinner's way
to God by a Mediator; and the splendour of this ephod
was to have attracted Israel's eyes to the true way of
approaching Jehovah, and so keep them after their vic-
tories from self-righteousness, and from the gods of the
heathen.   But, being a scheme of human wisdom—like
the invention of rites and ceremonies in some Christian
churches—it led to sin.   Hence, also, the sin of Micah's
ephod, in Judges xvii.   The words of Hosea (iii. 4) mean
that Israel should no longer have even the simplest elements of a priesthood: as we see at this day! It may be
objected, however, that Samuel (1 Sam. ii. 18) and David
(2 Sam. vi. 14) wore a linen *ephod*, and they were not
priests.   True: but let it be observed, that both these
men of God were in some respects extraordinary, as if
intended to be typical, in regard to office.   Samuel was
judge in the land, as well as *prophet;* and though not
of Aaron's line, God authorised him to act as *priest*
on many occasions—a threefold office in his own person!
So, also, David combines the same three offices, the *king*
and *prophet* fully, the *priestly* more dimly—a threefold

office in his one person; and yet he is not of Aaron's line! Is there not a type here? Did it not foreshadow our Messiah, in his threefold offices? Upon the whole, there seems little doubt that the *ephod* was the *rudimental* dress of the priesthood. And in this light, it is interesting to see that the onyx-stones, on which the names of the twelve tribes were engraven, were fixed " on the shoulders of the Ephod" (Exod. xxviii. 12).

2. We now come to the second stage in the inquiry. In addition to this simple original dress, the Lord commanded Moses to provide for every priest of Aaron's line (Exod. xxviii. 5) a broidered *coat*, with its girdle, and *trowsers* for the limbs, all which were to be worn below the ephod, covering closely the whole body of the priest. This coat is said to have been without a seam (ἄρραφος), like our Lord's (John xix. 23). Is there not here an intimation of our need of every complete clothing, in order to appear before God? The Lord multiplies the types of our need by this provision, while he shews our need supplied in the priest. And, at the same time, he ordered that the same priests should wear " *bonnets for ornament and beauty*," as if to say, that they, whose persons were thus fully clothed, would be so acceptable in his sight, that they need not be ashamed to lift up their face before God. When some of the priests at Calvary saw the seamless robe of Jesus in the soldiers' hands, must they not have felt a flash of conviction? It was God in that hour bringing to light his *priestly character*.

3. But yet more was to be shewn. The full-length portrait of our Priest and Substitute was not yet drawn. Accordingly, the *High Priest* was to be one superior to all his brethren. He claims all the coverings that belonged to them: only, in his case, each one is made of finer mate-

rials. All his garments are "*for glory and beauty*," to set off the person of him who is to make complete atonement. His *ephod* has a "*curious girdle*," *i. e.* a girdle wrought and embroidered with skilful workmanship. With this girdle he binds up his ephod, and goes forward to work for God, unentangled and undistracted. The rare workmanship of it prefigured the pre-eminent qualifications of the Lord Jesus—his zeal more fervent and pure, more beautiful in its acts and stronger in its efforts, than any ever seen among the children of men. Every quality was in its proper place; nothing was out of proportion; all was graceful. "*He bound to him the curious girdle.*"

But this, and the fine quality of the vestments already named, was only the beginning of the high priest's pre-eminence in the dress he wore—the clothing of office. Next, we find a robe called "*the robe of ephod*" (מְעִיל). It was worn below the ephod; it reached down to the feet, and at the feet was set with a row of bells and pomegranates alternately. Is there not here a further hint, or rather a plain intimation, that in a full priest there must not only be nothing wanting, but there must be something, also, to spare—a *superfluity of righteousness* to cover the needy? He must have fold upon fold of the pure linen, for he needs a righteousness "like the waves of the sea." And these *bells*,* like the bells in Zech. xiv. 20, speak to the ear, giving notice of his approach; while the *pomegranates* speak to the eye, telling that he comes laden with Canaan-fruit for those that hunger and thirst for righteousness. His is a robe unsoiled, though it touches the ground. Its pomegranates

---

* It is interesting to find, in the British Museum, small bells, about an inch in diameter, and nearly of the shape of a pomegranate, brought from Egyptian tombs.

proclaim that it is rich in righteousness to the very skirts, while its bells warn off the approach of pollution. This is the robe, so peculiarly characteristic of the *high priest*; the " ποδήρης" of Rev. i. 13, in which our Lord appears, thereby proclaiming himself to be the true Aaron. Besides, being " *all of blue*," it had a heavenly tinge— the " sky-tinctured grain" pointing to the firmament.

But there remained still something to be put on which might be superior to " the bonnets" of the common priests, and would yet more significantly declare that the *high priest* was accepted of the Lord.   There was, there-fore, a *mitre* (ver. 9) on his brow, and a *breastplate* (ver. 8) of very singular use and form, having on it four rows of precious stones, and in each row the names of three of the tribes of Israel.

> Ver. 8. *And he put the breastplate upon him; also he put in the breastplate the Urim and the Thummim.*

Israel now saw their name—the name of each tribe— blazing on the precious stones of the breastplate, as Moses lifted it up to bind upon Aaron's heart.* They see that their high priest carries on his heart the memo-

---

* It is curious to notice a connexion between *New Jerusalem* glories and the *breastplate*, and yet more, to observe that both point back to *Eden*. It may thus be shewn.   The first precious stone mentioned in the Bible is the *onyx-stone* (Gen. ii. 12); and it was this stone that formed the " stones of memorial" on the shoulders of the high priest's ephod (Exod. xxviii. 9), on which the names of the twelve tribes were engraven.   Then, farther, and more directly as to the breastplate, there is mention in Ezekiel (who is the prophet that describes the *cherubim*, and most frequently refers to *Eden*) of the following precious stones having been in Eden:—" The sardius, topaz, and diamond, the beryl, and the onyx, and the jasper, the sapphire, the emerald, and the carbuncle" (chap. xxviii. 13).   It would almost appear as if the *breastplate* of the high priest pointed back to Eden, promising to God's Israel re-admission into its glories; while *New Jerusalem* speaks of the same, presenting to the redeemed all, and more than all, the glory of Paradise, into which they are introduced by the Lamb, the true High Priest, who bears their names on his heart.

rial of every tribe, a token of his love for all, and care for all, and a pledge that he will offer sacrifice and intercede for all.   Jesus, yet more fully still, bears on his soul, and writes on the palms of his hands, the name of every individual of all that innumerable company, from every kindred, and tongue, and people, given him by the Father —and for each he offers himself as the Atonement, and for each he intercedes.   Oh, how unutterably blessed to know that it is so!   "Set me, Lord, as a seal upon thine heart" (Song viii. 6), may well be our prayer; and his reply is already given, "I pray for them" (John xvii. 9).   Truly it is blessed to be here, fighting with Amalek in the valley, when our Intercessor, whose hands never hang down, is pleading for us before the throne.   How quietly we may rest ourselves, free from all care, enjoying the sleep of his beloved, when we know that our Priest bends over us, and, pointing the Father to us, prays, " Father, I will that they also whom thou hast given me be with me where I am."

But the " *Urim and Thummim*" are on the breast-plate of the high priest.   What are these?   The first word means " *lights*," just as sun and moon are called (אוּרִים) "lights" in Ps. cxxxvi. 7; and the second means " *perfections*," or, perhaps, " *perfect rules*."   The terms would be appropriate to express some revelations of God's mind and directions given by him; and, accordingly, much has been said to prove that these terms denote *the law*, or two tables on which the commandments were written.*   For anything we know, these may have been

---

* See a good statement of this in *Edzardus*, page 202 of his notes and translation of the treatise of the Gemara, " *De Avoda Sara seu de Idolatria*."   I suppose he may have had in view 2 Cor. iii. 7—" The ministration of death, written and engraven in stones, was glorious."   The whole subject is obscure.

engraven on precious stones; but the point to be observed is, that Moses needed to get no description of them. As in the case of the *cherubim,* which were known as emblems of redemption ever since the days of the Fall, so here, there was no need of special description; for the things were known. The Lord bids him (Exod. xxiv. 30) "*put* THE *Urim and Thummim on* * *the breastplate.*"

We find from Exod. xxxii. 15, that there was much writing on the tablets given by God to Moses. Like the seven-sealed book, they were written "*on both sides by the finger of God.*" The Lord, in Exod. xxiv. 12, spoke of "tables of stone, and *a law* and *commandments.*" These were *written ere Moses went up;* for it is said, "WHICH I HAVE WRITTEN." They were lying, therefore, within sight when Moses went up to meet God on the hill; and he saw them engraven in some form, just as John saw the sealed book in the hands of him that sat on the throne. Hence it is we might account for the manner in which Moses was told (Exod. xxviii. 30) to put "THE Urim" on the breastplate. The Lord, referring to the "law and commandments" already written, and seen by Moses, calls them "*the lights, and the perfect rules*" for Israel; and bids him place them on the breastplate. How this was done we know not : it may have been simply on tablets, or in the form of a roll. And it may have contained more than the ten commandments. It is to these that reference is supposed to be made in Psalm xix., where "*the law* of the Lord" is said to be "*perfect*" תָּמִימָה, and the "*commandment*" to be the "*enlightener* of the eyes," as if referring to אוּרִים.

Our Lord refers to the breastplate, if not to the Urim and Thummim also, when he says, in Psalm xl. 8, "*Thy*

* אֶל, "*on,*" not "in."

law is within my heart"—not merely on it. And this is
his plea on our behalf. He pleads his obedience, and sinks
our disobedience therein. Pointing to us, he pleads as a
favour to himself, "Lord, withhold not thou thy tender
mercies *from me"* (ver. 11), identifying *us* with *himself.*
We are in this glorious "ME."

It has been suggested by one who is a "ready scribe in
the law of his God," that the stones of the breastplate
were arranged in the manner in which the tents were
pitched round the ark : thus—

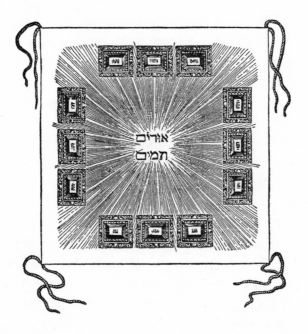

Lightfoot has the idea that the precious stones of New
Jerusalem (Rev. xxi.) were placed in such a way that
there were three layers of them on each side of the square
city ; and so each wall exhibited three varieties of precious
stones in its structure. This arrangement corresponds
to what we suppose to have been the arrangement of

the breastplate stones. The *Urim and Thummim* would be in the midst, corresponding to the place of the ark; and the stones in rows on each of the four sides. If so, do we not see Israel encamped in safety, *with The Law in the midst?* or, in other words, with The Revealed God* in the midst. The redeemed abide secure because his revealed will is their rule.

The mode of consulting the Lord by the Urim is uncertain. It may have been simply this;—the priest put on the breastplate with all it contained, when he drew near the Lord's presence. And this was an appropriate action; for *the Urim* was a sign or testimony of the Lord being in the midst of Israel, ready to be consulted in time of need (1 Sam. xxviii. 6; Neh. vii. 65).

> Ver. 9. *And he put the mitre upon his head; also upon the mitre, even upon his forefront, did he put the golden plate, the holy crown; as the Lord commanded Moses.*

There would be a thrill of deepening interest in the assembled Church of Israel when they saw the *breastplate* put on; but not less so when *the mitre* was put on his head, and the arraying of the high priest completed. Some represent the "*golden plate*"† as different from the "*holy crown*;" but this is a mistake; these are but two names for the same thing. The "*golden plate*" was no doubt bound round the head *like a diadem,* or crown, though it was only half a circle, encompassing the forefront of the mitre. On this diadem, or plate of gold, was written, "*Holiness to the Lord*;" and hence its name, "the *holy* crown." The typical meaning seems to be this;—our High Priest atones and intercedes and reconciles, yet does all to the glory of Jehovah's *holiness.* The manifestation

---

* The תּוֹרָה (*the law*) means *somewhat taught to us*—the revealed teachings of God, whether doctrinal or preceptory.

† See, *e. g.*, Warden *on the Types.*

of the Divine character appears in the high priest—love to man, and tender mercies, combined with rich displays of righteousness and holiness.   There is not one frown, not one look of terror in the high priest, though there is purest holiness.   The deep love and compassion of his soul make that holiness appear most desirable.

In reference to this scene, and to any such that were similar, the Psalmist writes, " I will clothe her priests with salvation, and her saints shall shout aloud for joy" (Ps. cxxxii. 16).   The eye of the guilty fell upon this exhibition of Divine love and righteousness harmonised, and their heart leapt for joy.   It is somewhat remarkable that the Church itself did not use the word "*salvation,*" but prayed (ver. 9), "Let thy priests be clothed *with righteousness,* and let thy saints shout for joy."   The conscience of the believing multitude sought for *righteousness* to cover their guilt; this was the uppermost desire of their heart, and the chief suggestion of their conscience. But when the Lord replies to them, in ver. 16, he gives *more* than merely forgiveness—he sends "*salvation*" in its fulness.

> Ver. 10, 11. *And Moses took the anointing oil, and anointed the tabernacle and all that was therein, and sanctified them. And he sprinkled thereof upon the altar seven times, and anointed the altar and all his vessels, both the laver and his foot, to sanctify them.*

Aaron was now for a time left alone.   Clothed and arrayed as high priest, with his sons at his side, all eyes gazed upon him.   Blessed type of Jesus, with his " many sons" (Heb. ii. 10), whom all creation beholds with wonder and delight!   And, that the high priest might arrest every eye, he is left alone, like Jesus when the voice was past on the transfiguration-hill.   " *Consider the High Priest*

of your profession!" is the voice proceeding from this
scene to every believing soul. Ye are complete in him.
And why look ye elsewhere, self-righteous souls? All
that gives peace, all that can speak of God reconciled, is
here. The *person of Immanuel, and what hangs upon
that person,* furnish you with all your soul can long for.

But, meanwhile, Moses has gone into the tabernacle,
and is busy there. Already all things therein had been
sprinkled with blood, according to the remark in Heb. ix.
21, though at what precise time is difficult for us to say.
That *blood* had cleansed them: and now *the oil* sets them
apart for holy purposes. The dust of sin having been
laid, the Spirit breathes freely over every part of the
tabernacle, and through every apartment. The Holiest of
All, as well as the altar; the laver and "its foot," or basin
into which its waters were poured, are solemnly set apart
to the Lord. None can ever claim the use of them again.
They must be used by no other but the Lord; nothing
must be done with them but what bears directly on the
Lord's glory. This is "*sanctifying them.*" Let us learn
what we should be, if really set apart for God.

And this explains to us John xvii. 19, "*For their
sakes I sanctify myself, that they also might be sanctified
through the truth.*" There Jesus speaks of himself as like
a temple-vessel, or like the Holiest of All, when set apart
to be used for the Lord's purposes. Just as that sanctuary and all it contained was to be used only for setting
forth the sinner's way to God—so, *Jesus,* of his own free
will, presented himself to be used by the Father wholly
for the purpose of providing for the sinner a way to the
holy God! Glorious truth! The use for which the incar-
nate Saviour is set apart is, to make a way for sinners to
God! *The Father* used him in this manner in coming to

us; *we* are to use him thus in going to *the Father!*   A
Saviour set apart for the use of sinners!   No angel may
touch that Saviour—he is not for angels.   But the guiltiest
soul out of hell may use him—he is for the unlimited use
of sinners!

We thus see the purpose of God in anointing; but next
we see yet more the *person.*

> Ver. 12. *And he poured of the anointing oil upon Aaron's head,
> and anointed him, to sanctify him.*

This is typical of the Spirit fully poured out on Jesus
to set him apart for his public office—his office as Saviour
of the world.   Aaron was not merely *sprinkled,* but had
the oil poured out in full measure on his head.   To this
reference is made in Psalm cxxxiii. 2, "It is like the precious ointment upon the head, that ran down upon the
beard, even Aaron's beard; that went down to the skirts
of his garments."   It was to foreshew that Jesus was to
have the fulness of the Holy Spirit poured upon him
And inasmuch as this oil was composed of myrrh, cinnamon, calamus, and cassia (Exod. xxx. 25), the variety
of the Holy Spirit's gifts and grace was shewn.   In that
Psalm, the *unity of brethren—many* persons, yet *one soul*
and mind—is compared to the oil composed of such varied
ingredients as cassia, myrrh, cinnamon, and calamus,*
and yet forming one sweet fragrant oil.   But besides this
point of comparison, there is another, viz. the *abundance
of the oil,* "that ran down upon the beard of Aaron, that
went down to the skirts of his garments"—or, "to the
collar of his robe."   The unity of brethren is not a bare,
scanty love, but is overflowing feeling, full and abundant
affection.

* In Ps. xlv. 8, we find, "All thy garments smell of myrrh, and *aloes,* and
cassia."   I suppose "*aloes*" comprehend the *cinnamon* and *calamus.*   The
anointing of Messiah in that Psalm is thus pointed out as done with the *holy oil.*

> Ver. 13. *And Moses brought Aaron's sons, and put coats upon them, and girded them with girdles, and put bonnets upon them; as the Lord commanded Moses.*

The priests receive *girdles, coats,* and *bonnets*—all of which were "*glorious and beautiful,*" for so Exod. xxviii. 2, and xxviii. 40. But they must look up to Aaron; he only had the complete title to enter the *Holiest of all.* It was only the high priest that had "*Holiness to the Lord*" on his mitre, and so had right to go into the Holiest, even as Christ's "many sons brought to glory" owe all to him. Their clothing is his in miniature, and standing, two on his right hand and two on his left, himself in the midst, form a representation of the company who shall be all "*priests* to God and his Christ."

> Ver. 14. *And he brought the bullock for the sin-offering: and Aaron and his sons laid their hands upon the head of the bullock for the sin-offering.*

When Aaron and his sons had been thus arrayed, and the attention of the people more than ever fixed upon them, Moses proceeded to another act. He brings forward the *bullock for the sin-offering.* Immediately the high priest and the four priests beside him come forward, and together lay their hands upon the bullock's head, confessing their sins. They transfer their guilt to this victim. This was done for themselves personally, as sinners bringing their individual sins to the sacrifice, teaching the people to do the same with their sins: even as ministers must themselves set an example to their people, of constant dependence on Jesus, and unceasing application of his death. In proportion as they who lead others do themselves make use of that atonement, will their people also be convinced of their need of it. And, observe, they use the *sin-offering,* for their special personal sins, ere they bring the "*burnt-offering*" for more general and comprehensive application to the body of sin.

> Ver. 15–17. *And he slew it; and Moses took the blood, and put it upon the horns of the altar round about with his finger, and purified the altar, and poured the blood at the bottom of the altar, and sanctified it, to make reconciliation upon it. And he took all the fat that was upon the inwards, and the caul above the liver, and the two kidneys, and their fat, and Moses burned it upon the altar.* But the bullock and his hide, his flesh and his dung, he burnt with fire without the camp; as the Lord commanded Moses.*

From the order of the original, it seems that *Moses* slew the bullock on whose head Aaron and his sons had laid their sins; and then took the blood in one of the bowls. We are told what was done with the *blood*, the *fat*, and all that then remained. The *fat*, and the *remainder*, are used as in chap. iv. 9–11, where the sacrifice of the priest, for sins of ignorance, is mentioned. But *the blood* is used to set apart *the altar* on which that high priest was hereafter to present the daily offerings. He thoroughly put the blood on it—on its *horns* and *whole framework*—and the remainder is used to bathe *its base*. Thus the *whole altar* is completely washed in blood, and thereby is "*purified*" † and "*sanctified*," *i. e.* set apart for these ends. Perhaps in this typical action we are to see the shadowing forth of the truth, that the *person of the Son of man* (who was the altar) was set apart for the purposes of the Lord's will. He was to be the Lord's alone; not appearing on earth for himself. " I came,

---

* Heb. הַמִּזְבֵּחָה, "*toward* the altar;" so chap. ix. 6, 10, 14, 20. But in chap. v. 10, עַל מִזְבֵּחַ. The expressions are nearly equivalent, only the former intimates *going towards*, or *carrying* the portions mentioned *towards*, the altar, perhaps in such a way as to fix attention on the act.

† יְחַטֵּא. Onkelos in the Chaldee gives דְּכִי, " cleanse from sin, make pure."

not to do mine own will, but the will of him that sent me." The new and living way was "consecrated for us."

But why "*purify*" the altar? I suppose that here we are shewn another truth. The sin laid on the altar would have polluted that altar itself, steeping it, in a manner, in the filth of these sins, had not this blood been previously laid on it to preclude this danger. So, the Son of man was prepared by the depth and intensity of his purity—by the abundant indwelling of the Holy Ghost—for bearing the sin laid upon him without being thereby polluted at all. He was so set apart and purified before-hand, in the body prepared for him, that the sins of a world lying upon his person communicated no stain whatever to him.

> Ver. 18–21. *And he brought the ram for the burnt-offering: and Aaron and his sons laid their hands upon the head of the ram. And he killed it; and Moses sprinkled the blood upon the altar round about. And he cut the ram into pieces; and Moses burnt the head, and the pieces, and the fat. And he washed the inwards and the legs in water; and Moses burnt the whole ram upon the altar: it was a burnt-sacrifice for a sweet savour, and an offering made by fire unto the Lord; as the Lord commanded Moses.*

The *burnt-offering* was the most marked and fully significant of all the sacrifices, being the basis of the rest. But in this case the *priest's sin-offering* precedes it, on the ground, that the priest's special personal sinfulness should first be spread out and forgiven; and then the altar, which had received the stroke of justice, could be freely used for other purposes—for all the purposes that the *burnt-offering* might be applied to—by the ministering priest.

The rites observed are the same as in chap. i. 6–8,

but more briefly stated. Christ offers *himself* as the burnt-offering.

It may be asked in what respect *Christ* could be said to offer a *sin-offering;* for, if He is represented here as offering the *burnt-offering*, did he not also offer the *sin-offering?* He did, but it was not for *personal sin:* it was for what he calls his " own sin," viz. our imputed guilt. Thus, in Psalm xl. 12, " *Mine* iniquities have taken hold upon me." Psalm xxxviii. 4, " *Mine* iniquities are gone over my head ; my wounds stink, and are corrupt, because of *my foolishness.*" Psalm lxix. 5, " O God, thou knowest *my foolishness: and my sins* are not hid from thee." The sins of his body the Church are the sins he can call *his own.*

> Ver. 22. *And he brought the other ram, the ram of consecration: and Aaron and his sons laid their hands upon the head of the ram.*

Instead of a special *trespass-offering*, as we might have expected from the order of chap: v. and vi., there is, in the priest's case, an offering presented which includes both what the trespass-offering signified, and also whatever specially concerned the priest's personal state. Indeed, we might call " the *ram of consecration* " by the name of " *The priest's trespass-offering.*"

It may be asked, " Why does the priest bring no *peace-offering* on the day he enters upon his office ?" Because, perhaps, all that was signified by the *peace-offering* was taught by the priest's remaining in the sanctuary in the Lord's presence. He remained in the Lord's presence ; therefore there is reconciliation and peace between God and him. They who are not at peace with God, quickly go out from his presence, and are found in the world ; and God, also, on his part, drives them out of his garden:

but those that are his reconciled ones remain in his presence, entranced and chained to the spot by the beauties of his Divine grace, and kept by the mighty hand of him who so loves them that he will not let them go.

> Ver. 23, 24. *And he slew it; and Moses took of the blood of it, and put it upon the tip of Aaron's right ear, and upon the thumb of his right hand, and upon the great toe of his right foot. And he brought Aaron's sons, and Moses put of the blood upon the tip of their right ear, and upon the thumbs of their right hands, and upon the great toes of their right feet; and Moses sprinkled the blood upon the altar round about.*

By this type, *the whole person* is visibly dedicated to the Lord. Every power and faculty is consecrated. The Lord touches with blood his right ear, right hand, right foot, as if to say, "I claim from thee the exercise of every faculty and property of body and soul, to be used in my service." From head to foot he is marked by blood, and set apart. He is to *hear* for God; and at the slightest whisper of the Divine voice to stretch out that *right hand* for immediate activity, and move with *that foot* in the Lord's ways. "Here am I; send me!" If we are "*priests to God*," such must be our position and readiness to obey. Our *High Priest* in the heavens was the full example of this true consecration, set apart to the Lord, wholly, and for ever.

Perhaps it is to this that Psalm xl. 6 refers. Our version has rendered it, " Mine ears hast thou opened." The Hebrew is, אָזְנַיִם כָּרִיתָ לִּי, " Ears thou hast provided for me;"* and the reference seems to be to this day of the priest's consecration. The Psalm speaks of Christ's

---

* In Heb. x. 5, כָּרִיתָ is rendered " κατηρτίσω," as in the Septuagint: " κατεσκεύασας " is used by Symmachus.

coming forth as the Great Priest and Sacrifice who was
to supersede all other; and in Hebrews x. it is quoted
for that end.   Now, in the Psalm, we see one who
says, " Lo! I come"—even Jesus, who appears before us,
casting his eye round about upon all the scenery of a
priest's consecration-day.   He looks at the bullock and
rams (ver. 6, " burnt-offering, and sin-offering, and sacrifice"), and at the meat-offering (מִנְחָה, " offering");
at the " great congregation" also (ver. 9); but above all,
at the *high priest*, whose *hand, foot*, and *ear* are wet
with the warm blood just sprinkled upon them.   He
comes forward—he looks up to his Father, and says
(ver. 6)—" Thou art not pleased by the *material* things
presented here, but only by what they typify.   ' Sacrifice
and meat-offering' thou didst not desire further than as a
type of me; and *this priest, whose ear is sprinkled with
blood, gives place to me, for thou hast provided ears to
me, which I consecrate to thee;* and this burnt-offering
and sin-offering thou no more requirest.   ' For, lo! I
come to do thy will, O God.' "

In this view of the passage, we suppose Christ to say
of himself, that, having assumed human nature in order
to be our Mediator, *he* was the true Sacrifice and the
true Priest.   And, *pointing to his own human body*, he
says, " *Ears*** hast thou provided me*,"—meaning, that
now he had ears, hands, feet, to be sprinkled as were
Aaron's.   It is thus that the writer of the epistle to the
Hebrews has been led to say at once, " *A body* hast thou
prepared me" (Heb. x. 5).

---

* The Septuagint version has " σῶμα;" but I suspect this reading has
been inserted by later writers, who were familiar with the New Testament : just
as in some other cases—Prov. xi. 31 compared with 1 Pet. iv. 18, and Ps. iv. 4
compared with Eph. iv. 26.   If it is genuine, they may have given *the sense*,
understanding it somewhat as we have done.

Ver. 25–27. *And he took the fat, and the rump, and all the fat that was upon the inwards, and the caul above the liver, and the two kidneys, and their fat, and the right shoulder: and out of the basket of unleavened bread that was before the Lord he took one unleavened cake, and a cake of oiled bread, and one wafer, and put them on the fat, and upon the right shoulder: and he put all upon Aaron's hands, and upon his sons' hands, and waved them for a wave-offering before the Lord.*

In ver. 25 we have a summary of the parts of the different offerings presented. Some pieces of them all are taken—pieces that represented the inward and most deep-seated feelings (viz. fat on the inwards and kidneys), pieces that represented richness and fulness of feeling (viz. fat in general, and the marrow of the rump), and that piece which represented the devotion of the person's whole strength (viz. the right shoulder). Then there is, in ver. 26, a summary of the different kinds of meat-offering. The "*oiled bread*" belonged to the third sort, and the "*cakes and wafers*" to the second; thus selecting neither the highest nor lowest, but the medium, as a proper specimen of all.

All these *cakes* were put on "*the fat pieces*"* just mentioned, and *the right shoulder;* and thus a type was exhibited of *soul and body* together offered to the Lord. Moses, therefore, put these into each individual priest's hand in succession; and as each priest stood with them in his full hands, Moses stood by and waved his hands over them, as a symbol and token of their being wholly the Lord's. As Moses spread his hands over them, and next waved them from north to south, east to west, he signified their acknowledgment that they were the Lord's in every feeling of their souls, and every faculty of their minds, and every power of their bodies.

---

* חֲלָבִים is the expression.

Thus each man presented the fatness of his soul, the strength of his body, and the richness of his substance to God. *That* was the gift which *filled the hands* of a consecrated priest. What manner of persons, then, ought we to be, if we are "priests to God!" Each of these priests was a type of him who came forward to the Father, saying, "*Lo! I come.*" Each of these, with his full hands, represents Christ in that position. And such ought each believing man to be—"a holy priesthood" (1 Pet. ii. 5).

> Ver. 28, 29. *And Moses took them from off their hands, and burnt them on the altar upon the burnt-offering: they were consecrations for a sweet savour; it is an offering made by fire unto the Lord. And Moses took the breast, and waved it for a wave-offering before the Lord: for of the ram of consecration it was Moses' part; as the Lord commanded Moses.*

Moses put them all "*on the burnt-sacrifice,*" which lay on the altar. The *whole burnt-offering* was, in a manner, the primary sacrifice; it expressed *atonement*, full atonement. Therefore, the putting on it of those pieces which represented the giving up of feelings and desires, and the meat-offering, which represented the person's whole substance, was a declaration that all we offer to God must be on the foundation of atonement. "*By him,* therefore, let us offer the sacrifice of praise to God continually" (Heb. xiii. 15).

"*They*"—these pieces—"*were consecrations.*" They were parts of the consecrating offering, each part a sweet savour; and the whole sacrifice together formed an offering made by fire to the Lord. It was a transaction which the Lord approved and accepted.

There still remained one—*the breast* of the ram. This had been mentioned so far back as Exod. xxix. 26, when first the order of consecration was appointed. This *breast* is waved before the Lord, over all the pieces on the altar, and over Aaron and his sons. The waving of it is the last sacrificial act. It seems to declare the heartfelt concurrence of the parties in all that had been done ;—by one concluding act they give up their heart to the Lord.

But why was this *breast* to be Moses' part? Perhaps for the following reason :—The dedication was that of Aaron and his sons ; and Moses kept this last part of the offering as a *pledge*, or token, that they had really given up themselves to God. The pledge, of course, must be deposited in other hands than their own ; and, therefore, it is not given to the priests, but to Moses. The type may represent Jesus as depositing in the Father's hands the pledge of his complete consecration, when he said, " Lo! I come."

Ver. 30. *And Moses took of the anointing oil, and of the blood which was upon the altar, and sprinkled it upon Aaron, and upon his garments, and upon his sons, and upon his sons' garments with him; and sanctified Aaron, and his garments, and his sons, and his sons' garments with him.*

Moses takes the prepared oil and mixes it with the blood of the ram of consecration (Exod. xxix. 21),— blood already accepted. At first sight, this seems to be no more than a repetition of what was already done (ver. 12). But there the act was meant to set apart the *man;* here it is meant to set apart the *priest.* In the former case, the *oil* was first poured on them, and then *blood* sprinkled (ver. 24) on their persons; as if to say, Thus does the Holy Spirit point out these persons to be set apart, and thus are those who are set apart cleansed with blood. When this was done, they were constituted priests ; and, now that they are actually invested with

office, oil and blood are sprinkled on them and their garments again, intimating that they need, as priests, a double
portion of the Spirit, and a doubly complete cleansing.
Such was Jesus! "without spot or blemish," and endowed
with the Spirit "without measure."

Their very *garments* are thus set apart and cleansed.
To this Jude (ver. 23) may allude, " Hating even the garment spotted by the flesh." Believers are priests to God;
therefore, not their persons only (as verse 24 in this
chapter shews), but their garments also—not their personal character alone, but every act and outward manifestation—must be unspotted by the world. Perhaps
Rev. iii. 4, " A few names . . . who have not defiled their
garments," may refer to this also ; and xvi. 15, " He that
watcheth and keepeth his garments."

> Ver. 31. *And Moses said unto Aaron and to his sons, Boil the
> flesh at the door of the tabernacle of the congregation; and
> there eat it with the bread that is in the basket of consecra-
> tions, as I commanded, saying, Aaron and his sons shall
> eat it.*

The priests must eat of the sacrifices in order to shew
that these sacrifices have brought peace and reconciliation. But first they " *boil the flesh at the door of the
tabernacle;*" in the immediate sight of God they do this.
The type represents Christ's sufferings—every joint re-
laxed—" I am poured out like water" (Ps. xxii. 14).
The fire was, of course, taken from the altar, which was
fire from heaven—to intimate that Christ's agony proceeded directly from the Father. But in the very place
where this wrath fell on him, there is peace found for sinners,—the offerers feast upon the boiled flesh. And then
they rise and take the " *meat-offering,*" or bread, also;
for now they can freely dedicate themselves to the Lord.

> Ver. 32. *And that which remaineth of the flesh and of the bread*
> *shall ye burn with fire.*

There must be nothing left to corrupt, and nothing left neglected. Either it must be wholly consumed, or wholly eaten—a type of the fact, that all things must be either wholly visited with Divine wrath, or wholly enjoy Divine favour.

> Ver. 33, 34. *And ye shall not go out of the door of the tabernacle*
> *of the congregation in seven days, until the days of your con-*
> *secration be at an end: for seven days shall he consecrate*
> *you.   As he hath done this day, so the Lord hath com-*
> *manded to do, to make an atonement for you.*

During some days, the truths represented and expressed in the preceding types were to be kept before the minds of the priests themselves, that they might meditate on them and be imbued with them. So continually was this to be done, that for seven days they were not to leave the precincts of the tabernacle—" the door of it " (ver. 35), day nor night. Thus they were taught their office; and thus *Christ* was set forth as a priest who should ever, day and night, be found at his work of satisfaction and mediation.

> Ver. 35. *Therefore shall ye abide at the door of the tabernacle of*
> *the congregation day and night seven days, and keep the charge*
> *of the Lord, that ye die not: for so I am commanded.*

The last clause is added lest the strict injunction should seem too severe. " So I am commanded." It is the Lord's will; therefore, it will be pleasant.

Such passages as, " Blessed is the man that heareth me, watching daily at my gates, waiting at the posts of my doors" (Prov. viii. 34), seem to refer to this case. Blessed are they, who, like these priests, are wholly the Lord's, night and day,—unwearied and unexhausted, they serve him and rejoice in him. Thus, too (Ps. lxxxiv. 4)— " Blessed are they that dwell in thy house; they shall be still praising thee!" Many a song was heard ascending from the lips of these sons of Aaron during these seven days. And in these priests, during these seven days, we see a type of real believers. The *seven days* is the expression for fulness, *q. d.* the whole space filled, from beginning of life to the end. Then, there is not the alternate approach to the altar, and withdrawal from it, to go back to other duties; there is continual, uninterrupted service. This ought to be the characteristic of believers as "priests to God:" not a few minutes' service at morning and evening, but the whole day filled up by successive acts of service.

It shall specially be so in glory. It is thus with our High Priest, who "appears in the presence of God *for us.*" He never retires from his blessed position; *he* always beholds the face of his Father. The nearer we come to this, the nearer we resemble him. "Pray without ceasing," "Rejoice evermore," indicate what ought to be our state, even now on earth. The calm, blessed, glorious rest of our High Priest within the Tabernacle, with the Father's love upon him every hour, and his soul reposing on the Father every hour, represents to us what we should be. Oh! how sad the long intervals in our adoration, and in our seasons of communion! How sad, how unlike priests, our intermittent flow of love and joy! When shall we be for ever the same as to the kind of feeling, and ever rising higher as to the degree!

Ver. 36. *So Aaron and his sons did all things which the Lord commanded by the hand of Moses.*

The Lord ceased to speak; and now, therefore, they began to act. We see them solemnly engaged seven days in these appointed rites.

Looking back on this chapter, the subject of the *consecration* of the priests leads us to an interesting investigation. The *consecration* was the time when a priest was fully brought into the duties of his office, and all the privileges of his office. Though of Aaron's line, still he was not fully a priest till he was consecrated. This is to be kept in mind; for, with a reference partly to this idea, and partly to the Hebrew term for it (מִלֵּא יָד), "filling the hand," the Septuagint were led to adopt the Greek "τελειόω," to express *consecration*. Hence, ver. 22, "κριον τελείωσεως;" ver. 28, "τὸ ὁλοκαύτωμα τῆς τελείωσεως;" ver. 33, "ἡμέρα τελείωσεως;" chap. xxi. 10, "ὁ τετελειωμένος," is the *consecrated priest;* and Exod. xxix. 9, τελειωσεις Ααρων τὰς χείρας αὐτου."* These are specimens.

If we keep this in remembrance, we are prepared to understand several passages of the New Testament that otherwise are difficult and obscure. In the epistle to the Hebrews, Christ is spoken of (chap. ii. 10) as "*made perfect by sufferings;*" and more specially (chap. v. 9), "*being made perfect*" is connected with his priesthood; and in chap. vii. 28, this is the term used to describe his consecration, "εἰς τὸν αἰῶνα τετελειωμένον." There is no difficulty left, when we see it is *office*, not character, that is spoken of. Now, in a figurative way, but with a reference to this idea, Heb. x. 14 represents Jesus as "*perfecting*" (τετελείωκε) those that are set apart by his blood; *i. e.* he puts them, by his one offering, into the possession of all the privileges of fully pardoned and justified ones. The "*spirits of just men made perfect*" (Heb. xii. 23) bears the same reference; they are entered into posses-

---

* Perhaps it is in this sense that our Lord uses "τελειοῦμαι" (Luke xiii. 32), "On the third day, lo! I am fully consecrated!"

sion of what was intended for them.   Like Aaron's sons,
looking forward to privileges inasmuch as they were
priests' sons, but not entered on possession till the day
of " τελείωσις"—so these just men.   James (ii. 22) says,
" By his works was faith *made perfect*" (ἐτελειώθη).
Faith was carried out to its proper purpose; it entered on
its proper work; it was inaugurated visibly by his works.
It is thus, too, in 1 John ii. 5, " *Whoso keepeth his word,
in him verily is the love of God perfected.*"   The love of
God, which he feels, is carried out to its proper extent,
or is made use of for the purpose intended, when it leads
a man to walk holily.   It has got its *consecration-day*—
it has fully entered on its office.

This is still better seen in 1 John iv. 17, " Herein is
our love made perfect," &c.   The Greek words are, 'Εν
τούτῳ τετελείωται ἡ ἀγάπη μεθ' ἡμῶν.   It is *God's love to
us* that is the theme—" *the love that is with us.*"   He calls
it (as if the name *Immanuel* were running in his mind)
" *the love with us;*" i. e. God's display of love to us (ver.
16) in his Son; which is now our property.   Now, he
says this love of God to us "*is made perfect*" (τετελείωται)—has got its consecration-day—has fully entered on
its office.   "*Herein* (viz. as ver. 10, in the sending of his
Son) *has God's love to us reached its perfection.*"   The
ocean has been filled with love; it is an ocean which we
may call "*ours;*"* angels cannot call it "*theirs.*"   And
so complete is this display of God's love to us, that at the

---

* " *Ours,*" because bestowed on us; just as, in Milton's *Comus*, " She has
a hidden strength," says the elder brother.   The other asks, " What hidden
strength, unless the strength of Heaven, if you mean that?"   The other, in reply
says—

" A hidden strength,
Which, if Heaven gave it, may be termed *her own!* "

Is not Judg. vi. 14, " Go in this *thy might*," the might which I give thee?

day of judgment we shall have no fear; and even at
present, in spite of indwelling sin, we are as really righteous
as our Surety—" as *He* is, so are *we!*"   Hence it is that
they altogether mistake the gospel who cherish fears and
doubts, as if they were part of its results.   This love has
no element of fear in it; nay, *" He that feareth is not
made perfect in love"* (οὐ τετελείωται ἐν τῇ ἀγάπῃ), ver.
18.   He who still fears, and has suspicious doubts
remaining, has not entered upon his consecration-day—
has not fully entered upon the enjoyment of the privileges
to which this love entitles him : for *this perfect love* casts
out all fear.†

† In "*Jehovah Zidkenu*," a small work by F. Sanders, Pastor in Barmen,
this passage is explained in a similar way. " He by whom the love of God is
so perfectly believed, known, experienced, and enjoyed, that he can comfort himself with it against all the condemnations of the law, against all the accusations
of conscience, and against all the assaults of Satan, such a one is said in this
respect to ' *have boldness for the Day of Judgment.*' This ' *perfect love*'
casteth out all ' fear.' "—(P. 51.)

CHAPTER IX

Aaron's Entrance on his Office

" Being made perfect, he became the author of eternal salvation unto all them that obey him."—Heb. v. 9

> Ver. 1. *And it came to pass, on the eighth day, that Moses called Aaron and his sons, and the elders of Israel.*

THE priests were now " *made perfect,*" that is, consecrated to their office. There is now to be a specimen given of the High Priest actually engaged in his office. The *elders of Israel* are special witnesses, that they may tell the people with what confidence they may now approach the altar; for Aaron is fully consecrated—" *made perfect.*" And his four sons, also, stand by as witnesses.

It was thus that witnesses of Christ's completeness have assured us of his being a true and every way complete priest. They proclaim, " Being made perfect, he has become the author of eternal salvation unto all them that obey him" (Heb. v. 9). The Father bears witness that he did consecrate him completely; and, on earth, saved souls bear witness that they have seen and felt the power of his priesthood, for they took their sins to him, and received atonement from him.

> Ver. 2. *And he said unto Aaron, Take thee a young calf for a sin-offering, and a ram for a burnt-offering, without blemish, and offer them before the Lord.*

Aaron, now actually in office, is to begin his official
acts before all the people, by again offering (as in chap.
viii. 14, 18) a sacrifice of sin-offering and burnt-offering.*
He is ever to keep the people in mind that there must
another priest arise, greater far than Aaron; for Aaron
needs atonement himself.   On all great public occasions,
the high priest began by presenting these two offerings
for himself.   The *consecration-offerings* of chap. viii. 22,
26, he had, of course, no more to do with.   Now, in so
doing, he was "the voice of one crying" at the altar,
"Prepare ye the way of the Lord!   I am not the Christ.
There cometh one after me, mightier than I, the latchet
of whose shoes I am not worthy to stoop down and
unloose!   One who shall not need daily, as I need, 'to
offer up sacrifice, first for his own sins, and then for the
people's'" (Heb. vii. 27).

> Ver. 3, 4. *And unto the children of Israel thou shalt speak, saying,*
> *Take ye a kid of the goats for a sin-offering; and a calf and*
> *a lamb, both of the first year, without blemish, for a burnt-*
> *offering; also a bullock and a ram for peace-offerings, to*
> *sacrifice before the Lord; and a meat-offering mingled with*
> *oil: for to-day the Lord will appear unto you.*

The people bring all kinds of offerings, except the
trespass-offering, which, at the entrance of the priest on
his duties, and while the congregation, therefore, were
only beginning to be shewn *their* duty in holy things,
might not be needed.   A *trespass* in holy things (see
chap. v. 15) could scarcely have yet occurred.   But all
other kinds are brought.   Foremost is the *sin-offering*,
whereon they lay their individual, special guilt.   Then, a
twofold *burnt-offering*—a calf and a lamb—to shew their

---

* The *young calf* here, and the "young bullock" of Exod. xxix. 1, seem
the same.   The Hebrew in this chapter is עֵגֶל בֶּן בָּקָר, and in Exodus פַּר בֶּן בָּקָר.
The Jews say it put Aaron in mind of the matter of the golden calf.

trust in the grand primary sacrifice. Next, the *peace-offering*, in its fullest form—a ram and a bullock (שׁוֹר, ox)—to shew the complete peace bestowed, and reconciliation to God. Lastly, the *meat-offering*, mingled with oil —their own persons consecrated to God and his service.

The people were called to do this, on the ground that "*the Lord would appear to them that day.*" As if Moses had said, " Thus shall you meet the Lord : his way to the sinner is through the shedding of blood; and the sinner's way to him is through the same." A glorious truth for the chief of sinners ! " He has been to you a God that hideth himself; but approach with the blood that has been shed for you; this day approach; and this day shall the Lord appear unto you!"

> Ver. 5, 6. *And they brought that which Moses commanded before the tabernacle of the congregation : and all the congregation drew near, and stood before the Lord. And Moses said, This is the thing which the Lord commanded that ye should do ; and the glory of the Lord shall appear unto you.*"

The congregation gathered themselves together in front of the tabernacle, with the offerings, and " *stood before the Lord*"—an expression denoting a setting themselves in the solemn posture of worshippers, as Abraham in Gen. xviii. 22. Moses then said to them, " This, which the Lord commanded, do" (see the original), and in so doing, expect that he will appear. We are taught that the Lord appears as our God, reconciled and gracious, when we are approaching him through the work of his Son— the same lesson inculcated in ver. 4.

> Ver. 7. *And Moses said unto Aaron, Go unto the altar, and offer thy sin-offering, and thy burnt-offering, and make an atonement for thyself, and for the people : and offer the offering of the people, and make an atonement for them; as the Lord commanded.*

The people being ready, Aaron is now to offer for them. But, that they might know him to be only a type and shadow, and not "the Christ," the true anointed Priest, he first of all presents a sacrifice for himself. It being thus understood by all that he acts in the name of another yet to come, he goes forward to the work.

> Ver. 8–11. *Aaron therefore went unto the altar, and slew the calf of the sin-offering, which was for himself. And the sons of Aaron brought the blood unto him; and he dipped his finger in the blood, and put it upon the horns of the altar, and poured out the blood at the bottom of the altar: but the fat, and the kidneys, and the caul* above the liver, of the sin-offering, he burnt upon the altar; as the Lord commanded Moses. And the flesh and the hide he burnt with fire without the camp.*

As soon as Aaron had slain his sin-offering, his sons caught its blood in the bowls of the altar; and as each of the four stood—perhaps one at each corner of the altar— Aaron bent down and dipt his finger in their bowl of blood, and sprinkled the horns of the altar. Thus, the four horns were seen by the people wet with blood, a loud voice of atonement thereby ascending to heaven, crying, "Pardon to the guilty! for this is his penalty." Then Aaron emptied out of the bowls, and out of the body of the animal, the blood that remained, till a torrent of red crimson blood flowed round the altar's base. In ver. 10, 11, the view is the same as chap. viii. 16.

> Ver. 12–14. *And he slew the burnt-offering; and Aaron's sons presented unto him the blood, which he sprinkled round about upon the altar. And they presented the burnt-offering unto him, with the pieces thereof, and the head; and he burnt*

---

* The Hebrew in this place is not the same as in chap. iii. 4. The caul is said to be מִן הַכָּבֵד, "*from* the liver;" and מִן הַחַטָּאת, "*from* the sin-offering." This may be, *q. d.* the caul which he takes *from the liver, from out of the sin-offering.* So ver. 19. The expression for "upon the altar" is the same as in chap. viii. 16, הַמִּזְבֵּחָה.

them upon the altar.   And he did wash the inwards and the
legs, and burnt them upon the burnt-offering on the altar.

This is the other part of Aaron's offering for *himself,*
ere he presented the people's.   His own peculiar sins
being washed away by the sin-offering, and its blood
being put on the altar's horns to cry in his behalf, and
bring down better things than the blood of Abel, he
presents this *burnt-offering,* to shew that he had equal
interest in all that signified atonement, this being the
grand primary type of redemption.

The expression, in ver. 12 and 13, for *"presented"* (the
same as at ver. 9), suggests to us the reason why Aaron's
sons were there to do this.   The word (יַמְצִאוּ, Hiphil) is
one which is generally used when a person has a thing
in his own possession, and then offers it to another for
his.   It is used of one who gives up another into an
enemy's hand.   Hence on this occasion we are led to
consider Aaron's sons as stationed there by God to *ex-*
hibit to their father the blood and the other parts of the
sacrifice.   They are his instruments for *holding out* to
Aaron *the offer* of an atonement; and thus more fully
than before is the high priest exhibited to all the people
as one who himself needs atonement.   Their eyes are,
thereby, fixed on him only as he is the shadow of One
greater far, who is yet to come; and he himself is kept
from being at all lifted up by the honour done to him.
He is made to feel that he sustains a representative
character.

Ver. 15–17. *And he brought the people's offering, and took the*
goat which was the sin-offering for the people, and slew it,
and offered it for sin, as the first.   And he brought the burnt-
offering, and offered it according to the manner.   And he
brought the meat-offering, and took an handful thereof, and
burnt it upon the altar, beside the burnt-sacrifice of the morning.

Aaron now took up the people's offering. Here, and in chap. vi. 26, the most striking expression occurs that we anywhere meet with in regard to atonement. "*He offered it for sin*," might be rendered, "*He sinned it*," or, "*He made it sin*" (יְחַטְּאֵהוּ). The sense of "*offering for sin*," is evidently taken from the fact, that every such sacrifice had the sin laid on it, or imputed to it. This may have suggested the expression used in 2 Cor. v. 21, "*He made him sin for us*" (ἁμαρτιαν ἐποιησεν). It is not "*made him to be a sin-offering*," but much more;* the *sin-offering itself* was "*made sin;*" and not on this occasion only, but on all occasions, as we may infer from the clause "*as at the first*" (ver. 8). The true idea appears in Gen. xxxi. 39, אֲחַטֶּאנָּה: "I bare the loss of it,"—I was made sin for it. The idea seems to be, "He put the sin of the people on this victim till it became one mass of sin." The priest's using it as the atonement for those who presented it, made the victim become, in a manner, the receiver of their sin and of the penalty it deserved. And so our Great Sin-offering, Jesus, when slain for us, was treated as if he were the reservoir of the sin and curse that flowed, in so many streams, over man. In this sense, "The Father made him to be sin for us!"

The *burnt-offering* was presented in the usual way, "according to the manner." The *meat-offering* also.

---

* Chrysostom gives one of his best criticisms here, when he says, that it means more even than that he made the Righteous One a sinner in order to make sinners righteous. " Οὐ γὰρ ἕξιν ἔθηκεν, ἀλλ' αὐτην την ποιοτητα. οὐ γὰρ εἶπεν, ' ἐποιησεν ἁμαρτωλον,' ἀλλ' ' ἁμαρτιαν.' οὐχι ' τον μη ἁμαρτοντα' μονον, ἀλλα ' τον μηδε γνοντα ἁμαρτιαν.' ἱνα και ὑμεις γενωμεθα οὐκ εἶπεν ' δικαιοι,' ἀλλα ' δικαιοσυνη,' και ' Θεοῦ δικαιοσυνη'" (Comment. on 2 Cor. v.)—He does not say, "He made him *a* sinner," but "he made him *sin*"—not, "Him who *did not sin*," but "him that *did not know sin*." All this in order that we might become, not "*righteous*," but "*righteousness*," and "*the righteousness of God*."

And these two, offered on that occasion, were in addition to the morning sacrifice and meat-offering. For we are not required to set aside regularly-appointed duty, when engaged in more extraordinary and solemn exercises.

> Ver. 18, 19. *He slew also the bullock and the ram for a sacrifice of peace-offerings which was for the people: and Aaron's sons presented unto him the blood, which he sprinkled upon the altar round about, and the fat of the bullock and of the ram, the rump, and that which covereth the inwards, and the kidneys, and the caul above the liver.*

As before. In ver 19, it is literally "the *fat pieces* from the bullock and from the ram." " *That which covereth,*" is filled up by a reference to chap. iii. 9.*

> Ver. 20, 21. *And they put the fat upon the breasts, and he burnt the fat upon the altar: and the breasts and the right shoulder Aaron waved for a wave-offering before the Lord; as Moses commanded.*

The fat pieces of each were laid on the breasts of each; thus intimating that the inmost desires, and all nearest the heart, is a ready offering to the Lord. Then the fat was removed, and consumed in the flames; as if to express how the fire of Divine wrath descended upon Jesus, on his inmost soul, when that soul had offered all its strength and affections to God. The fat was laid on the breast, thereby to intimate the fullest and most cordial willingness.

These breasts, more fully expressive of complete devotion to the Lord now that *the fat* had lain on them, are waved before the Lord; and *the right shoulder,†* also, of each animal, as already appointed. All are thus heaved

---

* Jarchi supplies " הקרב," *the inwards,* as our version does.

† The singular is used; but this is in reference to chap. vii. 34. It means *the appointed* right shoulder, which always was the right shoulder of each peace-offering.

up toward the dwelling-place of Jehovah, that the giving up of the whole people to him for ever may thereby be openly expressed. This is the concluding act. Aaron *has presented* the people in virtue of his office ; and lo! the Lord has accepted them! There *is* a restoration to the fellowship of an offended God ; for here is the example. This first day's acts confirm Israel's faith in the truth, " *There is forgiveness with thee,*" and at the same time in that other awful truth, " *Without shedding of blood there is no remission.*"

> Ver. 22–24. *And Aaron lifted up his hand toward the people, and blessed them ; and came down from offering of the sin-offering, and the burnt-offering, and peace-offerings. And Moses and Aaron went into the tabernacle of the congregation, and came out, and blessed the people: and the glory of the Lord appeared unto all the people. And there came a fire out from before the Lord, and consumed upon the altar the burnt-offering and the fat: which when all the people saw, they shouted, and fell on their faces.*

Probably these offerings were presented at the time of the morning sacrifice. Then (ver. 23) Moses and Aaron retired into the tabernacle. At the time of the evening sacrifice they came forth again, and stood at the altar. At this hour, Aaron stood still and looked upon all the people as they crowded the space in front of the brazen altar. As he thus stood, the eyes of all the multitude turned toward him ; whereupon, amid the awful solemnity and deep silence, he lifted up his hands—the very hands that had been wet with blood—and blessed the people. It was as if he were pouring over them all the grace and peace that flow from the blood of Jesus! And this done, " he came down from offering the sin-offering, and the burnt-offering, and peace-offerings." It was thus that Jesus blessed his people—his faithful witnesses who stood around their altar on the Mount of Olives—lifting up the very hands that so lately had been nailed to the cross. And having so done, he left the place of sacrifice and went into the Holiest of all, there to receive more communications from his Father, and then to come forth again to give more blessing.

Aaron, leaving the altar, went into the Holy Place. There Moses stood with him, and, as representative of Jehovah, handed over to his care all the vessels of the sanctuary, and committed the ordering of all to him ; even as Jesus, on his ascension—on his leaving the place where he had made the sacrifice—received from the Father (Rev. i. 1; Ps. lxviii. 18; Eph. iv. 8) authority as Mediator, or as the Captain of salvation now made perfect (Heb. ii. 10), to administer the affairs of the sanctuary. It was in reference to this that he said, as he was entering in, " All power is committed unto me in heaven and on earth" (Matt. xxviii. 18). He is there now, managing their interests for them above, preparing many mansions. " The Father hath committed all things into his hand."

His coming out again will be like Aaron's, in order to bless the people anew. The people remained in the courts, expecting the re-appearance of Aaron and Moses. And so the Lord's people remain with their eye and heart on the altar, looking for the second coming of their Priest, in the Father's glory as well as his own. " The glory of the Lord appeared unto all the people" of Israel that day; and some of the bright fire of that glory shot down on the altar and consumed the pieces of the sacrifices, thus giving the last attestation required of complete acceptance. In all this we see the very figure and outlines of the Redeemer's second coming " to those that look for him." His glory will thus appear, when it is now the evening of the world's day, and that glory, investing the person of the Son of man—the Lamb of God—will give the last and most indubitable proof that he is well pleasing to the Father. He shall appear the second time, " *without sin, unto salvation.*" The sin consumed, and for ever done away, nothing is left for the people but the completing of their joy and their holiness. What a shout of ecstasy shall burst from them all then! Yet how deeply awed and reverent they shall be! even as forgiveness * produces holy awe, wherever felt. The people shout and fall prostrate before him. " To him shall *every knee bow,* and *every tongue confess* that he is Lord, to the glory of God the Father." O! our High Priest, now within the tabernacle not made with hands, perfect that which concerneth us! Put the bread on the golden table, that we may never want our better than angels' food. Pour in daily the olive-oil, that the lamps of thy golden candlestick may never be dim in this dark, gloomy world. Present thy incense with every prayer of ours, with every groan, with every sigh of the prisoner! And soon, soon come forth again! yea, even before we have slept with our fathers, if it seem good in thy sight; come forth to bless us, and to receive the shout of multitudes adoring and confessing that thou art Lord alone!

* Heb. xii. 28, 29 receives a beautiful illustration here. " Grace," or forgiving love, teaches to serve God with " reverence and godly fear;" for while it brings us to his nearest presence, it shews him to us as a God who consumes iniquity. " *Our God* is a *consuming fire.*" The light that guides us into his presence is the very blaze of the sacrifice on which our sins are laid.

CHAPTER X

Ⓣhe Ⓕencing of the Ⓟriestly Ⓡitual

" See that ye refuse not him that speaketh. For if they escaped not who refused him that spake on earth, much more shall not we escape, if we turn away from him that speaketh from heaven."—Heb. xii. 25

Ver. 1, 2. *And Nadab and Abihu, the sons of Aaron, took either of them his censer, and put fire therein, and put incense thereon, and offered strange fire before the Lord, which he commanded them not. And there went out fire from the Lord, and devoured them; and they died before the Lord.*

THIS event occurred at a time when its effect was likely to spread the most solemn awe over priest and people ; and occurring, as it did, in the persons of Aaron's sons, who were men of station and office, the influence of the lesson taught would diffuse itself over all ranks of men in the camp.

After spending the day in the manner mentioned in the former chapter—after presenting the blood (ver. 12, 13, 18), and seeing their father, Aaron, go in with Moses into the Holy Place—they seem to have felt impatient at not being allowed to take a more prominent part in conducting the service. Perhaps they thought that they, too, might enter the Holy Place and offer incense. Accordingly, next morning, it would appear, they both engaged in a most daring and presumptuous project.   If, as many believe from ver. 9, 10, they had drank too freely, and so become elated, their sin might be reckoned a sudden temptation.   But I rather suppose that it was a deliberate sin, proceeding from a jealous, sullen heart , and the injunction in ver. 9, 10, like that of Ezekiel xliv. 21, was suggested at this time by the fact, that what they did *deliberately*, others would be much and often tempted to do *suddenly*, through the influence of such excitement.

The expression, " *Which he commanded them not*," applies to the many ingredients that were contrary to God's will ; and the force of it is equal to, "*which he had expressly forbidden.*"   Their motive, the strange fire used, the time when it was done, were all opposed to the Lord's command; and the example of disobedience thus set was fitted to be extensively pernicious in the camp.

It was probably done in the morning of the day following the events of last chapter.   For ver. 16, where the question about *eating the sin-offering* is asked, shews that certainly it did not take place *later* than the second day; since the law required all remnants of the sin-offering to be *burnt*, if kept beyond that time.   And ver. 16 would also lead us to think that the sons of Aaron had been occupied with other sacrifices since the consecration-day ; for Moses *searches for* the goat of the sin-offering. If, too, the goat had been burnt on the very day of the consecration, Moses could scarcely have failed to observe the flames, as on that day there were no other offering but the priest's.

Nadab and Abihu took a censer, and kindled their incense. But they did so,—1. At a *time* not commanded : *Aaron* should have been consulted for this. 2. In a *place*, or in a part of the tabernacle, not commanded ; for they were in the open court (ver. 4, where Uzziel's sons, who were only Levites, went to them), not at the golden altar. 3. In a *manner* contrary to the Lord's declared will: for the priests understood that the only fire to be used in the tabernacle was to be fire *from the altar*—fire that had come from heaven. Probably, too, they used what spices were at hand, not the proper incense. The Lord had commanded neither the time, place, nor manner. But if the sinner's eye be blind to God, it sees not anything of the Lord's authority. And neither education, nor station, nor privileges (see Exod. xxiv. 9), are sufficient to keep men from this presumption. The heart may continue unrenewed amid all such blessings.

The Lord forthwith vindicated his own honour. These are priests, and they stand in the holy courts, and they hold the censers of the tabernacle in their hands, and the cloud of incense is ascending from them ; but the Lord is dishonoured under that cloud of incense, and therefore he must go forth in majesty. The stroke comes "*from before the Lord*"—the fire shoots across the mercy-seat, and through the Holy Place, and finds the sinners under their cloud of incense ! How awful to observe that it crosses the mercy-seat to reach them ! And though their cry reaches his ear over the mercy-seat, it is too *late now!* The Lord has risen up. It is like the events that will attend Christ's second coming, when from *Himself* (the mercy-seat itself), fire shall consume his foes, and their cry, though the *Lamb* himself hear it, is in vain. He consumes all that have defied him ; and many among these shall be found in the act of holding up the incense of vain worship to the Lord.

Will-worship in any form, Popery, Puseyism, formality,

idolatry, is hateful to the Lord's holy nature. *His will is holiness.*

> Ver. 3. *Then Moses said unto Aaron, This is it that the Lord spake, saying, I will be sanctified in them that come nigh me,** *and before all the people I will be glorified. And Aaron held his peace.*

The news spread through the camp. Moses and Aaron hastened to the spot. They stood together and gazed on the dead bodies. As they gazed in awful amazement, Moses turned to his brother and said, " *This is that the Lord spake, saying,*" &c. This is an illustration of the same holiness we saw at Sinai, when he said, " *Let the priests which come near to the Lord sanctify themselves, lest the Lord break forth upon them*" (Exod. xix. 22). Aaron felt what Moses said; he bowed in silent submission—one look on his lost sons, another on his exalted and glorified God.

It may be thus at the last day. The Father will point to the ungodly as objects of his just displeasure ; and the Intercessor, who used to yearn over these sons of men, shall then say, "Let them go down quick to hell ;" and the redeemed respond, over the smoke of their burning, " Hallelujah !" We can *understand* Aaron's silent submission, as he saw God's holy act of judgment on these presumptuous sinners ; but could we have gone farther, and *sympathised.*with him, had he even lifted up his hands to his God, and, with a holy gladness in his countenance, cried, in presence of the camp, " Hallelujah, hallelujah ?" Such shall yet be the feeling of the redeemed over their

---

* It has been remarked, that *priests* are the persons chiefly denoted by this term (as in Ezek. xlii. 13, and Exod. xix. 22) ; the people learning reverence by them. If so, then Heb. x. 22, " *Let us draw nigh,*" and Eph. ii. 13, " We are *made nigh* by the blood of Christ," assume a new aspect, viz. referring to *all believers being now priests.*

own kindred who offer strange fire. Standing in Aaron's
position, with all Aaron's submission, but with a pro-
foundly holy triumph, to which Aaron was a stranger,
" the righteous shall rejoice when he seeth the vengeance!
He shall wash his feet (*i. e.* be refreshed) in the blood of
the wicked" (Ps. lviii. 10). Angels are able now to
feel thus toward devils, who once were most dear and beloved brethren! The glory of God will so appear as to
hide all else from our view. His glory will cause us to
cry, " Hallelujah!" (Rev. xix. 3.)

> Ver. 4–7. *And Moses called Mishael and Elzaphan, the sons of
> Uzziel, the uncle of Aaron, and said unto them, Come near,
> carry your brethren from before the sanctuary out of the camp.
> So they went near, and carried them in their coats out of the
> camp; as Moses had said. And Moses said unto Aaron, and
> unto Eleazar and unto Ithamar his sons, Uncover not your
> heads, neither rend your clothes, lest you die, and lest wrath
> come upon all the people: but let your brethren, the whole house
> of Israel, bewail the burning which the Lord hath kindled.
> And ye shall not go out from the door of the tabernacle of the
> congregation, lest ye die: for the anointing oil of the Lord is
> upon you. And they did according to the word of Moses.*

Whoever saw the dead bodies saw at once that it was
the Lord's stroke! for *the coats*—the priestly coats—were
left unconsumed. The Lord directed the fire, as he often
directs lightning, in such a manner that *the persons* were
struck, but nothing besides. The stroke came on *guilt*
alone! And *all in the camp* saw them; for the dead bodies
were " *carried out*" before all. A prophet might have
pointed Israel forward from that sad scene to the coming
day of shame and vengeance—" They shall go forth, and
look upon the carcases of the men that have transgressed
against me" (Isa. lxvi. 24). All saw their presumption;
all must see their doom. All saw the law broken by

their hands; all must see the broken law honoured in their death.

And the honour done to the law is made the more apparent, and brought closer home to the heart, by the circumstance that nothing is done that could have been avoided. No feeling of the tender, paternal heart of Aaron is needlessly injured; none of the feelings of brother to brother are violated. In order to preserve these natural affections untouched, neither Aaron nor any of his family are asked to take part in the mournful duty of removing the consumed bodies—the ashes—of the men who have themselves become a burnt-offering in the Lord's sore displeasure. This duty is laid upon the sons of Uzziel, cousins of the dead. The mourning family receive a message (ver. 6) to sit still without putting aside their priestly character,—not to dishevel their hair, or rend their clothes, for they could not execute their duties in the sanctuary if they were to give themselves to mourning. Priests must restrain even the strongest natural feelings when these come into collision with duty to God. Our Master, who wept at the grave of Lazarus, and spoke to his mother on the cross, yet would not be turned aside from duty by such feelings. "*Considero te in cruce de matre sollicitum, cui volenti loqui tecum quum evangelizares, negâras colloquium.*" (Cyprian, *de Pass.*)—" I think of thee, how thou shewedst such concern on the Cross for thy mother, though, when thou wert preaching the Gospel, thou wouldst not allow her to speak with thee."

But the special reason seems to be this,—they bore a public character, as representing to the people God's views of truth and God's opinion upon all matters. Therefore, as his representatives, they must shew that such an act of judgment, however severe, was quite deserved, and brought glory to his name. They who had most to do in exhibiting the mercy of God at the altar were thus foremost in testifying that Jehovah continued to be holy and righteous, true and faithful.

It was for a similar reason that Ezekiel was not to lament his wife (xxiv. 16, 17). He stood as representative of God; for it is there expressly interpreted as being done with this view—" Ezekiel is unto you a sign" (ver. 24). And here, verse 7 says, " For the anointing oil of the Lord is upon you," *q. d.* you are men set apart for his use.

It is not because the Lord disapproves of our mourning over the dead, for he permits all Israel to lament this " *burning*"—both in its cause and in its effect—both for the sin that occasioned it, and the sorrow that resulted. But it is to shew how hereafter even friends shall approve of the Lord's acts of justice on the ungodly, while the smoke ascendeth for ever and ever. The sons of Aaron are to shew this, being representative characters.

> Ver. 8–11. *And the Lord spake unto Aaron, saying, Do not drink wine, nor strong drink, thou, nor thy sons with thee, when ye go into the tabernacle of the congregation, lest ye die: it shall be a statute for ever throughout your generations; and that ye may put difference between holy and unholy, and between unclean and clean; and that ye may teach the children of Israel all the statutes which the Lord hath spoken unto them by the hand of Moses.*

Oftentimes have seasons of affliction been the times when the Lord gave new communications to his people. And this season of judgment brought out a new precept; a precept fitted to prevent the recurrence of the offering of strange fire, or any similar will-worship. It appears from Ezek. xliv. 21 (if we are to use analogy as a guide), which speaks of the "*Inner court*," that this command refers to the times when the priests engaged in any holy service, whether in the court, or in what was more properly *the tabernacle.*

A priest must have his soul calm, clear, steady. He is to be "filled with the Spirit," not with "wine, wherein is excess" (Eph. v. 18). In a holy frame, discerning between clean and unclean, ready to teach others also, he is to enter the tabernacle. In two things he is to be the opposite of Nadab and Abihu : he is not to be excited with any false, vain desire ; and then he is to be exactly observant of the Lord's statutes (ver. 11), so that he may be ready to teach others also to keep them. Hence, he must keep away from every indulgence and every appearance of evil; from every tempting object, and every excitement not drawn from him to whom he is approaching.

O what a baptism of the Holy Ghost ministers now need, in order to be free of every foreign aid and false excitement, and be able to minister calmly, holily, and according to the Lord's revealed message !

Ver. 12–15. *And Moses spake unto Aaron, and unto Eleazar and unto Ithamar, his sons that were left, Take the meat-offering that remaineth of the offerings of the Lord made by fire, and eat it without leaven beside the altar; for it is most holy. And ye shall eat it in the holy place, because it is thy due, and thy sons' due, of the sacrifices of the Lord made by fire : for so I am commanded. And the wave-breast and heave-shoulder shall ye eat in a clean place; thou, and thy sons, and thy daughters with thee: for they be thy due, and thy sons' due, which are given out of the sacrifices of peace-offerings of the children of Israel. The heave-shoulder and the wave-breast shall they bring, with the offerings made by fire of the fat, to wave it for a wave-offering before the Lord; and it shall be thine, and thy sons' with thee, by a statute for ever; as the Lord hath commanded.*

The "*holy place*" here meant is defined by "*beside the altar*" (ver. 12). It is *the court made holy* by what was done in it (see chap. vi. 16). The "*clean place*" is any spot in their dwellings not defiled ceremonially.

The reason for this reiteration of injunctions which have been already given—at least in substance—in former chapters, seems to be, lest Aaron and his sons should suppose that they had forfeited their privileges by that awful sin committed by some of their number. But here they are assured that all their privileges remain to them as full as ever. They are thus gently led into the true consolation under all that had happened. They are reminded of the Lord's continuing friendship and love ; and with this assurance the Lord binds up those whom he has wounded. He wipes away their tears by presenting to them his unvarying and unchangeable love ; for this is what is exhibited to them in receiving the allotted portions of the sacrifices of peace-offering. Herein the love of God our Saviour appears ! O what tender, considerate kindness is discernible under this veil of types ! He has here made his love abound "in all wisdom and prudence"—so seasonable and so full. A new manifestation of a reconciled God is the oil he pours into their wounds.

Ver. 16–18. *And Moses diligently sought the goat of the sin-offering, and, behold, it was burnt: and he was angry with Eleazar and Ithamar, the sons of Aaron which were left alive, saying, Wherefore have ye not eaten the sin-offering in the holy place, seeing it is most holy, and God hath given it you to bear the iniquity of the congregation, to make atonement for them before the Lord? Behold, the blood of it was not brought in within the holy place:* * *ye should indeed have eaten it in the holy place, as I commanded.*

See here Moses manifesting great jealousy for the

---

* To the inner holy place (Ezek. xliv. 21).

honour of his God. " Moses was faithful *in all* his house" (Heb. iii. 2). He does not address Aaron, but his sons— yet it seems, from ver. 19, that Aaron, too, was present. He suspected that there might be some deviation from prescribed rules at such a time ; and hence, before he spoke, he " *diligently sought.*"

It should not have been " *burnt,*" but " *eaten ;*" for, in chap. vi. 30, the rule was laid down. If the blood of the sin-offering was brought into the Holy Place (as was done if it was the sin-offering of a public person, or of a public nature), then it was to be burnt ; but if otherwise, it was to be eaten. But the *sin-offering* here was one offered for the priests as individual sinners, and therefore was not to be brought into the Holy Place to reconcile withal. Hence, Aaron and his family should have eaten it, accord- ing to chap. vi. 26–29.

Besides, Moses perceived that by this deviation from the prescribed order, they had lost a privilege. He says, " *Seeing it is most holy, and God hath given it you*" (ver. 18), hinting that it was a privilege they would have found comfort in availing themselves of at such a time, it being a token of God's kindness to them. God may tenderly allow us to omit *the duty,* while it may be foolish in us to use the permission, as thereby we lose the *privilege.*

The subject of ver. 17 deserves more particular notice. The sense of that verse is, " God has given it to you that, in bearing the iniquity of the congregation, you may have an atonement for your own souls first of all." It is only incidentally that the expression " *Bearing sin*" occurs in Leviticus, viz. here and in chap. xxii. 9. But it may be right to notice what we may gather from these two references.

We gather from this passage—1. That the individual who *bears the sin of others* must himself be pure from these sins. This was signified by the priest's offering a sin-offering by which all his own sins were borne away. 2. That this expression means more than *enduring the effects* of sin. For a personally guilty substitute might have done this. But farther; chap. xxii. 9 teaches us—3. That to "*bear sin*" implies that the person is *reckoned guilty* of the sin. Hence, when it is said that the priests *bore the iniquity of the sanctuary* (Numb. xviii. 1), the sense is,—they were reckoned guilty, until they had put that guilt upon the sacrifice, and had seen that sacrifice burnt to ashes. Isa. liii. 6–11, and 2 Peter ii. 24 must be understood in this manner. For we now see that to "*bear the sin of others*" implies that the priest is reckoned guilty, by imputation, of sins with which he was not personally chargeable at all, up to the moment when he has cleared these sins away in the fire of wrath which consumes the sacrifice.

> Ver. 19. *And Aaron said unto Moses, Behold, this day have they offered their sin-offering and their burnt-offering before the Lord; and such things have befallen me: and if I had eaten the sin-offering to-day, should it have been accepted in the sight of the Lord?*

Aaron first defends his sons, and then himself. It seems clear to me that "*the sin-offering and burnt-offering*" *of his sons*, spoken of here, must have been presented by themselves, and are not the offering of chap. ix. 8–12. I understand this to have occurred the day after Aaron's consecration, and his sons had that morning presented sin-offering and burnt-offering for themselves.* Hence,

---

* There remains one difficulty, viz. where is it said that the common priests were to begin as Aaron began, by presenting a sin-offering and burnt-offering for themselves? The answer is, that from Heb. vii. 27, Lev. xvi. 16, 17, and other places, it appears that *no priest* could proceed to offer the sacrifices of others without first presenting these offerings for his own sins. Now, that morning the people had begun to bring their offerings, and Aaron's sons had entered on their duties.

Moses addressed them (ver. 16), and Aaron, in replying, says, " They have done part of the duty"—" *they have offered.*" Now, as *this sin-offering* was for *Nadab and Abihu,* now dead, as well as for Eleazar and Ithamar, it could not be used as other similar sin-offerings were ; for the Lord had interrupted the usual rites attendant on such a sacrifice. It could not be said to be *accepted,—* how, then, could Aaron and his sons eat of it, as if it had been accepted ? Had they sat down to feast on it, they would virtually be declaring their belief that the Lord had not refused to accept the sin-offering in which *Nadab and Abihu* had taken part, whereas there were manifest tokens of displeasure all around. In these circumstances, could Aaron and his sons eat in faith? No ; *the family* felt that there was a cloud over the Sun of Righteousness !

Ver. 20. *And when Moses heard that, he was content.*

" It seemed good in his eyes" (Heb.) He saw that Aaron entered into the spirit and meaning of the rites he ministered among ; and was satisfied. And it is to be noticed that this attention to the *spirit,* and not to the mere *letter,* of the ceremonial law, at the very outset, indicated to Israel that the *things signified* by these types were their chief concern, not the bare types themselves. And how interesting to find Aaron thus exhibiting his understanding of the emblems of the tabernacle ! Aaron's service was not formality; it was a worship done in the spirit ; and where the spirit could not be brought along with the rite, he left the rite undone. Herein he glorified God,—he gave him the honour due unto his name ! He felt that it was not worship at all, if his soul was not engaged ; for " *God is spirit.*"

Thus we have a glimpse into the hidden life of Israel's worship, at the very moment when undeviating attention to the appointed statutes is enforced by a stroke of severe righteousness.

But after these calamities befalling men of the priestly line, and testifying that they are sinners, and after so many various ceremonies that all spoke of the need of atonement, it is sweet for us to turn for a moment to the One High Priest, in whom all was summed up and perfected. We take Daniel's well-known prophecy, to find a full-length portrait of our Priest. It runs thus :—

> " Seventy weeks are determined
>   Upon thy people, and upon thy holy city ;
>   To finish the transgression,   [margin, *to restrain.*]
>   And to make an end of sins,   [margin, *to seal up.*]
>   And to make reconciliation for iniquity,
>   And to bring in everlasting righteousness,
>   And to seal up the vision and prophecy,   [margin, *prophet*]
>   And to anoint the Most Holy." —(Dan. ix. 24.)

Perhaps it might be rendered as literally, and more forcibly, by a few alterations. The prophet is told that seventy weeks must yet run on ere these events take place—that is, the proposed, determined time for the accomplishing of these six great ends :—

1. For the restraining of the transgression ;
2. For the putting the seal on the sin-offerings ;
3. For making atonement for iniquity;
4. For bringing in an everlasting righteousness ;
5. For putting the seal on vision and prophet ;
6. For anointing the Most Holy One.

We have here Gabriel's message regarding Messiah's work for men. In the course of seventy weeks, 1. *The transgression shall be restrained.* "The law entered, that *the offence* (τὸ παράπτωμα, הַפֶּשַׁע) might abound" (Rom. v. 20) ; but no sooner is the Saviour come, than lo! the offence is no longer overflowing. *Grace* has the opposite effect from *law;* it restrains sin. "Sin shall not have dominion over you ; for ye are not under the law, but under grace" (Rom. vi. 14). And the grace that brought salvation, flowing from the Saviour, Messiah, was soon felt to be thus powerful ; "Teaching us to deny ungodliness and worldly lusts, and to live soberly, righteously, and godly in this present world" (Titus ii. 12). 2. *The seal shall be put on the sin-offerings.* The article is prefixed to הַחַטָּאוֹת, as if to make it plain that it was "sin-offerings." The *sealing* is in the sense of giving them sanction—shewing that they gave proper views of man's sin and God's justice. This Jesus did by fulfilling the whole of their typical meaning, being made sin for us, and consumed to ashes without the camp, on Calvary. Thus he "set to his seal" (ἐσφράγισεν) that these were true representations of God's holy law and man's sin (John iii. 33, and Rom. iv. 11). Then, 3. *The atonement for iniquity shall be actually brought.* Hitherto it had all been done in type ; but the Saviour, by his one suffering and obedience, presents the reality to God and to man. He actually does what the ceremonies of the law pledged should be done. 4. *Everlasting righteousness shall be brought in.* The Saviour brought us a real righteousness, as real as was the imputation of our sins to him. It was no more a ceremonial purification only, or a cleansing from defilement, which lasted only for a season, and was lost by the next touch of pollution. He gives an *everlasting* righteousness—" eternal redemption." 5. *The seal shall be put on vision and prophet.* Whatever prophets have uttered, or seen in vision, concerning Messiah, was now all fulfilled by Jesus. Thus the seal of truth was stamped on them all, and they were set apart as attested and verified. 6. *The Most Holy One shall be actually anointed; i. e.* inaugurated into his office as Redeemer, by actually being born in our nature, and anointed with the Holy Ghost from the moment of his birth. In other words, he that is to accomplish all those blessings shall appear, viz. he that is the true High Priest, " Holy of Holies," on whom God's anointing oil shall be poured, even " the Spirit without measure."

The only doubtful clause here seems to be the last. Many apply "Most Holy" to the sanctuary, whereas we here apply it to *Messiah*, as the antitype of the high priest. Is the high priest, then, ever called קֹדֶשׁ קָדָשִׁים ? Yes; in 1 Chron. xxiii. 13. Let any one who understands Hebrew read that verse, and say if it ought not to be there rendered, " And Aaron was separated, setting him apart as holy of holies (קֹדֶשׁ קָדָשִׁים), himself and his sons for ever, to offer incense." And in a Jewish song, chanted by Joseph Wolff, and which he heard Jews sing in their own tongue, Messiah is praised not only thus—

> " The King, our Messiah, shall come,
>   The Blessed of the Blessed is He ;"

but, besides, he is celebrated, as in Daniel—

> " The King, our Messiah, shall come,
>   The Holy of Holies is He."

Oh, glorious Messiah! True High Priest! Thou art all that the prophets said of thee! Thou givest us everlasting righteousness and real atonement! Thou satisfiedst every claim made by justice, whose payment was pledged by sacrifice ! Thou alone hast stayed the torrent of sin ! Soon wilt thou again appear " without sin unto salvation," and present to thyself and to the Father a Church " without spot, or blemish, or any such thing !"

CHAPTER XI

Remembrancers of the Broken Law—The Clean and the Unclean

" Sin is the transgression of the law."—1 John iii. 4

Ver. 1. *And the Lord spake unto Moses, and to Aaron, saying unto them,—*

HITHERTO *atonement* has been the theme. A fallen world should relish that truth more than any. God shews himself willing to save, by thus fully setting atonement before us. And were he to do no more, the blame of being unsaved would all rest on *man*.

But now, as if it were to " compel men to come in," he opens up the state of sinfulness in which this world lies. The Lord wishes to make the sinner flee to the Atonement, by creating in his mind a loathing of sin, that so pollutes and defiles. For this end, he lays before us instructions of a peculiar kind, containing distinctions that would every day need to be attended to. He first so arranges the beasts they were to eat, and those they were not to eat, that an Israelite would every day meet an object that called for the exercise of his discrimination between *clean* and *unclean*. Thus they were to be taught God's discernment of sin, and the stigma he had set upon it. Though there was nothing *morally* different between one beast and an-

other, yet, if God put his difference between them, they
must so regard them ; and it was thus that every beast
became to them a remembrancer of the law, calling upon
them to distinguish between what was right and what
was wrong—what was permitted and what was forbidden.
The Lord set up so many finger-posts that pointed Israel
to the Fall, and reminded them that they were in a fallen
world.

This chapter begins the subject of *sin*—its existence in
the world all around us.   Then, chapter xii. teaches the
transmission of sin ; chapters xiii. and xiv., the vileness
of sin, and the mode of putting away this loathsome evil;
and, lastly, chap. xv., original sin in all its deformity.
The Holy Spirit would shut up the world to righteousness through the blood of Jesus shed for the most guilty.
The first fifteen chapters of this book treat of *sin and its
atonement.*

> Ver. 2. *Speak unto the children of Israel, saying, These are the
> beasts which ye shall eat among all the beasts that are on the
> earth.*

Some have suggested * that the object of these regulations might be to restrain the appetite, and might be
given after the murmuring for quails recorded in Numbers, chap. xi.   In this view, that incident would be considered as suggesting these rules, in the same manner as
Nadab and Abihu's sin, in last chapter, suggested the
restriction about the priests taking no wine before going
into the sanctuary.   But this seems a very ungrounded
supposition ; for the distinction of *clean* and *unclean* existed in Noah's days.

It is, however, to be noticed, as a remarkable fact,
regarding the regulations laid down here for the food of

* *E. g.* Townsend.

Israel, that all the *clean* animals are wholesome for food ; and the fish that have fins and scales—viz. the clean— are not only safe, but nutritious. Still, this is only a secondary consideration, taken into account, no doubt, by God, while he, in wisdom and love, appointed this arrangement for higher ends. It is also worthy of notice, that the wisdom which selected the clean and the unclean as early as the days of Noah, foresaw what animals· would be worshipped and used by idolaters. Hence we find them answering that use also, while still something far higher is the main thing in view.

To imbue the mind of Israel with moral distinctions was the grand and primary use of this arrangement. It was so in Noah's days, and probably in Adam's ; but now the development of that system takes place more fully ; just as in the case of the various sorts of offerings.

In proof that to teach Israel to put a difference between the clean and unclean in things moral was the end of *these typical distinctions*, we might refer to verses 44, 45. And also we might refer to Peter's vision, in Acts x. 12, 14, where he is shewn that the idolatrous Gentiles, so long unclean, are now to be admitted into fellowship with Israel. There we are clearly taught that there was a typical reference to sin in these ordinances.

We should join the last clause with ver. 3, and read thus—" These are the living creatures (הַחַיָּה) which ye may eat. Of all large beasts (בְּהֵמָה) that are on the earth, whatsoever parteth the hoof," &c.

Ver. 3, 4. *Whatsoever parteth the hoof, and is cloven-footed, and cheweth the cud, among the beasts, that shall ye eat. Nevertheless, these shall ye not eat, of them that chew the cud, or of them that divide the hoof: as the camel, because he cheweth the cud, but divideth not the hoof; he is unclean unto you.*

We have another table of the clean and unclean in Deuteronomy, chap. xiv., and some apparent differences occur. But the reconciliation is easy. It is this. In *Leviticus*, the principles of the distinction are laid down, and illustrated by only a few instances, either in regard to beast or fowl. In *Deuteronomy*, specific cases are given ; and though, at ver. 6, the rule is noticed, yet the object of the writer there is to set down special instances of the clean and unclean, rather than to state the rule.

The grand rules as to quadrupeds are, 1. *The clean* are those that *have their feet completely cloven* (above and below) ; and, 2. They *must also chew the cud.* The complete dividing of the hoof is very fully expressed in the Hebrew; it is, *q. d.* " Whatever not only divideth the hoof, but cleaveth a cleft in the hoof." This part of the rule was sufficient to exclude all such animals as the *lion* and the *dog*, whose foot has a membrane below that unites the claws together, and so interferes with the *complete cleft ;* or such as the *horse*, which has no cleft at all. And when the next part of the rule demanded that the animal should be one that *chews the cud*, this secured that it should never be a *carnivorous* animal ; for all that chew the cud live on vegetable food. No carnivorous animal was clean ; they had qualities that made them unfit to be acknowledged as proper for God's people to touch. But some of those not carnivorous were also unfit to be taken as food, possessing some peculiarity that fitted them to be types of things which the holy should avoid.

In ver. 4, " *nevertheless*," is אַךְ, equivalent to " *for example.*" There was a difficulty in determining the case of the *camel*, whether or not it really divides the hoof wholly, and the case of the *hare*, whether it really chews the cud ; therefore these cases are decided by authority.

And along with each of these a sample is given where no
ambiguity existed, viz. the coney and the swine.

In doubtful cases, we should decide on the side of *abstaining* from the thing.   See 1 Thess. **v.** 22, " Abstain
from all appearance of evil."

> Ver. 5–8. *And the coney, because he cheweth the cud, but divideth
> not the hoof; he is unclean unto you.   And the hare,* because
> he cheweth the cud, but divideth not the hoof; he is unclean unto
> you.   And the swine, though he divide the hoof, and be cloven-
> footed; yet he cheweth not the cud: he is unclean to you.   Of
> their flesh shall ye not eat, and their carcase shall ye not touch:
> they are unclean to you.*

The *coney*† is an animal called the *wuber*, resembling
the hare in size, and living in holes of the rock. The *swine*,
in the East, if eaten, produces a tendency to itchy diseases,
to leprosy, and, in short, to cutaneous diseases of all kinds.

We see here how the Lord multiplied in Israel the
memorials of sin.   In Noah's day, the distinction between
clean and unclean was known; but only in its rudiments.
That general rule is now branched out into particulars.
By this new constitution, *sin* was much oftener brought
before the eyes and into the thoughts of the godly men of
Israel.   For, suppose an Israelite of " quick discernment
in the fear of the Lord" going forth to his labour.   As he
goes forth, he meets one leading a *camel* along.   The
sight of this animal, marked as unclean in the law, stirs

---

* Hebrew, אַרְנֶבֶת.   It is stated by a Jewish writer, that the Seventy interpre-
ters were much puzzled by this word.   They hesitated to render it by " λαγωος,"
or " λαγως," because Ptolemy, whose father and uncle were of the family of the
" λαγοι," might take offence at finding his name registered among the unclean
animals.   But neither could they retain the Hebrew term, " *Arnebeth*," because
Ptolemy's queen was named " *Arnebet*;" and she might think herself insulted.
They, therefore, resorted to the expedient of rendering the word by the descriptive term, " Δασυπους," q. d. " rough-foot."

† The *Hyrax Syriacus*, or Wuber, is now agreed upon as the *Shaphan* of
the Hebrew.

up his soul to reflect upon God's having his eye on his
people to see if they avoid sin and remember his revealed
will ; and just because this animal was one of those that
it would have been difficult to determine whether it belonged to the clean or unclean, had not express authority
decided, he is reminded that it will be safe for himself to
observe the Lord's positive decision in things that have a
doubtful aspect. He walks onward. As he crosses the
field, a *hare* starts from its form, and speeds past him.
Here he is reminded that there are things which God has
expressly forbidden, and which he must avoid with as
much fear as this timid hare hastens its escape from him.
As he passes near some rocky part of his farm, the *coney*,
or *wuber*, attracts his eye, and deepens the remembrance
that God has made a difference between good and evil ;
while it teaches him to hide from the approach of the
least appearance of evil, even as that *coney*, at the sight of
a foe, betakes itself to its rocks. In the more woody and
wild scenes, he sees the *swine* and the *wild boar* enjoying
their retreats in savage filthiness. There he again is reminded of the law of his God ; and there he reads at the
same time, the filth of iniquity—its impure loathsome
aspect—the swine wallowing in the mire, and the wild
boar stretching his carcase at ease, or sharpening his tusks
for some effort of destruction.*

We have, in Deuteronomy xiv., an enumeration of
the principal *clean* animals. These would, in like manner, remind the Israelite of what was holy. One went
forth to his flocks, and there the *sheep*, feeding in their

* The peculiar abhorrence entertained of *swine* has been supposed to have
arisen in part from the fact, that the heathen used them in their feasts and
sacrifices. But this is not satisfactory ; for the Egyptians held them unclean.
It has been from the peculiar style of the animal ; just what gave occasion to the
proverb, 2 Peter ii. 22.

pastures, spoke to him of the clean and holy ones whom the Lord watches over as their Shepherd. Another, who beheld the *wild goat*, amid solitary rocks where scarcely any foot ever trod, feels himself taught that the Lord has kept up the difference between holy and unholy even in the deepest solitude ; while, at the same time, he reads the doctrine of a sustaining providence in the safety of the wild goat on its precipices. The *hart*, leaping in its joy, or hastening to quench its thirst in water-brooks, leads his thoughts to holiness. It is a clean animal ; it may guide his thoughts; it may remind him of the saint's panting after God. Again; the *roe-buck*, or gazelle, amid the fragrant shrubs, spoke of holy distinctions, and might lead up his soul to the beauty of holiness amid the enchanting beauty of earth's rich scenery. It may have been thus that it was first seen by Solomon, in the hills of Bethlehem ; and often, in after days, it would tell an Israelite of Him who was to come as a " roe on the mountains of spices." They could not gaze on the beautiful antlers of the *fallow-deer*, nor on the *pygarg* (or *lidmee*), with its double-sized horns and double strength, on the *buffalo's* wild might, or the *chamois*, sent out by God to people the very cliffs of the rock—they could never gaze on these merely with the feelings of one admiring a *creating* God ; they were led to think of them as connecting them with a holy God, who discerned between the clean and the unclean, and sought the redemption of his fallen creatures. And thus there was a check in Israel upon the mere sentimentalist and the admirer of nature ; their God superadded the idea of *sin* and *holiness* to all the objects they beheld.*

* I think it was not their *natural qualities*, so much as the *Divine appointment* of the animals, that taught Israel. Yet, at the same time, we need not exclude the other altogether. In the old poet, *Beaumont* (in his *Psyche*, ix.

They were not to make use even of the dead bodies of
such animals. Living or dead, by them they must be
reminded of sin, and refuse to come near it. Our hatred
of sin must be eternal hatred ; our forsaking of sin must
be everlasting; our farewell to sin must be for ever and
ever. The difference between sin and holiness is everlasting, not temporary; therefore, our protest against sin, and
in favour of holiness, must be without interruption and
without end.

> Ver. 9–12. *These shall ye eat, of all that are in the waters: what-
> soever hath fins and scales in the waters, in the seas, and in
> the rivers, them shall ye eat. And all that have not fins nor
> scales in the seas, and in the rivers, of all that move in the
> waters, and of any living thing which is in the waters, they
> shall be an abomination unto you. They shall be even an abo-
> mination unto you; ye shall not eat of their flesh, but ye shall
> have their carcases in abomination. Whatsoever hath no fins
> nor scales in the waters, that shall be an abomination unto you.*

It is a well-known fact, that all fish that have *both
scales and fins* are at once wholesome and nutritious. This
provision, therefore, secured to the people the free use of
what was certainly profitable, and kept them back from
the uncertainty of choosing among the others what might

106-108), there is an illustration of how such associations as the above might
be used, when he represents Jesus in the wilderness with the wild beasts :—

> " When *oxen* he, and *asses* had descried,
>   Lowing and braying their desires of grass,
>   He kindly thought of what did him betide
>   When in their house he entertained was ;
>   How Bethlehem's stable, with the hay and manger,
>   Welcomed the new-born, man-rejected stranger.

> " A flock of *sheep* went bleating after them,
>   Whose sucking sons made him reflect again
>   Upon himself—God's everlasting *Lamb*,
>   Born in proud Salem's shambles to be slain.
>   He blest them all, and for their sustenance,
>   Engaged his magazine of providence."

have injured them. Again, therefore, they were taught
that it is better far to lean to the side of abstinence, in
doubtful cases, than to run the risk of doing evil. They
were trained to the principle, " If meat make my brother
to offend, I will eat no flesh while the world standeth"
(1 Cor. viii. 13).

Those " *without fins and scales*" are partly creatures of
the mud and marsh; whereas the others swim through the
clear, limpid waters of " seas and rivers." There are others
of them that are " without scales," such as the voracious
shark; so that it was only those " with scales and fins"
that were naturally fitted to exhibit *purity.*

In ver. 9, we are to read " *in the waters,* i. e. *whether
seas or rivers.*" In ver. 10, " All that move in the
waters," is rather, " All that *crawl* in the waters ;" and
includes every living thing there that has not the specified
qualities. In the same verse, and at ver. 11, " They shall
be an abomination," is more emphatic if read thus—
" *They are an abomination to you, and they* SHALL *be an
abomination.*" * And it is thus strongly stated, because
the people might be ready to neglect the rule in the case
of some of the smaller creatures in the waters. Many of
the forbidden creatures are exceedingly small in size ; yet,
nevertheless, even that atom is to be abhorred, if the
Lord has given the command. It is not the importance
of the thing, but the majesty of the lawgiver, that is to be
the standard of our obedience. " Sin is the transgression
of *the law*" (1 John iii. 4).

There were tribes that were to dwell by the waters.
Thus Simeon and Dan had a sea-coast from the river of
Egypt up to Joppa. Ephraim and the half-tribe of

---

* Exactly as Ezekiel xix. 14, קִינָה לְקִינָה וַתְּהִי הִיא, " This is a lamentation,
and shall be for a lamentation ;" so here, הֵם שֶׁקֶץ לָכֶם יִהְיוּ וְשֶׁקֶץ לָכֶם.

Manasseh had a sea-coast as far as Carmel—the glorious
plain of Sharon descending to the water-side. Zebulun
and Asher, too, had their creeks and bays; while Naph-
tali, as well as Zebulun and the other half-tribe of
Manasseh, encircled the lake of Galilee, so plentiful in its
supply of fish; and the waters of Merom, no doubt,
swarmed with their kinds. Others of the tribes lay near
Jordan, or had some lesser streams and lakes at hand.
Hence there was not probably one tribe but had some
need of these laws, and opportunity for exercising faith
by attending to them.* The Lord also thus evidenced his
care over the spiritual health of the seamen and fishers of
Israel. It tried their faith when they needed to cast away
whatever unclean fish they had enclosed in their net.

Some, indeed, might reckon such minute and arbitrary
rules as these to be trifling. But the principle involved
in obedience or disobedience was none other than the
same principle which was tried in Eden at the foot of the
forbidden tree. It was really this—Is the Lord to be
obeyed in *all* things whatsoever he commands? Is he a
holy lawgiver? Are his creatures bound to give implicit
assent to his will?

But this discrimination between holy and unholy penetrated farther. It reached Israel's hours of recreation,
and kept them, even then, in mind of their Holy One.
A wealthy Israelite, who has his villa by the lake of
Gennesaret, goes forth on the bosom of the lake. In its
clear waters he finds fish, darting on before the slow-sail-
ing bark in the strength of their *fins*, and reflecting back
to the surface, from their *scales*, the light that fell on the
waters. All here speaks of purity—conformity to what

---

* Our Lord's parable, Matt. xiii. 47, 48, of "every kind of fish," would be
very significant to Jews who recognised an allusion to these Mosaic distinctions.

the law pronounced clean. But at another time he strolls along by some shallow, or is compassing the waters of Merom, and there he finds the crawling reptiles of the mud and marsh—teaching him to draw back in haste from the touch of uncleanness. In like manner, far within their land, at the little brook flowing through the valley of Elah, fringed by its green terebinths, the youth of Judah, in their sports, were taught to keep before them the difference between good and evil, while they scrupulously rejected the unclean minnows, and chose the clean, amid their easy angling at the stream. " Holiness to the Lord"—obedience to his revealed will—thus pervaded Israel's land and Israel's families, in public and in secret, in business and in recreation; their youth and their aged men, in their fields and by their river-sides, must remember " The Holy One of Israel !"

And now we shall see that the very air and sky had its signs, in the fowls that flew in the midst of heaven.

> Ver. 13–16. *And these are they which ye shall have in abomination among the fowls; they shall not be eaten, they are an abomination; the eagle, and the ossifrage, and the ospray, and the vulture, and the kite after his kind; every raven after his kind; and the owl, and the night-hawk, and the cuckoo, and the hawk after his kind, and the little owl.*

The *ossifrage* is a *sea-eagle*, frequenting cliffs and promontories; and the *ospray* is the *fish-hawk*, subsisting on fish, which it darts down upon from its watch-tower. The *vulture* and the *kite* are known in all these countries, as familiarly as the *eagle* and the *raven*. These are *birds of the air*. The next are mere *birds of earth*. But what is here called " the owl"(יַעֲנָה) is the *ostrich*. The *night-hawk* is a species of owl known in Syria, very ravenous, so that it will attack infants. The *cuckoo* (שַׁחַף) is probably one of the lesser fowls, the *sea-swallow* or *sea-gull* on their shores. The *hawk* is well known.

All these are ravenous in their nature ; and therefore there is an obvious ground of difference between these and other fowls, without there being need to lay down any general rule such as is laid down in the case of quadrupeds and fish. These are *specimens;* other fowls of a similarly ravenous nature are to be classed along with them, as the clause, "*after his kind*," may intimate. Hence, in Deuteronomy xiv., "*the glede*" (רָאָה) is added to the list, unless there the same bird be meant under a different name. The "*little owl*" should also be taken in here, from ver. 17. It is the common *barn owl*.

The *eagle*, darting down from the hills of Moab or Bashan, or from the heights of Lebanon, would often teach the shepherd who saw his flock endangered by this unclean bird. Those by the sea-shore would have the same lesson taught them when the sight or cry of the *sea-eagle* and *fish-hawk* called to their mind that God had made a difference between the clean and the unclean even in the fowls of the air. The *vulture*, in their streets or highways, allured by the scent of death, and the *kite*, poised on its wings till it found a prey on which to dart down, and the hoarse unpleasant note of the *raven*, would constantly recall the same distinctions ; while their loathsome qualities would serve to make the feeling of uncleanness more and more detestable to the men of Israel. So long as they were in the wilderness, and ever afterwards on their borders, they would meet with the *ostrich*, whose disagreeable cries, voracious habits, and parental unkindness, would all contribute to deepen their aversion to whatever was unclean. And not less so the small but most ravenous *night-hawk*, that flies in at their open windows and seeks the life of

infants; and the *sea-gull* incessantly watching for its victims, over whom it screams in savage delight; and the
hawk, so furious in its attack on the birds of the air; and
the *owl* at evening, awake for designs of destruction. All
these, every time they were seen, helped to deepen
Israel's remembrance of the difference between holy and
unholy, and to give them intimations of the hateful qualities of sin.

> Ver. 17–19. *And the cormorant, and the great owl, and the swan,
> and the pelican, and the gier-eagle, and the stork, the heron
> after her kind, and the lapwing, and the bat.*

The *cormorant* might be seen all over the surface of
the Mediterranean, near its shores, sailing gracefully on
the calm waves, or fluttering boldly amid the foaming
billows in the storm, seeking its victims.. The "great
owl," or "*bittern*" * (יַנְשׁוּף), might be heard booming from
the sedges of the waters of Merom or of Jordan, busy all
the time in industrious search for what would fill its appetite; and along with it the "swan," or "purple-bird"
(porphyrio hyacinthine, תִּנְשֶׁמֶת), seeking its supply of
fishes by the side of lakes and rivers. By the shore of
the sea of Galilee, the *pelican* fished for its prey, and
stored what it found in the bag wherewith it is provided.
The *gier-eagle* (רָחָם) is very tender of its young,† according to its Hebrew name, yet in their behalf unsparingly
seizes fish or winged fowl. It manifests evil in combination with good, and being pronounced *unclean*, led Israel
to entertain abhorrence of any mixture of good and
evil. The same lesson might be learnt from *the stork*. It

---

* Consult Robinson's *Clavis*, Rosenmüller, the Pictorial Bible, Calmet, and
others, for a fuller inquiry into the natural history of the above. Many suppose
the *ibis* is meant by the יַנְשׁוּף.

† Hence some think *the swan* may be meant, which will attack even man in
defence of its young.

was a bird familiarly known, nestling in the roofs of their houses, possessed of strong social and parental affections, yet feeding on lizards, frogs, serpents, and other living things. Last of all, *the heron* (אֲנָפָה), angry and irritable, would often startle the man of God in some solitary spot, where it stood watching for its prey; the *hoopoe*, also, or *lapwing*, beautiful in feathers, yet filthy in habits, and noisy in its cry; and *the bat* (into whose retreats the shining idols of the heathen shall yet be cast, no more to catch the eye by their gaudy show, Isa. ii. 20), coming forth at evening-tide, when the air was still, hunting in the dusk for its food, and often flapping its wings most unexpectedly on the passer by, and unpleasantly disturbing his quiet thoughts. All these, not only kept up to remembrance that there was a difference between clean and unclean—sin and holiness—good and evil—but, by their individual qualities, impressed dislike for the unclean, and taught Israel to associate most unpleasant ideas with whatever was forbidden.

> Ver. 20–23. *All fowls that creep, going upon all four, shall be an abomination unto you. Yet these may ye eat, of every flying creeping thing that goeth upon all four, which have legs above their feet, to leap withal upon the earth ; even these of them ye may eat; the locust after his kind, and the bald locust after his kind, and the beetle after his kind, and the grasshopper after his kind. But all other flying creeping things, which have four feet, shall be an abomination unto you.*

Some writers notice four species of locusts that are supposed to be meant here. There is the *locust* (אַרְבֶּה), properly so called, the general representative of the class. It has neither tail nor protuberance. Then there is the locust (סָלְעָם) called here *bald locust*, which has a protuberance ; then another (the תַרְגֹּל), here called *beetle*, that has both the protuberance and a tail ; and a fourth,

called here *grasshopper* (חָגָב), that has a tail but no protuberance.*

All *insects* are unclean except these four classes; for it
is *insects* that are here meant by " the creatures that
both fly (הָעוֹף) and creep," using feet in the manner of
quadrupeds. All reptiles, worms, and insects, *e. g.* flies
and bees, are thus pronounced *unclean*—except only the
four classes that have *springing legs*, in addition to the
legs used in creeping.

The sight of insects, without number, in their groves,
on the leaves of their fig-trees, or the vine-leaves that
shaded them—the innumerable hosts that thickened the
air at sunset, or that played on the waters, and from time
to time alighted on the head of the solemn Jew who
marked the sight—could not fail to remind the soul that
it was encompassed with unholy things. I remember
(while in Palestine in 1839) the vast number of such insects, some of them very beautiful and rare, which we saw
one afternoon by the lake of Galilee, near Magdala; and
also, on a previous day, at the pools of Solomon near
Bethlehem. They skimmed along the waters, or flew
gaily through the air, or kept their seat upon a sappy
leaf—and the eye could not but be attracted by them.
Now, an Israelite would feel in these insects a memorial
of sin, however fair the external form appeared. No re-
tirement into quiet seats and bowers could give freedom
from the presence of what was unclean. The dragon-fly
that wafted itself past their eye, and the many magnificent insects, though fed amid the fragrance of Lebanon
and the excellency of Carmel and Sharon, were all made
to speak of God having set a mark on this earth as no

* Thus Robinson in his *Clavis*, from Ludolph. Some say the locust, the
domestic cricket, the mole-cricket, and the green grasshopper.

longer a Paradise. These creatures on the wing were like messengers sent to admonish the saints of God that the sweetest spots of earth were polluted, and, therefore, they must watch and keep their garments. The only clean insects were the locusts—the insects so often used by God to punish a guilty land and an unclean people.

THE CARCASES OF UNCLEAN CREATURES

Ver. 24–28. And for these ye shall be unclean: whosoever toucheth the carcase of them shall be unclean until the even. And whosoever beareth ought of the carcase of them shall wash his clothes, and be unclean until the even. The carcases of every beast which divideth the hoof, and is not cloven-footed, nor cheweth the cud, are unclean unto you: every one that toucheth them shall be unclean. And whatsoever goeth upon his paws, among all manner of beasts that go on all four, those are unclean unto you: whoso toucheth their carcase shall be unclean until the even. And he that beareth the carcase of them shall wash his clothes, and be unclean until the even: they are unclean unto you.

In ver. 24, "And for *these*" is to be connected with ver. 26. "*For these*," viz. *the carcases of every beast which divideth the hoof*," &c.—not the carcases of insects, which would have been quite overwhelming in number, and in every spot. The four-footed creatures that " go upon their paws" are such as the *jerboa* (the mouse of Isa. lxvi. 17), which uses its fore-paws for holding its food, and leaps with its hind ones.

The *carcase* defiles; thus keeping up in Israel awful impressions of *death*. It defiles because its speaks of *the fall—sin—wrath*—CURSE. They must remember that even Palestine is not Eden. "*Thou shalt die*" is written over all its dwellings; and every dead carcase is a voice crying in their ears, like Abel's blood in the ears of God, "*Thou shalt die!*"

In ver. 25, it is said, " *Whosoever beareth ought of the carcase of them.*" To carry a single portion of the carcase in their hands seemed to intimate the wish or intention to use it for some purpose. Hence they are warned that to be found " bearing the carcase" (ver. 28), or " any part of the carcase" (ver. 25), such as the skin, or bones, would pollute them ; for it connected them with the sign of the first threatening, " *Thou shalt die.*"

The defiled remained unclean "*until the even*" (ver. 25), even after washing their clothes. The washing of the clothes plainly represents the cleansing in the blood of Jesus. The pollution is washed away by Christ's death, applied to them by his Spirit. But why, then, remain unclean " *until even ?* " Why not enter the dwelling of a man of Israel till the day is done ? Why never cross the threshold of a clean and undefiled Israelite until the sun set ? I suppose it was in order to represent the truth, that fallen man, though justified wholly and completely from the sins lying to his charge, and though receiving the Holy Spirit to sanctify his polluted nature, is, never-theless, not entirely free from the effects of his fall till his night has come. At death he lays down his polluted rai-ment and is reckoned quite clean. But in truth it is not till *next morning* that his complete deliverance is apparent to all. It is at the resurrection-morning—after both even-ing and night is past—that it is undeniably evident that all effects of yesterday's defilement are gone. He can now enter the dwellings of the righteous ; he can go up to the' sanctuary; he can stand in the holy hill.

Thus the man, defiled by the touch of death, represents a sinner's state. His washing represents the sinner's using the appointed cleansing given him in the Lord Jesus. His waiting, nevertheless, till evening, ere the effects of

that connexion with death and sin be annulled altogether,
represents the justified—represents you, believer, fully
sensible of your cleansed state, yet aware that your deliverance from *all* the consequences, the misery, and the
shame, and the debasing effect of the fall, will not be
either fully enjoyed or really seen by others till this present day is past, and " the morning star" of the day of
God has risen.   Then you will go forth with joy—though
now you sit in conscious imperfection, often saddened and
often tempted, often groaning and often oppressed.   To
you Paul says, " Now is our salvation nearer than when
we believed"— for not only is the day of our uncleanness gone, but " the night" that intervenes between us
and the coming morn " is far spent; the day is at hand"
(Rom. xiii. 12).

> Ver. 29–31. *These also shall be unclean unto you among the creep-*
> *ing things that creep upon the earth; The weasel, and the*
> *mouse, and the tortoise after his kind, and the ferret, and the*
> *chameleon, and the lizard, and the snail, and the mole.   These*
> *are unclean to you among all that creep: whosoever doth*
> *touch them, when they be dead, shall be unclean until the*
> *even.*

A man of Israel, within the limits of his own field and
farm, is kept in view of memorials of sin; the *mole,*[*]
working up the earth in search of its prey below, attracts
his eye in the heaving ground—or the *mouse* (jerboa) of
the same race that afterward devoured the Philistines'
corn fields (1 Sam. vi. 4)—is seen burrowing in the sandy
soil as he approaches.   Or near some stream,[†] the slow-
moving tortoise drops down into the water at the sound of

---

[*] "*Weasel*" is not the true rendering of חֹלֶד.

[†] I remember multitudes of them at a stream near the lake of Galilee, and in
similar situations.

man's footsteps; and then the doleful cry of the (אֲנָקָה) *gecko*-lizard (not *ferret*), that by its very touch injures the victuals over which it passes its cold body; and the *strong lizard* * forcing its way into the sand to escape its pursuer; and the (לְטָאָה) poisonous, *filthy lizard,* that wallows in dirt and rubbish,—all these keep before him the great truth, that he is in a fallen world, where not only the birds of the sky above, and the animals that roam at liberty around, and the insects of the air, but even the reptiles which his foot might crush, are polluted. Look up, or look around, or look down, memorials of sin abound.

Then, the *snail* and the *chameleon* † on the trees or shrubs; the one filthily spreading its slime over every leaf, the other hanging from a twig, greedily intent on drawing into its mouth the gnats and almost invisible insects that play " in the web of the sunbeams," and changing colour according to the green or yellow hue of the leaf;—these are memorials of uncleanness to the Israelite, held up before him by the sides of his house, or among the tender branches which he is examining. At every point he is startled with some object that speaks of the difference between the clean and the unclean—the holiness of God, and the sin of man.

THINGS ABOUT THEIR HOUSES BECOMING UNCLEAN

Ver. 32–35. And upon whatsoever any of them, when they are dead, doth fall, it shall be unclean; whether it be any vessel

---

* כֹּיחַ is not *chameleon.*

† תִּנְשֶׁמֶת is not the *mole.* It is from נָשַׁם, *to breathe.* Bochart has been followed by most writers in the opinion that this name describes the *chameleon,* which has *lungs* of such vast dimensions, that, when filled, the body is made to appear transparent. It alters the colour of the skin by thus exposing more or less of the blood to the air.

of wood, or raiment, or skin, or sack, whatsoever vessel it be
wherein any work is done, it must be put into water, and it
shall be unclean until the even; so it shall be cleansed. And
every earthen vessel whereinto any of them falleth, whatsoever
is in it shall be unclean; and ye shall break it. Of all meat
which may be eaten, that on which such water cometh shall be
unclean: and all drink that may be drunk in every such vessel
shall be unclean. And every thing whereupon any part of
their carcase falleth shall be unclean;- whether it be oven,
or ranges for pots, they shall be broken: for they are un-
clean, and shall be unclean unto you.

These are the plain, undoubted cases of defilement.
The domestic in the family, engaged in the duties of his
humble lot, has sign-posts set up by God to warn him of
sin. The wooden vessels on his shelves, the skin bottles
that were filled with water, or ready to be used, the
wardrobe of the family, all must be watchfully kept from
pollution.

Their finest cakes, and the richest wines, must be set
aside and cast away, if the touch of the unclean creature
came upon them. The ovens for baking their food, and
the ranges where their pots for boiling stood, must be
disused if a spot of pollution fell upon them.

In this manner *cleanliness* was taught; but much more
holiness. Every vessel must have on it, " *Holiness to the*
Lord;" and the garment spotted by the flesh must be
hated.

Our private walk must be under the Lord's eye. It is
not abroad only, in public, but it is alone and before our
household, that the Lord's will must be done. In the
minute and apparently trifling things of domestic arrangement, we must regulate our actions by a regard to the all-
present, holy Jehovah. In putting on our raiment, instead
of allowing pride to arise, we must ask, Is there not pol-

lution even here ; for the air of earth is tainted? In all things we must have our hearts watchful, and our eye awake, to discern between the holy and the unholy. We must sing Psalm ci. in every room of our house, and with every movement of our hands.

Earthen vessels were to be broken ; other kinds were to be steeped in water for cleansing. The Lord's *two* ways of cleansing the pollution of this earth may be illustrated here. The water of the Deluge steeped earth till it was purified for a time ; but the next mode of cleansing is, " *Seeing all these things shall be dissolved.*" Or rather, it may refer to the Lord's two ways of treating *the polluted.* He either cleanses the polluted sinner by making him the temple of the Holy Ghost, or **he** at length destroys him. Now, the vessel of wood or skin at once parted with the stain and scent of the unclean thing when washed :—so does the justified soul, when washed in the blood of Jesus, and sanctified by the washing of regeneration. On the other hand, the porous earthen vessel imbibes the flavour and will not part with it, even though it be the flavour, of putrefaction :—so the unconverted soul retains his sin and his love to it, imbibes it and does not let it go ; " his taste remaineth in him, and his scent is not changed" (Jer. xlviii. 11) ; he must be broken in pieces and cast away. As a potter's vessel, he shall be dashed in pieces, and with the rod of iron broken for ever (Psalm ii. 9).

> Ver. 36. *Nevertheless a fountain or pit, wherein there is plenty of water, shall be clean : but that which toucheth their carcase shall be unclean.*

Rather read, " *a fountain or pit; in short, any collection of water,*" *e. g.* a pond or lake. An unclean thing falling into these did not pollute the waters ; it was only any thing, or person, " *that touched them*," *e. g.* a man in drawing them out of the pit, that became unclean. Perhaps there was a double reason for this : 1. The wells and water were themselves the means *of washing and cleansing.* 2. This water was typical **of** Him in whom all may find cleansing, without conveying to him any of their defilement. Any other but He, would be polluted by the touch; the man who drew out the carcase would be defiled —but not so the water. Christ can let the leper come near, and can touch him safely, communicating health, while the leprous man cannot convey defilement to his Deliverer. Christ can receive sinners and eat with them, sending forth health and salvation into their polluted souls. John can lean his body of sin and of death upon the bosom of the Saviour. A similar type we have in Naaman, whose leprosy is left in Jordan, and yet Jordan flows on as pure as before.

> Ver. 37, 38. *And if any part of their carcase fall upon any sowing seed which is to be sown, it shall be clean. But if any water be put upon the seed, and any part of their carcase fall thereon, it shall be unclean unto you.*

The husk, or skin, of the seed was between it and the polluting object. But if the seed was not in a sowing state, *i. e.* if it was bruised or ground, then pollution entered. So, if water fell on it, then the water's insinuating qualities, working its way through the pores, would rot the heart. Israel was taught the danger of coming in contact with sin. You must be shielded from its touch : the *husk* taught this. You must shrink back from all appearance of it : the soaking water taught this.

> Ver. 39, 40. *And if any beast of which ye may eat die; he that toucheth the carcase thereof shall be unclean until the even. And he that eateth of the carcase of it shall wash his clothes,*

and be unclean until the even: he also that beareth the carcase
of it shall wash his clothes, and be unclean until the even.

Even clean beasts were polluting if they died by disease, or in course of nature. The remembrance of *sin* entering into the world, and its fatal consequences, was thus kept up. In such cases as these, the *tendency* of all things to corruption was seen.

CREEPING THINGS

Ver. 41–43. *And every creeping thing that creepeth upon the earth shall be an abomination; it shall not be eaten. Whatsoever goeth upon the belly, and whatsoever goeth upon all four, or whatsoever hath more feet among all creeping things that creep upon the earth, them ye shall not eat; for they are an abomination. Ye shall not make yourselves abominable with any creeping thing that creepeth, neither shall ye make yourselves unclean with them, that ye should be defiled thereby.*

The Lord now looked down to the meanest things that moved on the earth, and pointed Israel to them. This notice of them was incidentally a good security against cruelty to insects; it would prevent even their children wantonly injuring them in sport. But, besides, we thus are taught how the Lord, whose eye scans the form of the archangel, and rests on the beauties of holiness throughout his holy heavens, " humbleth himself to behold the things that are on earth."

Those tribes are meant that both *creep and walk*, not as ver. 21, where mention is made of those that fly and leap. It is such tribes as the caterpillar, the worm, and the centipede, whose feet are so short as to be almost unseen, as if it went on its belly. But probably the *serpent-race* is chiefly aimed at; and the others that go on their belly are included because of their connexion with the serpent in their form, or mode of life. These all are unclean; they must remind man of *the fall.* They must recall to

him Satan, the great deceiver (Gen. iii. 14, 15), slily, un-
heard, and unseen, winding his way into the heart of Eden,
and then into the soul of Eve and Adam. The *creeping*
things were natural types of the Fall, representing men
degraded to the very dust, as if bowed on their bellies by
the weight of the curse. And thus, by contrast, the promise of the *Seed of the Woman* would daily be brought
into the minds of Israel. Association would be sufficient
to cause a godly Jew to remember the First Promise every
time a creeping thing crossed his path. A thought of a
coming deliverer would thus dart into his soul, as often
as a serpent darted along. His eye was thus trained to
remember Messiah at all times of the day, and his soul
drawn-forth to expect the time when He should come to
set free creation itself from the bondage of corruption.
The lowest stage of degradation was the very means of
lifting his heart to the hope of the highest blessing—" that
blessed hope !"

How beautiful is this arrangement, by which the Lord
has thus brought us to the feet of his Son, at the close of
so singular an enumeration of the clean and unclean! We
are left to rejoice in Him who sets us free from the uncleanness, and who will also set creation itself free from
the same. " For the creation was made subject to vanity,
not willingly, but by reason of him who subjected the same,
in hope; because the creation itself also shall be delivered
from the bondage of corruption into the glorious liberty
of the children of God" (Rom. viii. 20, 21).

WHAT SHOULD CONSTRAIN TO OBEDIENCE

Ver. 44–47. *For I am the Lord your God: ye shall therefore
sanctify yourselves, and ye shall be holy; for I am holy:
neither shall ye defile yourselves with any manner of creeping
thing that creepeth upon the earth. For I am the Lord that*

> *bringeth you up out of the land of Egypt, to be your God: ye*
> *shall therefore be holy; for I am holy. This is the law of the*
> *beasts, and of the fowl, and of every living creature that*
> *moveth in the waters, and of every creature that creepeth upon*
> *the earth; to make a difference between the unclean and the*
> *clean, and between the beast that may be eaten and the beast*
> *that may not be eaten.*

Nothing, however minute, is to be left undone, if the
Lord has commanded it; and hence ver. 44 joins "*I am
holy*," with "not defiling themselves with *creeping things*."
The infiniteness of his holy authority is seen in its extending from the height of his throne to this low descent.
Holiness in what we call *small matters*, is the surest test
of *real* holiness; for it shews a proper understanding of
the *wide extent and full reach* of Jehovah's holy nature
and law.

It is beautiful, also, to notice, that the Lord now follows up all his statutes by the grand motive, viz. *redemption.* In ver. 44, "I am YOUR GOD," reconciled to you,
and you to me; *therefore,* be holy. In ver. 45, "I am he
that is *bringing you up from Egypt,* your deliverer and
your guide—your Saviour; *therefore,* be holy." His love
to them is the motive that is to constrain them. And if
they ask, *What is holiness?* it is keeping even these laws
(ver. 46, 47).

And thus, in the end, it is seen that *holiness* is the
Lord's design and aim. He longs to have his creatures
freed from all uncleanness, and made holy. He seeks to
hear on earth no longer the cry of wickedness and woe,
but the blissful cry that seraph utters to seraph, "Holy,
holy, holy!"

CHAPTER XII

Original Sin —What has been transmitted to us

"By one man's disobedience, many were made sinners."—Rom. v. 19
"In sin did my mother conceive me."—Ps. li. 5

> Ver. 1, 2. *And the Lord spake unto Moses, saying, Speak unto the children of Israel, saying, If a woman have conceived seed, and born a man-child: then she shall be unclean seven days; according to the days of the separation for her infirmity shall she be unclean.*

It was not needful to give Aaron, whose "lips were to keep knowledge," the regulation of this statute; for it related to a thing of which none could pretend ignorance.

The woman is made unclean by the birth of a child. Why is this? Because the child is born a sinner, an heir of hell! She that bare him is therefore held as unclean. So decided is the Lord's view of the sin of a new-born babe.

She continues unclean for seven days, until the time come when her son is to be recognised as received into the visible Church by circumcision. This attests that *the babe* is born *out of covenant*, and so refers us back to Adam, *outside of Eden.* "Thy *first father* hath sinned" (Isa. xliii. 27), is the fact brought to their mind. *Adam's imputed guilt* rests on his posterity.

Ver. 3, 4. And in the eighth day the flesh of his foreskin shall be circumcised. And she shall then continue in the blood of her purifying three and thirty days: she shall touch no hallowed thing, nor come into the sanctuary, until the days of her purifying be fulfilled.

Iniquity is imputed to the mother for having brought a sinner into the world.   After he is circumcised, *i. e.* recognised as received into covenant with Abraham's God, her imputed sin is reckoned as in some. measure removed.   But still, though she shares to some extent in the benefits which her child receives from the covenant of circumcision, she is to touch nothing hallowed, nor come to hallowed ground for thirty-three days.   *Forty days* is a very common portion of time in all Scripture, *e. g.* forty days the flood advanced; Moses was on the hill forty days; Elijah at Horeb; Christ tempted.   Now, the *seven* and the *thirty-three* are just forty days.*

The child, in after days, must have learnt the lesson of his depravity very deeply, when his mother told him of her forty days' defilement.

Ver. 5. But if she bare a maid-child, then she shall be unclean two weeks, as in her separation; and she shall continue in the blood of her purifying threescore and six days.

The female child keeps the mother unclean double the time.   Perhaps one reason of this was, that the *male* child had had the advantage of the covenant of circumcision, and brought thereby blessing to his mother. Another reason, however, was, "because *the woman was in the transgression*" (1 Tim. ii. 14), and led Adam into

---

* Here let us indulge a conjecture: it is no more than a conjecture. May it have been the case that *Adam and Eve remained only forty days unfallen?* This forty days would thus be a reminiscence of that *only holy time on earth.* The second Adam was *forty days* on earth after his resurrection, recalling to mind earth's time of Paradise.   If this be so, every "*Forty*" that struck upon the ear would be a knell of Paradise lost!

it.   It kept up the remembrance of the Fall, and of the
first sin.

It may have been in reference to such restrictions on
the *female* children that Paul said, " There is neither Jew
nor Greek, there is neither bond nor free, *there is neither
male nor female;* for ye are all one in Christ Jesus"
(Gal. iii. 28).

> Ver. 6–8. *And when the days of her purifying are fulfilled, for a
> son, or for a daughter, she shall bring a lamb of the first year
> for a burnt-offering, and a young pigeon, or a turtle-dove, for
> a sin-offering, unto the door of the tabernacle of the congrega-
> tion, unto the priest: who shall offer it before the Lord, and
> make an atonement for her; and she shall be cleansed from the
> issue of her blood.   This is the law for her that hath born a
> male or a female. And if she be not able to bring a lamb, then
> she shall bring two turtles, or two young pigeons ; the one for
> the burnt-offering, and the other for a sin-offering : and the
> priest shall make an atonement for her, and she shall be clean.*

Her sin is to be brought to the altar at the end of the
appointed time.   And she offers, through the priest, first
of all, a *burnt-offering.*   The burnt-offering was, as we
have often noticed, the basis of all the other sacrifices ;
it was a broad recognition of all the principles of a sinner's acceptance.   After this the specialties of her case
are presented on the altar in the sin-offering, which sin-
offering is to be a pigeon, or a turtle-dove.   This was an
emblem of the child's tender years and apparent innocence,
though guilt lay hid within.   Oh ! how impressively the
mother was taught the need of her infant being washed
in redeeming blood !

All mothers in Israel were to act thus.   And, that none
might plead the excuse of poverty, there is permission to
take a *pigeon* or *turtle-dove* for the burnt-offering.   The
tender lamb and the gentle dove were both appropriate

when offered for a little child ; and the love of God is seen in extending his regard to the poorest by this arrangement. Indeed, there was in it a prospective regard to *Mary and Joseph's* poverty (Luke ii. 22), or, rather this provision was made in order that, when Jesus should be born, he might manifest, by his own poverty, that his salvation was for the poorest on earth—the beggar on the dunghill. In every view we recognise the features of the same glorious Gospel. The voice here may be only a whisper, but it speaks the same truth as at other times ; " Ho ! *every one* that thirsteth, come ye to the waters, and *he that hath no money.*"

And now the mother returnèd home rejoicing, to train up her child for the Lord, who had accepted her; and had taken her pledge that she would do this for him.

CHAPTER XIII

The Leprosy. Indwelling Sin—its horrid Features

"For out of the heart proceed evil thoughts, murders, adulteries, fornica-
tions, thefts, false witness, blasphemies."—Matt. xv. 19

Ver. 1. *And the Lord spake unto Moses and Aaron, saying,—*

AARON is present as well as Moses on this occasion; for the priests were to be judges of leprosy. Hence, the high priest is one of the original receivers of these laws. Jehovah opens up sin under the figure of leprosy—sin, as an evil seen, and disgusting when seen; sin, diffusive as well as penetrating.

An Israelite would naturally turn his thoughts to this chapter when he read such language as Isa. i. 6, "The whole head is sick, and the whole heart faint; from the sole of the foot even unto the head, there is no soundness in it; but wounds, and bruises, and putrifying sores." In Isa. liii. 5, "*Smitten of God*" is connected with "*stricken*" (נָגַע) as if the *stroke of leprosy* (נֶגַע) were a direct infliction of God. The expressions of Psalm xxxviii. are borrowed in many of their turns from the leprosy. Thus, "*My wounds stink and are corrupt*" (ver. 5). "*My loins are filled with a loathsome disease, and there is no soundness in my flesh*" (ver. 7). And these verses are beyond doubt descriptions of the horrid

features of sin.   Job's fearful disease was that more awful
leprosy called *elephantiasis.*

It was a disease which man could never heal; and therefore our Lord manifested no less than Divine power and
Godhead by healing the lepers as much as by raising the
dead.   To turn the pale, loathsome, putrid leper to all
the beautiful vigour and health of a little child, was what
only God could do—only the arm that could raise the
mouldering carcase from the grave.

The pain of common leprosy is not acute, but it
keeps the man restless and sad.   It is like *sin* in fallen
man—the cause of his restlessness and sadness, the root
of his unsatisfied desires ; yet not itself felt keenly.

Leprosy is also corrosive, and penetrates unseen—
almost unfelt—till it has wasted the substance : like *sin*
in the soul, eating out its beauty and its very life, while
outwardly the sinner moves about as before.   At length
it bursts forth externally, too—the man becomes a skele-
ton, and a mass of noisome corruption.   So does sin at
length deface the whole image of God, and every faint
vestige of comeliness that was left.   And *death* is the
sure end.

The Lord sent forth such a disease on earth after the
Fall,* to form, it would seem, a type of sin.   The workings
of the leprosy seem appointed by him on very purpose to
shew forth *sin* in all its features.

Ver. 2. *When a man shall have in the skin of his flesh a rising, a
scab, or bright spot, and it be in the skin of his flesh like the
plague of leprosy; then he shall be brought unto Aaron the
priest, or unto one of his sons the priests.*

Here are three indications of leprosy begun :—1. "*A*

* Perhaps, too, in greater frequency before Christ's coming than afterwards,
as in the parallel case of the Demoniacs; in order to give greater emphasis to
the felt necessity for a Deliverer.

rising," or boil.   2. "*A scab,*" or small tumour.   3. "*A bright spot.*"   There is inquiry to be made into the slightest indications of the disease ; if not prominent as a boil or a tumour, yet as a "bright spot" it may be there. Observe the first appearances of evil in your soul.   Detect the leprosy by what you see in your heart's desire, if not in your words, or in acts.   It is said, that "*the bright spot*" which indicates a leprosy begun is often so small that it is like pustules made by the pricking of a pin ; and so may be your first slight, passing wish, or half-curious look upon forbidden fruit.

It is also known that one infected with this disease may live long ; one born with it may live fifty years ; one who got it by contagion, twenty years (Jahn's *Archæologie*) ; and then in the end die suddenly, and leave the same awful disease to his children.   It was thus with *Adam ;* in him it began with no more than a small "bright spot" —yon fruit so fair, pleasant, to be desired. It then wrought in him all the 930 years of his lifetime—and he left it to us.

A *special* sin often resembles the beginning of leprosy ; as, for example, Noah's drinking too freely of the wine that was the produce of the first grapes that grew on the new earth.

GENERAL RULES AS TO ALL THE THREE SYMPTOMS

> Ver. 3. *And the priest shall look on the plague in the skin of the flesh ; and when the hair in the plague is turned white, and the plague in sight be deeper than the skin of his flesh, it is a plague of leprosy: and the priest shall look on him, and pronounce him unclean.*

Leprosy begins far within—in the bones and marrow ; and sometimes three or four years elapse ere it come out to sight (Jahn's *Archæol.*)   This typical view of sin we see

realised in the case of the tender infant, who lies so inno-
cent-like on the mother's breast.   Or, if we take the case
of special sins, we see it in David, who seemed of all men
the least likely to be guilty of adultery and murder on
the day when he sang Psalm xxxvi. or Psalm xxxii.   Or
in Hazael, when he honestly exclaimed, "Is thy servant
a dog, that he should do this great thing?" (2 Kings
viii. 13.)

If the "*hair was turned white*," and the plague evidently
"*deeper than the skin*," then two things were evident, viz.
that corruption was begun in the blood, and that it was
not superficial.   There was a tendency to decay, and a
tendency in this decay to advance inwards.   Were it a
mere external deformity, there might be little alarm felt;
but not so when there are tokens that decay is begun
near the seat of life.   By this the Lord taught Israel that
mere acts of sin would not be so alarming, were it not
that they indicated evil in purpose and feeling—a sinful
nature—deep-seated depravity within.

The priest was to examine and pronounce him unclean.
Our Priest, Jesus, has eyes of fire, to discern sin in his
people.   He detects its first risings.   We ought to be of
the same mind with our Priest; as anxious as he to detect
sin.   For it is not as *Judge*, but as *Priest*, that he lays it
bare to our view.   These eyes of flame are in our *Priest*
(see Rev. i. 14) when he visits his golden candlesticks.
And so we may willingly submit to have our filthiness
brought to light, when One standeth by who is ready that
very moment to cleanse it away.   Oh! there is sweet comfort in the words, "*The priest* shall pronounce him unclean."
To be completely convicted of sin casts us completely
into the hands of that High Priest who does not drive us
from the sanctuary, but fits us for its holy services.   The

deep convictions which his Holy Spirit works are meant
to direct the eye of the unclean to the cleansing Priest.
Our High Priest sends the Spirit to the sinner, and the
Spirit sends the sinner to the High Priest. "So," says
one, "when the Prodigal *had spent all*, and was famishing
with hunger, the blessing came."

THE BRIGHT SPOT

Ver. 4-8. *If the bright spot be white in the skin of his flesh, and in
sight be not deeper than the skin, and the hair thereof be not
turned white; then the priest shall shut up him that hath the
plague seven days : and the priest shall look on him the seventh
day : and, behold, if the plague in his sight be at a stay, and
the plague spread not in the skin, then the priest shall shut him
up seven days more. And the priest shall look on him again
the seventh day; and, behold, if the plague be somewhat dark,
and the plague spread not in the skin, the priest shall pronounce him clean ; it is but a scab: and he shall wash his
clothes, and be clean. But if the scab spread much abroad in
the skin, after that he hath been seen of the priest for his cleansing, he shall be seen of the priest again: and if the priest see
that, behold, the scab spreadeth in the skin, then the priest shall
pronounce him unclean : it is a leprosy.*

If no proof appeared of deep-seated corruption (which
is meant by its being "*in the skin*," and "no *whiteness* in
the hair"), it was not a leprosy ; but, until it be ascertained that there is none such, the man must be kept
apart from others seven days. "Abstain from all appearance of evil." The six days of his confinement might be
expected to be a season wherein the disease would take a
turn ; God had appointed that period of probation.

God taught Israel that he is not in haste to condemn.
"He is slow to anger." Time is afforded for full proof.
He allows the sinner a long day, during which the man's
leprosy is plainly manifested. He allows the fallen world

its six days—its 6000 years—during which time no
judgment is pronounced on it.   He waits for the seventh
day, when the priest, who has examined already into the
case, shall come and see the " shut up " leper, and declare
his doom.   " God hath concluded them all in unbelief,"
said Paul, in Romans xi. 32.   The original is " hath
shut them up together " (συνεκλεισε), and seems to be borrowed from this case of the leper.   And so in Gal. iii.
22, " The Scripture hath concluded "—shut up together
—" all under sin, that the promise by faith of Jesus
Christ might be given to them that believe."   The whole
world is allowed time to prove itself sinful—utterly sinful ; and then the priest comes and deals with them,
either for their cleansing, or for their eternal exclusion
from the camp !

If in the leprous-looking spot there was no *spreading*
of the disease (ver. 5), this was so far well.   Corruption
is stayed, or else never was begun.   Such a man is to
have the trial of six days, and on the seventh to be examined.   And if, on the seventh day, there is proof that
there is no spreading (ver. 6) of the plague, and that the
hair is darker than it was, the man is set free.   Now,
here we have the case of *souls pardoned*—God's company of *pardoned ones,* whom he treats for 6000 years
in the way of probation.   They shew that the disease
has been stayed—pardon has brought in the new principle
of holiness.   They are not to be excluded from the camp
on the seventh day.   The staying of the leprosy in the
soul—the ceasing from sin—proves that there has been
forgiveness of sin.   If the lower waters of Jordan are
ever getting shallower, then the upper waters must have
been cut off.

But if, after an *apparent* healing, the scab spread (ver.

7), then the man is a leper after all. Is this not typical
of him who, after appearing to be one of the justified,
returns to his old sins? True, believers have a *scab*
remaining—they have remnants of corruptions; but if
this scab—these remnants of corruptions—spread over
the soul, is not the man an unforgiven man? This is
not opposed to the doctrine of perseverance to the end,
any more than are Christ's words, "If a man abide not
in me, he is cast forth as a branch, and is withered"
(John xv. 6). It is speaking to us according to external
appearance.

THE RISING

*Ver. 9–11. When the plague of leprosy is in a man, then he shall
be brought unto the priest; and the priest shall see him: and,
behold, if the rising be white in the skin, and it have turned the
hair white, and there be quick raw flesh in the rising, it is an
old leprosy in the skin of his flesh: and the priest shall pronounce him unclean, and shall not shut him up; for he is
unclean.*

Where there is a rising or tumour, which has the skin
white, and the hair in it white, and quick raw flesh also
in the swelling, then there is no doubt of the disease
being there. "*It is a leprosy grown old* (נוֹשֶׁנֶת) *in the
skin.*" Not only the flower has died, but also the very
soil in which it grew is dead.—(Procopius apud Patrick.)
These symptoms put the case beyond doubt. Treat the
man, then, as unclean.

Here we see that the discovery of *inward corruption*
is the strongest reason that can occur for at once pronouncing the man unclean. It is stronger far than any
abundance of external marks. And so, in God's view,
the *existence of corruption in the heart* is far worse than
all its effects on the life. The fact that the sinner's soul

is long ago corrupt—that it is infected by a leprosy that is grown old—that it inherits depravity and enmity to God,—this aggravates the sinner's awful state. On bringing out this to light, the Judge at once may say, " What need we any further witnesses ?" The *white rising* and the *white hair,* and the *quick raw flesh,* are traced back to a deep-seated disease within that manifests itself in these forms ; so, the foolish talk, the giddy conduct, and the worldly heart, are traced back to their source, viz. a nature totally depraved. The proof is complete. The sinner is utterly lost. " Who can bring a clean thing out of an unclean ?" Let him take his true position—out of the camp—among the unclean!

> Ver. 12–17. *And if a leprosy break out abroad in the skin, and the leprosy cover all the skin of him that hath the plague from his head even to his foot, wheresoever the priest looketh; then the priest shall consider: and, behold, if the leprosy have covered all his flesh, he shall pronounce him clean that hath the plague: it is all turned white: he is clean. But when raw flesh appeareth in him, he shall be unclean. And the priest shall see the raw flesh, and pronounce him to be unclean; for the raw flesh is unclean: it is a leprosy. Or if the raw flesh turn again, and be changed unto white, he shall come unto the priest; and the priest shall see him: and, behold, if the plague be turned into white, then the priest shall pronounce him clean that hath the plague: he is clean.*

Some think a reference is made to this verse (ver. 12) in Isaiah i. 5, " *From the sole of the foot even unto the head, there is no soundness in it.*" If there be, the reference is to the entireness of the outward, visible spread of corruption in the land, in Isaiah's days.

At first sight it seems strange, to ordain that the man should be reckoned *clean,* if the leprosy were out upon him, and covered him wholly. The reason, however, may be, first, natural ; secondly, moral. If *natural,* then it is either because the leprosy is not so infectious when it has thus come all out on the body, the hard, dry scurf not being likely to spread infection, whereas the ichor of raw flesh would have this effect ; or, because it really is not a proper leprosy if it so come out—it is a salt humour cast out by the strength of the man's constitution, and is not deep-seated. It is rather a relief to the constitution ; even as when measles or small-pox come out to the surface of the body, recovery is hopeful. If it was for *a moral* reason, then it seems meant to teach that the Lord has a deep abhorrence of a *corrupt nature* —deeper far than merely of corrupt actions. We are ever ready to take home the guilt of *evil deeds,* but to palliate the evil of a *depraved heart.* But the Lord reverses the case. His severest judgment is reserved for *inward* depravity. He hates Sodom's lewdness and open vice ; but he hates yet more Bethsaida's *heart of unbelief,* wherein, as on a couch, all Sodom's vice could softly repose within its inner chamber. And yet more. Is it not when a soul is fully sensible of entire corruption, as Isa. i. 5, that salvation is nearest ? A complete Saviour for a complete sinner ?

If there appeared any "*raw flesh,*" then the man is unclean. For this indicates inward disease—not on the surface only. It is working into the flesh.

But if the "*raw flesh*" turn and be "*changed into white,*" then it is plain that the disease is not gone inwards ; it is playing on the skin only. Let him stand, therefore, as clean.

Perhaps the case of a *pardoned man* may be referred to again in this type. His iniquity comes *all out to view,* when it is thrown into the fountain opened ; and the

inner source of it is checked. The seat of corruption has
been removed. But if, after the appearance of pardon,
the man turn aside to folly (if "raw flesh" appear), he
is to be counted unclean. If, however, this turning aside
to folly be checked, if this backsliding be healed, then it
is like the "raw flesh" turning "into white"—it evi-
dences that his *nature* is sound—it has not returned to
its state of thorough depravity.

THE BOIL

Ver. 18–23. *The flesh also, in which, even in the skin thereof, was
a boil, and is healed, and in the place of the boil there be a
white rising, or a bright spot, white, and somewhat reddish,*
and it be shewed to the priest; and if, when the priest seeth it,
behold, it be in sight lower than the skin, and the hair thereof
be turned white, the priest shall pronounce him unclean: it is
a plague of leprosy broken out of the boil. But if the priest
look on it, and, behold, there be no white hairs therein, and if
it be not lower than the skin, but be somewhat dark, then the
priest shall shut him up seven days. And if it spread much
abroad in the skin, then the priest shall pronounce him unclean: it is a plague. But if the bright spot stay in his place,
and spread not, it is a burning † boil; and the priest shall pronounce him clean.*

Old ulcers were to be carefully watched, lest they
became means of the infection more easily insinuating
itself into the person. If the healed ulcer have any
mark like a white rising or bright spot, wherein the hair
is turned white, then corruption is at work below the
skin. As in former cases, however, if there was no sign
apparent of its spreading, there must be seven days' pro-

---

* אֲדַמְדֶּמֶת, " exceedingly shining," the inflammation being very red, or glisten-
ing so as to be even like snow.—*Patrick.* Hence ver. 24, " *reddish* or *white.*"

† Rosenmüller, from the Arabic root of צָרֶבֶת, renders it, " it is the *mark* of a
boil ;" and so the Vulgate, Septuagint, and Syriac.

bation. The spreading would shew that the blood was much vitiated.

Israel were thus taught to watch against new sins, after old ones were healed; or, more especially, the danger of coming near infection after being once delivered from the vicious atmosphere. Pardoned men must be jealous men. " Avoid it, pass not by it; turn from it, and pass away."

It taught, also, that marks, or remnants of former sins, may remain, though the *leprosy* be not there. Remains of an old peevish temper, of a proud, haughty demeanour, of a hasty judgment, of a taste for some earthly things, may exist in a pardoned man. They are remnants— scars—of an old wound. But if these indicate a tendency to spread, or shew that they are " deeper than the skin," then the leprosy is there—the man, in spite of other appearances, is really an unforgiven, unsaved man.

THE HOT BURNING

Ver. 24–28.   Or if there be any flesh, in the skin whereof there is a hot burning, and the quick flesh that burneth have a white bright spot, somewhat reddish or white, then the priest shall look upon it: and, behold, if the hair in the bright spot be turned white, and it be in sight deeper than the skin, it is a leprosy broken out of the burning: wherefore the priest shall pronounce him unclean: it is the plague of leprosy.   But if the priest look on it, and, behold, there be no white hair in the bright spot, and it be no lower than the other skin, but be somewhat dark, then the priest shall shut him up seven days: and the priest shall look upon him the seventh day; and if it be spread much abroad in the skin, then the priest shall pronounce him unclean: it is the plague of leprosy.   And if the bright spot stay in his place, and spread not in the skin, but it be somewhat dark, it is a rising of the burning, and the priest shall pronounce him clean: for it is an inflammation of the burning.*

* " *Mark of the burning,*" as at ver. 23. And so ver. 10 and 25, מִחְיַת is

For ver. 24 see note on ver. 19.   The meaning of the expression, "*hot burning*," is rather obscure.   Some think it was an *erysipelas;* others, that it was a hurt caused by the falling of some hot iron on the spot.   The rules to be observed in examining it are the same as above.   God is still the same holy, jealous God, but also the same long-suffering God—waiting calmly till the sin be undoubted, not swift to take advantage of mere symptoms. O how ungodlike it is "to make a man an offender for a word!"

We seem, also, to be taught another lesson here, viz. that in all keen suffering there is a tendency to sin.   In all diseases that made the flesh raw, there was a tendency to leprosy.   A time of suffering, of whatever sort be the suffering, should be a time of vigilance on our part, lest it end in sin.   Many things provoke, many things gall and irritate, many things tend to make us selfish, and so to lead us to forget God.

Again : the *staying* of the symptoms was to be taken favourably.   In this we see our God again—ready to forgive.   If Ahab put on sackcloth, then the Lord turns away from immediate vengeance.   If Nineveh repent, and "the bright spot is somewhat dark," then the Lord pronounces them *clean*.   If Ephesus lose her "first love," there is a " bright spot ; " but as yet there is no "white hair on the bright spot," and possibly it may not be "lower than the skin;" therefore Ephesus is shut up seven days, with the warning, "Remember from whence thou art fallen, and repent, and do thy first works, or else I will come unto thee quickly, and will remove thy candlestick out of his place, except thou repent" (Rev. ii. 5).

rendered by Rosenmüller from the Syriac, "*a mark*."   Onkelos in the Targum has rendered it so.

DISEASE IN THE HEAD, OR IN THE BEARD.

Ver. 29–34. *If a man or woman have a plague upon the head or the beard; then the priest shall see the plague: and, behold, if it be in sight deeper than the skin, and there be in it a yellow thin hair, then the priest shall pronounce him unclean: it is a dry scall, even a leprosy upon the head or beard. And if the priest look on the plague of the scall, and, behold, it be not in sight deeper than the skin, and that there is no black hair in it; then the priest shall shut up him that hath the plague of the scall seven days. And in the seventh day the priest shall look on the plague: and, behold, if the scall spread not, and there be in it no yellow hair, and the scall be not in sight deeper than the skin; he shall be shaven, but the scall shall he not shave; and the priest shall shut up him that hath the scall seven days more. And in the seventh day the priest shall look on the scall: and, behold, if the scall be not spread in the skin, nor be in sight deeper than the skin; then the priest shall pronounce him clean: and he shall wash his clothes, and be clean.*

Leprosy might begin, not only in the skin, but even under the hair of the head, or in the beard. Sin may originate in most unlooked-for ways and places, and must be watched against everywhere. The *head* and the *beard* are the proper seat of honour, or of what is seemly and lovely to look upon. When the hair became "*yellow,*" corruption was at work, changing the bushy hair into lank tufts, and the healthy colour into a yellow paleness. Herein the change of external aspect, produced by sin, is declared.

But as it was possible that the hair might really be drawing its nourishment from the vitality of the body, notwithstanding this unfavourable symptom, there is to be caution shewn. The inner parts may be sound; this may be only a scall on the head, and not a leprosy.

Again we see the character of our God. 1. *How holy*

is he! The first rising of evil is watched and pointed at
with hatred. 2. *How loving* is he! He deals most tenderly with the suspected man. 3. *How just* is he! It
must be noonday clearness ere he pronounces sentence;
all doubt must be gone!

> Ver. 35-37. *But if the scall spread much in the skin after his*
> *cleansing; then the priest shall look on him: and, behold, if*
> *the scall be spread in the skin, the priest shall not seek for*
> *yellow hair; he is unclean. But if the scall be in his sight at*
> *a stay, and that there is black hair grown up therein; the*
> *scall is healed, he is clean: and the priest shall pronounce him*
> *clean.*

The examination is never allowed to go into other
hands than the priest's, whose skill, and experience, and
compassion fitted him best for the work.   Oh, how sweet
to know that "the Father judgeth no man, but hath
committed *all* judgment unto the Son"! (John v. 22.)
He leaves us to be judged by no new standard, but just
by that same standard whereby Jesus judged when on
earth.   Therefore, we may be assured that, for *every* sin
that the Judge will bring to light in us, there is a remedy
in the blood of his own atonement.

The unchecked spread of the disease proves him a
leper.   So does the unchecked flow of sin prove a man a
child of hell! you need not to insist on "the yellow hair"
—the *outward* indications; if the man's *heart* be as before, he is unclean!   "For he that is born of God sinneth
not."

We have a God ready to bless!   If the "*hair be black,*"
and "*the scall at a stay*"—the conduct changed and the
heart cleansed—then there is no waiting, no suspense of
seven days; but, on the contrary, immediate acquittal.
No man, who was clean, was to be kept in uncertainty of
his cleanness; and no man, when cleansed from every

symptom, to be detained in a probationary state. We
see the very features of the Lord's merciful haste to the
sinner. *Immediate* pardon—*full and present* assurance
—restoration to his love and favour *on the spot*—liberty
that hour.

FRECKLED SPOTS NOT LEPROSY

Ver. 38, 39. *If a man also or a woman have in the skin of*
their flesh bright spots, even white bright spots; then the priest
shall look: and, behold, if the bright spots in the skin of their
flesh be darkish white; it is a freckled spot that groweth in the
skin: he is clean.

These spots might be only a cutaneous eruption; but
they were grounds of suspicion, because leprosy often
begins in this form. But spots so small, not altering the
colour of the hair, appearing only on the neck and face,
are only the sign of what they called "*Bochak,*" an eruption that passed away soon.

The Lord as carefully guards against imputing to a
man more than is due, as against letting a man escape
from what is his due. He holds the balance even. "A
God of truth and without iniquity"—he turneth neither
to the right hand nor left.

BALDNESS

Ver. 40–44. *And the man whose hair is fallen off his head, he is*
bald; yet is he clean. And he that hath his hair fallen off
from the part of his head toward his face, he is forehead bald:
yet is he clean. And if there be in the bald head, or bald
forehead, a white reddish sore, it is a leprosy sprung up in his
bald head, or his bald forehead. Then the priest shall look
upon it: and, behold, if the rising of the sore be white reddish
in his bald head, or in his bald forehead, as the leprosy ap-
peareth in the skin of the flesh, he is a leprous man, he is un-
clean: the priest shall pronounce him utterly unclean; his
plague is in his head.

The falling off of hair from the forehead indicated some decay; yet it might not be any more than on the surface. The Great Physician knows what are not indications of deep corruption, as well as what are. Ceasing from some busy undertaking may, at one time, be no proof of any real decay of inward love; whereas, at other times, it may be the outward discovery of lukewarmness which had been long going on within secretly. When the disciples all fled, this was "*the hair of the forehead*" decayed; yet still there was no "white, reddish sore." When, however, the many, in John vi. 66, went back, and walked no more with Jesus, this falling off of hair that looked fair before, brought into view the leprosy that had been working its way behind this concealment. When *John Mark* left Paul and Barnabas, there was a call for the physician examining. Paul suspected a hidden leprosy. It turned out that there was none. When *Simon Magus* offered money to Peter, "his bald head and forehead" too plainly revealed "the rising of the sore, white, reddish."

> Ver. 45, 46. *And the leper in whom the plague is, his clothes shall be rent, and his head bare, and he shall put a covering upon his upper lip, and shall cry, Unclean, unclean. All the days wherein the plague shall be in him he shall be defiled; he is unclean: he shall dwell alone;* without the camp shall his habitation be.*

The leper, in this state of declared uncleanness, is the awful type of a sinner under sentence of wrath.

His "*clothes are to be rent*,"† just as in all cases of

---

* The Septuagint here use the expression, " κεχωρισμενος καθησεται." Thorough separation from other men may be the thing expressed. So, when Jesus is said to have been " κεχωρισμενος ἀπο τῶν ἁμαρτωλῶν " (Heb. vii. 26), as thorough a separation as this here is meant—only, men are the lepers, HE is the Untainted One.

† The word פְּרֻמִים, is "*ripped up—seamed;*" perhaps as a sign that the passages of death were opened. Death enters by these rent seams, and the curse

mourning and woe. This indicated that the leper was now exposed to the full view of God and man in his state of decay and corruption. It is added, " His *head bare.*" All coverings are stript off, as in the case of one mourning for the dead. For the leper was counted as dead in his flesh; as we read in Num. xii. 12, when Miriam's leprosy was prayed for, " Let her not be as one dead; of whom the flesh is half consumed when he cometh out of his mother's womb." So, also, he "*covers his upper lip*" —another token of woe. His mouth is regarded as shut; he cannot speak to men any longer, only through the shroud comes the half-suppressed cry, " *Unclean, unclean!*" The pale, ghastly face—the covering spread up to the sunk and hollow eyes—the unsightly form muffled up from view to hide corruption and putrefying sores—all conveyed the idea of one already cut off from the number of living men, lingering at the gates of death and hanging about its door-posts, impatient for entrance there. He is forced to dwell alone, "as those who have long been dead;" permitted to come only within sight of the camp, but not to enter; tantalised by seeing afar off the happy tents of healthy, holy Israel. He sits without,* in mourning and sadness, pining away in his woe—every vein in every limb running down with putrid blood, his head sick and pained, his countenance disgusting the on-looker by the sallow hue of death, his mind filled with sad remembrances and gloomy imaginations. A gray blister, indicating the rising boil, now and then spots his temples;

---

follows it. " He in whose flesh evil prevails is preparing sorrow for himself, and bringing himself, in his wilfulness, into the condition of a mourner."—*Dealings of God with the Leprous Man* (tract).

* Ps. lxxxviii. 4 is to be thus understood : " *Free,*" is חָפְשִׁי, the peculiarly appropriate term for one " set apart as a leper." It is used of Uzziah. Then, " *Among the dead;*" like one dead, as we see above in the leper's case.

the hair hangs dry, lank, and sapless on his brow; the
nails of his bony fingers are discoloured and tainted. He
moves his body slowly, tottering along on feet that are
nearly powerless; and men "hide their faces from him"
(Isa. liii. 3) as he draws near. Even the wild Arab,
scouring past on his swift steed, starts at the loathsome
spectacle, and hastens away. The leper himself feels life
ebbing slowly; the blood still flows, but it is not with the
freedom of health; and the arteries have no longer their
full floods, like rushing torrents, but are clogged with
thick, clammy, sluggish moisture.

Here is the state of the sinner, not in the second
death, but in this world, in his exclusion from the Lord's
presence and dead in sin. The inner man has lost every
principle of holiness; his powers are withered, and every
sinew shrunk. Any attempts at spiritual motions are
slow and lifeless. Streams of putrid impurity burst forth
in his soul. His eye has none of the brightness of one
gazing on a holy God and a reconciled countenance, but
indicates an absence of all that can really cheer or delight.
The deathlike hue of the whole form proclaims the total
departure of the breath of God and the Divine nature.
From such a soul, God turns away his face. Nor can
the sinner pretend to any fellowship with the saints, or
any right to a place in the camp of Israel. Often he sees
their joy; he is present in their solemnities, and looks on
from afar, and feels his misery deepened by the contrast
of these happy multitudes. His own conscience compels
him to cry, "Unclean, unclean!"

Such was Isaiah's experience for a time, when, with
no more than the remnants and remembrance of his
leprosy, he entered the holy sanctuary above. Such is
every convinced soul's experience in the day of the

Spirit's dealing with it; when the High Priest has begun his treatment of the sin-sick soul, compelling it to uncover its head and rend its garment, and, with lips covered up, to take the position of one exposed to death and curse.

Yet all this is but *the shadow* of death. Convictions here, and fears and terrors here, are only faint shadows. Death itself—the second death—which casts this shadow, is behind. And then the leprous soul is eternally loathsome, eternally abhorred, eternally dead and corrupt, eternally excluded from the fellowship of saints, eternally hid from the face of God, and eternally within hearing and sight of happy Israel, though there is a gulf that cannot be passed, between! And none will or can offer sympathy to the eternally exiled man!

Oh, leprous soul, a High Priest passes through thy country now, who could deliver thee from thy diseases! Come, come, though thou hast sat alone under thy juniper-tree, apart from men, these many, many days! Come, though in vain thou hast hitherto looked for any abatement of thy disease! Perhaps no man ever cared for thy soul? Perhaps thou hast looked on the right hand, and there was no man that would know thee? Perhaps it is long since refuge failed thee? But a High Priest is in the land, who can deliver thee. He takes thee as thou art; he pronounces thee as thou really art, "*Unclean, unclean;*" and then he stoops down and says, "*Look unto me, and be saved!*" He passes by; he walks on the outside of the city, where the lepers are sitting, wistfully looking in through its gates, yet not daring to enter; he will soon enter in, and shut its everlasting gates! Invite him near; nay, he is near. "He it is that talketh with thee!" He has blood that cleanses from all sin. His touch is healing ; his look is life ! But if once in hell, thou art for ever and for ever miserable. No balm of Gilead is there : no tidings of a leaf of the healing tree! The High Priest that can deliver never passes through that cursed land. Leprosy is eternal there ; and therefore wailing and woe never end. " He that hath ears to hear, let him hear !"

LEPROSY IN GARMENTS

Ver. 47, 48. The garment also that the plague of leprosy is in, whether it be a woollen garment or a linen garment, whether it be in the warp or woof, of linen, or of woollen, whether in a skin, or in any thing made of skin;—

This *leprosy in garments* is to represent something quite different from leprosy in the man himself. It is to be a type of sin and defilement, not in his person, but in *the things around him.* Anything *round about the man* is this *garment;* the circumstances in the midst of which he is placed, the business he engages in, the comforts that impart a warmth to his person, the occurrences that affect his daily feeling. When Jude (ver. 23) speaks of " the garment spotted by the flesh," he evidently means the person's external contact with the world around him; and when the few names in Sardis are commended because "they *have not defiled their garments*" (Rev. iii. 4), reference is made to the allurements and sinful habits of all around them.

A *clothes-leprosy* and *house-leprosy* may have existed then, though it does not now ; just like the case of the *demoniacs,* in the time of our Lord. And the plague that was called *leprosy* in garments, was correlative to that disease in the human subject. It is like (as observed by others) the application of the term " *cancer*" to a disease of trees, and of "*rot*" to a disease among sheep. As the skin of the leper is fretted away, so there is a mode in which garments may be affected analogous to this—when vermin or animalculæ settle secretly in the garment, and fret away the threads. *Michaëlis* mentions, what is called "*dead-wool*," that is, wool of sheep that died by disease ; and it is found to be bad, losing the points, and ready to be settled in by vermin. Cloth made of it soon becomes very bare, and then full of holes. Such is the literal circumstance from which the type is taken. Learn, reader, to wear no garment that is exposed to corrosive influences. Frequent no company that has a *fretting leprosy*—unsound at heart, and communicating its unsoundness to you. Withdraw from the wells of *Esek* and *Sitnah* (Gen. xxvi. 20, 21), like Isaac, when you feel that there is evil in the situation, and the men who are there. If much prosperity is apt to make you settle on your lees, like Israel (Deut. viii. 11) when they had eaten to the full, and walked among their countless flocks, and heaped up silver and gold—then, shake the garment ; beware of Atheism ; " beware that thou forget not the Lord thy God."

It was of little consequence how goodly the garment appeared. Be not deceived by a fair show. Whether the garment was wrought of materials got from the animal creation (" wool "), or from the vegetable world ("linen"); or whether it was composed of a mixture of threads, those in the warp being of wool, those in the woof of linen, or flax ; nay, though it were a strong garment of skin, or of some manufacture of skin *—whether of simple, primeval strength and roughness, or fashioned into a finer texture —still, if there was the least ground for suspicion, it must be subject to instant examination, however costly, and

---

* מְלֶאכֶת עוֹר, " work—manufacture of skin."

however esteemed for comfort.   You must not judge of
the innocuous nature of an employment or a possession
by its appearance only, nor by its suitableness to your
taste, nor by the estimation in which it is held; you must
be prepared to admit examination.

Ver. 49–59. *And if* the plague be greenish or reddish in the
garment, or in the skin, either in the warp, or in the woof,
or in any thing of skin; it is a plague of leprosy, and
shall be shewed unto the priest.   And the priest shall look
upon the plague, and shut up it that hath the plague seven
days.   And he shall look on the plague on the seventh day: if
the plague be spread in the garment, either in the warp, or in
the woof, or in a skin, or in any work that is made of skin,
the plague is a fretting leprosy; it is unclean.   He shall therefore burn that garment, whether warp or woof, in woollen or
in linen, or any thing of skin, wherein the plague is: for it is a
fretting leprosy; it shall be burnt in the fire.   And if the priest
shall look, and, behold, the plague be not spread in the garment, either in the warp, or in-the woof, or in any thing of
skin; then the priest shall command that they wash the thing
wherein the plague is, and he shall shut it up seven days more.
And the priest shall look on the plague after that it is washed:
and, behold, if the plague have not changed his colour, and the
plague be not spread, it is unclean; thou shalt burn it in the
fire: it is fret inward, whether it be bare within or without.†
And if the priest look, and, behold, the plague be somewhat
dark after the washing of it; then he shall rend it out of the
garment, or out of the skin, or out of the warp, or out of the
woof.   And if it appear still in the garment, either in the warp,
or in the woof, or in any thing of skin, it is a spreading
plague: thou shalt burn that-wherein the plague is with fire.
And the garment, either warp or woof, or whatsoever thing of*

· * "*And if.*"   Connect this verse with ver. 47, "The garment, *if there be*
in it . . . *and if* the plague be *greenish*."   The Hebrew is so, בּוֹ יִהְיֶה כִּי and
וְהָיָה.   The word for *greenish* is יְרַקְרַק, intense green; such as is seen in the
wings of a peacock, or leaf of a palm-tree.—*Maimonides apud Patr.*

† Rosenmüller renders this rightly.   It is a fretting leprosy, whether on the
left side of the cloth (the bare side) or on the right side (the shaggy side)—
whether on one side or other.

*skin it be, which thou shalt wash, if the plague be departed
from them, then it shall be washed the second time, and shall
be clean. This is the law of the plague of leprosy in a
garment of woollen or linen, either in the warp or woof, or
any thing of skins, to pronounce it clean, or to pronounce it
unclean.*

A garment really infected must be *burnt.* There must
be a final forsaking of every real sin. " If thy right
hand offend thee, cut it off ; " or if not, " thou goest to
hell-fire, where their worm dieth not, and *the fire* is
not quenched."

Every approach to sin is hateful to God; therefore, even
on suspicion of evil, examine anxiously. If there be even
suspicion as to a garment, the priest shuts it up—lays it
by. So you give over the company which you are afraid
has an injurious influence on you; you give up the meats
about which you are *in doubt* (Rom. xiv. 15), or about
which your brother is in doubt. If you can really rend
out the spotted part, this is well. David's pride of heart
when he numbered the people, must be rent from him
by the sharp stroke that cut off 70,000 threads of life.
Hezekiah's pride must be rent off by the sword that is
to destroy his people, and carry his wealth to Babylon.
Peter's self-confidence must be torn from him, by his
being placed among the other disciples in abasement ;
" Lovest thou me *more than these ?* "

If, however, again the plague break out, the garment
is no doubt deeply spoiled. It is to be burnt. Thus,
when Israel's plenty and security—their garment of
beauty and comfort—led them to indulgence and sin, the
Lord rent off the pieces. But when, at last, the same sin
unceasingly returned, then he cast them away into an
enemy's land.

But lastly, if the garment out of which the piece was

rent be found remaining clean, then " *let it be washed a second time.*" Let *Peter*, after his recovery from his fall, be warned once more, to impress the special need he has of securing himself against the temptation in time to come. There is to be no doubtful holiness with God. He requires in his people definite and distinct purity. He likes us to make much use of his Holy Spirit, so that our freedom from the world's snares and the world's maxims may be plain to every eye. Oh, how holy is our God! How holy in himself! His heart has no other than *holiness* as its feeling. And when his eye looks abroad on us, it is *holiness* it searches for. He seeks for holiness in our *person*, and holiness in our *circumstances* —a holy people moving amid holiness! Hence it was that when Isaiah was enjoying a truly spiritual and heavenly gaze of the Lord of Glory, he perceived at once that both the *person* and *his circumstances* ought to be holy before such a God. He felt, " Woe is me, because *I* am a man of unclean lips!" but even had he been himself holy and pure, still, before such a God, how distressing the thought, " I dwell *among a people* of unclean lips!" Alas! alas! *I* am a leper myself—" Unclean, unclean!" And *my garments* have the fretting leprosy also! " I dwell among a people of unclean lips!

There remains yet the mention of an unclean *earth*. That subject is taken up in chap. xiv. 33. But it is not mixed up with the *person and his garments*, because these two may be clean, while still the earth remains unpurified. There is to be a cleansing of our persons and of our circumstances now; but not a cleansing of the land and of its properties till an after period. Perhaps it was to shew this the more, that the laws about the *person and his garment* came into full operation while they

wandered in the desert. But those laws that concerned
the land—typical of *the earth*—did not come into operation till they reached Canaan. See chap. xiv. 34, " *When
ye be come into the land of Canaan.*" We are journeying
onward to a pure land, to a New Earth ; but, meantime,
we are to watch carefully that our persons and circumstances be pure. No sight is more peculiar, and perhaps
more attractive to the eye of angels and of God, than
holiness in full bloom, though springing up from the soil
of a *cursed earth !* Such a magnificent plant, with such
waste sands, and barren clay, and rocky soil all around !
This recalls the image of the Son of Man, when, in Nazareth, " he grew up before him as a tender plant !"

Oh, seek to be holy in heart and life, in circumstances
and situation! Breathe holiness from within, and breathe
holiness on all around ! Send a fragrant gale of holiness
along the wild desert ; it may slacken the pace of some
weary, miserable wanderer, as the spices breathed from
" Araby the blessed" delay the ship that passes by. Send
up the incense of holiness to the Lord, giving him back
his own ; and let it be known above that the Spirit who
goeth to and fro in all the earth, striving with men, has
found a dwelling-place in some souls, and has begun to
create a heaven below !

CHAPTER XIV

𝕮𝖍𝖊 𝕷𝖊𝖕𝖗𝖔𝖘𝖞 𝕽𝖊𝖒𝖔𝖛𝖊𝖉

" But God, who is rich in mercy, for his great love wherewith he loved us, even when we were dead in sins, hath quickened us together with Christ; (by grace ye are saved;) and hath raised us up together, and made us sit together in heavenly places in Christ Jesus ; that in the ages to come he might shew the exceeding riches of his grace, in his kindness toward us through Christ Jesus."—Eph. ii. 4–7

Ver. 1–4. *And the Lord spake unto Moses, saying, This shall be the law of the leper in the day of his cleansing : He shall be brought unto the priest. And the priest shall go forth out of the camp : and the priest shall look, and, behold, if the plague of leprosy be healed in the leper ; then shall the priest command to take for him that is to be cleansed two birds alive and clean, and cedar-wood, and scarlet, and hyssop.*

HERE is the remedy in the case of the *person*. Some have thought that this was used not only in cases of *real healing*, but in cases also where the leprosy being fully spread, there was no more of the disease in the man than had already appeared. It seems likely that both are meant. In Israel, there were cases, no doubt, wherein symptoms of real leprosy led the man to use means for a cure, and to call on the Lord, who sent his word and healed him. And, no doubt, also, there were those in whom the full-blown leprosy had come forth and who were cleansed, or *pronounced legally clean.* At this day, in some Eastern countries, it often happens that, after eating away the

hands or feet, the stumps of the limbs heal, and the disease is in fact cured.   It spreads no further.*   These
latter cases were types of justified men—having still a
polluted nature, yet really forgiven, and no longer conveying infection to others, but "preaching the faith which
once they destroyed."

The leper that was to be cleansed was to direct his
steps to the priests and ask an audience ; like the four
men at the gate of Samaria (2 Kings viii. 10), when they
called to the porter of the city, standing afar off ; or like
the ten men (Luke xvii. 12) at the entrance of the village, who stood afar off and lifted up their voices and
said, "Jesus, Master, have mercy on us."

As much depended on the priest's willingness to listen
to his imploring cry, a leprous Israelite would often go
up to the spot whence he could call on him, desponding
or fearful.   And the priest, however willing, might be
busy, so as not to be able to come at once. As, with most
wistful eye, the man gazes on the living, cheerful camp,
he sees one and another meet the priest and pour some
message or entreaty into his ear—so that the priest is
detained, and hurried away to this and that part of the
camp, while the trembling, weary leper waits at the gate.
In this we see that our High Priest hath the pre-eminence
—never too busy—never unwilling—never unable. "He
waits that he may be gracious" (Isa. xxx. 18).   Neither
the business nor the bliss of heaven will detain him from
a wretched soul.   He who in the days of his flesh forgot
to eat, and even ceased to feel faintness, when a soul
stood before him in his leprosy, has nothing now to keep
him from instant compassion.   He who on the cross,
under the dark shade of the approaching cloud of wrath

* Malcolm's *Travels in the Burman Empire.*

and of death, heard the heaving of his mother's bosom
and the rush of anguish through her heart, has nothing
now to hinder him freely to direct his ever-ready compas-
sions towards the coming leper.   Even as this is true in
regard to those already come, so also is it to the coming.

> " Thy risen life but whets thee more
>   For kindly sympathy;
> Thy love unhinder'd rests upon
>   Each bruised branch in thee."

The priest directs the man to take *two birds*.   He
was thus shewing him a surety's death and resurrection.
The living birds must be "*clean,*" because signifying him
who is spotless; and are brought to the spot "alive."
Beside them are—1. "*cedar-wood,*" a stalk of it to form
the handle of what was to be used in sprinkling the
blood; 2. "*scarlet,*" *i. e.* scarlet wool, as Heb. ix. 19;
and, 3. "*hyssop,*" along with the scarlet wool.   The wool
and hyssop form a kind of sponge, put on a stalk of
cedar.   Some say (and Abarbinel has explained it thus)
that the *cedar* indicates undecaying, enduring vigour—fit,
therefore, for use when the leper is to be restored; the
scarlet colour indicates the expulsion of the putrefying
humours and the restoration of the blood to its proper
redness—just as in Numb. xix. 16, in the case of the heifer
for one that touched *the dead;* and as *hyssop* is somewhat fragrant, it is supposed to shew the opposite of the
decay and corruption.   But while all this is included, still
the chief intention is to shew pollution cleansed away.
The *cedar* intimated the reversal of decay and corruption,
and being a kind of wood of which they had none in
the desert, but must get in the Promised Land, it shewed
the man's connexion with Israel's blessing; while the *hys-*

sop, used so often* in bunches for sprinkling, spoke of *cleansing* as directly as the *scarlet* colour of the wool did of the *blood* that takes away sin.

> Ver. 5-7. *And the priest shall command that one of the birds be killed in an earthen vessel over running water. As for the living bird, he shall take it, and the cedar-wood, and the scarlet, and the hyssop, and shall dip them and the living bird in the blood of the bird that was killed over the running water: and he shall sprinkle upon him that is to be cleansed from the leprosy seven times, and shall pronounce him clean, and shall let the living bird loose into the open field.*

The method of a sinner's recovery could not be fully shewn forth by only one type. Here, therefore, is a twofold type—death and life in one. "*Running water*" is in Hebrew (מַיִם חַיִּים) "*living water*," *i. e.* fresh from a running stream, in opposition to the stagnant, dead water of a pool. This prefigured one who was to have the living water, which is ever-vital, ever-fresh, ever-sparkling with motion, instead of the stagnant, dull, languid flow of leprous blood. Now, the cleansed man was to be *legally* put in this state, by these rites being applied to him. And thus it is with the sinner—brought into a state of life and vital motion when the cleansing has been applied to him.

Notice, then, the mode of cleansing. We see one held forth in these symbols who was to have in him the ever-living Divine Spirit as a well of water. This is the holy nature of *Jesus*—the fulness of the Spirit in him. This holiness is in a human frame; the Holy Spirit dwelling in him "bodily," as is held forth by the

---

* When our Lord on the cross saw the sponge held up to him on a stalk of hyssop, or like the scarlet wool, perhaps, *along with* the hyssop-branch, it would call to mind the shadows and ceremonies of the law. His eye was on this shadow when he cried, " It is finished " (John xix. 29, 30).

"*earthen vessel*" (כְּלִי חֶרֶשׂ) into which the living water is put.   Men are elsewhere spoken of as like this earthen vessel, as when the prophet calls them "חַרְשֵׂי אֲדָמָה," potsherds of earth ; and Paul (2 Cor. iv. 7), in describing ministers, calls them " earthen vessels," in contrast to Divine nature and power.

The first bird, bearing the uncleanness of the leper, is then slain, its blood dropping into the clear, living water over which it is slain.   Two streams meet—blood and water !   Satisfaction for a broken law by suffering even unto death (the stream of *blood*, which is the life) ; and obedience rendered by a holy, unsinning observance of the law written on the heart (the stream of *pure water*).   It might not be to this type peculiarly that John referred, but certainly it was to these symbols of the law, when he called us to notice that, when the spear pierced the side of Jesus (John xix. 34), " then came there out *blood and water*."   The apostle who had said, that Jesus, " knowing all things were now accomplished, that the Scripture might be fulfilled, said, I thirst"—he is the apostle who records the circumstance of the *hyssop* being with the sponge, and who tells us the cry, " *It is finished*."   It is he, too, who quotes the reference to the Paschal Lamb, " A bone of him shall not be broken."   He specially seems to call our attention to every type being fulfilled in Jesus.   Hence, I suppose, he considered, under the guidance of the Spirit, the *blood and water* from the side of Jesus to be a circumstance that indicated him as the fulfiller in his own person of all that these symbols set forth under the law.   And so in 1 John v. 6, " This is he that came by water and blood." He points to Jesus as the Righteous One who came not only with a holy nature (" water "), but also in order to take away whatever was contrary to holiness by his atonement ("blood"), summing up in himself the figures of the law.*

The *living bird* was then to be brought forward. It was to be dipt in *the blood* of its fellow, and also in the *running water* (ver. 51). It typified the Saviour, after his work of suffering, on the resurrection-morning, imbued (so to speak) with the blessed virtue that had come out of his undertaking—bearing both the satisfaction rendered and the obedience so fully given to the last. The living bird, perhaps at the time of the morning dawn, is thus dipt in the vessel, and then flies forth free and joyful in the rays of a glorious sun. How beautiful the type! Jesus risen, in all his merit of death and obedience, basks in the rays of his Father's well-pleased love! And then, as the bird in its gladness would light upon some palm, and gaze around, and sing, He looks around on a world from whose imputed guilt he is for ever free, and over which he can rest in his love, and "joy with singing" (Zeph. iii. 17). All the time, the living bird has the marks of recent death upon its wings; and so the *Lamb slain* bears his marks in heaven, in his Father's very presence.

And oh! how precious for us that we can regard all this as *our* case, too! Dipt in the blood of the Almighty's Fellow, we may be as free and gladsome. Reckoned to have died, we may also rise, with him, and may sing, "bearing about with us the dying of the Lord Jesus." We may fly over the open field, up to the gates of heaven,—nay, to "thine altars, O Lord of hosts, my King and my God."

* Perhaps this constant reference to types will best explain John iii. 5, " born of *water* and of the Spirit"—the latter being exegetical of the former. So again, xiii. 10, in allusion to the priest at the laver.

What a picture this of a leprous man regaling himself after his long, sad, lonely days! And yet it is only the shadow of what a sinner justified enters upon and enjoys! "He hath put a new song in my mouth, even praise unto our God."

Ver. 8, 9. *And he that is to be cleansed shall wash his clothes, and shave off all his hair, and wash himself in water, that he may be clean; and after that he shall come into the camp, and shall tarry abroad out of his tent seven days. But it shall be on the seventh day, that he shall shave all his hair off his head, and his beard, and his eyebrows, even all his hair he shall shave off: and he shall wash his clothes, also he shall wash his flesh in water, and he shall be clean.*

Being now brought into the state of acceptance, one thing only remains, viz. his former habits of life and conduct must of course be altered, and then he is ready to join the happy congregation. This is typified by the man washing his clothes and body, that is, all outward, external things; and shaving off his hair, or removing all about him where old corruption might be still lurking. This done, he may enter the camp, mingle with its inhabitants, partake in the shadow of its pillar-cloud, join in its worship, and help to swell its notes of praise. A justified man is at once joined to the saints on earth: converted Paul is taken by Barnabas and led to the company of saints, who at first shrank from the once leprous man. Still, as the cleansed leper was not to enter his tent for seven days more, so no justified man enters on his *rest*, or finds his final settlement till his seven days are ended—his state of waiting here. But each saint is thoroughly cleansed; and so the whole Church, at the Lord's coming, which is the end of the time appointed—the *seven* days—the *complete* time in the Lord's view. This may be said, in some degree, of each saint at death; but it is specially at the Lord's coming that *all* his privileges begin, and *all* his wants are satisfied. The very "*eye-brows*" are shaved off now (ver. 7)—not even the possibility left of any lurking-place for pollution; and his whole person and all his external circumstances undergo their final and complete purification.

He is all clean now—"all fair; there is no spot in thee." He can join the worship fully, and can claim his own dwelling among the thousands of Israel.

> Ver. 10, 11. *And on the eighth day he shall take two he-lambs without blemish, and one ewe-lamb of the first year without blemish, and three tenth-deals of fine flour for a meat-offering, mingled with oil, and one log of oil; and the priest that maketh him clean shall present the man that is to be made clean, and those things, before the Lord, at the door of the tabernacle of the congregation.*

To shew that now he is entirely free, the man is to bring all manner of sacrifices; and each is accepted for him. He brings one *he-lamb* for a trespass-offering, another for a sin-offering—both without blemish, according to the usual manner. Also, a ewe-lamb, yet tender, "of the first year," to be for a burnt-offering. The strength of the two previous victims, and the tenderness of this one, are happily blended; and these *three* sacrifices sum up all the general offerings of a man of Israel. Then, the *three* tenth-deals of flour are the meat-offering for each sacrifice, one tenth-deal for each (compare ver. 21), of the finest flour of the land, and mingled with oil, to shew that it is set apart. Besides, there is a log of oil (a half-pint) set by itself in a vessel, to be poured on the head of the once leprous man, that he may be publicly received as an acknowledged Israelite, set apart for God.

Once the man was set apart from his fellows; but now every proof of acceptance is heaped upon him. And all is done by the priest, that so it may be authoritatively done. To all this Christ refers in Matt. viii. 4; Mark i. 44; and Luke v. 14. "Go, shew thyself to the priest, and offer for thy cleansing according as Moses commanded,* for a testimony unto them."

These rites on the eighth day were meant to testify, in the most complete way, that the leprous man was acknowledged to be fully clean. Just as the whole Church, and each member of it, on the day when Christ appears to those who wait for him, shall be declared to be altogether clean, receiving the antitype of every gift and offering, and presented as set apart for ever to Jehovah.

Ver. 12–20. And the priest shall take one he-lamb, and offer him for a trespass-offering, and the log of oil, and wave them for a wave-offering before the Lord. And he shall slay the lamb in the place where he shall kill the sin-offering and the burnt-offering, in the holy place: for as the sin-offering is the priest's, so is the trespass-offering; it is most holy. And the priest shall take some of the blood of the trespass-offering, and the priest shall put it upon the tip of the right ear of him that is to be cleansed, and upon the thumb of his right hand, and upon the great toe of his right foot. And the priest shall take some of the log of oil, and pour it into the palm of his own left hand: and the priest shall dip his right finger in the oil that is in his left hand, and shall sprinkle of the oil with his finger seven times before the Lord. And of the rest of the oil that is in his hand shall the priest put upon the tip of the right ear of him that is to be cleansed, and upon the thumb of his right hand, and upon the great toe of his right foot, upon the blood of the trespass-offering. And the remnant of the oil that is in the priest's hand he shall pour upon the head of him that is to be

---

* In Matt. viii. 4, " Offer thy *gift*," the sacrifices of the eighth day may be specially meant. And Jesus delighted in the exhibition of those types that shewed forth his death and resurrection.

cleansed: and the priest shall make an atonement for him before the Lord.   And the priest shall offer the sin-offering, and make an atonement for him that is to be cleansed from his uncleanness; and afterward he shall kill the burnt-offering.   And the priest shall offer the burnt-offering and the meat-offering upon the altar: and the priest shall make an atonement for him, and he shall be clean.

The priest slays the he-lamb "*in the holy place;*" that is, in the consecrated courts, and on the very spot where the sin-offering is slain.   A place is called "holy," if holy acts are done there; even as heaven is holy because every act done there is by holy worshippers, and done in a holy manner.

The priest's waving the trespass-offering and the log of oil, intimated that this offering for the leper was presented to the Lord.   It declared his dedication to the Lord anew (the *oil* shewed *dedication*), and seemed to say, first, "*Against thee, thee only, have I sinned;*" and then, "Lord, *truly I am thy servant; I am thy servant, and the son* of thy handmaid."

Some of the blood of this offering is put on the man's *right ear;* as if to say, "Thou art cleansed; go and hear in the camp the joyful sound."   Some is put on the thumb *of his right hand,* as if to say, "Thou art cleansed; use thy clean hands for God's work."   Some is put upon the *great toe of his right foot,* as if to say, "Thou art cleansed; walk in the Lord's ways; go up to his courts, and ever walk before him in the land of the living."

Some of the oil is then taken from the log.*   And first, it is. sprinkled before the veil seven times.   Now, as in the case of *blood* so sprinkled, the meaning was that by this *blood-sprinkled* way the sinner had boldness to enter the Holiest; so, by *this oil* thus spread on the

---

* *A log* contained half a pint of our measure.

same spot, there is a declaration to the effect that *the man*, the leper, now cleansed, offers himself as a consecrated one to serve the Lord who dwells within that veil.

The oil is put on the man's ear, as if to say, "Lord, I will hear for thee,"—and on his right hand, as if to say, "Lord, I will act for thee,"—and on his right foot, as if to say, "Lord, I will go up and down, to and fro, for thee." He then pours all that remains on his head (ver. 18), that, as it ran down in copious streams over all his person, he might hear every drop cry, "Thou art his that saves thee."

But farther; there is a double type here, as in the case of the two birds. Inasmuch as *the oil* was to be put upon *the blood* of the trespass-offering, there was implied the glorious truth, that the blood which *cleanses* also *sanctifies*. If you are forgiven, you are not your own. If the price is paid for you, you are now the Lord's; he bought you. If pardoned by Jesus, then you are inhabited by the Holy Spirit. Jesus cleansed away the guilt that there might be a fair tablet on which the Spirit might re-write his holy law. If freed from guilt and Satan, you are handed over to the Lord, to serve him in holiness and righteousness.

This being done, and atonement made by the trespass-offering (ver. 19), the priest shall offer the sin-offering, and then the burnt-offering also. Some think this the "δῶρον," meant in Matt. viii. 4, "The gift that Moses commanded." Thus, he is assured of acceptance by every kind of offering; and is sent home rejoicing. "*He shall be clean.*"

THE POOR LEPER.

Ver. 21–32. *And if he be poor, and cannot get so much; then he shall take one lamb for a trespass-offering to be waved, to*

*make an atonement for him, and one tenth-deal of fine flour
mingled with oil for a meat-offering, and a log of oil; and
two turtle-doves, or two young pigeons, such as he is able to
get; and the one shall be a sin-offering, and the other a burnt-
offering. And he shall bring them on the eighth day for his
cleansing unto the priest, unto the door of the tabernacle of
the congregation, before the Lord. And the priest shall take
the lamb of the trespass-offering, and the log of oil; and the
priest shall wave them for a wave-offering before the Lord.
And he shall kill the lamb of the trespass-offering, and the
priest shall take some of the blood of the trespass-offering, and
put it upon the tip of the right ear of him that is to be cleansed,
and upon the thumb of his right hand, and upon the great toe
of his right foot. And the priest shall pour of the oil into the
palm of his own left hand. And the priest shall sprinkle with
his right finger some of the oil that is in his left hand seven
times before the Lord. And the priest shall put of the oil that
is in his hand upon the tip of the right ear of him that is to
be cleansed, and upon the thumb of his right hand, and upon
the great toe of his right foot, upon the place of the blood of
the trespass-offering. And the rest of the oil that is in the
priest's hand he shall put upon the head of him that is to be
cleansed, to make an atonement for him before the Lord.
And he shall offer the one of the turtle-doves, or of the young
pigeons, such as he can get; even such as he is able to get,
the one for a sin-offering, and the other for a burnt-offering,
with the meat-offering: and the priest shall make an atonement
for him that is to be cleansed before the Lord. This is the
law of him in whom is the plague of leprosy, whose hand is
not able to get that which pertaineth to his cleansing.*

All these minute directions are in behalf of *the poor
leper.* Similar provision was made for *the poor,* in chaps.
i., ii., and v. He may substitute *one* he-lamb and two
turtle-doves, putting his special sin on the *lamb,* by making it a trespass-offering, and then using one of the doves
for a sin-offering, and the other for a burnt-offering.
Probably the Lord was pleased with this arrangement

for another reason, viz. it gave occasion to the more frequent display of Jesus as the *dove*—the holy, harmless, undefiled One, made sin for us.   And it is beautiful to observe how the exigencies of his creatures, instead of puzzling Divine wisdom, call forth a display of his resources, and furnish to him opportunities for manifesting his love.

The directions in the case of the poor man are quite as special as in the case of any other.   The Lord would thus assure him of his care—that he feels for him the same deep interest as for others in his state, and brings the same atonement to his hand.   And the words of ver. 32 are a special clause to prevent any man overlooking this provision for the poor: for men will despise and overlook those whom *the Lord* regards and remembers.   Surely here is the heart of the same *Father*, who anointed Jesus to preach glad tidings " to the poor;" and the heart of the same *Spirit*, who was himself *the oil* that so anointed Jesus for declaring his message " to the poor;" and the heart of the same *Son of man*, who was thus set apart by the Father and the Holy Spirit to proclaim tidings of great joy " to the poor."   Is not Jesus standing here to-day, and saying, " Go, and tell John what things ye have seen and *heard;* to *the poor the gospel is preached*"?   Tell my disconsolate, dejected ones, " *To the poor is the gospel preached*."   Their God selects the saddest case for the discovery of his finest skill and purest grace.   " *This is the law for him whose hand is not able to get*."   O ! words of grace!   " Glory to God in the highest, peace on earth, good-will to man!"

THE LEPROUS HOUSE

Ver. 33, 34. *And the Lord spake unto Moses and unto Aaron, saying, When ye be come into the land of Canaan, which I give*

*to you for a possession, and I put the plague of leprosy in a
house of the land of your possession ;—*

To teach that *this earth* is under a curse, God sent
this leprosy on *houses;* just as to teach that men are
under a curse he sent leprosy in their bodies.   This
plague on houses may have been something like what
Michaëlis calls "*saltpetre, or mural salt,*" an efflorescence
or incrustation on walls of damp cellars.*   The walls
become mouldy, and at last give way.   It may, however,
have been some special infliction in these times; and the
name was given, as *Bush* remarks, on the same principle
that Easterns call certain diseases in trees "*leprosy in
trees,*" and the Swiss call some disorders in buildings
"*cancer in buildings.*"   In Israel it may have been sent
on special occasions, where the owner of the house was
too much engrossed with his pleasant dwelling.   Jewish
writers say, it was as if the beam of the house had cried
to the inhabitant, "*Turn to the Lord thy God.*" It made
the person suspect evil from the Lord, *q. d.,* "Our dwellings have cast us out."   It came like a family affliction,
saying, "This is not your rest, because it is polluted."
We must look for the New Earth wherein dwelleth
righteousness.

Ver. 35–38. *And he that owneth the house shall come and tell
the priest, saying, It seemeth to me there is as it were a plague
in the house ; then the priest shall command that they empty
the house, before the priest go into it to see the plague, that
all that is in the house be not made unclean; and afterward
the priest shall go in to see the house. And he shall look on
the plague: and, behold, if the plague be in the walls of the
house with hollow strakes, greenish or reddish, which in sight
are lower than the wall; then the priest shall go out of the
house to the door of the house, and shut up the house seven
days.*

* Jahn calls it a " nitrous acor," that wastes away the stone.

The owner of the house is to tell. It is the head of the family that is to be on the watch at all times, in regard to whatever takes place in his house. Upon him rests the authority, and so also the responsibility.

Preparation is made for the priest's coming by removing everything that might impede examination. The furniture is taken out, that nothing may be between the priest and the walls he is to scrutinise. Just as, in the case of searching our hearts, or self-examination, *fasting* removes from us all intervening objects, and leaves the eye nothing to rest upon but only the bare walls of the chambers of imagery.

But God judges truly and righteously; and his decisions are deliberate and well-weighed. It is this deliberate decision that renders his judgments so terrible. Here we find the priest examining ; and if the plague appear in the form of *"hollows"* * that are deeper than the surface of the wall, then there is room for suspicion, but there is also time given for further development. It is to be left on trial for seven days. † It is to be an emblem of this earth's state and condition, exhibiting all the symptoms of decay and of pollution, yet left for a season to develop its symptoms, and to prove undeniably its state of decay. Its wines tempt men to intemperance ; its beautiful groves hide the idolater's licentiousness ; its gold and silver tempt thousands to acts of violence and fraud. Every object of beauty draws off some man's heart from God.

---

* שְׁקַעֲרוּרֹת means "low-lying." The Septuagint has " κοιλαδες ;" the Vulgate, "valliculas." Hence Bush renders it " *depressed cavities.*" The appearance was *hollow spots; pitted.*

† The Septuagint use the expression, " ἀφοριει την οἰκιαν." Some quote Isa. xxiv. 10, as illustrated by this. The city is like a city of leprosy, " *every house is shut up, that no man may come in.*"

Ver. 39–42. *And the priest shall come again the seventh day, and shall look: and, behold, if the plague be spread in the walls of the house; then the priest shall command that they take away the stones in which the plague is, and they shall cast them into an unclean place without the city. And he shall cause the house to be scraped within round about, and they shall pour out the dust that they scrape off without the city into an unclean place. And they shall take other stones, and put them in the place of those stones; and he shall take other mortar, and shall plaster the house.*

The removing of the decaying, infected stones seems to typify such an event as that of sweeping earth's surface by the flood, and then ornamenting it anew by a fresh covering of verdure, and establishing it anew by a new arrangement of its rivers and hills, while the old " plaster " and the " scrapings of the house" were carried out of sight. They are carried to an *" unclean place "*—for there is here no application of atonement ; all is destruction.

The *decayed stones* are quite removed; so the palaces, the gardens, the cities, the temples of the antediluvian world were entirely swept off. But then, besides this, the *whole surface* is scraped, and plastered afresh; even as every part of earth's surface was visited, and its former aspect retouched. This done, earth was left once more, by its Priest and Judge,* for further trial. Its groves and forests wave again in strength and greenness; its fields yield their fruit ; its orchards hang out their heavy-laden branches ; its pastures are clothed with flocks. Is the plague stayed? Shall earth ever again exhibit corruption like the former? The Lord sits on his throne, and waits to see.

* There was much of the *judicial* character in the *priest;* that is, he judged much in regard to all ceremonial affairs, and all sanctuary laws. Hence, in Isa. xxxiii. 22, " The Lord is our *Judge,*" seems to refer to the *priestly* office judging in holy things.

Ver. 43–45. *And if the plague come again, and break out in the house, after that he hath taken away the stones, and after he hath scraped the house, and after it is plastered; then the priest shall come and look, and, behold, if the plague be spread in the house, it is a fretting leprosy in the house: it is unclean. And he shall break down the house, the stones of it, and the timber thereof, and all the mortar of the house; and he shall carry them forth out of the city into an unclean place.*

If, amidst earth's restored beauty, when its wide regions are again blooming with all their former produce, and the sky over them is serene as before, with its covenant-rainbow spanning all below—if, then, corruption burst forth again, there will be here proof of deep, inveterate disease. In anticipation of this result, the Lord said, " I will not again curse the ground any more for man's sake ; for the imagination of man's heart is evil from his youth " (Gen. viii. 21). The same remedy shall never be tried a second time. But now, there shall be a removal of the old materials. The house must be broken down— stones, timber, mortar—and all swept away. "The earth and the works therein shall be burnt up." "All these things shall be dissolved," says Peter (2 Pet. iii. 11). There must be a new building raised on the same spot—"a new earth." It is the *priest* himself that removes the old building ; it is Jesus that comes to say, " Behold, I make all things new."

Ver. 46, 47. *Moreover, he that goeth into the house, all the while that it is shut up, shall be unclean until the even. And he that lieth in the house shall wash his clothes; and he that eateth in the house shall wash his clothes.*

Any one going into the shut-up house for any of his stuff is unclean for a day. If one go to sleep there, even in order to escape the dews of the night, or go to eat there, to escape the burning sun, that man must wash his clothes, as well as be reckoned unclean. It shews us that there is woe befallen us by the very circumstance of our being on this earth, which is under a curse, even if we ourselves were holy. For it is not a holy place—the Lord's curse has been spread over it. There must be blessing on our dwelling and on our possessions, if we are to enjoy them in true peace. But there is a secret tendency in all earthly things, at present, to provoke indulgence in sin, as if a secret poison were pervading all nature. Hence, even our meat and drink so draw down the soul, that we need to fast, if we would be quite free from the influence of even lawful things.

> Ver. 48–53. *And if the priest shall come in, and look upon it, and, behold, the plague hath not spread in the house, after the house was plastered; then the priest shall pronounce the house clean, because the plague is healed. And he shall take to cleanse the house two birds, and cedar-wood, and scarlet, and hyssop: and he shall kill the one of the birds in an earthen vessel over running water: and he shall take the cedar-wood, and the hyssop, and the scarlet, and the living bird, and dip them in the blood of the slain bird, and in the running water, and sprinkle the house seven times: and he shall cleanse the house with the blood of the bird, and with the running water, and with the living bird, and with the cedar-wood, and with the hyssop, and with the scarlet: but he shall let go the living bird out of the city into the open fields, and make an atonement for the house: and it shall be clean.*

This case of the plague arrested in its course, represents a case like that of Job v. 24, " *Thou shalt know that thy tabernacle shall be in peace; and thou shalt visit thy habitation, and shalt not sin.*" The house is purified after the leprosy is arrested; and it is purified by the very same means as the leper himself was purified. There is the same blood, the same sprinkling, the same running, or fresh, water, and the same type of resurrection exhi-

bited in the live bird.   Probably we are taught by this
case, that during the days wherein earth remains, since
the removal of the infected stones by the great visitation
of it at the flood—during the days of "the earth that now
is" (2 Pet. iii. 7)—a believer may enjoy his dwelling in
peace and safety, free from all share in the curse, by
means of the same atonement that gave him pardon.
His dwelling and property may be purified for his use by
the glorious redemption that so purified his soul.   Our
dwellings are set apart as well as ourselves.   The curse
on them is arrested.   *They are clean.*   The priest does
all this for us; Jesus by his glorious work secures that
"all things shall be ours."

The concluding ceremony must have been very striking.
The living bird was carried through every apartment of
the dwelling, and then at some open window, or from
the flat roof of the house, allowed to fly at liberty.
The inhabitant would often afterwards, as he sat in his
dwelling, remember the concluding act of cleansing.   He
would remember the cheerful song of the bird set free,
and its joyful flight through the sky, while drops of the
living water fell; and the marks of its fellow's blood were
observed as it shook its wings.   It is thus a believing
soul feels.   He remembers Christ's *resurrection* as the
concluding act that completed cleansing; he remembers
Christ's joy on the resurrection morning—his words, "All
hail," and "Peace be unto you,"—and he remembers the
freedom with which he traversed the heavens, even the
heaven of heavens, returning to his Father's bosom still
bearing the marks of the nails and spear, and shedding
down the purchased Spirit.   This, this is truly the source
of all our peace from sin within us, from sin in those
around us, from sin on the earth that lies under a curse

—from leprosy in our persons, our garments, and our dwellings.

"Bless the Lord, O my soul, and forget not all his benefits: who forgiveth all thine iniquities, who healeth *all* thy diseases!" We must sit at the window of our purified dwelling, and with cleansed soul and anointed eye look out for the Return of the priest who has brought us such blessings. Shall we not rejoice at the sound of the tread of his footstep? Shall we not welcome the very rumour of his coming this way again? Shall the first sight of his form not fill us with holy gratitude? In the meantime, let our dwellings resound with the melody of "rejoicing and salvation" (Ps. cxviii. 15); and in our out-goings let us sing, "I shall not die, but live, and shall declare the works of the Lord. The Lord hath chastened me sore; but he hath not given me over unto death."

CONCLUSION OF THE LAW OF LEPROSY

Ver. 54–57. *This is the law for all manner of plague of leprosy, and scall, and for the leprosy of a garment, and of a house, and for a rising, and for a scab, and for a bright spot; to teach when it is unclean, and when it is clean: this is the law of leprosy.*

In ver. 57, the literal rendering is, "To teach *in the day* of the unclean and *in the day* of the clean;" meaning, to instruct us regarding what is right to be done at the seasons when things are unclean, and what is right to be done when they are clean. The Lord keeps ever before us the solemn truth that we are in a world of sin, moving amid evil; and he is the same Jehovah who prayed "not that thou shouldest take them out of the world, but that thou shouldest keep them from the evil" (John xvii. 15). He leads his people through the same wilderness, then and now—or rather through the same

Red Sea. He does not dry up the waters, but makes his own pass between their overhanging walls.

That this is a summary of the preceding chapters appears clear if we notice that mention is made first generally, ver. 54, "*of leprosy and scall.*" Then, the leprosy is subdivided in ver. 55 into "*leprosy*" in a man, garment, or house. Lastly, ver. 56, "*scall*" is subdivided into rising, scab, or bright spot.

However various the symptoms and forms, yet the discerning priest observes all, and pronounces righteous judgment "in the day of the clean and of the unclean." There is a time and season when sin of any shape and aspect appears before him ; and *the law* decides unerringly on each case. "Behold," he says to us, "I come quickly—he that is unjust, let him be unjust still : and he that is filthy, let him be filthy still : and he that is righteous, let him be righteous still : and he that is holy, let him be holy still." As of old, to Israel (Mal. iii. 18), who asked, "What profit is it that we have kept his ordinance ?" he said, "Then shall ye return and discern between the righteous and the wicked ; between him that serveth God and him that serveth him not."

CHAPTER XV

The Secret Flow of Sin from the Natural Heart, typified in the Running Issue

"I know that in me (that is, in my flesh) dwelleth no good thing."—
Rom. vii. 18

Ver. 1–3. And the Lord spake unto Moses and to Aaron, say-ing, Speak unto the children of Israel, and say unto them, When any man hath a running issue out of his flesh, because of his issue he is unclean. And this shall be his uncleanness in his issue: whether his flesh run with his issue, or his flesh be stopped from his issue, it is his uncleanness.

MOSES and Aaron are both addressed, as in the case of the disease of leprosy (xiii. 1). Wherever there is only *a law* laid down, Moses alone hears the voice. God speaks only to the *lawgiver*. But, in cases where *disease* is pre-scribed for by special rules, Aaron is joined with Moses. Is this because a priest—a high priest—ought to have much compassion, and might be more likely to learn com-passion while hearing the tone of pity in which the Lord spoke of man's misery ?

This secret uncleanness, known only to the person's self, represents the secret sins, or the secret, quiet, oozing out of sin from the natural heart—its flow of pollution while not a word is spoken, not an act done, not a motion in the eye of our fellow-men. The more disgusting the images, the more is it meant to express God's extreme

abhorrence of the sinful state ; just as in 1 Kings xiv. 10,
and elsewhere, indignation at the ungodly is expressed by
most contemptuous language.   O that we felt the shame
of sin !   O to be confounded because of our inward hardness ! Ashamed   as not to look up, because of secret
unbelief, secret pride, secret selfishness, secret lusts, secret
painting of the walls with imagery!

Some th'nk this disease was sent as a judicial punishment; for it is so referred to in 2 Sam. iii. 29; and Mark
v. 29, calls it " $\mu\acute{a}\sigma\tau\iota\xi$," " a scourge."

To a Jew it was the more hateful, as being pollution
where *the seal of circumcision* had been.   Indwelling sin
thus shews its existence in closest neighbourhood to the
blood-sprinkling of Jesus.

The difference in the kind of the disease (ver. 3) does
not change its polluting character.   Sin may be flowing
freely as a stream, or may be brooded over till the soul
is like a stagnant pool—in any form it is hateful to the
Holy One of Israel.   The lively imagination of a gay,
poetic mind is not less sinful when it showers forth its
luscious images, than the dull, brutal feelings of the stupid,
ignorant boor.   " Thou desirest truth in the inward
parts."   " The righteous Lord loveth righteousness ; his
countenance doth behold the upright"—his countenance
shines in upon the cleansed, blood-sprinkled soul, gazing
on its purity with true delight, while he turns away from
the sickening sight of the unwashed conscience and the
" sinner lying in his blood."

> Ver. 4–12. *Every bed whereon he lieth that hath the issue is un-*
> *clean: and every thing whereon he sitteth shall be unclean.*
> *And whosoever toucheth his bed shall wash his clothes, and*
> *bathe himself in water, and be unclean until the even.   And he*
> *that sitteth on any thing whereon he sat that hath the issue*
> *shall wash his clothes, and bathe himself in water, and be un-*

clean until the even. And he that toucheth the flesh of him that hath the issue shall wash his clothes, and bathe himself in water, and be unclean until the even. And if he that hath the issue spit upon him that is clean, then he shall wash his clothes, and bathe himself in water, and be unclean until the even. And what saddle soever he rideth upon that hath the issue shall be unclean. And whosoever toucheth any thing that was under him shall be unclean until the even: and he that beareth any of those things shall wash his clothes, and bathe himself in water, and be unclean until the even. And whomsoever he toucheth that hath the issue, and hath not rinsed his hands in water, he shall wash his clothes, and bathe himself in water, and be unclean until the even. And the vessel of earth that he toucheth which hath the issue shall be broken; and every vessel of wood shall be rinsed in water.

We have already had occasion to notice the limited time—"*until even*" (chap. xi. 25). But let us further observe, that under the law we seldom find *immediate* pardon. The legal ceremonies were thus like the pool of Bethesda—*imperfect* types of Christ. What joy there is in immediate pardon! To pass at once from hell to heaven, from the fangs of Satan, the smoke of hell, the angry recrimination of a tossed conscience, and the dread of a frowning God, to the peace and love of the Saviour's holy bosom! The law had a shadow of good things to come, but was not the very image of those things.

Again; let us notice that one touch conveyed uncleanness—so full is the cup, that if shaken at all, its pollution trickles over. What a glorious contrast have we in Jesus! He touches (Mark i. 41), and lo! the holy stream of health flows from him. Or another touches Him, and disease flies away (Mark v. 28) in the moment of contact.

We are here taught the disgusting constancy with which our original, deep-seated corruption will naturally discover itself. In all situations, towards all persons, at all seasons, this filthiness of the secret soul may be detected. In ver. 4 the man is represented as unclean when he lieth down to sleep, or even to rest at noon.* Ah! yonder lies a sinner, and the very ground under him is accursed! His very pillow may shortly become a spear under his throat; just as Jonah's couch in the side of the ship soon became a tempestuous sea. A friend comes to see him, and gently awakes him, but touches his couch in so doing, and becomes thereby *unclean* (ver. 5); for the man is all polluted. However amiable the friend you visit, yet, if still in his unhealed corruption, your intercourse with him spreads its baleful influence over you. You have insensibly been injured by the contact. How we should watch our souls in mingling with a world lying in wickedness! Oh! how holy, how marvellously strong in holiness was Jesus! who breathed this polluted air, and remained as holy as when he came.

If the man leave the spot, and another occupy it, that other has seated himself in the sinner's place (ver. 6), and the trace of his sin is not gone. He is in contact with a polluted thing. As, when one of us now reads the details of a sinner's career and our mind rests thereon, we are involved in his sin.

If a physician (ver. 7) or an attendant touch the sick man's flesh, he is in contact with sin, and becomes polluted. This legal consequence of any actual contact with the defiled, shews us, no doubt, the danger and hazard of even attempting to aid the polluted. It is at the risk of being ourselves involved in their sin. Therefore, it must be watchfully done, not boldly and adventu-

---

* So מִשְׁכָּב is used in 2 Sam. iv. 5, when Ishbosheth was reclining in the heat of the day.

rously. You breathe an impure atmosphere: proceed with caution.

If (ver. 8) any even accidental touch occur—as if the diseased man spit or sneeze, so as anything from him reaches the bystander, pollution is spread. An accidental word, a casual expression, an unexpected look, may suggest sin ; and if it does, forthwith wash it all away ere evening comes. " Let not the sun go down upon thy wrath." Leave no stain for a moment upon thy conscience.

When the man rides forth, lo! yonder is a sinner ; and his saddle is polluted; and the mattress he spread on the floor of his tent for a temporary rest in his journey (ver. 10) is so polluted, that the attendant who lifts it is defiled. Oh! sad, sad estate of fallen man! In going out or coming in, in the house or by the way, his inward fountain of sin flows on unceasingly, and the Holy One of Israel follows him with his eye to mark him as a sinner.

Nay, if he put his hand forth (ver. 11) to touch any one—to give him a friendly welcome, or aid him in any work—he conveys pollution, unless he have first " rinsed his hands in water." The sinner whose natural heart is still unhealed cannot do even a kind act without sin—his only mode of doing so would be first to "wash in clean water." And the vessels he uses (ver. 12) must be broken or rinsed in water ; even as the earth, on which the sinner has stood as his theatre for committing evil, shall be broken in pieces by the fire of the last day (" all these things shall *be dissolved*," 2 Pet. iii. 11), the trial by water being already past.

Ver. 13–15. *And when he that hath an issue is cleansed of his issue, then he shall number to himself seven days for his cleansing, and wash his clothes, and bathe his flesh in running water, and shall be clean. And on the eighth day he shall take to*

him two turtle-doves, or two young pigeons, and come before
the Lord unto the door of the tabernacle of the congregation,
and give them unto the priest: and the priest shall offer them,
the one for a sin-offering, and the other for a burnt-offering;
and the priest shall make an atonement for him before the Lord
for his issue.

The time of cleansing is to be "*seven days*"—a full
time. During each of these days he is to wash his clothes
and bathe himself " in running water"—the emblem of
the purity of the Holy Ghost. And it is the indwelling
Spirit, like living water, that our corrupt heart requires
in order to its sanctification. During seven days he thus
declared his need of the Holy Spirit by his repeated
washings. Then on the eighth day he comes to receive
" atonement" (ver. 15), as the means to this true purification. He brings two " *turtle-doves*, or two *young*
pigeons;" perhaps because, whatever difference might be
made by circumstances in regard to the *actions*, or *actual*
sins, of rich and poor, yet, in regard to original sin and
depravity of heart, both are alike; and so the offering of
" *turtles* or *pigeons*" is fixed upon for the poor man, as
bringing down the rich to the level of the poorest. Yet,
perhaps, there is a further reason—the *turtle-dove*, or the
pigeon, being so frequently the emblem of *purity* (Song,
vi. 9; v. 12; Psalm lxxiv. 19), they may have been chosen
in this case as reminding the offerer that *personal purity*
is required in coming to God.

A full atonement is as much required for our inward
secret sins as for open and flagrant sins. The sinful vision
that our fancy spread out before us for a moment must
be washed away by blood. The tendency which our soul
felt to sympathise in that act of resentment or revenge
must be washed away by blood. The hour or minutes we
spent in brooding over our supposed hard lot, must be

redeemed by blood. The selfish wish we cherished for special prosperity in some undertaking that was to reflect its credit on us only, is to be washed away by blood. The proud aspiration, the sensual impulse, the world-loving glance our soul casts on earth's glories, must be washed away by blood. The darkness, ignorance, suspicion, and misconception we entertain toward God and his salvation, must be washed in blood. "Behold, thou desirest truth in the inward parts; and in the hidden part (hidden region of the soul) thou shalt make me to know wisdom" (Psalm li. 6).

> Ver. 16–18. *And if any man's seed of copulation go out from him, then he shall wash all his flesh in water, and be unclean until the even. And every garment, and every skin, whereon is the seed of copulation, shall be washed with water, and be unclean until the even. The woman also with whom man shall lie with seed of copulation, they shall both bathe themselves in water, and be unclean until the even.*

It is supposed that this law was intended to mark God's holy abhorrence of uncleanness, even in the desire. Hence, he puts in the class of the polluted, any one who even accidentally discovered inordinate desire, married or unmarried. Indeed, so far was such a state of feeling from being overlooked by the Lord, that he enjoins pollution to be attached to the very neighbourhood thereof. "Every garment and every vessel made of skin" that comes in contact with the defiled man must be washed and held unclean until the even. And so with the persons; they must not cast off the thought of their sad depravity, but all day long go mourning over this fall, though known only to God; and must use the water which was the emblem of a cleansed and pure nature. "Having, therefore, these promises, dearly beloved, let us cleanse our-

selves from all filthiness of the flesh and spirit, perfecting
holiness in the fear of the Lord" (2 Cor. vii. 1).

> Ver. 19–24. *And if a woman have an issue, and her issue in
> her flesh be blood, she shall be put apart seven days; and
> whosoever toucheth her shall be unclean until the even. And
> every thing that she lieth upon in her separation shall be un-
> clean; every thing also that she sitteth upon shall be unclean.
> And whosoever toucheth her bed shall wash his clothes, and
> bathe himself in water, and be unclean until the even. And
> whosoever toucheth any thing that she sat upon, shall wash his
> clothes, and bathe himself in water, and be unclean until the
> even. And if it be on her bed, or on any thing whereon she
> sitteth, when he toucheth it, he shall be unclean until the even.
> And if any man lie with her at all, and her flowers be upon
> him, he shall be unclean seven days; and all the bed whereon
> he lieth shall be unclean.*

As in the case of the man noticed at the beginning of
the chapter, so now, the same law is laid down in the case
of the woman who has any issue. An issue of blood,
such as that referred to here, brought the woman of Israel
from time to time into great trial. We may conceive her
miserable state during the time she was ill. Separated
from general society (for so Num. v. 2 seems to declare),
she was like a leper. She was " a fear to her acquaintance." Everything she touched became defiled ; every
couch she rested on at noon (ver. 20); every one that
touched her, even the very physicians (ver. 21) she
went to consult, or who came (ver. 23) to see her when
she could not visit them because of her distress, were unclean for a day after. Her husband himself (ver. 24) was
in like manner separated from her, or polluted and defiled
if he did not live apart from her. She was a living picture of the awful truth, that sin, however hidden to the
view of men, is so virulent in its nature and tendency,

that it dissolves every relationship, and sets apart the sinner for misery and sadness.

In chap. xx. 18, death is the penalty if this uncleanness were known and disregarded by the parties. But the treatment here seems severe enough, and we are led to inquire into the cause. Why is *the woman's* case dealt with so severely? Perhaps, to keep up the memory of "*The Fall.*" The woman was in the transgression. "Remember whence thou art fallen." Our original sin, inherited from our first parents, is not to be forgotten. The Lord never forgets that time of the fall, even as he never forgets the day when the angels left their first habitation. Of what parents have we come! See the rock out of which we were hewn! "Thy father was an Amorite, and thy mother an Hittite."

> Ver. 25–30. *And if a woman have an issue of her blood many days out of the time of her separation, or if it run beyond the time of her separation; all the days of the issue of her uncleanness shall be as the days of her separation: she shall be unclean. Every bed whereon she lieth all the days of her issue shall be unto her as the bed of her separation: and whatsoever she sitteth upon shall be unclean, as the uncleanness of her separation. And whosoever toucheth those things shall be unclean, and shall wash his clothes, and bathe himself in water, and be unclean until the even. But if she be cleansed of her issue, then she shall number to herself seven days, and after that she shall be clean. And on the eighth day she shall take unto her two turtles, or two young .pigeons, and bring them unto the priest, to the door of the tabernacle of the congregation. And the priest shall offer the one for a sin-offering, and the other for a burnt-offering; and the priest shall make an atonement for her before the Lord, for the issue of her uncleanness.*

The case here referred to is such as that of the woman in Mark v. 29 ; an unnatural issue, called in that passage

" a plague," or " scourge," as if it were something sent
judicially. She is treated as in the former cases, all the
time this plague or disease lasts, though it should be
twelve or twenty years. Every new view of these cases
seems intended to impress on us the inward shame which
we ought to cherish for our defilement. We may well be
confounded for the secret loathsomeness of sin that no
eye of man ever could have discerned.

Take the case of the woman in Mark v. 29, twelve
years thus deeply distressed, groaning over her misery,
living alone, in vain trying every physician, and keeping
aloof from friends as much as possible, lest she should
spread defilement on them by her presence. What a
picture of a sinner! a sinner conscious of her nature's
fearful pollution mourning over her weak and wicked
heart, trying every remedy that man can suggest, yet still
sad at heart, and her sore still running down with its new
outflowings of sin. But one tells her of Jesus. She
hears of his having, the night before, calmed the sea at
its height of storm, and having gone over to the other
side for the sake of saving one soul. She comes; she sees
and hears him for herself, and is persuaded that he has
the very fountain of life in his person. In this faith she
touches the hem of his robe, as if to say, " He is full of
love and power, even to the very skirts of his garment."
She brought no gift; for she had spent all her living
already on physicians. She brought nothing like a begun
cure ; for she was "nothing bettered, but rather grew
worse." She had not long-waiting to shew as a plea ; for
she came only that morning. She had no repentance to
offer ; for hitherto her regrets were simply that she had
in vain sought to other physicians. She had no love to
allege; for she was only now coming to see what reason

for love there was. She offered no prayer; she simply
drew near, and placed herself in contact with the fountain
of life and healing! The result was immediate cure! *Sin*
and *grace* met! and this is ever the singular result of
their meeting. How often now, after presenting at Jerusalem her turtle-doves, would she walk at that sea-shore
with the daughter of Jairus—who was born the very year
she took her disease, and who was raised from the dead
the very same day that she was healed—and together
would they sing and praise the Lord, one saying, " Who
healeth all thy diseases," the other responding, " Who
redeemeth thy life from destruction" (Ps. ciii. 3).

When Jesus healed *the leprosy* and *the issue of blood*,
was he not tacitly explaining the type couched under
these diseases and their cleansing ? Was it not like his
healing the man at the pool of Bethesda? There was an
emblem in it all, though he said not at the moment that
this was what he wished to shew. It was enough that he
had declared himself " *come to fulfil the law.*" They were
thus warned to expect that his every action would tend
in that direction. It is in reference to this chapter that
Zechariah (chap. xiii. 1) calls Christ the "*Fountain for
uncleanness*" (נִדָּה) ; and Isaiah (iv. 4) speaks of washing
away " the *filth of the daughters* of Zion, and purging
away the *blood of Jerusalem*," by judgments that will
drive them to this fountain. Thanks be unto God for
his unspeakable gift!

Ver. 31–33. *Thus shall ye separate* (q. d. " *make Nazarites of*") *the
children of Israel from their uncleanness, that they die not in
their uncleanness, when they defile my tabernacle that is among
them. This is the law of him that hath an issue, and of him
whose seed goeth from him, and is defiled therewith; and of her
that is sick of her flowers, and of him that hath an issue,* of*

* The force of the clause is, " *even of any one that has an issue*, male or

*the man, and of the woman, and of him that lieth with her which
is unclean.*

No commandment of God is trivial; hence there is
here a summary of all, in order to fix the contents on the
memory.   The threatening, in ver. 31, teaches us that
our worship in the sanctuary must be offered with *inward*
purity, as well as outward. We must be conscious to ourselves of having been cleansed. To come while aware of
unremoved pollution, is to defile the tabernacle and ex-
pose ourselves to immediate curse. " The Lord our God
is holy." " Let us have *grace*, whereby we may serve
God acceptably" (Heb. xii. 28).

female."   As the masculine, הָאָדָם, in Gen. i. 27, is generically used for *mankind*,
so הַזָּב here.

CHAPTER XVI

The Day of Atonement

" Who his own self bare our sins in his own body on the tree, that we,
being dead to sins, might live unto righteousness."—1 Pet. ii. 24

> Ver. 1, 2. *And the Lord spake unto Moses after the death of the*
> *two sons of Aaron, when they offered before the Lord, and*
> *died; and the Lord said unto Moses, Speak unto Aaron thy*
> *brother, that he come not at all times into the holy place within*
> *the veil, before the mercy-seat which is upon the ark, that he*
> *die not: for I will appear in the cloud upon the mercy-seat.*

ALL the laws about uncleannesses that disqualified worshippers from coming to the sanctuary may have been
delivered after the death of Nadab and Abihu, on purpose to shew, at such a solemn time, how holy is the
Lord, and that he must be approached with fear and
reverence. So now also, while that event is still fresh in
Aaron's remembrance, this command is given, ver. 2.
The event was thus made useful to qualify Aaron more
fully for his solemn duties; he learns, and all generations
after him, how profound must be the reverence wherewith
the Lord is approached. It is thus still that a minister's
afflictions are not in vain; they affect his office; they prepare him for it, as Paul wrote (2 Cor. i. 4) to the Cor-
inthians in his day. It is, at the same time, significant,

that before the Day of Atonement is spoken of, there should be a spreading out to view of *sin*, and of *death*, which is its desert.

Aaron must enter *within* the veil only at appointed times; for *within the veil* the cloud of glory rests, at these appointed times,* and Jehovah is there, as it were, in his inaccessible light. He that comes in must be led in by God himself. "For through him we have access by one Spirit unto the Father."

> Ver. 3, 4. *Thus shall Aaron come into the holy place; with a young bullock for a sin-offering, and a ram for a burnt-offering. He shall put on the holy linen coat, and he shall have the linen breeches upon his flesh, and shall be girded with a linen girdle, and with the linen mitre shall he be attired: these are holy garments; therefore shall he wash his flesh in water, and so put them on.*

Here is Aaron's *personal* preparation. After the usual morning sacrifice (see Num. xxix. 11), and a sacrifice of *seven lambs* at the same time—to indicate the *complete offering* up to God that was that day to be made, and the *complete dependence* on atoning blood that day to be shewn in all that was done—Aaron approached the holy place; for ver. 3 says, "come *to* the holy place." In so doing, he led along a bullock for his sin-offering, and a ram for his burnt-offering—both of these for himself, as an individual, and for his household.† On these he was to lay his sins. But ere he did this, he retired, and put off his golden garments, putting on the plain linen ones —pure, but unadorned—like Jesus on earth, holy, yet in a servant's form. The priest must put aside both ephod

---

* It is doubtful if this cloud of glory rested there all the year round, or only occasionally.

† Some think "*his house*" (ver. 6), means "the house of Aaron," in its widest sense, namely, all the body of priests and Levites, as in Ps. cxv. 12.

and breastplate ; he appeared simply as head of the people. He washed himself in water ere he put them on, that *holiness* might still be proclaimed by him, though putting on this unattractive dress; even as our Surety, in entering Mary's womb, was declared to be "that Holy One that shall be born of thee."

> Ver. 5. *And he shall take of the congregation of the children of Israel two kids of the goats for a sin-offering, and one ram for a burnt-offering.*

These were brought to him by the people after he had put on his linen robes; and they were for themselves. It was these that were to be specially typical of Christ's work; for wherein Aaron offered for himself he could not resemble Jesus, as Heb. vii. 26–28 declares.

It is to be remarked, that no details are given respecting any of the *burnt-offerings* of this day. The details are all confined to the *sin-offerings*. Hence, though "*seven lambs*" * are mentioned, besides "the *continual burnt-offering*," yet nothing more about them is recorded. The *ram of Aaron's* is mentioned as to be offered, yet no particulars are given; and the *ram of the people* is also specially noticed, but its offering up is not described. The reason is, all these were "*burnt-offerings.*" Now, on this day the Lord wished to fix the attention of all upon the *sin-offerings*, as it was a day of expiation for the confessed, defined, specified sins of Israel.†

> Ver. 6–10. *And Aaron shall offer his bullock of the sin-offering which is for himself, and make an atonement for himself, and for his house. And he shall take the two goats, and present*

---

* Perhaps there was also a *bullock* and a *ram* along with these; see Num. xxix. 8.

† This seems to me the true reason for the omission. On this point I can find nothing satisfactory in any of the commentators. Their accounts of these rites are very confused on the whole.

them before the Lord at the door of the tabernacle of the congre-
gation. And Aaron shall cast lots upon the two goats; one lot
for the Lord, and the other lot for the scape-goat. And Aaron
shall bring the goat upon which the Lord's lot fell, and offer
him for a sin-offering. But the goat, on which the lot fell to be
the scape-goat, shall be presented alive before the Lord, to make
an atonement with him, and to let him go for a scape-goat into
the wilderness.

These verses describe no more than the *order and
manner* of arranging the transactions of the day—Aaron's
bullock first ; then the lot to be cast on *the two goats*,
whose different destinations are determined.

There is little ground for doubting that the rendering
" scape-goat" is the best. But two other views have been
vigorously maintained; *one*, that the word (עֲזָאזֵל) means
the devil; *the other*, that it was the Jewish people in their
state of apostasy and rejection.   Among the maintainers
of the former view, Faber is by far the most powerful,
for he repudiates the idea of any offering to Satan, and
considers the transaction as intended to signify *Christ
handed over to Satan for the bruising of his heel.*   Hengstenberg also maintains this, but applies it differently.*
The *latter* view is held by *Bush*, who tries to shew that
it was appropriate, on an occasion that shewed forth
Christ's death and atonement so fully, to introduce his
rejection by Israel as one of the accompaniments of that
momentous transaction.

The objections urged to the common rendering " *scape-
goat*," however, are, after all, quite unsatisfactory.   It is
evidently the most natural meaning.   The word, עֵז, for *a
goat*, had just been used, ver. 5, and אָזַל, " to depart, go
away," was likely enough, even on account of its similar
sound, to be the term employed to express the fact of the

* See *Egypt and Books of Moses.*

goat's being dismissed. Then, as to the two strong objections alleged by some against this view, when examined, they have no force. For the first is, that if the clause, "the one lot *for the Lord*," intimate that the goat is *appropriated to a person*, so should the next clause, "the other *lot for* (עֲזָאזֵל) *Azazel*," also signify *appropriation to a person*. But the answer to this is, that the proper sense is not *appropriation to*, or *designation for persons*; it is *designation for use*, viz. the first for the purpose of being killed at the *Lord's altar*; the other *for the purpose of sending* away to the wilderness. The second objection is more serious. It is said that the words in ver. 10, יְכַפֵּר עָלָיו, never can mean, "make atonement *with* him," but must mean "*for him*," as the object. And it is on this ground mainly that *Bush* defends his strange idea of this goat being a type of apostate Israel. But, in reply, we assert that the words may have the meaning which our version gives them; and that בַּעֲדוֹ would probably have been used if "*for him*" had been meant, seeing this is the phrase used all throughout this chapter to express that idea. In Exod. xxx. 30, the phrase (כִּפֶּר עַל) occurs twice in the sense of "*atone over* or *upon*"—"Aaron shall make atonement *upon the* horns of it once in a year;" and "once in the year shall he make atonement *upon it*" (יְכַפֵּר עָלָיו). So here, the priest is to make atonement *over* the scape-goat, by putting Israel's guilt upon it ere he sends it away. And if one say, that surely it is strange that this mode of expression should occur so rarely, the answer is, the *act described by it occurred rarely*, and no other words could better express the act intended.

Probably, the root of all these objections has been the secret feeling that there was something quite unsatisfactory in explaining the passage as a type of *death* and *resur-rection*. How the *scape-goat* could mean *resurrection*, has been secretly felt to be very puzzling. But this diffi-culty will vanish when we come to see that it does not mean resurrection. Let us proceed, therefore, to consider the whole transactions of that memorable day.

> Ver. 11-14. *And Aaron shall bring the bullock of the sin-offering which is for himself, and shall make an atonement for himself, and for his house, and shall kill the bullock of the sin-offering which is for himself. And he shall take a censer full of burn-ing coals of fire from off the altar before the Lord, and his hands full of sweet incense beaten small, and bring it within the veil. And he shall put the incense upon the fire before the Lord, that the cloud of the incense may cover the mercy-seat that is upon the testimony, that he die not. And he shall take of the blood of the bullock, and sprinkle it with his finger upon the mercy-seat eastward: and before the mercy-seat shall he sprinkle of the blood with his finger seven times.*

All the victims having stood before the Lord—types of all our race standing before him, shuddering under the curse—Aaron, first of all, offers for himself and his house. He takes the *sin-offering bullock,* slays it on the altar, and pours out its blood. With the blood he fills one of the bowls of the altar. Then, with this in one hand, he places in the other a pan of live coals from the very same altar—out of the very same flames that had fed upon his sacrifice—and on this he sprinkles a handful of incense, whose sweet fragrance instantly fills the courts of the Lord's house. What a glorious scene for sinners! This sinner's offering is accepted! The sweet savour breathes over it and ascends to heaven. The very fire * that preyed upon the bullock till it was consumed into ashes,

---

* Notice, the fragrance is drawn out by the *fire*, to shew that acceptance is effected by justice itself.

is that which causes this fragrance to be felt; the very righteousness that sought for an atonement ere it could forgive delights to proclaim that the law is magnified, Jehovah glorified, the sinner justified. The holy law, having met with its requisitions, exults in declaring the sinner free!

But Aaron's next step is yet more wondrous. He advances to the *Holiest of All*, passing through the *Holy Place*, blood and sweet incense all the time held up in his hands; yea, not only a censer full of incense, but a cup of it, besides, held in his hand. The light from the golden candlestick directs his reverent step to the veil, which he draws aside. Forthwith the bright cloud of glory pours its full radiance upon him—too bright for his feeble eye, were it not softened by the cloud of incense that arises from the censer in his hand. Thus enveloped, he sprinkles the blood on the mercy-seat seven times. But what a moment was this! It is his own sins that he is thus confessing; his own death, his own deserved wrath, is what is spread out before the Lord in that sprinkled blood! His tears drop on the floor as he again and again spreads out this symbol of his life forfeited and of his life saved. It seems that offering of incense was always accompanied with prayer (Rev. viii. 4); it was so here. Elijah's prayer for rain, when seven times in succession he urged the plea that in the end prevailed, was not more awfully earnest than Aaron's now. When first he sprinkles the blood, oh, how deep his agony! "O God, be merciful * to me a sinner!" Yet oh, how sweet his hope as he waves the censer over it, and feels the savour of life! Again and again he thus presents his atonement, till the seventh

---

* The very word there used seems to point the finger to the " ἱλαστήριον," *the mercy-seat.* It is ἱλάσθητί μοι, Luke xviii. 13.

time ends the whole transaction, and he stands alone with God, justified, accepted, loved, and blessed. Happier man than Adam! More holy spot than Eden! Happier man, because escaped from the curse for ever, and entered into an everlasting fellowship with the Almighty. More holy spot, because encircled with such amazing discoveries of the infinite perfections of holiness. In every way more blessed! for here are springs from the Godhead gushing forth as they never did in Paradise—new forms of love, joy, peace, blended with righteousness, and wisdom, and truth.

It was thus with Jesus in atoning for others. He all along carried the *blood* and the *sweet incense** with him. If he is baptized in Jordan, lo! the cloud of incense ascends "This is my beloved Son." If he talk of his decease, which he is to accomplish at Jerusalem, lo! again, "This is my beloved Son." If he is troubled in the temple, and the consuming fire be felt in his bones, lo! the incense again, "I have glorified thee, and will glorify thee again." He enters the sepulchre, rending asunder the veil; then, lo! the cloud of incense settles on his head! All is favour now; God meets with man, and man rests on God! "It is finished."

Christ's resurrection may have been typified by Aaron's coming out to the court again, after thus entering the

---

* "*Incense*," because of its smell being pleasing, is the type of service offered acceptably; see Rev. viii. 4; Ps. cxli. 2. But here notice, that in Rev. v. 8, the "*golden vials*" are not *censers*. The *censer* is, in the Septuagint, "τὸ πυρεῖον;" and "τα πυρεία" (2 Kings xxiv. 15) are distinguished from "τας φιάλας." "*Vials*" are the bowls of the altar, or the like. In Rev. v. 8, the saints see Christ about to enter on his glorious reign, and forthwith take their harps to praise, and also hold up their bowlfuls of still unanswered prayers, because these prayers will be fully granted now. As Ps. lxxii. 20. The saints here do not intercede for others; they have no *censers*; they only present their own prayers to the high priest.

Holiest.   He came forth, and once more stood at the altar.   And now he prepared to offer for the people.

> Ver. 15–17. *Then shall he kill the goat of the sin-offering that is for the people, and bring his blood within the veil, and do with that blood as he did with the blood of the bullock, and sprinkle it upon the mercy-seat, and before the mercy-seat.   And he shall make an atonement for the holy place, because of the uncleanness of the children of Israel, and because of their transgressions in all their sins: and so shall he do for the tabernacle of the congregation that remaineth among them in the midst of their uncleanness.   And there shall be no man in the tabernacle of the congregation when he goeth in to make an atonement in the holy place, until he come out, and have made an atonement for himself, and for his household, and for all the congregation of Israel.*

He now kills the people's sin-offering, confessing over it their uncleanness, transgressions, and sins.   He enters the Most Holy Place, as before, to sprinkle the blood. This he does on *the mercy-seat*, and also on *the floor* before it, or on the side of it ; thus filling the Holiest with the cry of atoning blood.   Over it he stands, confessing Israel's sin, with strong crying and tears ; he enumerates their departures from the holy law, and spreads out before God, in the light of his countenance, their endless sins, their transgressions of every form, their uncleannesses of deepest dye.   But that blood sprinkled there raises its cry—the life of the Living One is taken for the guilty —and to this blood Aaron points for pardon.   This is none other than a Gethsemane !   The Man of Sorrows, bearing our sins, is here.   "O God, thou knowest my foolishness, and my sins are not hid from thee" (Ps. lxix. 5).   "Surely he hath borne our griefs and carried our sorrows."   "The Lord laid on him the iniquity of us all."   And his precious life—the life of the true Living One—is taken for our life, and is poured out before the

Lord.   The cry of blood was to rise both from the *floor* below, and the *mercy-seat* above; so, the Saviour's atonement pleaded for us both from earth below, while he was here, and in heaven above, when he ascended.

This act of the high priest's was reckoned to be a cleansing of the Holy Place itself.   For the presence of guilty Israel defiled the courts, and the bringing in of their case in the person of their representative was reckoned as a defilement.   Therefore, there was need of a cleansing; and this took place when their representative was accepted, and all he confessed was thoroughly forgiven.   The forgiveness went forth in all its power through the Holy Place, carrying cleansing virtue with it to the worshippers, and to the ground whereon they stood.   But thus we see how it is written in Heb. ix. 23, that heaven needed purification if sinners were to enter : "It was therefore necessary that the patterns of things in the heavens should be purified with these ; but the *heavenly things themselves* with better sacrifices than these ;" viz. as ver. 24 declares, by Christ himself entering into them with the sacrifice himself.

This may shew us, by the way, why God not only drove out the man from Eden, but removed Eden itself very soon.   The *place* was polluted by having been the scene of the Fall—polluted by the most heinous of sins.

While all this was transacting, no one whatsoever was to be seen in the court of the tabernacle round the holy place—the Most Holy.   It was to be evident that the priest alone made atonement, and none else.   On one man dependeth their atonement.   How often would the idea of *another Adam* cross their minds—*all* leaning on *One!*   And oh, how tremblingly alive would they be to the danger of that óne mán, their representative, failing

in any point of duty that day! If he fail, Israel's guilt
remains. The high priest himself feels his awful responsibility; if he sin in this matter, he quenches the light
of Israel, extinguishes their hopes, sends them away in
blank despair. This one person is intrusted with their
life and their all. And thus the Holy Spirit painted
Jesus to the view of those who had clear, Abraham-like
faith. He will be alone in his undertaking, " *One for
all.*" Heaven and hell will look on intensely interested;
for "now is the judgment of this world;" now is the
crisis in the hopes of perishing men. He himself feels the
awful responsibility, and often, often as he goes onward,
raises a cry, "Make haste to help me, O my God!" "O
my strength, haste thee to help me!" "Save me from
the lion's mouth!" All alone he stands on Calvary; nay,
not one draws near to offer help; his own Father keeps
aloof, and the Mediator cries, "Lover and friend hast
thou put far from me, and mine acquaintance into darkness."

The priest entered in awful solemnity, pressed beneath
such a weight; Jesus also, in like manner, entered in
fear and anguish. But on this very account, to us all
bitterness is past; we go boldly into the Holiest of All
through that blood.

> Ver. 18, 19. *And he shall go out unto the altar that is before
> the Lord, and make an atonement for it; and shall take of
> the blood of the bullock, and of the blood of the goat, and put
> it upon the horns of the altar round about. And he shall
> sprinkle of the blood upon it with his finger seven times, and
> cleanse it, and hallow it from the uncleanness of the children
> of Israel.*

Some consider the altar of incense to be here meant,
simply because it is said, "the altar that is *before the*

Lord." But this expression determines nothing. Nay, it applies to the *altar of sacrifice*, as being under his special eye (see chap. iv. 24; or i. 5). The *holy* and *most holy* have been purified already; we are told now of the purifying of the *courts* and *the altar.*

Strange that *the altar* should need to be purified! And yet what spot had more connexion with sin? Was not every sin confessed there? Was not every sin laid down there? Was not that the spot where wrath was ever falling? Here is a strange combination—sin, and the atonement for sin. It may have been typical of the fact, that the foulest sin and the fullest atonement were found at the cross. Never was sin committed equal to that of the men who put Christ to death. Hell's darkest malignity and man's consummate infatuation and enmity were brought together to form this sin. And yet his dying took away sin. Thus, the eye of God sees on that spot, at one moment, the blackest of sins, and the most glorious atonement. Or, perhaps, it was meant simply to shew how he that was to make the atonement would himself contract no pollution. The *altar purified* is an imperfect way of shewing that *Christ continued spotless.*

Once more; the courts where the altar stood shared in this purification. Earth must be purified, because stained by sharing in the murder of the Son of God. When Jesus comes out from the Holiest of All, then it is that he shall purify these courts. It shall be a thorough cleansing; even as the blood was "seven times" put on the altar's horns, till in this manner the cry for pardon, or rather the cry of atonement accepted, had "seven times" sounded through all the courts of the tabernacle from the four "horns"—the emblems of strength and power.

Ver. 20–22. *And when he hath made an end of reconciling* the
holy place, and the tabernacle of the congregation, and the altar,
he shall bring the live goat: and Aaron shall lay both his hands
upon the head of the live goat, and confess over him all the
iniquities of the children of Israel, and all their transgressions
in†* all *their sins, putting them upon the head of the goat, and
shall send him away by the hand of a fit man into the wilderness.   And the goat shall bear upon him all their iniquities
unto a land not inhabited: and he shall let go the goat in the
wilderness.*

Aaron is now to shew atonement in another form.
To leave no doubt that sin has been carried away, there
is to be a putting away of it which the people can see,
as there had been one unseen in the Holy of holies.   The
live goat is brought forward, and all Israel hear the high
priest's voice confessing their sins and iniquities and transgressions.   Most solemnly, and no doubt even with weeping, did Aaron confess his people's sins over the head of
the scape-goat.   He felt on his heart the load which he
was laying on the victim.

These confessed sins being thus laid on its head, the
goat stood laden with the curse.   Against it alone will
the lightning be directed now—on this one point will
vengeance fall.   Israel is now clear—the stroke must
slope over their heads toward their substitute.   And a
"fit man," one appointed for the purpose, leads it away
down the courts, in presence of all the people, slowly and
carefully, till he has gone out of sight and reached the
wilds of some rugged spot, or uninhabited waste.‡   The

---

* May Col. i. 20, "By him to *reconcile all things* to himself which are in
heaven," be explained by a reference to the above transactions?

† לכל, perhaps, "*according* to all their sins." As if he were reading the
pages of the book of remembrance, he must read according to what has been
actually before him.

‡ Some "regio invia," or γῇ ἀβατος, as the Septuagint render it.

"*fit person*" returns and attests that he left it there; and Israel feels the joy of pardon.   Wrath against these confessed sins will now alight in the desert, not upon them. " *The Lord hath laid on him the iniquity of us all*," is their song.

We may remark the opinion of a learned man, that Jesus, driven into the wilderness to be tempted of the devil after the scene of his baptism, where our sin was openly confessed by him as laid on himself, is the antitype of what follows in the scape-goat.   We think, however, much more is meant.

Follow the scape-goat, and see its doom.   Is there not here a criminal led along?   There is something that speaks of the Man of Sorrows, made sin for us.   Is there not here a criminal led away to unknown woe?   There is something that speaks of one "made a curse for us." Why is he left alone, defenceless, trembling amid a wilderness?   There is here enough to remind us of Jesus left to suffer without sympathy.   "He looked on his right hand, and there was none; refuge failed him; no man cared for his soul."   The scape-goat's solitary cry is re-echoed by the barren rocks, and the howling of beasts of prey terrifies it on all sides; the gloom of night settles down upon it and shrouds it in deeper terror. Perhaps, too, it was not uncommon for Jehovah himself to direct his lightning's stroke toward this victim, and to cause it to perish amid the tempest's roar.   Wounded by beasts of prey, from whom it has scarcely escaped, it is now stretched on the ground by a stroke from that thunder-cloud (for " lightnings in the night" are frequent in that country at this season), its eyes glaring with convulsive fear, and its piteous cries echoing through the dismal wilderness.   Perhaps it was generally thus that the sin-bearing scape-goat died. "Lover and friend hast thou put far from me, and mine acquaintance into darkness." And to Israel there was the same meaning in its suffering unto death as the thief saw in a dying Saviour. "That victim's sufferings are my sufferings," would a man of Israel say, even as Ambrose has said of the thief on the cross, "Scivit latro quod illa in corpore Christi vulnera non essent *Christi* vulnera, sed *latronis*" (*Serm. de salv. latr.*) "The thief knew that those wounds in the body of Christ were not the wounds of *Christ*, but of *the thief.*"

> Ver. 23–28. *And Aaron shall come into the tabernacle of the congregation, and shall put off the linen garments which he put on when he went into the holy place, and shall leave them there: and he shall wash his flesh with water in the holy place, and put on his garments, and come forth, and offer his burnt-offering, and the burnt-offering of the people, and make an atonement for himself, and for the people. And the fat of the sin-offering shall he burn upon the altar. And he that let go the goat for the scape-goat shall wash his clothes, and bathe his flesh in water, and afterward come into the camp. And the bullock for the sin-offering, and the goat for the sin-offering, whose blood was brought in to make atonement in the holy place, shall one carry forth without the camp; and they shall burn in the fire their skins, and their flesh, and their dung. And he that burneth them shall wash his clothes, and bathe his flesh in water, and afterward he shall come into the camp.*

All that was absolutely required toward the people's forgiveness being now done, no doubt through the assembled congregation there ran a thrill of joy and expectant hope. All felt the heavy burden raised off their persons; and they now only waited for the final issue—the appearing of Aaron in his robes of beauty. Thus far it was as when Jesus cried, "It is finished:" but one thing remains; let him return in his glorious person, no more connected with sin, shining in the beams of the Father's love. This he did on the third day when he rose.

Aaron had gone into the Holy Place, and there laid aside his linen garments, and washed his person in pure water, preparatory to his coming forth again—a type of Jesus laying aside the likeness of sinful flesh, and ceasing from all connexion with sin. Putting on his other garments, which were embroidered with gold, he appeared in glory ; for the sunbeams fell bright and dazzling on his golden mitre and on his gold-adorned vestments, expressive of the acceptance and favour of God shining on him as representative and head of Israel. As their accepted intercessor, he completed that day's solemn atonement by offering up his own burnt-offering and the burnt-offering for the people, shewing thereby that there was free access opened up to Israel by One ; and that One stood as priest over them. Then, in sight of all, he burnt "the fat ;" that is, the two kidneys and the fat on them (iii. 10), and all the fat about the inwards, that the blazing flame of these portions of the sacrifice might indicate the dedication of his whole heart and inmost desires, all sent up in one flame to God. And while he was thus engaged, the man who had carried away the scape-goat shewed himself at the gate of the camp, testifying that he had fulfilled his commission. So truly had the sin laid on the goat been transferred to it, that this man was polluted by being at its side ! So in Num. xix. 8. But having bathed himself in pure water, to shew that all connexion between him and the sin-bearing goat had ceased, he now entered among the worshippers as a man who could testify that their sins had been laid there and were carried away.

Last of all, the relics of the offerings already presented viz. of the bullock and goat sin-offering, are removed. The sacrifices were offered, the blood sprinkled, the scape-goat sent to its desert; the burnt-offerings were blazing on the altar; the fat of the offerings were consuming away; the conductor of the scape-goat present to testify to the completeness of the transference of sin—like ministers who are eye-witnesses of Christ's sufferings, and partakers of the effects. What then remained, but only to remove the relics of the sacrifices that began that day's solemn proceedings? It is soon done. The relics are carried out of the camp and burnt there, in the place of the curse (see chap. iv. 12), leaving all Israel assured that their own and Aaron's sins are for ever gone—the smoke bending its curling volumes towards the wilderness, as far from view as the scape-goat that had borne thither their heavy load. And thus, all done, the sun sets in stillness over a calm, solemnised, and peaceful camp.

It had been a wondrous day from the very first dawn to the last streak of setting sun. At the third hour of the morning (nine o'clock) every street or way of the camp had been trodden by a people going up to peculiar service—each moving along serious and awe-struck. As many as the courts could contain enter—specially aged men and fathers of Israel; the rest stand in thousands near, or sit in groups under green bushes and on little eminences that overlook the enclosing curtains. Some are in the attitude of prayer; some are pondering the book of the law; some, like Hannah, move their lips, though no word is heard; all are ever and again glancing at the altar, and the array of the courts. Even children sit in wonder, and whisper their inquiries to their parents.

The morning sacrifice is offered; the priest's bullock and ram standing by, and other victims besides. They wait in expectation of what is to follow when the smoke of the morning lamb has melted into the clouds. They see the lots cast on the two goats, the priest enter the sanctuary with his own offering, and return amid the tremblings of Israel, who all feel that *they* are concerned in *his* acceptance. They see one goat slain and its blood carried in. The scape-goat is then led down their trembling ranks, out of the camp; and at length Aaron re-appears to their joy. The murmur of delight now spreads along, like the pleasant ruffling of the water's surface in the breeze of a summer's evening. The silver trumpets sound—the evening lamb is offered; Israel feels the favour of their God, and returns home to rest under his shadow. "O Lord, thou wast angry with me, but thine anger is turned away, and thou comfortest me."

How intensely interesting, to have seen this day kept in Jerusalem! The night before, you would have noticed the city become silent and still, as the sun set. No lingerers in the market; no traders; no voice of business. The watchmen that go about the city sing the penitential Psalms, reminding themselves of their own and the city's secret sins, seen through the darkness by an all-seeing God; and the Levites from the temple sing responsively as they walk round the courts. When the sun has risen over the Mount of Olives, none go forth to the streets; no smoke rises from any dwelling; no hum of busy noise; for no work is done on a holy convocation day. The melody of joy and health ascends from the tabernacles of the righteous. But at the hour of morning sacrifice, the city pours out its thousands, who move solemnly toward

the temple, or repair to the heights of Zion's towers, of
the grassy slopes of Olivet, that they may witness as well
as join in all the day's devotion.   They see the service
proceed—they see the scape-goat led away—they see the
priest come out of the Holy Place; and at this comforting sight every head in the vast, vast multitude is bowed
in solemn thankfulness, and every heart moves the lips
to a burst of joy.   The trumpet for the evening sacrifice
sounds; Olivet re-echoes; the people on its bosom see
the city and the altar, and weep for very gladness; all
know it is the hour for the evening blessing.   When the
sun set, an angel might have said to his fellow, "Look
upon Zion, the city of solemnities! behold Jerusalem, a
quiet habitation!"

> Ver. 29–34. *And this shall be a statute for ever unto you, that
> in the seventh month, on the tenth day of the month, ye shall
> afflict your souls, and do no work at all, whether it be one of
> your own country, or a stranger that sojourneth among you.
> For on that day shall the priest make an atonement for you,
> to cleanse you, that ye may be clean from all your sins before
> the Lord.   It shall be a sabbath of rest unto you, and ye
> shall afflict your souls, by a statute for ever.   And the priest
> whom he shall anoint, and whom he shall consecrate to mini-
> ster in the priest's office in his father's stead, shall make the
> atonement, and shall put on the linen clothes, even the holy
> garments.   And he shall make an atonement for the holy sanc-
> tuary, and he shall make an atonement for the tabernacle of
> the congregation, and for the altar; and he shall make an
> atonement for the priests, and for all the people of the con-
> gregation.   And this shall be an everlasting statute unto you
> to make an atonement for the children of Israel, for all their
> sins, once a year.   And he did as the Lord commanded
> Moses.*

We see, in ver. 29, that the true heart-service of the
day was enjoined as much as the external observances—

as much "*afflicting their souls*,"* as "*doing no work at all.*" Nor was the presence of strangers to be the least hindrance ; our friends must join us in God's service, but no politeness must lead us to leave God for them.

Once a year all these rites were to be observed. The *seventh month* was to be to them as memorable as the *seventh day* of every week. The prophet Isaiah very sorely reproves the neglected observance of this holy day in chap. lviii. He says, ver. 3, "In the day of your Fast ye find pleasure," not afflicting your souls, " and exact all your demands of labour," instead of doing no work at all. God saw them in their houses, and observed that they secretly carried on their worldly business, and that their soul was unhumbled. Hence, he says, " *Ye shall not fast as ye do this day. Is it such a fast that I have chosen, a day for a man to afflict his soul?* " That is, is it such a fast as yours ? Is that like a day of soul-affliction ? your bowing down your head as a bulrush ? And ye have added external rites of your own, to hide the inward leanness, "*putting sackcloth and ashes under you*" (ver. 5). "Nay," saith the Lord, "loose the burdens which ye wickedly impose on the poor, and set free the bankrupt,† and thus make the day a real *Sabbath.* Also, let the poor have food (ver. 7), and help thy impoverished brother. Then, indeed, thou mayest expect to feel the joy of the Expiation-day (ver. 8, 9), and all the year long thou shalt be kept and blessed" (ver. 11,

---

* See chap. xxiii. 29.

† This may refer to the times when the year *of jubilee*, " the year of release," began on the evening of the day of atonement. Giving food to the poor (ver. 7) marked the year of jubilee also (Ex. xxiii. 11). The prophet chooses such a time, when there was double obligation on a Jew, in order to shew their hypocrisy in a more marked form.

12). As surely as morn arose, after the atonement-day was done; and as surely as in the year of release that morn was ushered in with the joyful notes of jubilee, so certainly should they have reaped the blessing. Oh! if thou wouldst keep all his solemn Sabbaths, how blessed wouldst thou be (ver. 13, 14), and thy land a land of fruitfulness to thee!

"Happy art thou, O Israel, a people saved of the Lord!"

CHAPTER XVII

The Use of Animal Food Regulated *

" Whether therefore ye eat, or drink, or whatsoever ye do, do all to the glory of God."—1 Cor. x. 31

Ver. 1–5. *And the Lord spake unto Moses, saying, Speak unto Aaron, and unto his sons, and unto all the children of Israel, and say unto them, This is the thing which the Lord hath commanded, saying, What man soever there be of the house of Israel that killeth an ox, or lamb, or goat, in the camp, or that killeth it out of the camp, and bringeth it not unto the door of the tabernacle of the congregation, to offer an offering unto the Lord, before the tabernacle of the Lord, blood shall be imputed unto that man; he hath shed blood; and that man shall be cut off from among his people: to the end that the children of Israel may bring their sacrifices, which they offer in the open field, even that they may bring them unto the Lord, unto the door of the tabernacle of the congregation unto the priest, and offer them for peace-offerings unto the Lord.*

HERE *the people* are addressed, as well as Aaron and his sons ; for it was needful to shew them that, in requisitions that affected their private affairs, the scrutiny was made by the all-seeing God. It was important that the people should see plainly that this inspection of private matters was the Lord's ordinance, not originated by the priests nor by Moses. They would naturally be more jealous

---

* We may call this portion of the book *the second section of the Levitical code.* The *public services* of the worshippers are over. Here begin some rules affecting their private morality and their secret devotions.

in regard to those institutions that touched upon their domestic habits.

There was little *flesh* used as common food in these Eastern countries; it was used chiefly on feast days.* Hence the restrictions here were not burdensome. And when they reached Canaan, if they needed more animal food, and were further off from the tabernacle, these restrictions ceased, as Deut. xii. 13–15 declares, and as the constant use of " camp" in this place might lead us to suppose. The grand object of this law was to prevent idolatry. Heathen nations (see Ps. xvi. 4) used to take the blood of animals and pour it into a hole or trench in the earth, for food to their gods ;† and there the dead were consulted. Now, a law like this insured that the blood should not be so used. *The ox, sheep, and goat* (ver. 3) are selected as specimens; but no doubt *any* species of animal food was subjected to the same restrictions. They came with the animal to the door of the tabernacle; saw God revealing himself there; left the blood as an offering to him; and then returned home to their tent to feast. How solemn and how sweet to a true Israelite! He brings his food to the Lord, sees his majesty, acknowledges himself worthy to die, but redeemed by atoning blood; and thus goes to his table and eats his meat with gladness and singleness of heart! All their meat became a " peace-offering" (ver. 5).

Are we not here taught the duty of coming to the Lord at every season of food? owning him as Preserver? feeling that blood has redeemed our life? and so going forward with hearts ever impressed and awed? We

---

* It has been noticed by some that Reuben, Gad, and half Manasseh were the only tribes that had herds (Num. xxxii.) ; the other tribes possessed very few, and may even have borrowed from these when they needed sacrifices.

† As we see in Homer's celebrated Νεκυΐα, *Odyss.* B. xi

should eat our daily bread in his presence.* We should remember the time when the grant of animal food was made, viz. after the deluge ; and thus we would feel our common food to be a memorial of wrath passed and new mercy begun.

In ver. 5, "the *sacrifices in the open field*" mean all things slain ; which they had hitherto killed anywhere, at home or publicly. These are now to be presented as *peace-offerings;* that is, they are to be presented to the Lord through the priest, and then given back to him, like as was done in the case of peace-offerings.

> Ver. 6. *And the priest shall sprinkle the blood upon the altar of the Lord, at the door of the tabernacle of the congregation, and burn the fat for a sweet savour unto the Lord.*

The *fat* and the *blood* are taken (see chap. iii. 17). When this is done, the blessing rests on them; *sweet savour* breathes from them.

> Ver. 7. *And they shall no more offer their sacrifices unto devils, after whom they have gone a whoring. This shall be a statute for ever unto them, throughout their generations.*

The word here rendered "*devils*" (שְׂעִירִים) is equivalent to "*goat-gods.*" It is originally used of "goats ;" shaggy goats, whose appearance gave origin to the heathen idea of *satyrs.*† No doubt the Lord called *heathen gods* by this name, to cast contempt upon them ; and also *the devils,* or fallen angels, who suggested and fostered the idolatry of the heathen, were denominated by this term. Besides, *goats* were worshipped in Egypt.

---

* Cudworth, *on the Passover,* suggests that the coming up to the three annual feasts effected the same end when Israel reached Canaan ; for then they came up and ate before God, and carried home the solemn impressions then made for the rest of the year.

† Robertson, in his *Clavis Pent.,* adds "*monkeys*" to the class of hairy deities. The root of the word is שָׂעַר, used in Deut. xxxii. 17, and elsewhere, in the sense of "*fear.*" The derivative would thus express "*objects of dread.*"

Various passages shew that the Jews had gone aside to such idolatry during their sojourn in Egypt; and that they manifested a tendency to this same apostasy still.[*]

The Lord who says of disciples, "Inasmuch as ye have done it unto one of the least of *these*, ye have done it unto *me*," says in like manner, "If ye sacrifice to one of these idolatrous gods, ye sacrifice to the devils who have suggested them." The Lord saw, at the same time, how the devils allured Israel to make this idolatrous use of *the blood*, in order to bring *atonement* into disregard; or, in order to get them to suppose that devils needed to be, and could be, thus appeased and bribed to leave them unhurt.

> Ver. 8, 9. *And thou shalt say unto them, Whatsoever man there be of the house of Israel, or of the strangers which sojourn among you, that offereth a burnt-offering or sacrifice, and bringeth it not unto the door of the tabernacle of the congregation, to offer it unto the Lord, even that man shall be cut off from among his people.*

This law is different from the foregoing. It refers to animals offered in sacrifice. All sacrifice must be offered "at the door of the tabernacle," that is, in the presence of Jehovah, and to him alone. Some might have tried to evade the law already given by pretending that they killed their animals for sacrifice, and so were free to pour out the blood at the spot where they offered sacrifice; therefore, the Lord commands all sacrifices to be offered at one spot, viz. his own presence. And, lest *strangers* should mislead them, the law is laid on strangers too. The Lord is full and sincere in all he enjoins; he never intends reserve or mystery in his demands. His name is glorious. We can trust his heart; for he tells us plainly

---

[*] See Deut. xxxii. 16; Ps. cvi. 37; Amos v. 25; Ezek. xx. 7.

all he means.   And surely not less true are his promises
of life—his life-giving offers.

> Ver. 10–12. *And whatsoever man there be of the house of Israel,
> or of the strangers that sojourn among you, that eateth any
> manner of blood, I will even set my face against that soul that
> eateth blood, and will cut him off from among his people. For
> the life* (נֶמֶשׁ) *of the flesh is in the blood; and I have given it
> to you upon the altar, to make an atonement for your souls:*
> for it is the blood that maketh an atonement for the soul*
> (בַּנֶּפֶשׁ). *Therefore I said unto the children of Israel, No soul
> of you shall eat blood, neither shall any stranger that sojourn-
> eth among you eat blood.*

A former law is re-instituted or enforced afresh (see
chap. iii. 17; vii. 26).   While they must guard against
pouring out the blood to idols, they must equally guard
against using it for themselves, in the haste of hunger,
doing as Saul's soldiers are related to have done (1 Sam.
xiv. 32).

The grand reason for this jealousy over the use of the
blood is, " *The blood is the life*."   When poured out, it shews
atonement ; for it expresses the *life taken;* " Thou shalt
die."   To you, sinner, what should be more tremendous
than the sign of your own life taken ?   And to your God,

---

* Sykes, *on Sacrifices*, has collected some interesting quotations to shew the
general prevalence of the idea of substitution.   The Egyptians said over the
victim : " Εἰς κεφαλὴν ταυτην το κακον τραπεσθαι " (Herod. ii. 39).   In Ovid
Fast. vi. 161, we read, " Cor pro corde precor, pro fibris sumite fibras ; Hanc
animam vobis pro meliore damus."   Cæsar says of the Gauls, " Pro vitâ
hominis nisi vita hominis reddatur non posse deorum immortalium numen pla-
cari arbitrantur " (B. G. vi. 15).   Magee quotes from Plautus Epid. :—

> " Men' piaculum oportet, fieri propter stultitiam tuam,
>   Ut meum tergum stultitiæ tuæ subdas succedaneum."

And Porphyry uses " ψυχην αντι ψυχης."   If Bahr's rendering of ver. 11 be
admitted, there is greater force still in it :—" For *the soul* of the flesh is in the
blood—and it is the blood that maketh atonement by *means of the soul*," *i. e.*
by means of the life of the flesh being poured out.   This illustrates Isa. liii. 10,
" When thou shalt make his soul (*his life*) an offering for sin."

O sinner, nothing is more solemnly glorious than the blood of his own Son. Earth and heaven stand still when blood is poured out. " By the life is the atonement made."

When the spear reached the heart of Jesus, the blood was poured out from the very seat of life. The heart and the pericardium were both pierced, and, therefore, the blood that then gushed forth with the liquid fluid of the pericardium was blood from the warm seat of vitality (see John xix. 34). And as such was the type, so the reality. Jesus did then pour forth his whole soul; affections, feelings, faculties, and every power of his soul—all were laid down in suffering obedience to his Father. The heat of wrath melted all: and all thus melted flowed forth in that wondrous stream. The law took out its penalty from the very source of life.

But why *life taken?* Why "death" required? Because the essence of sin is an attack on God's holy throne and his very existence. It is, therefore, repelled by God crushing the sinner's life. And Jesus bore even this for men! " Ye have *slain the Prince of Life!* "

Yet more, however. How astounding must our Lord's words have been to the Jews; "*Except ye . . . drink the blood of the Son of man, ye have no life in you*" (John vi. 53). He abrogates the law, for he fulfils the type! You must *live by blood* now! You are to drink *the poured out life* of the Son of man.

> Ver. 13, 14. *And whatsoever man there be of the children of Israel, or of the strangers that sojourn among you, which hunteth, and catcheth any beast or fowl that may be eaten; he shall even pour out the blood thereof, and cover it with dust. For it is the life of all flesh; the blood of it is for the life thereof: therefore I said unto the children of Israel, Ye shall eat the blood of no manner of flesh: for the life of all flesh is the blood thereof; whosoever eateth it shall be cut off.*

Another opportunity is taken of solemnly charging Israel to remember the blood of atonement.   The hunter in his full career must keep atonement in his eye ; and, when he has his prey in his hand, must reverently stand still and pour out its blood to Jehovah, to cover it from the gaze of men and the ravenous appetite of creatures of prey.   God would have the sinner's soul send up its adoring thanks to him for atonement amid their forests, and in their wilds.   Redemption should be sung of by every man in every situation ; and none should be found in a situation wherein he cannot sing the song of Moses and the Lamb.

Israel's huntsmen were to be men of faith.   They were not to hunt for the gratifying of wild fiery passions, but for food and necessity.   The chastening solemnity of *"pouring out the blood"* was a check on the huntsman. None who would not stay, in their vehement, eager, keen pursuit, to realise redemption, must engage in this employment.   It is not for the gay, wild spirits of youth ; or, if fiery youth engage therein, it must lead them to the most solemn views of sin and righteousness.   Yea, it shall be even a way of life to them.   Let them go—let them ride furiously over rock and chasm—let them shoot the arrow—but lo! the field becomes an avenue to lead them to the presence of the Holy God.   They must stand still *at the blood!*   " He taketh them in their craftiness." After his most ardent chase, in the recess of the forest, the huntsman of Israel meets with God !

> Ver. 15, 16. *And every soul that eateth that which died of itself, or that which was torn with beasts, whether it be one of your own country, or a stranger, he shall both wash his clothes, and bathe himself in water, and be unclean until the even ; then shall he be clean.   But if he wash them not, nor bathe his flesh, then he shall bear his iniquity.*

The reason of this law is, that *the blood* is left in the body, if the animal die of itself or be torn to death. So also, if *strangled* (see Acts xv. 20), the blood coagulating in the veins and arteries. He that violates this law, even ignorantly, is guilty. He must forthwith wash in water and be unclean till evening. And the reflection awakened, the jealousy begotten, the view of atonement given, by his being that day set apart, will leave its indelible impressions on the man of Israel, that he may ever after walk with his eye solemnly resting on atoning blood.

CHAPTER XVIII

Private and Domestic Obligations—Purity in every Relation of Life

" Not in the lust of concupiscence, even as the Gentiles which know not God: that no man go beyond and defraud his brother in any matter: because that the Lord is the avenger of all such, as we also have forewarned you, and testified. For God hath not called us unto uncleanness, but unto holiness."—1 Thess. iv. 5-7

Ver. 1–5. And the Lord spake unto Moses, saying, Speak unto the children of Israel, and say unto them, I am the Lord your God. After the doings of the land of Egypt, wherein ye dwelt, shall ye not do: and after the doings of the land of Canaan, whither I bring you, shall ye not do; neither shall ye walk in their ordinances. Ye shall do my judgments,* and keep mine ordinances, to walk therein: I am the Lord your God. Ye shall therefore keep my statutes and my judgments; which if a man do, he shall live in them: I am the Lord.

THE Lord prefaces the laws he is to lay down in this chapter by very solemn declarations of his sovereignty—
"*I am Jehovah;*" and of his relation to them as a reconciled God—"*I am your God.*" He sets before them his authority and his constraining love. He knows our frame; and he sees that man resents interference with his liberty

---

* The general principles and precepts are, מִשְׁפָּטִים, "*judgments;*" the "*statutes,*" חֻקּוֹת, are special details under these heads. Others say מִשְׁפָּט is what your very nature binds you to observe, and חֹק, what depends on the arbitrary appointment of God.

in the things of daily life and private actions, more than in anything else; therefore, to silence objection, and to draw the will, he adduces the argument of his sovereignty and love.

Besides, nothing is so directly fitted to subdue lust as a full recognition of the glorious Godhead, and his presence in the soul. The sweetness and blessedness of a present God causes a holy, heavenly satisfaction in the soul that altogether banishes impure desire. Hence 2 Pet. i. 4, *" Partakers of the divine nature, having escaped the corruption that is in the world through lust."** And in Rom. i. 23, 24, the root of uncleanness is said to be, " They changed the glory of the incorruptible God." In ver. 25, 26, the origin of vile affections is declared to be, " They changed the truth of God into a lie, and served the creature ;" and in ver. 28, 29, it is plainly stated, that their " not liking to retain God in their knowledge" was the cause of the "things not convenient, unrighteousness, fornication," that followed.

In ver. 5, he subjoins another motive, namely, *life to be found in them.* This might mean here, that God's appointments are the sinner's sign-posts, by which he learns how to go to the city of refuge, and how to keep on the way of holiness. But if, as most think, we are to take, in this place, the words " *live in them,*" as meaning "eternal life to be got by them," the scope of the passage is, that so excellent are God's laws, and every special, minute detail of these laws, *that if a man were to keep these always and perfectly,* the very keeping would be eternal life to him. And the quotations in Rom. x. 5, and Gal. iii. 12,

---

* The original implies that " *partakers of the divine nature* " are " *fleers from—fugitives from the corruption—the lustful corruption—that is in the world.*"

would seem to determine this to be the true and only sense here.

> Ver. 6. *None of you shall approach to any that is near of kin to him, to uncover their nakedness : I am the Lord.*

These laws are not national, or peculiar to the Jews alone, for the violation of them is charged on the nations of Canaan as a violation of what nature itself teaches. The " nearness of kin," is sister, mother, daughter; the woman being born of the same flesh as the man is (Patrick). The following Latin lines (quoted in Poli Synopsis) sum up the forbidden degrees :—

> " Nata, soror, neptis, matertera, fratris et uxor,
> Et patrui conjunx, mater privigna, noverca,
> Uxorisque soror, privigni nata, nurusque,
> Atque soror patris, conjungi lege vetantur."

The Lord again sets forth his authority in beginning to enter upon the details that follow. By his Divine authority he issues these laws. And they are still binding. 1. They are really no more than an amplification of the seventh commandment. The different channels in which lust might flow are pointed out, and then filled up— choked up—by the Divine prohibition. 2. They are not *ceremonial* precepts, and therefore they are permanent in their obligations. They bind all nations, even as does the seventh commandment. 3. They are so truly *moral* obligations, that in ver. 24, 25, the Canaanites are stamped with infamy for not having recognised and observed them. It is plain, therefore,* that these laws were in force *before* the Mosaic ritual existed; and if so, they have *patriarchal* authority. 4. There is no hint in the New Testament that they have been repealed ; but, on the contrary, Paul's horror, expressed in 1 Cor. v. 1, unequivocally declares

---

* See Bush, *ad locum.*

that he recognised the precepts as both *moral* and *divine* in their authority.

The Lord would hereby preserve purity and peace throughout the wide circle of domestic intercourse. He wishes perfect confidence and a pure familiarity to prevail among relatives. Having, in former chapters, fenced his own tabernacle, he now fences the tabernacles of men.

> Ver. 7, 8. *The nakedness of thy father, or the nakedness of thy mother, shalt thou not uncover: she is thy mother; thou shalt not uncover her nakedness. The nakedness of thy father's wife shalt thou not uncover: it is thy father's nakedness.*

Whether thy full mother, or only thy step-mother; and although thy step-mother be now left a widow. The heathen story of Jocasta and Œdipus proves how deep this precept as to the mother is engraven in the nature of man; and not only the Divine stigma on Reuben (Gen. xxxv. 22), but even the heathen abhorrence of the same in 1 Cor. v. 1, " *not so much as named among them,*" shew how this same feeling extends to the case of step-mother.

May we not here, from the fact that in this instance *human* law and feeling among heathens coincided with the Divine, derive light as to the other commandments? If the law of God be thus recognised by the human conscience in such cases as these, is it not plain that the same conscience will yet testify to all other parts of this holy law in like manner? There is sufficient to prove that the law was once there, and sufficient also to prove that it was displaced. The *fragments* testify that it was there; yet, being *only fragments*, they also testify that it was effaced.

> Ver. 9–11. *The nakedness of thy sister, the daughter of thy father, or daughter of thy mother, whether she be born at home, or*

born abroad, even their nakedness thou shalt not uncover. The
nakedness of thy son's daughter, or of thy daughter's daughter,
even their nakedness thou shalt not uncover: for theirs is thine
own nakedness. The nakedness of thy father's wife's daughter,
begotten of thy father, (she is thy sister,) thou shalt not uncover
her nakedness.

The case of a sister, legitimate or not, and of a grand-
daughter, and of a step-sister, *i. e.* half-sister by the side
of the mother—each of these is here taken up. Of
course Cain and Abel were not under this law; they
married their sisters. Abraham marrying his half-sister,
Sarah, is an instance of the unsettled state of the law
then, and an instance of what Solon thought might be
allowed, viz. the marriage of " ὁμοπάτριοι," but not of
" ὁμομήτριοι," those who had the same father, but not
the same mother (Gen. xx. 12). But to prevent a recurrence of these unions, the law is clearly stated for the
future. Temporary considerations were allowed by God
to supersede these precepts on some occasions; but so
strong and binding are they in all other cases, that it
would need nothing less than Divine permission to make
them justifiable. All this was fitted to set up in families
a system of pure domestic peace; intercourse where no
impure principles had sway; affection flowing out in a
clear stream of disinterested kindliness. Families on
earth should bear resemblance to the heavenly family,
who walk in holy intercourse, receiving from the Father
himself, through the Son, an overflowing love. For the
love of God to them comes in upon the love they have to
one another; and forthwith, as when a massy rock glides
down into the bosom of some mountain-pool, there is a
gushing over of its waters on every side—on all around.

The case of *grandchildren*, in ver. 10, 11, has an interesting feature in it. It might happen that after a father's

death, the original family would be broken up. The
widow married again, and her new family grew up in
youth and beauty. These *daughters* are like strangers to
the original family; still, a relationship has been formed,
however slight it appear: these are to be reckoned sisters
of the original family. Thus the Lord multiplied the
links of connexion, and kept connexions unbroken. And
the more this is done, the less have selfishness and sen-
suality room to gain strength.

> Ver. 12–14. *Thou shalt not uncover the nakedness of thy father's
> sister: she is thy father's near kinswoman. Thou shalt not
> uncover the nakedness of thy mother's sister: for she is thy
> mother's near kinswoman. Thou shalt not uncover the naked-
> ness of thy father's brother, thou shalt not approach to his
> wife: she is thine aunt.*

Here is the case of aunts, paternal and maternal, and
the wives of paternal uncles; and of course, too, a maternal uncle's wife. This is always understood to include
the *niece* likewise, on the plain principles already stated;
and it, of course, includes the case of females not marrying uncle or nephew. The Lord would spread the feelings of relationship widely, and so expand our unselfish
feelings; but all the while he checks and restrains every
tendency to what would hinder the free flow of those
disinterested feelings.

> Ver. 15, 16. *Thou shalt not uncover the nakedness of thy daughter-
> in-law: she is thy son's wife; thou shalt not uncover her
> nakedness. Thou shalt not uncover the nakedness of thy
> brother's wife: it is thy brother's nakedness.*

In one particular case, namely, that referred to in
Deut. xxv. 5–10, the famous case brought forward to
Jesus by the Sadducees, Matt. xxii. 23–26, there is an
exception to ver. 16. But that express exception, or pro-
viso, in the particular case, just enforces it the more in all

others ;* and that one exception had in view the special object of preserving families and inheritances unbroken until Messiah should come. Daughters-in-law are reckoned truly *daughters*, and sisters-in-law really *sisters*. It seems that when such new relations are formed, God gives the affectionate feeling of kindred to the new relatives, and so cements the social fabric.

This verse seems plainly to forbid the marriage of a woman to the husband of her sister. Throughout this chapter, affinity and consanguinity are identified or spoken of as constituting relationships of equal nearness.

> Ver. 17, 18. *Thou shalt not uncover the nakedness of a woman and her daughter, neither shalt thou take her son's daughter, or her daughter's daughter, to uncover her nakedness; for they are her near kinswomen: it is wickedness. Neither shalt thou take a wife to her sister, to vex her, to uncover her nakedness, besides the other in her lifetime.*

It appears that God is anxious to draw as many men as possible into close relationships. Connexion so near, with persons who were previously unconnected with us, is well fitted to counteract the natural selfishness of men. Men are thus drawn outward to other circles of society; and the circles are none of them isolated, but each touches on the other, or passes through it. The disunion of the Fall, and the divisions of Babel, are thus repaired to some degree. And in all we see the traces of the same Father and Elder Brother who binds together his new family so thoroughly into one wide yet firmly knit and compact community.

It is declared to be "*horrid wickedness*" (זִמָּה) to marry the daughter of a man's own step-daughter; much more, then, to marry the step-daughter herself. So,

---

* Bush has good remarks on this chapter.

mutatis mutandis, in the case of a woman proposing to marry her step-son, or his son. But, in ver. 18, there is a difficulty. Some consider it as a prohibition of polygamy altogether, rendering the words thus : " Thou shalt not take one woman to another." But this sense cannot be demonstrated to be demanded by the words ; and Jewish practice seems to prove that it was not the sense attached to the words by Israel in ancient days. The true meaning seems to be, as in our version, " *Thou shalt not take a wife to her sister;*" and the design of the law was to prohibit such marriages as once took place in the case of Jacob, when he married *Rachel* and *Leah* in one week. Other laws imply that a *sister-in-law* must never be married to her brother-in-law ; and this verse still further fortifies society at a time when polygamy prevailed. For some might have tried to evade the prohibition by taking two sisters *simultaneously, i. e.* before one or other could stand in the relation of sister-in-law. The words, "in her *lifetime,*" should be joined to the first clause,* "*to vex her all her life*"—as we see took place in the case of Leah and Rachel. The Lord has a regard even to the personal feelings of the individuals, and to the probable results that might ensue in regard to domestic peace. While he does not in this place positively forbid polygamy, he guards it against one special evil that might be introduced by it, viz. the marrying of two sisters.

That the Lord permitted polygamy at all, seems to have been with a typical design. It was branded as a state of imperfection, and merely tolerated. Our Lord says of it, in Matt. xix. 8, that it was permitted "*because of*

* So ver. 19, בְּנֻדָּה. Bush has a full note on this passage, bearing on the disputes that have arisen in the American churches; and of late, in our own country, since the earlier editions of this work appeared, the subject has assumed importance.

the hardness of their hearts." This language implies that it was acknowledged to be an imperfection. As such, it was permitted to remain in Israel, in order to keep them in expectation of a higher and better order of things, resembling far more nearly the order of unfallen Paradise, where there was union between one man and one woman—a shadow of Christ and his Church. The Church's unholy alliances with the world, its mixed holiness, its imperfections, its inconsistencies, were to be set forth by the one husband with many wives. But, at all events, there was an intended imperfection in the system, pointing forward to the coming of the true Spouse and Bridegroom—Christ and his catholic yet one united Church.

> Ver. 19. *Also thou shalt not approach unto a woman to uncover her nakedness as long as she is put apart for her uncleanness.*

By this law, the Lord put a check even on lawful intercourse. There were times when the wife was not to be approached by her own husband. And in Ezek. xxii. 10, the transgression of this law is reckoned one of the marks of Israel's great corruptions. Every sensual feeling must be subordinated to the Lord's will; and men must live as the Lord appoints. Their happiness consists in letting their soul flow out in the channel of the Lord's will.

> Ver. 20–23. *Moreover, thou shalt not lie carnally with thy neighbour's wife, to defile thyself with her. And thou shalt not let any of thy seed pass through the fire to Molech, neither shalt thou profane the name of thy God: I am the Lord. Thou shalt not lie with mankind as with womankind: it is abomination. Neither shalt thou lie with any beast, to defile thyself therewith; neither shall any woman stand before a beast to lie down thereto: it is confusion.*

The word " confusion" means probably " *audacious*

depravity."* And such is the human heart that all these
forms of depravity were not too bad to be anticipated by
the Lord, who knew the heart. He knows the virulence
of the poisoned spring. The Syrian Hazael wonders that
any should fancy, far less say, that he could be capable
of a murderous deed; but the Lord Jehovah, looking on
the unrenewed heart, forms this estimate of it, even in
the case of his own Israel, viz. they might be tempted not
only to adultery (ver. 20), and to present † their children
to Molech, in reckless inhumanity, and perhaps in order
to be quit of them (ver. 21). By all this they brought
public reproach on the name of Jehovah ("profaning his
name"); yet even beyond this would they go. Some
might be led (ver. 22) to the grossest and most shocking
lust—man with man, and (ver. 23) man or woman with
beasts. How awful is the Lord's judgment of the human
heart! He believes that an Israelite, though surrounded
—as an Israelite of course was, with everything that could
fence in his morality—might nevertheless have a heart so
foul as to burst all bounds, and transgress all limits, and
overflow all banks. "The heart is deceitful above all
things, and desperately wicked; who can know it? I
the Lord search the heart; I try the reins" (Jer. xvii.
10). Surely in an unrenewed soul there is a secret connexion with hell and the devil, even as in a regenerate
soul there is a secret connexion with heaven and with
God!

---

* Rosenmüller derives the Hebrew noun נֵבֶל from the Arabic root, which
means "improbus fuit; adulterium commisit."

† The Septuagint reading here varies from ours. They read הַעֲבִד "δωσεις
λατρευειν," and מֶלֶךְ ἀρχοντι. Perhaps הַעֲבִיר means here, as Gesenius thinks,
simply *to present to*, though that implied, of course, passing them through the
fire in his honour. Some suppose, from 2 Kings xvi. 3, that Hezekiah had been
thus dedicated.

All these safeguards are needful to secure the peace and purity of human society. And this social order is, after all, but an external effect. What, then, must be needed to produce a real, inward, heart-pervading holiness!

> *Ver. 24–28. Defile not ye yourselves in any of these things : for in all these the nations are defiled which·I cast out before you. And the land is defiled : therefore I do visit the iniquity thereof upon it, and the land itself vomiteth out her inhabitants. Ye shall therefore keep my statutes and my judgments, and shall not commit any of these abominations ; neither any of your own nation, nor any stranger that sojourneth among you; (for all these abominations have the men of the land done, which were before you, and the land is defiled;) that the land spue not you out also, when ye defile it, as it spued out the nations that were before you.*

The land was to be cleared of its inhabitants, who had committed these sins. Iniquity done in its secret places was crying to God for vengeance, and the land itself was loathing the foul sins it was compelled to bear—the land itself was "spewing out"* the people.

Again we see, as at the beginning of the chapter, that these precepts have all of them a place in the conscience. The law is written on the heart even of these Canaanites; and for resisting that law they are punished.

See, again, how even a smaller degree of light renders a man liable to judgment. Canaan suffers for its guilt, though the law was not given in words and in writing to

---

* What *lukewarmness* is in His sight may be inferred from the use of this expression in Rev. iii. 16—the very expression applied to the most abominable state of society that could be imagined! O man, are you pleasing the world? Are you content with a hope? Are you going as far as possible to meet the world? Are you a decent, moral, nay, highly respected professor, who avoids being over-zealous? Satisfied with being saved, though still unholy? Are you trying to gain both worlds? Are you thinking to walk on to heaven in a way that a scoffing world will not discover? Then, tremble! He will as assuredly spew thee out of his mouth as if thou hadst all the lusts of lustful Canaan!

them.   How evident, then, that the slightest glimmer of gospel light will add tremendous force to the responsibilities of every one of us!

> Ver. 29, 30. *For whosoever shall commit any of these abominations, even the souls that commit them shall be cut off from among their people.   Therefore shall ye keep mine ordinance, that ye commit not any one of these abominable customs, which were committed before you, and that ye defile not yourselves therein: I am the Lord your God.*

If the people of Israel at large fell into these sins, then they were to be treated as the Canaanites.   If individual cases occurred, these souls were to be immediately punished.   They are to watch against the first symptoms.   "*Obsta principiis.*"   In the case of Benjamin— a whole tribe—taking part with Gibeah, they were compelled to act upon these commands to the extent of not only excommunicating them, but even cutting them off with the sword.

It was needful thus to denounce vice of every shape, ere Israel took possession of such a land.   It was so, not only that the memory of former days might be used to benefit them, but because it was a land where natural scenery—groves and vales and green trees—were all abused by former inhabitants to favour lust.   Its delicious climate and luxuriant fruits, if unsanctified, might tend to excite the gratification of fleshly lusts, like as did the fulness of Sodom (Ezek. xvi. 49).   Plenty and peace are safe for us only when our souls are partakers of Divine holiness.   *Israel's land* combined these two things, and so was the type of the " New Earth wherein dwelleth righteousness."   It was a land flowing with milk and honey;   and at the same time peopled by a nation whose heart felt the love and whose consciences bowed to the law of Jehovah.

EBAL AND GERIZZIM

Perhaps it was in order to purify the land from these abominations, in a manner, or solemnly to pledge Israel, at their entrance on it, not to share in the sins of the former inhabitants, that that transaction, mentioned twice, in Deut. xi. 29, 30, and xxvii., was appointed to take place. It is recorded as having taken place, Joshua viii. 30.

When they had penetrated into the very midst of the land, and had it all before them in consequence of the taking of Ai, there were preparations made to pledge the people to a holy occupation of these seats of former lewdness. It was to take place in the valley between *Ebal and Gerizzim*, a valley which is a mile broad at an average, and beautifully adapted for a large assembly. Besides, Jacob's well and Joseph's tomb had made it well known. Accordingly, the camp moved hither. Six tribes were posted along the base, and perhaps a little way up the sides, of fertile Gerizzim, " *the hill of reapers;*" and these, as they stood amid the luxuriance of the spot, were to seal *the blessings* pronounced with their united "*Amen.*" The other six tribes were posted along the base,* and a little way up the slope, of the bleak and frowning Ebal,† to respond to *the curses*. In the midst of the valley stood *the ark* of God, and around it the priests, with the judges, officers, and elders. A solemn silence spread over all; deep suspense and awe rested on the vast assembly.

Joshua then proceeded to erect on Ebal an altar of stone, unadorned, and so the better fitted to typify Him who had no attraction to the carnal eye. Burnt-offerings

---

* עַל Deut. xxvii. 12, and Joshua is still more express.

† Which, according to Gesenius, means " void of leaves."

and peace-offerings were presented on it to the Lord;
and Israel's conscience bathed in the peace-speaking
blood. Thereafter, while the fire still blazed, Joshua
wrote on the side of this altar, which faced the whole
assembly, a copy of *the law!* It was clear and distinct;
the holy law on the altar's sides! And no sooner was
this done, than the priests at the ark prepared to utter
the blessing and the curse.

Those nearest the hill of Gerizzim uttered the blessings, one by one; and were distinctly heard by the six
tribes on that side the valley. At each utterance the
tribes responded "*Amen;*" and the voice of the host
floated over the valley.

Next, those priests nearest *Ebal* uttered the curses,
one by one. But will Israel say "*Amen?*" Will their
soul not tremble? Have they ever already incurred the
curse? The six tribes, who hear the utterance of each
awful curse, hesitate not to respond, "*Amen, amen.*" It
is like the "Hallelujah" over the smoke of torment.
The whole camp feels the awe of Jehovah's holy law.

But we see how it is that they are able to respond so
calmly even to the curse. Their eye can rest on *that altar*
on Ebal, while Ebal's curses float along the vale. Do they
not see in that altar the blood of sacrifice? Do they not
see the peace-offering? And, more than all, do they not
see the law, the very law the violation of which insures
the curse, written on that altar's side, and brightly shone
upon by these flames of sacrifice? This is sufficient to
give peace. There is *the law,* receiving honour from the
sacrifice; illuminated by the flame and blaze of sacrifice,
as well as written on the altar's side. Here, then, is the
law honoured and magnified by that atonement which
their guilty consciences have free access to use.

It is with our eye on *the law thus honoured by the sacrifice* that we can bear to hear its whole demands made.   It is when we see its curse exhausted on the victim, while all the time its every sentence shines brightly to view—it is then we can so calmly respond, " Amen, amen! " We can look on Ebal, and hear Ebal's curse, as fearlessly as if it were Gerizzim's beauty, and Gerizzim's blessing.

And thus they depart, feeling that the way of pardon —the sacrifice—the peace-offering—has itself left the law's majesty and authority impressed on their soul. Israel must depart to their cities, carrying with them that day's solemn views of the holy law, which they will tell to their children's children.   And the land shall be full of men who " love righteousness and hate iniquity"—the law of Jehovah on their hearts.

CHAPTER XIX

Duties in the Every-day Relations of Life

" Follow peace with all men, and holiness, without which no man shall see the Lord: looking diligently lest any man fail of the grace of God; lest any root of bitterness springing up trouble you."—Heb. xii. 14, 15

> Ver. 1, 2. *And the Lord spake unto Moses, saying, Speak unto all the congregation of the children of Israel, and say unto them, Ye shall be holy: for I the Lord your God am holy.*

HERE are duties to be inculcated that for the most part depend upon the man's inward feeling. Hence, at the outset, the Lord presents himself again to our view. He speaks to reconciled children ; and with these what argument could be stronger than this: " Oh ! be ye as I your God and Father am?" Paul knew the force of this kind of persuasion when he said to the Galatians who so loved him, " Brethren, I beseech you, be as I am" (Gal. iv. 12). And so the beloved John, on whose soul this argument had continual effect—" Every man that hath this hope in Him purifieth himself, even as he is pure" (1 John iii. 3).

> Ver. 3. *Ye shall fear every man his mother and his father, and keep my sabbaths: I am the Lord your God.*

These two precepts are a summary of the whole law, or rather are a specimen of the two tables—duty to all men in their relations, and duty to the Lord. But besides this, the *principle* of both these special precepts is, regard for, and reverence towards, God in his ordinances, and man in his relation towards us. And the respect shewn to parents has an intimate connexion with the submission of our mind to authority in any other case ; such as this of the Sabbaths of the Lord.

> Ver. 4. *Turn ye not unto idols, nor make to yourselves molten gods:* * *I am the Lord your God.*

In your public life, be careful to honour God before all men. Turn not to other gods ; which implies the duty of being guided by the Lord's will in our public or common-life transactions. You are not to be led by Mammon, nor by the smile of the great, nor by the fear of the mighty. The fear of Jehovah is to pervade your actions.

> Ver. 5–8. *And if ye offer a sacrifice of peace-offerings unto the Lord, ye shall offer it at your own will. It shall be eaten the same day ye offer it, and on the morrow : and if ought remain until the third day, it shall be burnt in the fire. And if it be eaten at all on the third day, it is abominable; it shall not be accepted. Therefore every one that eateth it shall bear his iniquity, because he hath profaned the hallowed thing of the Lord; and that soul shall be cut off from among his people.*

Even in holy actions there must be care taken of the effect which our example would have on others. Peace-offerings are left to the free will of the offerers; only, when they do bring them, they must strictly follow the prescribed rules. And if, on leaving any of their offering

---

* Perhaps there is emphasis in each clause. " *Turn not,*" or look not to. The attire and elegance of idol-worship was attractive, like Popish splendour, to the natural eye ; therefore, do not cast even a glance on it. And perhaps there is ridicule in the other clause, " *molten gods*"—cast-metal gods ! It is a Divine sarcasm on idolatry.

to the third day, some one should eat of the portion left
(ver. 8), that soul must suffer for it by being shut out
from the congregation.

There is probably another view to be taken of this
precept. It prescribes nothing but what has been already
prescribed in former chapters ; but then we must notice
the *position in which it occurs.* It occurs among rules
regarding a man's relation to his fellows in common acts
of life. Hence, this precept may be intended here to
guide them in the circumstances wherein they were
placed toward others. It is meant to prevent ostentation
or any selfish ends in their free-will offerings. For it is
to be brought " of *their own will*"—spontaneous outflowing of gratitude to God. It is to be used *immediately*, and
on the spot. It is to be treated as one of the Lord's
"hallowed things." All this, of course, in no way interferes with the typical design of the ceremonies themselves,
which have been already spoken of in chap. vii. 16.

> Ver. 9, 10. *And when ye reap the harvest of your land, thou shalt
> not wholly reap the corners of thy field, neither shalt thou
> gather the gleanings of thy harvest. And thou shalt not glean
> thy vineyard, neither shalt thou gather every grape of thy vine-
> yard; thou shalt leave them for the poor and stranger: I am
> the Lord your God.*

The Jewish writers say that a sixteenth part was left
in every field. Then, if in reaping, or binding what was
cut, some fell out of the sheaves, it was to be left in the
field for the poor—for such as Ruth. And thus, too, in
gathering the clusters of their vines. Such as Ruth, who
was both "*poor* and *a stranger*" (ver. 10), must be
allowed to take what was left. This law was meant to
check selfishness and greediness; to encourage brotherly

kindness and liberality; and to condemn covetous, avaricious, griping tendencies in the people of Israel.*

God tried them to see if they would really act as *stewards* for him.   And when he sends the poor and the stranger to *Boaz*, he blesses the rich man who had the desire to act as the Lord commanded.

Besides, Israel were thus taught, that though *they* got *the best* of the substance, yet there were strangers who were to share in their blessings.   There were poor Gentiles often coming across their borders from Moab or from Egypt, from Syria or from Edom who must receive a share in Israel's blessings.   Here was a type of the Gentiles partaking in their spiritual things.   Such persons were *Ittai* the Gittite, *Hiram* king of Tyre, the *queen* of Sheba, the widow of Sarepta, *Naaman* the Syrian, *Jehonadab* the Kenite, *Ebedmelech* the Ethiopian ; and many, many unknown, but whose names are in the book of life, though they were not of the seed of Israel.

> Ver. 11, 12. *Ye shall not steal, neither deal falsely, neither lie one to another.   And ye shall not swear by my name falsely, neither shalt thou profane the name of thy God: I am the Lord.*

—In their civil transactions with each other—in business and trade.   In ver. 11, theft, or any dishonest deed, is forbidden, however plausible it appear—" Ye shall not steal, nor be guilty of any deceptive practice" (תְכַחֲשׁוּ).
Nor must they carelessly appeal to God in common affairs, when their truth may be doubted by a neighbour.

Christians need to be warned and admonished on these heads, as much as Israel.   There is a contamina-

---

* The "*corners*" of the field were the edges, or skirts.   Then (ver. 10),
" Thou shalt not gather the (פֶּרֶט) single grapes," that stood not in clusters.

tion of conscience too frequently found in even Christian men, from continual intercourse with an unconscientious world. Glorify God, therefore, by a jealous integrity, and by a noble uprightness. Cast reproach on the world's meanness, and shew you carry God's presence with you into every place, and at every hour, and in all engagements. Write "*Holiness to the Lord*" on the bells of the horses.

> Ver. 13. *Thou shalt not defraud thy neighbour, neither rob him: the wages of him that is hired shall not abide with thee all night until the morning.*

Far from defrauding, or withholding what is due to thy neighbour, thou shalt not even *delay* giving him what he is entitled to. This precept is directly pointed against incurring *debt.* Fraudulent bankruptcies, and pretexts for withholding payments, are condemned by it; but remaining in debt to any one is also pointedly condemned. "Owe no man anything, but to love one another." In James v. 4, this is spoken of as a sin of *the last days.*

> Ver. 14. *Thou shalt not curse the deaf, nor put a stumbling-block before the blind, but shalt fear thy God: I am the Lord.*

How great the hard-hearted selfishness of man, since such a precept is needed! and how deep the inclination to Atheism in practice, since such a testimony, "*I am Jehovah,*" needs ever to be repeated! The Lord abhors the meanness that would take advantage of a neighbour's defects, instead of aiding that neighbour in supplying the want he feels. O how unlike the Lord when a man acts so!

> " He that might the advantage best have took
> Found out the remedy."

When we think of this, we see double emphasis in the words, " *I am the Lord.*"

> Ver. 15. *Ye shall do no unrighteousness in judgment; thou shalt not respect the person of the poor, nor honour the person of the mighty; but in righteousness shalt thou judge thy neighbour.*

There must be in us no affectation of kindness to the poor, even as there must be no fawning flattery of the great. Especially in matters of judgment the judge must be impartial. The eye of God is on him ; and as he is a just God, and without iniquity, he delights to see his own attributes shadowed forth in the strict integrity of an earthly judge.

If these are God's holy principles, it follows that the misery and oppression and suffering of the lower classes will in no way serve as a reason for their acquittal at his bar, if they be found guilty. Suffering in this world is no blotting out of sin. Hence we find at Christ's appearing, " *the great men and the mighty men, and every bondman,*" cried to the rocks, " Fall on us, and hide us from the face of him that sitteth on the throne" (Rev. vii. 15).

> Ver. 16–18. *Thou shalt not go up and down as a tale-bearer among thy people; neither shalt thou stand against the blood of thy neighbour: I am the Lord. Thou shalt not hate thy brother in thine heart: thou shalt in any wise rebuke thy neighbour, and not suffer sin upon him. Thou shalt not avenge, nor bear any grudge against the children of thy people; but thou shalt love thy neighbour as thyself: I am the Lord.*

" *Standing against the blood of thy neighbour,*" is taking his life, or rising up to shed his blood. " *Hating in the heart,*" is either, thy virtually hating* him by restraining

---

* The *love* that is a true reflection of *God's love to us* is described as giving no quarter to a brother's sin (1 Cor. xiii. 6).

thy expressions of love ; or covering up thy grounds of anger instead of telling them to him.

Gossip, and idle talking, and meddling with our neighbours (being ἀλλοτριοεπίσκοποι, 1 Pet. iv. 15), and, more directly still, insinuating and hinting evil of him, are sins forbidden here. The villages and cities of Israel, their households and their friendly circles, were exposed to this pestilence. " The tongue is set on fire of hell :" and so long as Satan is loose from hell, he will not fail to kindle these flames.

If a brother defame us, or slight us, or give us cause for grief and anger, we are to tell it to the person face to face. There must be no self-satisfaction, as if you were in this better than he. Even for his sake, the evil must not be left on him.

There must be no revenge or grudge; no smothered ill-will. Let love run through your streets in a pure, full stream. Love as you would be loved.

" *I am Jehovah,*" is the authority and motive for all.

> Ver. 19. *Ye shall keep my statutes. Thou shalt not let thy cattle gender with a diverse kind. Thou shalt not sow thy field with mingled seed: neither shall a garment mingled of linen and woollen come upon thee.*

The introduction to these three enforcements of similar observances is very solemn, because they might otherwise seem trivial. "*Ye shall keep my statutes.*" They are to abstain from every action that seemed to exhibit a mingling and confusing of opposite things. Being a people familiar with types and emblems, it was natural (as in the case, chap. xi.) to teach them, by common occurrences, spiritual truths that must always be attended to. Hence, they are to testify their abhorrence of the immoral mixtures of heathen lewdness, by never mingling linen and

wool in the same garments ; by never sowing two different kinds of seed in one field ; and by avoiding any mixture of species among their cattle.   Perhaps, they thus
also expressed their adherence to the principle of one
true God, keeping themselves separate from all idols and
idolatry.   And thus, too, at this day ought the Lord's
people to have no fellowship with Belial, nor follow
Mammon while they profess to follow God.

This precept gives force to our Lord's words in Matt.
xiii. 24—the parable of *tares* in the field of *good seed ;*
and some others of a similar kind.

> Ver. 20–22.   *And whosoever lieth carnally with a woman that is a
> bondmaid, betrothed to an husband, and not at all redeemed,
> nor freedom given her; she shall be scourged: they shall not be
> put to death, because she was not free.   And he shall bring his
> trespass-offering unto the Lord, unto the door of the tabernacle
> of the congregation, even a ram for a trespass-offering.   And
> the priest shall make an atonement for him with the ram of the
> trespass-offering before the Lord, for his sin which he hath
> done; and the sin which he hath done shall be forgiven him.*

This law seems intended to prevent any one alleging
the force of circumstances on the one hand, or, on the
other, taking advantage of his superior station in society.
Here is the case of a bondwoman, not at all at her own
disposal, who had been betrothed to some other slave.
In ordinary cases, she and the master who seduced her
would both be put to death, according to the law (Deut.
xxii. 23–25).   But there is to be a difference made here.
The woman might be overawed by the master's authority,
or tempted by his apparent right and claim to obedience;
therefore she is not reckoned so guilty as in ordinary
cases.   Then, on his part, the master might be ignorant
of the betrothing of his bondwoman previously.   These
alleviations are supposed, and yet still there is a penalty.

"*She shall be scourged*" for not resisting and making the whole case known. And he shall publicly offer a trespass-offering, confessing his sin. The Lord is considerate and impartial, yet holy and righteous. "*By him actions are weighed*" (1 Sam. ii. 3).

> Ver. 23–25. *And when ye shall come into the land, and shall have planted all manner of trees for food, then ye shall count the fruit thereof as uncircumcised: three years shall it be as uncircumcised unto you: it shall not be eaten of. But in the fourth year all the fruit thereof shall be holy, to praise the Lord withal. And in the fifth year shall ye eat of the fruit thereof, that it may yield unto you the increase thereof: I am the Lord your God.*

There is said to be a natural reason for this precept, viz. trees yield better fruits afterwards, if the blossoms be nipt off ("circumcised") during the earliest years. It is even said, the fruit of the first three years is unwholesome. Others see in this precept chiefly a design to check the appetite of the people, and accustom them to self-denial.

Was this precept not a memorial of the *Forbidden Tree of Paradise?* Every fruit-tree here was to stand unused for three years, as a test of their obedience. Every stranger saw, in Israel's orchards and vineyards, proofs of their obedience to their supreme Lord—a witness for him. And what a solemn shadow they cast over the fallen sons of Adam there, reminding them of the first father's sin. Is it from this, too, that the parable of the barren fig-tree is taken?* *Three years* barren, it ought, in the fourth year, to yield its *first-fruits* for the Lord. The husbandman could bear disappointment during the *three* years; but not when *the Lord's* year of fruit came. In the fourth year, the Lord got the fruit. It was offered

* Luke xiii. 7.

up to him with songs of praise; perhaps with festival songs, like that scene in the vineyards of Shiloh (Judg. xxi. 19, 21). The grand lesson enforced is plainly this, "Seek ye first the kingdom of God, and all these things shall be added unto you."

> Ver. 26–28. *Ye shall not eat any thing with the blood; neither shall ye use enchantment, nor observe times. Ye shall not round the corners of your heads, neither shalt thou mar the corners of thy beard. Ye shall not make any cuttings in your flesh for the dead, nor print any marks upon you: I am the Lord.*

"*To eat with the blood*" (עַל) is supposed, by some, to mean, "eat *at* the blood," as the heathen; but it rather means, eating flesh while the blood was not fully drained from the new-killed animal, as in 1 Sam. xiv. 33. (But see chap. xvii.) *Enchantments*, observing lucky and unlucky *times*, leaving a tuft of hair on the crown of their head when all the rest of the hair was shaven off,* and shaping the beard in particular ways—all these were heathenish rites. So, also, tatooing the flesh, or even cutting themselves in mourning, by way of shewing deep sorrow.

Israel is to be a holy people. 1. Even in hunting, or in times when their food was hastily procured, they must stand still and witness for God in the manner of their eating. 2. Far more, when tempted to join in auguries by birds, or the appearance of the clouds. These things they must denounce; they must carry on their business, and prosecute their enterprises, irrespective of all these. Simple reliance on their overruling Jehovah is their safety; and he would have told them, if any of these

---

* This the Septuagint calls, making a "σισόη."

things were needed for their safety. 3. If they happen to visit among the heathen, when abroad, or if a heathen come among them, they are not to please and flatter the heathen by a false liberality. They are not to adopt their fashions in dressing their hair and their beards. Even here they are to be witnesses for God. And, 4. At funerals, nothing is to be done but what speaks of submission to their God, and holy reliance. There must be no extravagance of grief, and nothing indicating any wildness of spirit. Tears may flow silently, like those of the Man of Sorrows; but grief must not be distracting nor inconsolable.

> Ver. 29. *Do not prostitute thy daughter, to cause her to be a whore; lest the land fall to whoredom, and the land become full of wickedness.*

Perhaps the Lord here refers to the fact, that some parents would, through connexion with idolaters, become so depraved as to let their daughters become prostitutes in the heathen temples. Or it may be meant as a caution to parents to prevent their daughters gadding about, like Dinah, lest they should fall in with another Shechem. Parents are held responsible for the conduct of their daughters! So much influence have they, and so much blessing does God attach to proper training at the hands of parents, that neglect in using all these means is reckoned a conniving at, and participation in, the sin that follows. How heavily will wrath fall on those parents whose daughters are ruined for eternity by gaieties and fashions—their beauty and their natural qualities prostituted to the end of gaining a settlement in life, by drawing the attention of the rich and noble, and so matching them well for this life!

Ver. 30. *Ye shall keep my sabbaths, and reverence my sanctuary:*
I am the Lord.

Their streets must not only be free of trade and common business on Sabbaths, but be full of worshippers
going up to the house of the Lord.   This precept is
inserted here, as if to say, "The foregoing duties will
be remembered and enforced just in proportion as you
keep up in your souls my worship, by seeing me set forth
in the sanctuary, and by spending the Sabbaths in my
fellowship."   All immorality, and all manner of evil,
will attend upon the neglect of the Sabbath.   Take away
yon river that waters the roots of the tree, and soon you
will see the leaves wither and the sap dry up.

Ver. 31. *Regard not them that have familiar spirits, neither*
seek after wizards, to be defiled by them: I am the
Lord.

No secret worship is allowed—none but that of God
alone.   The messages you get in the sanctuary, on the
Sabbaths, or at other times, should be sufficient to satisfy
you as to providences and the ways of God.   Fellowship
with God is incompatible with a seeking after communi-
cation with devils, who may aid those that give themselves up to them.   *Persons that spoke as if inspired*
(ἐγγαστριμύθοι)—females—and men who pretended to,
and may have got, *singular knowledge* of unseen things
from Satan, are here meant.   Such were those Manasseh
sought, and such was she to whom Saul went at Endor.
Probably the devil was allowed to deceive his willing
slaves, by some extraordinary communications made to
them respecting common things.   Satan sees much, by
his sagacity, that men do not, though the future is unknown to him ; and there seems to be such a thing as

fellowship *with the devil* personally, even as there is *with God*. Oh, fearful enmity of men! They choose rather the fellowship of God's enemy!

> Ver. 32. *Thou shalt rise up before the hoary head, and honour the face of the old man, and fear thy God: I am the Lord.*

When you meet them in public places, or they come to where you are, shew them reverence. Infirmity, wisdom, nay, age in itself, have each a claim on us. *Age*, even apart from its qualities, has in it solemnity. The Lord would thus solemnise us in the midst of our pursuits. "Lo! the shadow of eternity! for one cometh who is almost already in eternity. His head and beard white as snow, indicate his speedy appearance before the Ancient of Days, the hair of whose head is as pure wool."

Every object, too, that is feeble seems to be recommended to our care by God; for these are types of the condition wherein he finds us when his grace comes to save. It is, therefore, exhibiting his grace in a shadow, when the helpless are relieved, "the fatherless find mercy" (Hosea xiv. 3), "the orphans relieved, and the widow" (Ps. cxlvi. 9) and the "stranger preserved."

> Ver. 33, 34. *And if a stranger sojourn with thee in your land, ye shall not vex him. But the stranger that dwelleth with you shall be unto you as one born among you, and thou shalt love him as thyself; for ye were strangers in the land of Egypt: I am the Lord your God.*

The stranger here spoken of is one who has come to reside in Israel, for the sake of Israel's God, or simply because he preferred their land. Such persons are to be so many memorials of Israel's former bondage. In public or private dealings with them, they must not oppress them by word or action. Their laws must not vex them.

Israel must have compassion and consideration, like the
great *High Priest* who was yet to arise.

God thus moulded his people into a pitying and kind
frame of soul, and undid their selfishness. And thus,
too, foreigners were likely to be attracted to inquire regarding *Jehovah*, when his people were known as merciful, and kind, and sympathising. Even as now, believers
must exhibit kindness and gentleness for the very end of
gaining men to Christ.*

> Ver. 35–37. *Ye shall do no unrighteousness in judgment, in
> mete-yard, in weight, or in measure. Just balances, just
> weights, a just ephah, and a just hin, shall ye have: I am the
> Lord your God, which brought you out of the land of Egypt.
> Therefore shall ye observe all my statutes, and all my judg-
> ments, and do them: I am the Lord.*

The closing precepts are a general, but very wide and
decided, command as to righteous and holy dealing. In
markets, in trade, in their shops—in meting out land
with the yard and cubit, or weighing articles in the balance, or trying the capacity of solids. The balance and
its weights, the *ephah*, and its subdivision the *hin*, must
be strictly exact. The Lord is a God of justice—unbend-
ing, holy rectitude. It is thus that he will himself deal
with us in judgment; hence he prefaced it by saying,
ver. 35, "Ye shall do no unrighteousness in judgment,"
i. e. nothing which would be reckoned unjust if the case
were tried. He ends by renewing the command, in ver.
37, twice repeating his authority, "I am the Lord;" and
intermingling, "Your God which brought you out of the
land of Egypt," as a motive of grace.

---

* It is in this form that holiness is recommended in 1 Cor. xiii. 4-7. *The
love that God felt* to the guilty, is the love which we are to feel to our fellow-
men. This alone is " *Charity.*"

Alas! who shall live when God doeth this—when he lays judgment to the line in his dealings with us? Or rather let us say, "Where is there room left to fear, if the Surety's work be tried and taken for us? if there be no unjust weight or balance in the sanctuary above, and yet we are acquitted on the ground of the full measure of righteousness meted out by Jesus!" "In that great hour," says Dr Owen, on Heb. v. 7, "God was pleased for a while, as it were, to hold the scales of justice in equilibrio, that the turning of them might be more conspicuous, eminent, and glorious. *In the one scale,* as it were, there was the weight of the first sin and apostasy from God, with all the consequence of it, covered with the sentence and curse of the law, with the exigence of vindictive justice—a weight that all the angels of heaven could not stand under one moment. *In the other,* were the obedience, holiness, righteousness, and penal sufferings of the Son of God, all having weight and worth given to them by the dignity and worth of his Divine person. Infinite justice kept these things for a season, as it were, at a poise, until the Son of God, by his prayers, tears, and supplications, prevailed to a glorious success in the delivery of himself and us." Glory to the Righteous One!

But here we may stay to reflect how bitter to the Lord Jesus it must have been to come to his own nation, whom he had thus taught, and yet to be treated so unkindly. *He* was the greatest *stranger* (ver. 33) that ever traversed earth. It was not his home; he had nowhere to lay his head. Yet his Father's laws as to *strangers* were not kept toward him. "They received him not."

> "A pilgrim through this lonely world
> The blessed Saviour pass'd;
> A mourner all his life below,
> A dying lamb at last.

> "That tender heart that felt for all,
> For us its life-blood gave;
> It found on earth no resting-place,
> Save only in the grave."

How bitter, also, to the "Holy One and the Just," to be treated with the most glaring injustice! In the hall of the Sanhedrim—in the court of Herod—at the tribunal of Pilate—"*his judgment was taken away*" (Acts viii. 33). Of this he might complain far more truly than Job, who so solemnly protested "by the living God, who hath taken away my judgment" (Job xxvii. 2; xxxiv. 5).

The reference to the perverting of law and equity in our Lord's case is brought out by the rendering of Isaiah liii. 8 given in Acts viii. 33—"*In his humiliation his judgment was taken away.*" This rendering has been a difficulty to many; but is it not the only true rendering? Throughout Isa. liii., the prefix מ means most frequently "*because of.*" Thus ver. 5, 8, 12. We would therefore expect the same in the case of מֵעֹצֶר. What seems to me probable is, that the "*ἐν τῇ ταπεινώσει*" of Acts viii. 32, is to be found in מֵעֹצֶר. And then the "*αὐτοῦ*" is found attached to מִשְׁפָּט. The true collocation of the words would in that case be מֵעָצְרוֹ מִמִּשְׁפָּט לֻקָּח, "*because of his oppression,*" *i. e.* his oppressed state, his humiliation, "he was taken away from judgment." In Psalm cvii. 39, מֵעֹצֶר is found in this sense. In translating Isaiah, the historian Luke (not the Sept.) inserts "*αὐτοῦ*" after "*ἐν τῇ ταπεινώσει,*" shewing how he read the

Hebrew. But, at all events, their awful perversion of all law and equity towards the Righteous One is set before us in full relief: "In his humiliation, from judgment (the sentence he was entitled to) was he taken away." The Judge of Israel, who shall yet sit on the great white throne, was hurried away out of sight of justice and equity. O how fearfully deep the descent our Surety made! But thus it was he drew us from the miry clay.

CHAPTER XX

𝔚arnings against the 𝔖ins of the former 𝔍nhabitants

"Have no fellowship with the unfruitful works of darkness, but rather reprove them: for it is a shame even to speak of those things which are done of them in secret. But all things that are reproved are made manifest by the light."—Eph. v. 11–13

Ver. 1, 2. *And the Lord spake unto Moses, saying, Again thou shalt say to the children of Israel,—*

THE Lord, knowing well the deep delusions of the heart, warns Israel against sins which had already been forbidden. But he does it here by a reference, throughout, to the former state of morality and idolatry in the land, lest Israel should say, "Let us try what was once done in the land before" (see ver. 22, which is the key to this chapter). How thoroughly the Lord knows the readiness of the corrupt heart to adopt a suggestion of evil! and how accurately he saw the tendency to what was afterwards really done by Israel.

Ver. 2, 3. *Whosoever he be of the children of Israel, or of the strangers that sojourn in Israel, that giveth any of his seed unto Molech, he shall surely be put to death: the people of the land shall stone him with stones. And I will set my face against that man, and will cut him off from among his people;*

because he hath given of his seed unto Molech, to defile my sanctuary, and to profane my holy name.

How startling the determination expressed here! The Lord employs the people of the land as his executioners, and then seems to preside himself over the execution— "*They* shall stone him, and *I* will cut him off, setting my face against him." And the sentence is fearful, *stoning to death.* What, then, is the sin? It is the worshipping of the god Molech, whose imagined qualities seem to be the very antipodes of the true God. Molech was worshipped by revolting cruelties, the cries of the sufferers being drowned in loud noise. An image of red-hot glowing brass was the form in which he was adored, and his arms received the children offered to him, forthwith consuming them by their red-hot touch. The child was put ("εἰς τὸ χάσμα πλῆρες πυρός") "into a gaping hole, full of fire," says a historian.* Everything was savage and demoniacal; fiendish tyranny and hellish hate. What a contrast to Jehovah —" God is love !" His everlasting arms take up the little child to bless and to save; and never is his heart satisfied with his worshippers till they believe his love to them. Rather than that *they* should suffer woe, He stretched out his arms on the cross, and opened his side to the spear, and made a way for the streams of the poured-out vial running over his own soul.

The man, therefore, who chose *Molech* in preference to *Jehovah,* proved himself to be in a state of most desperate enmity to God—"*defiling his sanctuary,*" casting contempt upon it by preferring Molech's court; and "*defiling his name,*" by his awful choice; as if saying, that the perfections of God were so loathsome to him, that he would rather burn in the furnace-heat of Molech's image than enjoy the sweet, holy love of the God of Israel.

* Diodorus Siculus *apud* Patrick.

Ver. 4, 5. And if the people of the land do any ways hide their eyes from the man, when he giveth of his seed unto Molech, and kill him not; then I will set my face against that man, and against his family, and will cut him off, and all that go a whoring after him, to commit whoredom with Molech, from among their people.

Fearful truth to men that "have not the love of God in them." Though you are not punished by the world, though the world is sheltering you and defending you, God is himself instituting a process against you. God was to become the prosecutor when the people of the land would not take measures against a worshipper of Molech. The Lord brought ruin on the man and his house, and all those who secreted the man and favoured him.

The expression, *"whoredom with Molech,"* is one of many similar phrases taken from the marriage-relation. It seems that the Lord thereby intimates that his view of our world is this—He came down in the person of Messiah to betroth and marry us; therefore, every turning aside to another Saviour and another God is breaking this marriage-union. It was in this form that, in Old Testament times, *unbelief* was spoken of. God's covenant with Israel as a people tended to deepen this view of likeness to a marriage-union, as we find in Jer. iii. 14, "I am married unto you;" and Hos. ii. 19, "I will betroth thee unto me for ever;" and in Mal. ii. 11, the reverse, "Judah hath married the daughter of a strange god." We may everywhere understand it as equivalent to the New Testament expression, *"Making God a liar."* All our love to God begins by our perceiving the love of God to us; therefore, a turning to other lovers is virtually a declaring that there is no satisfying love in God toward us.

Ver. 6. And the soul that turneth after such as have familiar spirits, and after wizards, to go a whoring after them, I will even set my face against that soul, and will cut him off from among his people.

Though the people of the land entice you, and though you be in perplexity and laden with care, yet never must you go to other counsellors than *the Lord.* Has not the Lord wisdom enough to direct you? and love enough to reveal sufficient discoveries of the future? May you not be satisfied with his spreading a veil over much of your path, rather than run to wizards, whose familiarity with Satan may enable them to suggest extraordinary views of your future case?

The Lord "set his face against that soul, and cut him off." As in the case of king Saul; He followed him to Endor, and there met him with a message of ruin. Is there not a tendency to this same sin in us when we refuse to sit still under apprehended evils—when we run backward and forward seeking intelligence—when we stop hastily in our prayer or meditation to rush away to some new sources of information that have occurred to us? Is all this running to and fro, this restless, unbelieving haste, this diving into every deep, this pulling at the veil over the future as if we could thus force it aside,— is not all this a going after wizards? *"He that believeth shall not make haste."*

Ver. 7, 8. *Sanctify yourselves, therefore, and be ye holy: for I am the Lord your God. And ye shall keep my statutes, and do them: I am the Lord which sanctify you.*

Some make this an *appendix* to the preceding; but it is rather a *preface* to the following precepts—as appears by *"for"* in the beginning of ver. 9. And yet in one view it has a retrospective reference also. It is placed in the position of a commemorative sign-post, to attract the

eye, and to tell that this road was once in a deplorable
state, but is now altered through the great kindness of
their King : therefore none of his fences must be broken
through. These calls to holiness often occur; for how
the Lord longs to see his people holy! And very tender
and persuasive is the argument which he uses with them!
It is always this—I, your God and Father, desire it! It
is I, the Lord, who sanctify you! He knows that they
who love the Lord, love to be like him! "I shall be
satisfied, when I awake, with thy likeness" (Ps. xvii. 15)
—but never wholly till then.

And now begins a dark and dismal scene! The Lord's
holiness is set before us, as if to make the after-gloom
more deep; or, the after-gloom is meant to make the
Lord's holiness the sweeter by its contrast. The rainbow
is reflected from the opposite dark cloud!

> Ver. 9. *For every one that curseth his father or his mother shall
> be surely put to death: he hath cursed his father or his
> mother; his blood shall be upon him.*

Like the heathen in Paul's days, the people of Canaan
had "lost *natural affection*" (Rom. i. 31). Israel needs
to be warned against their sin. And as this is the
strongest tie of duty towards any earthly friend, if it be
snapt, then the whole other duties and feelings of relationship between men are gone. "*He hath cursed his
father!*" "*he hath cursed his mother!*" seems written to
mark the crime as eminently heinous! It is so nearly
allied, also, to the utter renunciation of all our ties to
God our father, who has nourished and brought up children. The son has become a prodigal! The son has
gone to a far country! The son wishes to erase the very
memory of his father's home! "Be astonished, O ye
heavens, at this, and be very desolate!"

This is the porch. Now enter the chambers where deeds are done in the dark, of which it is a shame to speak; but which even the camp of Israel might be led to commit with greediness. Is it so? Are there sins of which it is a shame to speak? Then surely God's Israel cannot need to be warned against these? Alas! They need it like other men. The Lord sees their hearts' depraved tendencies, and how Satan will clear the channels for their easy flow. Amazing grace! Jehovah chooses for the fellowship of his bosom throughout eternity persons whose nature he knew to be capable of the foulest, filthiest, darkest profligacy! There is surely fulness of meaning in saying that Jesus "saves his people *from their sins!*"

Ver. 10–21. *And the man that committeth adultery with another man's wife, (even he that committeth adultery with his neighbour's wife,) the adulterer and the adulteress shall surely be put to death. And the man that lieth with his father's wife hath uncovered his father's nakedness: both of them shall surely be put to death; their blood shall be upon them. And if a man lie with his daughter-in-law, both of them shall surely be put to death: they have wrought confusion; their blood shall be upon them. If a man also lie with mankind as he lieth with a woman, both of them have committed an abomination: they shall surely be put to death; their blood shall be upon them. And if a man take a wif and her mother, it is wickedness: they shall be burnt with fire, both he and they; that there be no wickedness amony you. And if a man lie with a beast, he shall surely be put to death; and ye shall slay the beast. And if a woman approach unto any beast, and lie down thereto, thou shalt kill the woman, and the beast: they shall surely be put to death; their blood shall be upon them. And if a man shall take his sister, his father's daughter, or his mother's daughter, and see her nakedness, and she see his nakedness; it is a wicked thing; and they shall be cut off in the sight of their people: he hath uncovered his sister's nakedness; he shall bear his iniquity. And if a man shall lie with*

a woman having her sickness, and shall uncover her nakedness;
he hath discovered her fountain, and she hath uncovered the
fountain of her blood: and both of them shall be cut off from
among their people. And thou shalt not uncover the naked-
ness of thy mother's sister, nor of thy father's sister; for he
uncovereth his near kin: they shall bear their iniquity. And
if a man shall lie with his uncle's wife, he hath uncovered his
uncle's nakedness: they shall bear their sin; they shall die
childless. And if a man shall take his brother's wife, it is
an unclean thing; he hath uncovered his brother's nakedness:
they shall be childless.

What sins are here, and what sounds of the stroke of
the sword of wrath! "*Put to death—their blood upon
them!*" "*Burnt with fire!*" "*Cut off in the sight of
their people*" (ver. 17)—that all may see and fear, like
the witnesses of Babylon's destruction. "*Cut off from
among their people;*" driven out of holy fellowship (Rev.
xviii. 10). "*Die childless,*"—some left living as monu-
ments of wrath, seen by all like a leafless, fruitless, tree
which the lightning of God has blasted. Many are the
arrows in his quiver, shot even on earth upon transgressors! What, then, when his "bow is made quite
naked?"

But what a land of sin!—its cities and its plains
crying up to heaven! Children curse their parents!
Neighbours and relatives live in adultery with each
other! The son dishonours the bed of his step-mother;
the father-in-law that of his daughter-in-law! Men burn
in unnatural lust (Rom. i. 27); and the same man takes
mother and daughter as his wives! Men and women
go to the very beasts to gratify lusts! * Brothers disregard the holy ties that forbade him approach to sisters

---

* In ver. 15, Patrick observes that the slaying of the beast was quite accordant
with our feelings; just as they used to hang a forger with his pen and counter-
feit seals, and a conjuror with his magical books and characters.

and step-sisters. Aunts, and brother's wives—in short, all relations in turn—seem only to be fuel to lust, which consumes the fence, and rages till it expire in its own indulgence.

Was it not a land of enormous guilt? Who wonders that its people were rooted out! The only wonder is, that the Lord could have borne the very sight of the land any more! Should he not blot it out from his creation? He did so to Sodom and Gomorrah. But, lo! he rather will purge it, and people it with a new race! I think I can see in this how Jehovah gave a token that even so will he deal with this whole wicked earth! He will not blot it out of creation—nay, it shall remain for ever a monument of his long-suffering. He will cleanse it soon by the appearance of *Joshua* in flaming fire; and then shall it be "the New Earth wherein dwelleth righteousness!"

Even thus, also, O sinner, with thy polluted soul! Every sin and vice and lust and passion has had its seed in thee—if not its spring-time when it grew to flower and baneful fruit. But the Lord, instead of destroying thee, can cleanse and save! The *Priest on his throne* comes in to thee; thou art washed: "Be holy, for he is holy!"

Ver. 22–24. *Ye shall therefore keep all my statutes, and all my judgments, and do them; that the land, whither I bring you to dwell therein, spue you not out. And ye shall not walk in the manners of the nations, which I cast out before you: for they committed all these things, and therefore I abhorred them. But I have said unto you, Ye shall inherit their land, and I will give it unto you to possess it, a land that floweth with milk and honey: I am the Lord your God, which have separated you from other people.*

The Lord tells them of the inheritance he has provided for his Israel. They are to walk on the banks of streams

whose verdant slopes are fed upon by flocks and herds;
and in climbing their rocks they are to find honey flowing
forth for their use. "*Milk and honey*" are representatives
of all abundance. It is a land which the Lord is not
ashamed to give them (Heb. xi. 16). But here they
are to walk in holiness—separated from other people.
The former inhabitants were "abhorred" by the Lord for
their sins; they are to be loved, and to love in return.
Israel's land is to be a theatre whereon heavenly character
and heavenly joy shall be displayed, and the eye of the
Lord shall look with delight on holy deeds and holy
desires. All this is to be produced by their being made
to feel free grace and flowing love. They do not get the
land *on conditions*. It is given *freely*; and, being given,
they are then commanded to be holy. The God of grace
is visibly at work here—placing them in the midst of
blessing, and then saying, "Now wilt thou surely love
me." "*He first loved us!*" must be the spring of Israel's
obedience. What strength there must be in that spring!
It is sufficient to counteract all the sinful propensities of
Canaan! Sinai's loud thunder failed, but the silent love
of Zion overcomes!

> Ver. 25, 26. *Ye shall therefore put difference between clean beasts
> and unclean, and between unclean fowls and clean: and ye
> shall not make your souls abominable by beast, or by fowl, or
> by any manner of living thing that creepeth on the ground,
> which I have separated from you as unclean. And ye shall
> be holy unto me: for I the Lord am holy, and have severed
> you from other people, that ye should be mine.*

It is instructive to observe that God enjoins the observance of the *ritual* of worship very strictly; and this is
done with the view of severing them more completely (ver.
26) from the people of the land. The form of church

government is not in any way the essence of the truth, but it is the fence around the truth. It is not the jewel, but it is the precious case that encloses the more precious jewel. Whatever form of worship is best fitted to effect this purpose is surely the best for our adoption. If people, on the other hand, are led to mistake *the case* for *the jewel*, then the great design is lost. In Popery and Puseyism, and whenever the forms of worship are such as engross the eye and the heart, *the truth* is lost, out of sight. Our unattractive Presbyterianism is a rough case in the view of many; but it certainly answers the blessed end of preventing any from resting on the form, as if the form itself were the jewel. Its very plainness leads the inquirer to go deeper in, and find the glorious view of God manifest in flesh, which it is intended to fence and guard. How uninviting to Israel these laws as to "*clean* and *unclean!*"—and yet their observance led to humble and solid inquiry after the Holy One.

> Ver. 27. *A man also, or a woman, that hath a familiar spirit, or that is a wizard, shall surely be put to death: they shall stone them with stones; their blood shall be upon them.*

This is not the same as ver. 6. This is the case of the wizards themselves, not of those who go to consult them. If found, wizards, and all of that class, are to be put to death. Israel is to remove stumbling-blocks. Israel must keep so far from the evil as even to extirpate it. None but Jehovah shall be honoured.

Israel must live in open and avowed enmity with the serpent and the seed of the serpent. There is to be no compromise. And this shall throw them entirely upon the Lord for strength. They are to wage war with Satan; to storm his strongholds; to crush the adder and dragon in their den · to refuse any offer of peace on the part of their great foe.   Hell would hate no portion of earth so intensely as Canaan in the days of believing Israel.   And yet no region on earth was half so secure; for the strength of heaven—the breadth of heaven's shield, and the edge of heaven's keen sword, became Israel's safety.   " The Lord alone did lead him, and there was no strange god with him."   " Happy art thou, O Israel! O people saved of the Lord!"

CHAPTER XXI

Personal Duties of the Priests

"A bishop must be blameless."—1 Tim. iii. 2

Ver. 1–4. *And the Lord said unto Moses, Speak unto the priests the sons of Aaron, and say unto them, There shall none be defiled for the dead among his people: but for his kin that is near unto him, that is, for his mother, and for his father, and for his son, and for his daughter, and for his brother; and for his sister a virgin, that is nigh unto him, which hath had no husband, for her may he be defiled. But he shall not defile himself, being a chief man among his people, to profane himself.*

THE fourth verse assigns the reason why the priest is not to be allowed, like all other men, to defile himself for every relative or friend that dies. He is "*chief man among his people*" *—guardian, or superintendent of the community at large ; and of course, therefore, could never be out of mourning if he were to mourn for every one in the community that died. Whereas, he is a public character, sustaining important relations to the people in their religious rites and in their approach to God.

He is, however, not to be devoid of sympathy and feeling. Nay, he is fully permitted to pour out his grief over mother, father, son, daughter, brother, and unmarried

---

* Not "husband," for then אִישׁ would have been joined with בַּעַל ; but like the construction of בְּ מָשַׁל. And so Jer. iii. 14 has it.

sister (who still clung to him with unweakened affection, having no husband); and of course, also, over his own wife, "his own flesh."* A priest must have feelings of deep emotion; he must resemble *Jesus*, the Antitype, weeping over his own kindred most of all, and only restrained from weeping over all by express enactment of Jehovah. A priest must have in his soul the yearning of all affection, though he give not vent to all he feels. He must not place his regards too specially on any but near relatives, that so he may feel more generally for all under his care.

Ought not ministers of Christ to be of this same mind? There is exceeding great tenderness required of us! There is wide compassion! An eye, too, that will look out upon a lost world, and a heart that will feel anguish for what the eye beholds. O for that mind which was in Jesus!—such sympathy and pity—such full tides of loving-kindness that never had an ebb. "The earth was full of the loving-kindness of the Lord." How, then, did men contrive to escape from its blessed power? Alas! they fled from the advancing tide, and stood far off, and perished. So should our ministry be—men so compassed on all sides by the love we bring them, that they can escape salvation only by fleeing from the full tide of love that would have swept away their guilt and bathed their souls in bliss. Lord, keep us from selfish joys and selfish sorrows! Teach us to live for others, and for *thee!*

Ver. 5, 6. *They shall not make baldness upon their head; neither shall they shave off the corner of their beard, nor make any cuttings in their flesh. They shall be holy unto their God, and not profane the name of their God: for the offerings of the*

---

* Ezek. xxiv. 16-18 shews this inference to be true; for there we see that it needed an express prohibition, introduced for the occasion, to prevent the prophet's mourning.

Lord made by fire, and the bread of their God, they do offer; therefore they shall be holy.

Even when they do mourn in the instances specified, they are not to imitate the heathen, nor conform to the usages of any who express immoderate grief. There must be no baldness, or plucking off the hair (Ezra ix. 6) in such cases; no shaping of the beard into a corner; no cutting of the flesh. Priests are doubly bound to abstain from all appearance of evil: they are his near attendants, offering " *the bread of their God;* " as if they were cup-bearers at his table, always seeing his face. And being thus near him, they have access to peculiar joys, and they may be well expected to exhibit in consequence peculiar holiness. If otherwise, they "profane his name;" they leave on other men a bad impression of Jehovah's perfections, as if such men could live (as they profess) in the radiance of them, and yet be earthly-minded men.

It is still thus with ministers of Christ.* Paul was directed to charge one such to be "no striker, not a brawler;" that is, not imitating the heathen in revengeful and angry passions; but to be " *sober, and of good behaviour*" (σώφρονα, κόσμιον). This implies an absence of all worldly conformity; no immoderate grief, like the world's, in time of calamity; no excessive or extravagant tokens of affliction even under the sorest bereavement; and no unbecoming act even when tempted by a wish to comply with fashionable usages. The world must see the habit of our spirit and the manner of our actions to be such as might be looked for from men peculiarly set apart

* Not that ministers of Christ now are *priests* at all in the sense of offering sacrifice, or standing as mediators between God and the people. (See Archbishop Whately on this.) But they are servants who occupy a station in sight of the people, and are sent by God to point others *to the sacrifice already offered.*

to minister the bread of life to others, receiving it from the master's table.

> Ver. 7, 8. *They shall not take a wife that is a whore, or profane; neither shall they take a woman put away from her husband: for he is holy unto his God. Thou shalt sanctify him therefore; for he offereth the bread of thy God: he shall be holy unto thee: for I the Lord, which sanctify you, am holy.*

The priest must not marry one whose character was not publicly known to be blameless. One that had been guilty of uncleanness, or one who has become unhallowed ("*profane*") by any other circumstance, such as by being the daughter of such a mother, or a divorced woman,— these are all forbidden him. The priest was typical in all his public acts; he shadows forth our High Priest; therefore, he must shadow him forth in his espousals. The Saviour's bride is " without spot or wrinkle," "undefiled," " the choice one of her that bare her; the daughters saw her and blessed her" (Song, vi. 9). And as he " hateth putting away " (Mal. ii. 16), therefore the priest must not marry a divorced woman. The Saviour chooses for eternity; there must be nothing even to hint to his espoused that she may again be separated from him.

In a minister there is not the same *typical* reason for care in this matter ; but there is the same reason that is given in ver. 8, viz. his employment before God, and the character of the God with whom he has to do, and for whom he acts. The argument of ver. 8 is this: "I am holy; and I sanctify you, my people Israel, for mine. Now, the priest is my servant in offering my bread, or sacrifices; therefore, for my sake, since he serves me so nearly, let him be holy in your eyes." O man of God, do you hear? Do you observe what the Lord says of you? You are to be holy in the eyes of the people, in consider-

ation of the God whom you serve. If so, O how watchful
must you be! how circumspect! how unblemished! In
regard to the special subject of ver. 7, Paul writes (1 Tim.
iv. 12), "Be an example of the believers . . . . . in purity."
Very awful is your responsibility if you diminish your
zeal, love, spirituality, by marrying one who has more of
earth and a present world in her person and spirit, than
of heaven and a coming eternity. It seems to be a sin
in ministers to do anything whatsoever that might leave
an unholy impression on others; how much more, then, is
it a sin in them to have their own frame of spirit secu-
larised. Oh! to have the deep solemnity and unfeigned
holiness of "word and conversation" (1 Tim. iv. 12) that
well become servants of Jehovah, who is holy, and who
sanctifies us for his holy work! "Who can stand before
so holy a God?" "Purer than the rays of the sun ought
a minister of Christ to be," said Chrysostom. Lord, bap-
tize us with a full baptism of the Holy Ghost!

Ver. 9. *And the daughter of any priest, if she profane herself by
playing the whore, she profaneth her father: she shall be burnt
with fire.*

As in the case of New Testament pastors it is written,
"having faithful children, that are not accused of riot, nor
unruly" (Tit. i. 6) ; so here, in the case of the priest's
family. For the conduct of the family is noticed by the
world, and they lay the blame of their misdeeds at the
door of their parents. There is a responsibility connected
with belonging to a godly house ; the privileges enjoyed
there ought to have had a blessed effect on the children.
Woe to them if it be otherwise! Double woe! for thus
they hinder the usefulness of their father, who loses influence in the eyes of the world if his counsels and walk
have not succeeded in drawing his own family to God.

This is "profaning their father's name." The daughter mentioned here was to be burnt with fire—a type of the flames of wrath, the fire that never shall be quenched. "It is impossible but that offences come; but woe to them by whom they come!"

> Ver. 10-12. *And he that is the high priest among his brethren, upon whose head the anointing oil was poured, and that is consecrated to put on the garments, shall not uncover his head, nor rend his clothes; neither shall he·go in to any dead body, nor defile himself for his father, or for his mother; neither shall he go out of the sanctuary, nor profane the sanctuary of his God; for the crown of the anointing oil·of his God is upon him: I am the Lord.*

On a typical account the high priest was not to conform to the usages of his brethren in mourning;—"the anointing oil being poured on his head," he was thereby set apart, beyond all others; nay, "*the crown of the anointing oil*," *i. e.* the holy crown on his forehead (Exod. xxix. 6), placed him in a position too conspicuous as a public person to admit of his conformity to the usages of private life. The oil, and the holy crown bound around his anointed head, proclaimed him "*high priest*" between God and his brethren—an eminent type of Jesus.

The title "*High priest*" (literally "great priest") occurs here for the first time. It is given in order to shew that the *rank* of the man is the reason for this law being laid down. Now, Jesus exhibited no sign of mourning for himself—never "*uncovered his head nor rent his clothes*" because of personal bereavements; nor did he touch the dead, except to convey life back again; and even when his mother was feeling all a widow's and a mother's anguish at the cross, he still acted as High Priest; and while he exhibited excessive tenderness, he at the same time did so as one fulfilling public responsibilities; for, in the midst

of his woes as the smitten Shepherd, he took time to recommend her to John, and then, so to speak, resumed his
work of suffering. He truly was the Priest who never
went " out of the sanctuary," and who " never profaned
it " by the introduction of personal concerns. He ever
felt the streams of the anointing oil on his head; he saved
not, but hated and lost, his own life for us; he stood as
entirely a Substitute and Surety.

> Ver. 13–15. *And he shall take a wife in her virginity. A widow,
> or a divorced woman, or profane, or an harlot, these shall he
> not take: but he shall take a virgin of his own people to wife.
> Neither shall he profane his seed among his people; for I the
> Lord do sanctify him.*

Here is another type of our Great High Priest. His
Church is espoused to him " as a chaste virgin " (2 Cor.
xi. 2) ; and he says of her, " My undefiled" (Song, vi. 9) ;
and she says of him, " My first husband" (Hosea ii. 7).
The meaning of the clause, " *neither shall he profane his
seed*," may be to this effect, that he should not allow his
sons, who were to be priests after him, to marry in a way
forbidden by the law, and especially not allow the son
that would be high priest in his room to unqualify himself
for the office by marrying any one forbidden by this law,
and who was, therefore, " profane."

Christ is married to his Church in perfect holiness.
" She cometh to the king in robes of needle-work "—all
glorious. She was not thus fair when he found her;
but she is " all fair," " undefiled," " the choice one,"
when he marries her. The marriage of the Lamb is on
the day of his coming out of the Holy Place to bless his
redeemed. It is a holy people he is to rejoice in ; holiness becometh his house for ever ; no spot or wrinkle,
no blemish or any such thing, appears on his redeemed

when he is their Bridegroom (Eph. v. 27). We look for a holy heaven—an eternity wherein we shall never once think an earthly thought, or feel one desire that is less than divinely pure. The blood of the high priest's sacrifice speaks of such a demand as this; for that blood not only washes clean, but its testimony and demand are loud and vehement in behalf of perfect purity for the time to come.

Ver. 16. *And the Lord spake unto Moses, saying,—*

As it is a precept for the line of priests in all ages, " in their generations " (ver. 16), the Lord does not speak to Aaron personally, but to Moses, the lawgiver; especially as these precepts bore so much upon personal capabilities.

Ver. 17–21. *Speak unto Aaron, saying, Whosoever he be of thy seed in their generations that hath any blemish, let him not approach to offer the bread of his God: for whatsoever man he be that hath a blemish, he shall not approach: a blind man, or a lame, or he that hath a flat nose, or any thing superfluous, or a man that is broken-footed, or broken-handed, or crook-backed, or a dwarf, or that hath a blemish in his eye, or be scurvy or scabbed, or hath his stones broken: no man that hath a blemish of the seed of Aaron the priest shall come nigh to offer the offerings of the Lord made by fire: he hath a blemish; he shall not come nigh to offer the bread of his God.*

The sacrifices are the *"bread of God,"* as in other places. Can there be in this expression a reference to God giving us Christ as our *bread of life?* Can it mean the " bread which is set before God, in order to be handed to us when he has examined and accepted it?" And is it to this the Lord Jesus refers, when he says, " *The bread* which I give is *my flesh*, which I give for the life of the world ? " (John vi. 51.)

These precepts concerning the priests evidently originate in the necessity that, as being a type of Jesus, the officiating priest should be one that exhibited no blemish. The Song of Solomon may cast some light on this passage. In setting forth purity and loveliness under figurative terms, it uses almost all the references to the bodily qualities that are found here. *Here,* the defects are spoken of; *there,* the excellencies (see specially Song, v.)

If the priest were "*blind,*" * then the people would be led to misapprehend the type. He could not represent him whose "eyes are as a flame of fire." If the priest were "*lame,*" he could not represent him whose "legs are as pillars of marble." If "mutilated in the nose" (חָרֻם), he could not be the type of him whose Church and Spouse has this said of her, "Thy nose is as the tower of Lebanon." If "superfluous in any limb"—or rather if one limb was longer than another—he could not be a type of him who, in conscious completeness, "cometh leaping on the mountains." If "*broken-footed,*" he was unlike him whom his Church celebrates as planting his stately steps so firmly that his feet are "sockets of fine gold," on which the "pillars of marble" rest. His hands are "as gold rings, set with beryl;" and could not, therefore, admit of being represented by one "*broken-handed.*" He was to stretch out his complete and entire person on the cross; the nails were to pierce his hands and feet, but yet not a bone be broken. If the priest were "*crook-backed,*" then he would have represented the

---

* At ver. 20, the Septuagint have "$\pi\tau\ell\lambda\lambda$os τo$\grave{\upsilon}$s $\dot{o}\phi\theta\alpha\lambda\mu$o$\grave{\upsilon}$s" for תְּבַלֻּל בְּעֵינוֹ, on which the *scholia* of the Vatican edition, as quoted by Bos, has this somewhat quaint remark, "$\dot{o}$ $\ddot{\eta}\kappa\iota\sigma\tau\alpha$ $\mu\epsilon\nu$ τo$\hat{\upsilon}$ $\beta\lambda\epsilon\pi\epsilon\iota\nu$ $\dot{\epsilon}\sigma\tau\epsilon\rho\acute{\eta}\mu\epsilon\nu$os, $\dot{\upsilon}\gamma\iota\hat{\omega}$s $\delta\epsilon$ τo$\upsilon\tau$o πo$\iota\epsilon\hat{\iota}\nu$ o$\dot{\upsilon}\kappa$ $\ddot{\epsilon}\chi\omega\nu$. $\dot{o}\pi$oιoι $\tau\iota\nu\epsilon$s $\epsilon\dot{\iota}\sigma\iota\nu$ $\alpha\dot{\iota}\rho\epsilon\tau\iota\kappa\omega\nu$ υίοι."

High Priest of the Church as inferior to the Church her-self, " whose stature is like the palm-tree ;" her stately figure pre-eminent. If "*a dwarf,*" unable to reach up to the altar's height,* he would ill suit as a type of him whose " countenance is as Lebanon, excellent as the cedars." If in his eye were cataract, or any white spot or " *blemish,*" then he is not any more like him, whose "eyes are as doves by rivers of waters, washed in milk, and fitly set." If he be diseased, having the " *scurvy,*" or itch, or if he have any " *scab,*" or tetter (יַלֶּפֶת), how-ever unseen by the common eye, still he is not as He " who is all fair," who has " no spot or wrinkle." If in the most secret, hidden pore of his frame, there be any blemish or defect, he can no more claim to be type of one whose Church, made like himself, is "all glorious within."

The priest must be type of Him who is to give forth his own comeliness and perfection to the sinner. O how fair is Jesus! His person all perfect *;* virtue floweth out of it when it is touched by a sinner's hand, even as fragrance breathes forth from the leaf of the balm-tree when it is pressed by the hand of the passer-by. And this glorious person was *the sacrifice* as well as *priest—* " He offered up himself" (Heb. vii. 27).

> Ver. 22, 23. *He shall eat the bread of his God, both of the most holy, and of the holy; only he shall not go in unto the veil, nor come nigh unto the altar, because he hath a blemish; that he profane not my sanctuaries: for I the Lord do sanctify them.*

Many think that these precepts, forbidding any de-

---

* Or if קָן means " consumptive, lean; in his make indicating decay," how unlike him who is " white and ruddy," eternally vigorous in heavenly health !

formed person to minister as priest, were to some degree intended to prevent the people entertaining mean ideas of God's service. They must see nothing but what would leave the impression of dignity and completeness. On this ground, it may be, as well as on the typical grounds already noticed, these rules must be kept; and any one transgressing, however zealous he might appear—any one insisting upon being allowed to minister, though bearing such defects—did, in reality, profane the sanctuary.

It is said, "*my sanctuaries;*" meaning the courts of the tabernacle, which are often called "holy" (*e. g.* vi. 16), and the two chambers, "the holy" and "the holy of holies." Or perhaps, as ver. 23 indicates, the outer place where the *altar* stood, and the inner where the *veil* was hung, are *the sanctuaries.* The deformed priest is to be provided for, nevertheless; and, in this provision, he is to have the pledge and type of as full communion and friendship with God as any other priest. For he is to partake of "the holy things," such as those mentioned in Num. xviii. 19; the heave-shoulder, also, and wave-breast, and even the "most holy," such as the meat-offering mentioned in chap. ii. 3, and vi. 17. It was only in regard to *office* that he was to be treated as unfit. He must not presume to enter within the veil, or minister at the altar. Alas! what must they be exposed to who are conscious of being excluded by God from the ministry, and yet enter it for a piece of bread? What do they mean? They are unconverted, they have no call, they are blemished men; yet they venture to stand forth "as though God did beseech" men by them! Alas! they shall yet feel that to be true—"*I the Lord do sanctify* my sanctuaries."

Ver. 24. *And Moses told it unto Aaron, and to his sons, and unto all the children of Israel.*

Thus, all Israel knew what sort of priest to expect. Their eyes were fixed on One who was to be " altogether lovely," who would come to supersede all type and shadow.

CHAPTER XXII

Household Laws regarding Holy Things;

FIRST, AS TO PRIESTS, 1-16; THEN, AS TO PEOPLE, 17-33

" *Be ye clean, that bear the vessels of the Lord.*"—Isaiah lii. 11

" *If any man minister, let him do it as of the ability which God giveth,
that God in all things may be glorified through Jesus Christ, to whom be
praise and dominion for ever.   Amen.*"—1 Peter iv. 11

THE PRIEST AT HOME

Ver. 1, 2. *And the Lord spake unto Moses, saying, Speak unto
Aaron and to his sons, that they separate themselves from the
holy things of the children of Israel, and that they profane not
my holy name in those things which they hallow unto me: I am
the Lord.*

HERE is a general caution. The priest is to act as a
priest at all times.   He is to " *separate himself from the
holy things;*" that is, keep aloof from them at home, as
if the holy things were placed away from him to shew
reverence. The priests, at home, were not to handle holy
things familiarly; they must act, even there, with deepest
reverence.

Ministers may learn from this law.   Ministers of God
must beware of letting their spirituality be injured by
domestic occurrences; they must not let domestic comforts unhinge their soul, so as to lead them to speak of

holy things too familiarly.   Ministers are specially under
God's eye ; he sees whether they walk in the steps of
Jesus in their chambers and at their studies.   They
must be *ever* separated to the Lord.

> Ver. 3. *Say unto them, Whosoever he be of all your seed, among*
> *your generations, that goeth unto the holy things, which the*
> *children of Israel hallow unto the Lord, having his unclean-*
> *ness upon him, that soul shall be cut off from my presence: I*
> *am the Lord.*

If he go to the tabernacle in a careless state—unclean
through some ceremonial pollution—the Lord will frown
the priest out of his presence, nay, it may mean, will even
deal with him as he did when Nadab and Abihu were
smitten for offering their strange incense.

O how solemn the warning here to ministers !   If we
go forth to minister with unholy souls ! if the frame of
our souls be at the moment irreverent ! if it be engrossed
with earthly feelings ! Surely we need very special grace
at all times, and yet more than all when we stand in the
Lord's name.   How cruel is the prayerlessness and levity
of our people when they come up to the sanctuary with
easy-minded indifference !   Do they not know our dan-
gers ?   Do they not feel for our tempted souls ?   Would
they not be sufferers themselves, as well as we, if the
Lord were that day to cut us off from his presence?
" Great fear is due unto the Lord in the meetings of his
saints ; " and when it is added, " To be had in reverence
of all them that are about him " (Ps. lxxxix. 7), the special responsibility of ministering ones—who are " about
him," as if at his hand—seems marked out.

> Ver. 4–7. *What man soever of the seed of Aaron is a leper, or*
> *hath a running issue, he shall not eat of the holy things until*
> *he be clean. And whoso toucheth any thing that is unclean by*
> *the dead, or a man whose seed goeth from him; or whosoever*

*toucheth any creeping thing, whereby he may be made unclean,
or a man of whom he may take uncleanness, whatsoever uncleanness he hath; the soul which hath touched any such shall
be unclean until even, and shall not eat of the holy things, unless he wash his flesh with water. And when the sun is down,
he shall be clean, and shall afterward eat of the holy things;
because it is his food.*

The object of this law is evidently to keep the priest
at all times, even in the private intercourse of home,
vigilant, jealous of evil, abstaining from all appearance of
evil. These causes of defilement have been all noticed
in former chapters; some of them could be known only
by the man himself, yet in the most retired situation the
priest must be holy and clean. He must be the type of
Jesus.

That part of the ordinance which enjoins him not to
" *eat of the holy-things* " in such circumstances deserves
to be noticed. These " *holy things* " were the portions
of the sacrifices that were the priest's due. They were
pledges of God's fellowship and communion. But, to
shew that he is a holy God, he will not hold fellowship
even with an accepted man, if the man regard iniquity
in his heart. " If we say we have fellowship with him,
and walk in darkness, we lie, and do not the truth "
(1 John i. 6). He must " wash."

And it is to be observed that this was called for by
pollution even from " *creeping things,*" that is, arising
from the smallest causes. The eye of the Lord pierces
through any darkness, and the heart of the Lord is
jealous of all sin, however small.

" *Unclean till even.*" Though an accepted man, yet
he must, like Hezekiah, " walk softly." He must take
time to meditate on and feel his pollution. " O wretched
man that I am !"

In all this the minister of Christ is addressed. Moses speaks to us also. "Be ye clean, that bear the vessels of the Lord."

> Ver. 8–13. *That which dieth of itself, or is torn with beasts, he shall not eat, to defile himself therewith: I am the Lord. They shall therefore keep mine ordinance, lest they bear sin for it, and die therefore, if they profane it: I the Lord do sanctify them. There shall no stranger eat of the holy thing: a sojourner of the priest, or an hired servant, shall not eat of the holy thing. But if the priest buy any soul with his money, he shall eat of it, and he that is born in his house; they shall eat of his meat. If the priest's daughter also be married unto a stranger, she may not eat of an offering of the holy things. But if the priest's daughter be a widow, or divorced, and have no child, and is returned unto her father's house, as in her youth, she shall eat of her father's meat; but there shall no stranger eat thereof.*

Witsius (*de Vitâ Timothei*) describes a true minister in the language of the heathen Seneca, " Plus tibi et viva vox et convictus, quam oratio, proderit." And Jerome had said the same, " Cujus et sermo, et incessus, et habitus, doctrina virtutum est."

In his dwelling, the priest shall never set on his table anything that died a natural death, or was torn—that is, anything that spoke of death and violence. All he eats must have a savour of the tabernacle. A sin committed at his own table, by violating this rule, must be considered worthy of death. Man of God, what is thy soul's feeling at the table whereon thy food is set? Is God honoured by thee there? Is there a savour of his love breathed forth by thee in presence of those who sit at meat? Doth thy spikenard send forth its smell? Is the law of thy God seen there, even as in thy public life? Remember his words; " *I am the Lord.*" " *I the Lord do sanctify them.*"

And who are the company at the priest's table, as he partakes of the holy things ? *"No stranger"* shall partake of these with him; that is, no one who is not a priest.*

No one who is only a sojourner, no servant hired for a time ; but any inmate such as a perpetual servant, or one born in his house, may eat, being reckoned one of the family. How remarkably, by this law, does the Lord shew the unity of a household, and hold up the principle that the servants are a part of it, even as the children are ! What kindly treatment, what deep interest in the souls of servants, this was fitted to produce! The priest's family must be a model for the other families of Israel ; so must the minister's now.

If one of the family returned home—if the daughter's husband put her away or died, and she sought again her father's home—she is once more a part of the family. Formerly she was one with her husband, and so was not any longer properly a member of this family; and, if she have a child, then she is considered as having a separate household of her own. Whoever is *really* of the priest's household is to eat of the holy things, and none else. Why is this ? Because it is taken for granted that the household of the priest is consecrated to the Lord more than any other household. A peculiar air of holiness is understood to be breathed there. It is a holier spot, a more deeply sacred circle. As Paul writes, " One that ruleth well his own house, . . . with all gravity" (1 Tim. iii. 4).

Ver. 14–16. *And if a man eat of the holy thing unwittingly, then he shall put the fifth part thereof unto it, and shall give it unto the priest with the holy thing. And they shall not profane the holy things of the children of Israel, which they offer unto*

* זָר so means ; had it been נֵכָר, it would have meant, one of a foreign place, or nation.—See *Patrick*.

the Lord; or suffer them to bear the iniquity of trespass,
when they eat their holy things: for I the Lord do sanctify
them.

As there was a fence round Sinai, so round the holy
things given by God to the priests.   If any of the common people—not priests—partook of the dedicated food
even unwittingly, he was guilty.   Therefore, the priests
at home, when friends were present with them, must
carefully watch against being the occasion of sin to
others.   The priests will be counted as sharing in the
sin ; "*profaning the holy things;*" and this they must
not do, neither "*suffer any one to bear the iniquity of*
trespass."

Ministers of Christ may be guilty of leading others
into sin, if they do aught to create levity in the people's
minds, or aught that may lessen the holy feeling of
reverence toward God.   If by levity at home, in handling
what in the pulpit was treated very solemnly, they
destroy any one's godly fear of prying into the ark, then
are they exposing " holy things " to the unconscious pro-
fanation of those at their table.

The payment of "*the fifth part*," or double tithe, was
fitted to teach the transgressor that he had defrauded
God of his due, and must now repay what he could.   Discovered sins should excite us to be doubly zealous for the
future in repairing the Lord's honour.

THE PEOPLE

Ver. 17–21. *And the Lord spake unto Moses, saying, Speak unto*
Aaron, and to his sons, and unto all the children of Israel,
and say unto them, Whatsoever he be of the house of Israel, or
of the strangers in Israel, that will offer his oblation for all
his vows, and for all his free-will offerings, which they will offer
unto the Lord for a burnt-offering ; ye shall offer at your own
will a male without blemish, of the beeves, of the sheep, or of

the goats. But whatsoever hath a blemish, that shall ye not offer; for it shall not be acceptable for you.* And whosoever offereth a sacrifice of peace-offerings unto the Lord to accomplish his vow, or a free-will offering in beeves or sheep, it shall be perfect, to be accepted; there shall be no blemish therein.

When an Israelite, or one who has joined himself to Israel ("a stranger," ver. 18), has made a vow, or resolved to bring a free-will offering, one essential condition is, that it be *unblemished*, and that it be *a male*. The "holy, harmless, undefiled One" is ever set before our eyes. The Lord does not weary of the sight; and surely sinners may never weary of the sight of one who brings them life by his death. So, if the man brought any peace-offering, there must be no *blemish*. A holy God will hold no fellowship with man but in a blameless way; no peace or reconciliation, except through an unblemished sacrifice. But see chap i. 3.

Ver. 22. *Blind, or broken, or maimed, or having a wen, or scurvy, or scabbed, ye shall not offer these unto the Lord, nor make an offering by fire of them upon the altar unto the Lord.*

The glorious, perfect Antitype would be misrepresented if any animal was offered that was "*blind*" (chap. xxi. 18), or "*broken*" in its limbs, or "*maimed*" by any wound, rent in any way (חָרוּץ, Gesenius); or "*having a wen*" (μυρμηκιῶντα, Sept.), pimples that disfigured its form, or "*scurvy*," that made it actually disagreeable to the eye, or "*scabbed*," the dry scab making its touch polluting.

Ver. 23. *Either a bullock or a lamb that hath any thing superfluous or lacking in its parts, that mayest thou offer for a free-will offering; but for a vow it shall not be accepted.*

---

* Or perhaps rather, "It shall not seem to you fit for being offered to me," is the sense; and, literally, it may be rendered, "It shall not be acceptable to you," finding no favour in your eyes.

If given as a *free-will offering*, it shewed the offerer's view of the case, and not the Lord's view, nor yet the priest's. Hence, his presenting from his herd or flock an animal that wanted an eye, or an ear, or the like, shewed, indeed, his low sense of what was due to the Lord, and proper as a type ; but inasmuch as it was done of his own free will, to express the present state of his feelings, it might be taken with that understanding. Were it a *vow*, then it could not be received; for the priest was responsible in that case, pronouncing it suitable or unsuitable by rules that had reference to the perfection of the coming Antitype. O how different is the *free-will offering* of such an Israelite as this from God's own *free-will offering* of his Son ! The Lord has measured the narrowness of man's soul ; who has ever measured the unlimited fulness of the mind of God ? " It is *as high* as heaven, what canst thou do ? *deeper* than hell, what canst thou know ? The measure thereof is *longer* than the earth, and *broader* than the sea" (Job xi. 8, 9). Nor is his love—this one attribute—less wonderfully great in the eyes of Paul, who sought to comprehend " what is the *breadth*, and *length*, and *depth*, and *height*, and to know the love of Christ which passeth knowledge" (Eph. iii. 18, 19). If our faith were not too much straitened by our selfish, narrow nature, what might we not obtain? For Cyprian truly writes : " *Quantum illud fidei capacis afferimus, tantum gratiæ inundantis haurimus.*"—(*Ep. ad Donat.*)

Surely the *free-will gifts* of men discover their fallen, narrow souls ! and placed before such a God, they make us feel, " His ways are not as our ways, nor his thoughts as our thoughts !" And what *bondage to self* shines through these narrow gifts of men—in amazing contrast

with the full-souled liberality of him who for our sake
emptied his own bosom of his beloved Son!

> Ver. 24. *Ye shall not offer unto the Lord that which is bruised, or
> crushed, or broken, or cut; neither shall ye make any offering
> thereof in your land.*

Any mutilation was a misrepresentation of the Antitype; and especially any castration in any of these four
ways.   Never in their land was such an offering to be
made ; or, as some render it, never was there to be even
such a custom in their land.*   The Surety for us was
truly man ; and, as in all things but sin he was made
like his brethren, there must not be even a hint in these
types of any defect.   Then, as his own humanity was
truly complete, so also the Lord in his dealings with us is
bringing about our restoration to perfect humanity.   He
is so intent on this, that he says that he would not be
called the " God of the dead;" he must be " God of the
living," for these only are truly *men*—body and spirit.
Hence his care over the type, that it hint at no imperfection.   Lord, why carest thou thus for us?   What has
led thee to these kind designs?   " What is man, that
thou visitest him?"

> Ver. 25. *Neither from a stranger's hand shall ye offer the bread of
> your God of any of these; because their corruption is in them,
> and blemishes be in them; they shall not be accepted for you.*

Some understand this as forbidding them to let a
stranger supply them with animals for sacrifice, *q. d.*
Take it not out of a stranger's flock or herd.   But this is
contrary to practice approved of in after days; as when

---

* However, if this last were the meaning, there would scarcely have been need
for the minute prohibition of such animals in sacrifice. For who would be in
danger of bringing them in a land where there were none of them?

Cyrus gave, and Darius ordered others to supply (Ezra vi. 9).

But the true meaning is evidently, that the same rule shall hold in regard to a stranger's offering as in regard to their own. "*The stranger*" may be a proselyte, as ver. 18; or he may be such a one as Cyrus. "Neither from a stranger's hand shall ye priests offer a sacrifice of any of these maimed or imperfect animals."

The Lord must be known as "having no respect of persons," but adhering to his one way of salvation, viz. through the Perfect Substitute.

> Ver. 26, 27. *And the Lord spake unto Moses, saying, When a bullock, or a sheep, or a goat is brought forth, then it shall be seven days under the dam; and from the eighth day, and thenceforth, it shall be accepted for an offering made by fire unto the Lord.*

This precept guards the type. The animal sacrificed must have lived a *complete time*, "seven days." For the Antitype was not to be offered in infancy, but was to live the full life of a man of sorrows. As during the *six* days of creation there was time for God to unfold gradually his creating skill, so this period becomes symbolical, in a manner, of *sufficient time* to unfold and develop any purpose. Christ, our Surety, was to live far beyond infancy, tasting the world's sorrows as he breathed its air ; taking time to open out the law and exhibit conformity to it all, ere his set time came that he must die.

> Ver. 28. *And whether it be cow or ewe, ye shall not kill it and her young both in one day.*

Some say this was meant just to discourage cruelty. No doubt it had this effect. But a typical reason lies hid, and is very precious. The *Father* was to *give up* his Son ; and the *Son* was to be, as it were, torn from the

Father's care by the hands of wicked men. How could
this be represented if *both* the ewe and her young were
offered together? This part of the truth must never be
obscured, that "*God so loved the world, that he gave his
Son.*" And the bleatings of the tender lamb in its parent's
ears, as it was taken from the fold, filling the air with
sadness, represented the bleatings of "the Lamb led to
the slaughter," who so sadly wailed, "Eli! Eli! lama
sabachthani?" And as these rules apply to domestic
arrangements about what they were to carry out of their
house and folds for the altar, we see thus a picture hung
up in every house in Israel of that great truth, "*God spared
not his own Son,* but delivered him up for us all."

> Ver. 29–33. *And when ye will offer a sacrifice of thanksgiving
> unto the Lord, offer it at your own will. On the same day it
> shall be eaten up; ye shall leave none of it until the morrow:
> I am the Lord. Therefore shall ye keep my commandments,
> and do them: I am the Lord. Neither shall ye profane my
> holy name; but I will be hallowed among the children of
> Israel: I am the Lord which hallow you, that brought you out
> of the land of Egypt, to be your God: I am the Lord.*

When in their houses the first purpose was formed of
offering a thanksgiving, each one must see that the purpose sprang from a thankful heart. Let none be induced
to bring it because of the arguments of some of his
friends, or because it might appear fitted to produce an
impression in his favour among his neighbours. It must
be "*at your own will.*" It must flow spontaneously from
the heart.

So, also, it must not be laid by, as if you were intend-
ing to use it for a feast; leave none of it till to-morrow.
Use it at the time. As the *peace-offerings* represented
communion with God, reconciled to the sinner, they must
represent this as enjoyed by the sinner, as his feast, his

joy, his chief delight. Now, *thanksgivings* were of this class; and the offerer must not seek any *selfish* gratification on such an occasion, but must, on the spot, and at the time, offer all to his God, and in the presence of his God, satisfied with this full outpouring of his own soul to the God who pours out his fellowship in return.

Five motives are strewn on their path to constrain them to close obedience.   1. "*I am the Lord.*"   This is authority employed.   2. "*I will be hallowed among the children of Israel.*"   This is his holiness, and his desire to diffuse awe of his holy name.   3. "*I am the Lord which hallow you.*"   Here is an appeal to their privileges as Israelites.   Do you not feel that you actually are set apart for me?   4. "*I am the Lord which brought you out of Egypt.*"   Here is his claim as Redeemer, who paid the price and set free the captives.   Is there gratitude in your souls?   Is there sense of thankfulness for favour done?   5. "*Your God*"—as well as your Lord: his claim as Father, Shepherd, King, and whatever else there is that is tender in relationship, or beneficial in office, or sweet in character—all is summed up in " YOUR GOD !" Who is like "Our God?"   "Who *would not fear* thee?" (Jer. x. 6.)

CHAPTER XXIII

The Public Festivals, or Solemn Convocations

" Not forsaking the assembling of ourselves together."—Heb. x. 25
" They continued steadfastly in the apostles' doctrine and fellowship."
Acts ii. 42.
" A day in thy courts is better than a thousand."—Ps. lxxxiv. 10

THE SABBATH

> Ver. 1–3. *And the Lord spake unto Moses, saying, Speak unto the children of Israel, and say unto them, Concerning the feasts of the Lord, which ye shall proclaim to be holy convocations, even these are my feasts. Six days shall work be done : but the seventh day is the sabbath of rest, an holy convocation ; ye shall do no work therein : it is the sabbath of the Lord in all your dwellings.*

THE Lord begins with *the Sabbath.* " The assemblies (מוֹעֲדֵי) of the Lord which ye shall call (by sound of trumpet, Num. x. 10) to be holy meetings; these (that follow) are my assemblies." Of these, the foremost is *the Sabbath.*

It was with the rest of *the Sabbath* that unfallen man was blest ; and that unfallen rest is ever presented by the Lord to man as each week revolves.

That rest was the Lord's own refreshing rest, made known to man, to be shared in by man newly created. The eye of God rested on his holy creation, and He was refreshed; so was the eye of man to rest on the creation and the Creator, and his soul be refreshed.*

This *Sabbath-feast* is to be repeated each week, as a testimony of the Lord's good will to have men restored to their original rest. And it is to be kept when all other feasts have finished—a type of the deep rest yet to come when earth's sins are swept away, and creation itself is restored to holiness and the liberty of the sons of God.

It is beautifully supposed by some, that *Israel's feasts* represent the *Course of Time*—this earth's days, from creation down to the final end. The *Lamb slain* (passover) commences it, and the eighth day of the happy Feast of Tabernacles is its close; while *the Sabbath*, the rest—God's rest in himself, and his creatures' rest around him—both *precedes* and *follows* this *Course of Time*.

It is remarked, that "*no work*" whatever was to be done on this day; and no other festival has so strict an injunction put on it, except only *the day of expiation*. Thus, the rest in *atonement* is to equal the rest that was enjoyed in an unfallen *creation*. Is it so with thy soul, believer? Hast thou rest in God as if thou hadst never sinned? Hast thou no more conscience of sin? Was not the rest of Jesus as deep—nay, deeper, might we not say?—when he rested from his agony, as was the Father's rest after creation? And thou enterest into *his* peace. Israel's *Sabbath* was to be שַׁבַּת שַׁבָּתוֹן, "a rest-day of rest"—a thorough season of repose from care and toil (ver. 3): so, every week, ought thine to be, even in this tumultuous world. And thy soul should keep its constant Sabbath, too, since thy work is all ended by thy risen Lord.

* It is a Jewish remark, that "whoever does any work on the Sabbath denies the work of creation."—*Patrick*.

THE PASSOVER

Ver. 4, 5. *These are the feasts of the Lord, even holy convocations, which ye shall proclaim in their seasons. In the fourteenth day of the first month at even is the Lord's passover.*

The first feast is Passover, commemorating their escape from Egypt. The Lord finds Israel in bondage, and makes him free, that he may serve Him.

" THE LAMB SLAIN " is the first object held up to the view of Israel about to be redeemed. " Behold the Lamb of God ! " is still the cry that first reaches a sinner's ear and a sinner's heart. Here is the first feast for fallen man. What grace meets the sinner ! God meets him with the *Lamb*, and that Lamb is his beloved Son ; and shews him in that Lamb life out of death, even life to the sinner out of the death of the Son of God. The first altar we read of exhibited a *lamb slain;* the first act of God for Israel is the slaying *of the lamb;* the first deed of the new dispensation was, presenting the *true Lamb* to the view of all, and then offering it up to God; and the first opening of the sanctuary above (Rev. iv. 1), where the coming glory is preparing, exhibits the *Lamb that was slain*, loved, adored, ruling, reigning, with all heaven gazing on him in unutterable transports of delight and thankfulness.

We should notice, however, that *a people delivered* is essentially connected with *the passover*. The lamb is not slain in vain. Behold a people going forth in perfect freedom, in the fresh joy of recent deliverance from imminent peril. A people thus escaped, cheerful, thankful, solemn, with a heavenward eye, and a step lifted up to tread on Canaan's kingdom—this is as essential to the full idea of *the passover* as *the lamb*. Hence our Lord's words in Luke xxii. 16, " I will not any more eat thereof

until it be fulfilled in the kingdom of God." The Second
Coming of the Lord will exhibit the full line—the whole
company—of blessed ransomed ones, saved for ever from
wrath, and made heirs of a glorious kingdom.

THE FEAST OF UNLEAVENED BREAD.

Ver. 6–8. *And on the fifteenth day of the same month is the feast
of unleavened bread unto the Lord: seven days ye must eat
unleavened bread. In the first day ye shall have an holy convocation; ye shall do no servile work therein. But ye shall
offer an offering made by fire unto the Lord seven days: in the
seventh day is an holy convocation; ye shall do no servile work
therein.*

We might have expected that the direction which follows, in ver. 10, 11, should come in in the midst of this
week of unleavened bread ; but as they were then in the
wilderness, not in Canaan, it is stated apart.

The feast, then, of *unleavened bread* * was meant to
be a continuation of the same topics on which they had
begun to meditate on the passover-night. The *passover*
was the *cause,* the feast of *unleavened bread* the *effects,*
of their deliverance from the grasp of Egypt. To a believer now, the one exhibits the way of pardon, the other
exhibits the fellowship of God, and the holiness that
follows upon pardon

All Israel in one great family kept the first day as a
" holy convocation," wherein, though they prepared food,
no servile work was done. On that day they joined
together in remembering their escape ; the *community of
believers* felt on that holy day that all alike were ransomed from Egypt, and had common joys and common

---

* In Matt. xxvi. 17, and Mark xiv. 12, the passover is called the *first* day of
unleavened bread, because of its intimate connexion with it, and on *the evening*
of the passover the feast did actually begin.

remembrances of sorrow, and common reason for gratitude now. " *With all* saints" (Eph. iii. 18) they could
look back on the night when they hastily bound up the
unleavened dough on their shoulders and hasted out of
Egypt (Exod. xiii. 34). *Unleavened bread* was thus a
mark of begun deliverance.

Having thus, on the first of the seven days, mutually
excited each other's feelings, the rest of the days were
spent in remembrances and enjoyments of the same
things, but by each individual alone. Each day, after
the sacrifice had been offered, they called to mind their
hasty flight from Egypt in joy and fear, associating that
deliverance with every crumb of unleavened bread on
their tables.

The Lord had a reason for so ordering the matter,
that it should be necessary to leave Egypt before leaven
was put into their dough. He thus prepared a type
of the truth, that a delivered, redeemed man must shake
off his former connexion with pollution. His deliverance
from corruption (leaven) is to date its commencement
from the very hour he rises to forsake his house of bondage. And all saints rejoice to keep a feast to this effect
—seeking holiness more than joy in their festivals, and
rejoicing in deliverance from corruption as much as in
deliverance from the bondage of Egypt. " We are redeemed from our vain conversation" (1 Pet. i. 18) as well
as from our state of death and condemnation. " Purge
out the old leaven" (1 Cor. v.)*

Though not mentioned at this place, it was during
the time when this feast of seven days ran on that the

---

* *The bitter herbs,* elsewhere mentioned, may have taught sorrow over the
lost and ruined Egyptians, and over their own sin which exposed them to the
sword of destruction, but for the sprinkled blood.

sheaf of first-fruits of barley harvest was presented; thus casting in a new element of joy to the worshippers, sweetening their cup, and giving a relish to their food by the near prospect of abundance soon to be theirs. A *risen Saviour* and his benefits never fail to urge on the felt joy of every believer's soul; he returns ever to that pledge of plenty—"Christ is risen." But more of this at ver. 11.

On the closing day, the seventh, after each had spent the intervening space alone, there was a "holy convocation" again. Thus they fired each other's heart anew. They offered a sacrifice peculiar to the day, and rejoiced at the altar for all the great blessings they had been commemorating and receiving. The first and the last of the feast-days was thus a day of rest, for meditation on the past, and preparing for a return to ordinary duties.

THE SHEAF OF FIRST-FRUITS

Ver. 9–14. *And the Lord spake unto Moses, saying, Speak unto the children of Israel, and say unto them, When ye be come into the land which I give unto you, and shall reap the harvest thereof, then ye shall bring a sheaf of the first-fruits of your harvest unto the priest: and he shall wave the sheaf before the Lord, to be accepted for you: on the morrow after the sabbath the priest shall wave it. And ye shall offer that day, when ye wave the sheaf, an he-lamb without blemish, of the first year, for a burnt-offering unto the Lord. And the meat-offering thereof shall be two tenth-deals of fine flour mingled with oil, an offering made by fire unto the Lord for a sweet savour; and the drink-offering thereof shall be of wine, the fourth part of an hin. And ye shall eat neither bread, nor parched corn, nor green ears,* until the self-same day that ye have brought an*

---

* כַּרְמֶל is used here, and chap. ii. 14, and Num. xviii. 13. This term, for "*full ears of corn*" occurs only once elsewhere, viz. 2 Kings iv. 42. It was a term not used in common life, but appropriate to things presented for holy uses. Hence (see Hengstenberg on the *Gen. of the Pentateuch*, Dissert. II.),

*offering unto your God: it shall be a statute for ever through-
out your generations in all your dwellings.*

First notice this institution as, like the rest, bearing on
the people's present state. See its reference to their
harvest. It is the *barley*-harvest that is meant, for it
only is ripe at passover. A *sheaf* is taken as representative of the whole harvest. It was to be observed on the
first day after *passover-Sabbath;* and that happened to
fall sometimes on the third day after passover, sometimes later. The *priest* waved it before God, along with
the sacrifice of a he-lamb—intimating that even thanksgiving cannot be accepted but through blood and through
a mediator. There was a *meat-offering* besides—two
tenth-deals—double the usual amount, because here they
are expressly offering *property* to God; and the fourth
part of the hin of *wine* (the usual rate) indicates that they
did all this most cheerfully—no grudging, no reluctance*
(Ps. civ. 15). Till this was done, they had no right
even to a green ear (ver. 14). How forcibly it taught
dependence on the Lord! (Hos. ii. 8, 9; Jer. v. 24.)
Yet how gently did the Lord thus bind fast the bonds of
connexion between him and his people. They must dip
every temporal blessing in this fountain of life ere they
ventured to use it; but what was this but sweetening it
to their taste? They remembered that he who in the
desert daily gave them manna, had ripened this harvest
for their present use. They had found it ready on the
very week of their entering Canaan (Josh. v. 11).

Next, view it as typical. *The sheaf* is evidently *Christ
the first-fruits* (ἀπαρχὴ Χριστὸς, 1 Cor. xv. 23). Jesus rose

that man of Baal-shalisha appears to have been one who intended to recognise
Elisha as God's true Levite, while he refused to recognise the apostate church
which Jeroboam had organized.

* The Drink-offering has been spoken of, p. 46

on the third day after passover: and this has become *our Sabbath* ever since.* Jesus was the first-fruits. Being in our true and very nature, he rose as our Head. *The Father* was waiting for his presentation—his "being waved;" and this was done when, raised from the dead by the Spirit of holiness, he stood at the opened sepulchre, no more a Man of Sorrows. His life of sorrow had that morning ripened into the full ear of bliss; and there he stood in the sunshine of eternal love. And *He* stood, on our earth and in our nature, not for himself personally so much as "first-fruits"—pledge and earnest of all the harvest; because *He* was accepted by the Lord, therefore shall *we* also be. Until He was thus presented and accepted, none of us could speak of a harvest-day (ver. 14); no blessing was secured to us or free to our use.

The *first* time that the Jews ever waved the sheaf before the Lord must have been on their first entering the land. They entered and found the barley ripe for use. This was *"on the morrow after the passover"* (Josh. v. 11). On that day they would eat the old corn and unleavened cakes; and that very day would cut down the sheaf of first-fruits, to be waved "on the morrow after the Sabbath" (Lev. xxiii. 11). Thus the *first* employment of Israel in Canaan was *preparing* the type of the *Saviour's* resurrection, and their first religious act was *holding up* that type of a risen Saviour. Their land was to be renowned for this wonder more than any other,—*resurrection!* and that *resurrection* implying *redemption* and *completed deliverance.* The paschal lamb in Egypt shewed deliverance begun; this shewed it finished.

* Perhaps be himself *appointed* it to be so; ἡ κυριακὴ ἡμέρα (Rev. i. 10), may mean this as much as in 1 Cor. xi. 20, " κυριακὸν δεῖπνον" means the Supper instituted by the Lord.

This first *sheaf* is the pledge of *our resurrection*, as well as acceptance; or rather, of our *declared acceptance and full freedom by our resurrection.* Christ is "first-fruits of them that sleep" (1 Cor. xv. 20). It is type and pledge of our harvest—this earth's season of ripe increase—the day for which every providence, every event has been preparing—the day for which every blast and every hour of sunshine has been ripening the wide fields—the people, cities, and hamlets of the whole world. "*Christ the first-fruits; then they that are Christ's at his coming.*" The Lord himself will then rejoice with the joy of harvest. When Israel tasted the barley of Canaan, then were they fully sensible of completed deliverance from Egypt and from the desert. Tasting even *Marah-wells* made them know they were escaped from Egypt; but it must be receiving the harvest of the land that assured them of their complete escape from the desert. So the believing soul feels his escape from sin and the law even by the frowns of a self-righteous world, and his sorrow in the midst of its sin: but that *resurrection* (of which Christ was the earnest, or first-fruits) will be his blessed assurance that every hardship of the desert also—and so every remaining mark of having come from Egypt—is obliterated and for ever gone.

Thus the "*sheaf of first-fruits*" was like a "heap set about with lilies;" so many truths, so many visions of the future, so many tokens of Divine purpose begun, clustering round it when it was waved before the Lord.

FEAST OF WEEKS

or, as it is otherwise called, "*Feast of fifty days;*" in Greek, πεντηκοστή, Pentecost.

Ver. 15, 16. *And ye shall count unto you from the morrow after the sabbath, from the day that ye brought the sheaf of the*

wave-offering; seven sabbaths shall be complete.   Even unto
the morrow after the seventh sabbath shall ye number fifty
days; and ye shall offer a new meat-offering unto the Lord.

There is a way of viewing these feasts as containing
a prefiguration of the different dispensations which the
Lord has chosen for the manifestation of his ways to man.
In this case, we can easily see that the coming *Feast of
Tabernacles* refers to the millennial glory; but to what
do *Passover* and *Pentecost* refer? *Passover* seems peculiarly to describe *Israel's dispensation*—it is a time of
exhibiting blood poured out for the people's deliverance;
and if so, *Pentecost* may be considered as descriptive of
the dispensation that followed, viz. the apostolic Church
instinct with the fruits of a Saviour's death, resurrection,
and ascension.   Our Lord's stay on earth for forty days
after his resurrection, and his ten days in heaven before
the day of Pentecost, exhibited in earth and heaven the
blood of Passover fully poured out and needing no more
to be repeated, and thus brought that dispensation to a
close.

There were to be "*seven Sabbaths*" running their
course ere another feast came—to indicate a *full* and
complete period, during which ordinances and services
were carried on appropriate to the time.   Israel's system
had a full development during this passover-time.

At the close of the "*seven weeks*" the new *meat-offering* was to be brought forward; that is, the *first-fruits of
the new, or wheat-harvest.*

> Ver. 17–21. *Ye shall bring out of your habitations two wave-
> loaves of two tenth-deals: they shall be of fine flour; they
> shall be baken with leaven; they are the first-fruits unto
> the Lord.   And ye shall offer with the bread seven lambs
> without blemish of the first year, and one young bullock, and
> two rams: they shall be for a burnt-offering unto the Lord,*

with their meat-offering and their drink-offerings, even an.
offering made by fire, of sweet savour unto the Lord.   Then
ye shall sacrifice one kid of the goats for a sin-offering, and
two lambs of the first year for a sacrifice of peace-offerings.
And the priest shall wave them, with the bread of the first-
fruits, for a wave-offering before the Lord, with the two
lambs; they shall be holy to the Lord for the priest.   And
ye shall proclaim on the self-same day, that it may be an
holy convocation unto you: ye shall do no servile work
therein: it shall be a statute for ever in all your dwellings,
throughout your generations.

We here see that the *first-fruits of wheat-harvest* were
to be presented on the fiftieth day after the waving of
the *barley-sheaf.*   But they were not to be offered in the
form of a sheaf.   They are to be made into *two loaves of*
bread, which the priest (ver. 20) shall afterwards feed
upon.   A special quantity of flour, double the quantity
of a common meat-offering, was to be taken from some
Israelite's dwelling, and baked into loaves, and so waved
before the Lord.   There was to be *"leaven"* in the
loaves; for they were to be loaves found among men in
daily use—thereby presenting to the Lord a thanksgiving
for their supply of food, even of the finest of the wheat.

But of what was all this typical?   We reply—1. These
first-fruits do not seem to typify Christ himself; for then
there would have been no *leaven.*   2. Neither do they
seem to typify the gift of the Holy Ghost; for what is
there here significant of the Spirit peculiarly?   But, 3.
They typify *something made out of wheat-seed.*   If so,
then, we find in John xii. 24, that Jesus is the *corn of*
wheat; and here we will have *what was produced from*
that seed of wheat.   The *two loaves,* made out of the
wheat-seed, are *his Church,* which sprang from him
who died; made of finer flour than the Old Testament
economy (the passover economy) furnished, because the

Spirit is abundantly given; taken from the common abodes of men (John xvii. 5), and becoming part of the body of our High Priest.

They are *two* in number, also; just as in Rev. xi. 3 and Zech. iv. 3 *two* is the number—an adequate number, but not *seven;* for that would have signified a complete number. It seems, too, to be *Christ's Church after he was risen;* viz. his Church founded by apostles. Some, indeed, say that the *two* loaves point to the two dispensations of his Church—Jew* and Gentile; but the progressive order of the types is against this view. The types have shewn us Christ's *dying*—the passover lamb; then his *rising again*—the sheaf waved; and now what he accomplished at Pentecost in proof of his being *ascended.* The result was, the production of a Church, in which there was leaven or corruption still; but which was of fine wheat, the Holy Ghost being now given.

I suppose *"Christ ascended"* might have been typified by the waving of a *"sheaf of fine wheat"*—his own glorious body, when ascended, being fine wheat; but he prefers to shew how that body became food to a blessed *company of souls,* whom he called to be his Church, in whom there was imperfection still, as denoted by the leaven. These *two loaves* are the fruit of the *one corn of wheat* (John xii. 24), or a *specimen* of the harvest that has sprung from that One. Look over the land, and everywhere you find the ripe wheat ready to be gathered into the granaries; even so the Church, exhibited in its beginnings at Pentecost, was to increase and spread, and be found all over earth; but all originating in Christ, the Seed.

---

* There can properly be no symbolic type of the Jewish Church, for that Church itself was a symbol of what was yet to come—" good things to come."

And ever to keep us in mind that our blessings, and God's doings for us, are the effects and fruit of atonement, many sacrifices are to attend this offering of first-fruits. It is meant thereby to keep us on earth as intently fixing our eye on the Lamb of God, as those round the throne. Hence we have here the injunction to offer—1. A very complete burnt-offering, seven lambs, two rams, one bullock—victims of all the usual sorts. 2. The usual meat-offering. 3. The usual drink-offering. 4. A kid, as usual, for sin-offering. Then, 5. A special peace-offering. This last was to be two tender lambs, as if one along with each of the two loaves. And over these two lambs of peace-offering, the two loaves were to be waved.* The priest is thus directed to exhibit the peace between God and his Church by waving the two loaves over the two lambs! "We *have peace with God through our Lord Jesus Christ,*" is the voice of the whole Church of God. The *two witnesses* on earth ever cry, "*The chastisement of our peace was laid upon him,*" as they look on the slain Lamb. "We have fellowship one with another—truly our fellowship is with the Father—and the blood of Jesus Christ his Son cleanseth us from all sin." Peace and fellowship through blood is the experience of every saint—*the loaves* are presented to the Lord over the *lambs of the peace-offering!*

This day was to be proclaimed a "holy convocation" †—kept like a Sabbath, excepting that work might be done, if it was not "servile work." The reason for so specially saying, "*that self-same day,*" is, that on this

---

* " *With* the two lambs " is בְּ, " over."

† I do not see why our translators have adopted so awkward a rendering as we find in the text. It is quite literally rendered thus—" Ye shall proclaim, on the self-same day, a holy convocation to you."

occasion there was no long *season* or *space of time* kept, as at the offering of the sheaf: there was only *one day*.

The Jews say that this feast commemorated the giving of the law on Sinai; but not one word of this object is mentioned here, or in any of the passages of Scripture that refer to this feast. That idea is evidently an idea started by the Jews themselves; they did not receive it from God. And it is natural for them to adhere to it while they know not the glory of an ascended Saviour. For this feast has no meaning that can be discovered, except in Him who is "gone up, and has received gifts for men." But to us how significant! It tells of Jesus ascended, and of the proofs he gave of his ascension, in "shedding down the Spirit" (Acts ii. 33). Indeed, we may use these feasts as a symbolic language for the grand facts on which our hope and joy depend. The *passover* is just symbolic language for "Christ died for our sins." The waving of *the sheaf* is symbolic language for "Christ is risen from the dead, and become the first-fruits of them that sleep." The waving of the *two loaves*, at the commencement of wheat-harvest, is symbolic language to express the words of Jesus, "Verily, verily, unless a corn of wheat fall into the ground and die, it abideth alone; but if it die, it bringeth forth much fruit. . . . . And I, if I be lifted up from the earth, shall draw all men unto me." Here is the fruit of "the corn of wheat"—here are *two loaves!* a specimen and earnest of abundance beyond measure, all arising from the one seed of wheat! And in due time, the Feast of Tabernacles will express to us the truth contained in the words, "The tabernacle of God is with men, and he will dwell among them;" or in the saying of the Master himself, "I will not leave you orphans; I will come unto you."

O to be able to see the wonders of thy law, O God! Anoint our eyes with eye-salve. Lead us through these types thyself, as thine angel led John through the wondrous streets of New Jerusalem. Shew us here the precious stones, and the fine gold; yea, let the Lamb himself be our light, as he has said, "I will send you another Comforter; and when he, the Spirit of Truth, is come, he will lead you into all the truth," even as he shall, in person, lead us yet to fountains of living waters.

> Ver. 22. *And when ye reap the harvest of your land, thou shalt not make clean riddance of the corners of thy field when thou reapest, neither shalt thou gather any gleaning of thy harvest; thou shalt leave them unto the poor, and to the stranger: I am the Lord your God.*

See chap. xix. 9. In this manner, *love to man* was taught in these thanksgiving feasts, at the very time that *love to the God* who so kindly gave them their plenty, was called forth and increased.

This may be considered, further, as a rule applicable to both harvests, viz. *barley* and *wheat* harvest—being placed at the close of the directions given for both. Now, some have thought that this *gleaning* left to the poor, in *corners of the fields and scattered up and down*, may refer *figuratively* to the remnant to be gathered, during this dispensation of the Christian Church, from Israel. I should rather apply it to both dispensations. During Israel's dispensation (barley-harvest), there were to be handfuls left to the stranger. This may be the Gentile remnant brought to know Jehovah in that age, such as Rahab, Ruth, Ittai, the queen of Sheba, Hiram king of Tyre, the widow of Sarepta, Naaman, and the Rechabites. Then, during the Christian dispensation, there have been gleanings left for Israel, now a stranger, and poor and

needy, as at this day we see in the converted Jews of
our own land, or in the converts at Pesth, or even in the
late Bishop of Jerusalem.

A feast is coming on that will unite Jew and Gentile
in equal fulness.

THE FEAST OF TRUMPETS

Ver. 23–25. *And the Lord spake unto Moses, saying, Speak unto
the children of Israel, saying, In the seventh month, in the first
day of the month, shall ye have a sabbath, a memorial of blowing of trumpets, an holy convocation. Ye shall do no servile
work therein; but ye shall offer an offering made by fire unto
the Lord.*

Instead of "BUT ye shall offer," it is better, as it is
also more literal, to read, "AND ye shall offer."

The *seventh* month is a kind of *sabbatical month*, full
of feast and fast days. It was also the beginning of their
civil year. The heathen kept their new year with mirth
and folly; Israel keeps his with joy and solemnity. His
new year ever reminds him of the coming on of a period
of jubilee and joy, when the Feast of Tabernacles shall be
kept; so that their new year's mirth was, for the most
part, caused by the prospect of things to come.

No month opened to Israel such a scene of rejoicing as
did this; for no other had in it the *Expiation-day* and
the *Feast of Tabernacles.* Hence it is very probable
that this month's *Feast of Trumpets* was "the *joyful
sound*" referred to in Ps. lxxxix. 15, "Blessed are the
people who know the joyful sound" (תְּרוּעָה, as here).
Where else are there a people who know at once of full
atonement and of the joy of the *Tabernacle-feast*—present acceptance and future glory? At the same time, the
"*joyful sound*" might equally refer to the silver trumpets
which summoned the people to *all* the solemn services of

this chapter. For Num. x. 7, 8 proves that they were sounded on occasion of each of these solemnities, though more especially on "the *Feast of Trumpets.*" The people who know "justice and judgment, mercy and truth," all harmonised, enter fully into the blessedness of this joyful sound.

But why is it called "*a memorial?*" What does it keep in memory? Some say it kept the *Creation* in memory, being the first day of the common year;* as Abib, the passover-month, was the first day of the sacred year, celebrating *redemption.* If so, it might be held as a memorial of the "sons of God *shouting for joy*" at the world's foundation; for the original word is the same as that used for "*the glad sound,*" and "*the blowing of trumpets.*"† And we might take into view, also, the suggestion of others, that *the trumpet-sound,* which is so often connected with the voice of God (*e. g.* Exod. xix. 19; Rev. i. 10), was a special memorial of God having, in those days, spoken with man—a sound more joyful far than all the shoutings of the sons of God.

But I rather think this feast was a *memorial* in another sense. We read of a *memorial,* chap. ii. 9, in the sense of something taken or done to keep in view what was lying in sight, though not brought forward. In Leviticus, the term "*memorial*" does not mean the keeping in memory of a thing past. Many have erred from overlooking the sense of the term. It is, in fact, a ceremonial or tabernacle term, signifying something done in order to call attention to something yet remaining. It should be rendered "*a reminding*" of something present, or of

---

* Exod. xxxiv. 22 speaks of it as happening "in the end," or rather "*at the revolution* of the year," תְּקוּפַת הַשָּׁנָה.

† It is יָרִיעוּ, Job xxxviii. 7.

something just at hand ; rather than "*memorial,*" which suggests the past.   In Hebrew, the term is זִכָּרוֹן, from the same root as הַמַּזְכִּירִים, Isa. lxii. 6, " Ye who are the remembrancers of the Lord," reminding him of what is to be done.   So also Exod. iii. 16, "This is my name for ever, and my *memorial*" (זִכְרִי), *q. d.* to remind my people of what I still am, and may be expected to do. So also Acts x. 4, "Thy prayers and thine alms are come up for a *memorial* before God"—to remind him what to do for thee ; every prayer and every giving of alms *called the attention of God* to the centurion.   The word may, in other connexions, call attention to *the past,* but the above is sufficient proof of its very usual sense in calling attention to things coming on, and not yet actually arrived.   Now, it was in this sense that *Maimonides* understood this *Feast of Trumpets.*   It awakened (he thought) the people to repentance in prospect of the Day of Expiation.   It has, indeed, been objected to this view,* that תְּרוּעָה always signifies *a joyful sound,* and so could not be used in prospect of such a solemn fast.   But the objector forgets that that solemn day was not merely confession, but pardon also, and introduced the most joyful of all feasts, that of Tabernacles.

It was, then, a feast whose object was to rouse all Israel to joyful expectations, and summon their attention. The silver trumpets ever sounded a glad note, they being in reality *the voice of God* uttered to Israel. Whensoever these silver trumpets sounded, whether to proclaim a solemn sacrifice, or to call out Israel to the battle-field (Num. x. 7–10), their utterance was *the voice of Jehovah,* saying, "Come, my people."   Even as the trumpet on Sinai indicated God speaking ; and as

* *See* Jennings, " *Jewish Antiq.*"

Christ's voice, in Rev. i. 10, was heard as if a trumpet sounded. It is thus "the last trump," or the trump at the close of all things, shall intimate what is written in Ps. l. 3, "Our God shall come, and shall not be silent."

This feast, therefore, is to be considered as God's solemn call to attention in prospect of the very special causes for joy in this month. In short, it is just the symbolic language for that word "BEHOLD," which prefaces many a New Testament call in regard to the same truths. "Behold the Lamb of God, which taketh away the sin of the world!"—the expiation day is at hand. "Behold, the Bridegroom cometh!"—the day of joy is at hand—the feast of fat things.

There were several sacrifices (Num. xx. 1-10) offered on this day; but we are not called on here to specify them. Indeed, they were no way more special than others of a similar kind, offered on other solemnities. It was the *trumpet-sound*, heard from morning to evening, that was peculiar to this feast. On other occasions, the trumpet blew once or twice; but on this day they blew all day long; and the special reference of Ps. lxxxi. 3 * is not to every new moon, but to the new moon feast of trumpets in this one month—"our solemn feast day."

What a God of love have we! He calls us to bliss. If there be one time more blessed than another, then we find that to that time he calls our special attention. He would have our whole soul engaged in the enjoyment of those special prospects presented to our eye and heart in the coming feasts of fat things that follow the great day of atonement, as well as to atonement itself. He calls us

* Ps. lxxxi. 3, "Blow trumpets at new moons." If it be asked, Why is not the monthly festival of new moons noticed in this chapter? the answer is, There were additional sacrifices offered on the day of the new moon; but it was not set apart in any other way. It was not a Sabbath-day.

to the contemplation of both, that we may find holiness and happiness together.

Does not all this lead us at last to the true significance of this *Feast of Trumpets?*   It is the grand type of the *preaching of the Gospel.*   The *Gospel* is God's voice— "*See that ye refuse not him that speaketh*" (Heb. xii. 25).   It declares both the *sufferings* and the *glory* of the Saviour—both the day of atonement and the feast of tabernacles.   Or, we should rather say, it signifies the cry and testimony of God taken up by a host of witnesses, age after age; all of them sounding the silver trumpets, and saying, "Repent, for the kingdom of heaven is at hand."   *Passover* represented Israel's dispensation; *Pentecost* represented the Christian dispensation.   But this month's feasts are to unite and blend both.   Hence, it begins with a feast that sets forth God's voice of love and warning under both dispensations.   "How often would I have gathered you!" is equally true of God under both dispensations.

The interval between this feast and that of the Atonement-day and Tabernacles may be typical of the short time near the close of all, when it would almost seem as if God had spoken in vain.   Jew and Gentile have in turn been tried, and have in turn rejected him.   "When the Son of man cometh, shall he find faith on the earth?"   But this shall soon be followed by the breaking of a glorious day, when there shall be true mourning over sin, and then a universal scene of holy joy.

THE DAY OF ATONEMENT *

Ver. 26–32. And the Lord spake unto Moses, saying, Also on the

---

* Called by way of eminence יוֹמָא among modern Jews.   Bengel has an idea that is at least interesting, viz. that this day of atonement may have been the *anniversary* of THE FALL.

tenth day of this seventh month there shall be a day of atonement: it shall be an holy convocation unto you; and ye shall afflict your souls, and offer an offering made by fire unto the Lord. And ye shall do no work in that same day; for it is a day of atonement, to make an atonement for you before the Lord your God. For whatsoever soul it be that shall not be afflicted in that same day, he shall be cut off from among his people. And whatsoever soul it be that doeth any work in that same day, the same soul will I destroy from among his people. Ye shall do no manner of work: it shall be a statute for ever throughout your generations, in all your dwellings. It shall be unto you a sabbath of rest, and ye shall afflict your souls: in the ninth day of the month at even, from even unto even, shall ye celebrate your sabbath.

This special day of humiliation and atonement has been fully spoken of, chap. xvi. In verse 27, it is "a day of הַכִּפֻּרִים," expiations—atonements. It is remarkable that the chief view of it given in this place is that of its being a time for *"afflicting the soul."* We can perceive a propriety in this view. This *afflicting of the soul* withdrew the man from earthly joys; the world and its scenes faded away while he contemplated his guilt and the wrath of his God, and then the atonement provided by God. His afflicted soul is weaned from earth. In this manner, preparation is made for the holy joy of the Feast of Tabernacles.

Sorrow for sin seems to be like the rough sand that a man uses to rub off rust from iron; sorrow searches and rubs sore on the soul, but at the same time effectually removes what cleaved to the soul before. The vessel is thus rinsed of the flavour of former wines, and left quite clean for the new wine of the kingdom. *Sorrow* does not take away the *sin*, but it takes away the taste for it, and the pleasant taste of it; it does not empty out the vessel, but it frees the emptied vessel (the pardoned soul) from the former relish it had for earth. It is thus that the Lord's children pass through fire and water to the wealthy place. For this reason it is that their souls are tried with spiritual griefs and outward tribulation. It makes the joy of the Lord the fuller and sweeter to them.

The evening of the day, or rather, the afternoon of it, bathed their souls in the refreshment of pardon and assured acceptance. And is not this also a preparation for the joy of the kingdom? It is by these beginnings that the heart is tuned for the day of universal gladness at the Lord's appearing. By these beginnings are their souls fashioned into the feelings of heaven.

THE YEAR OF JUBILEE

Might have been expected to come in here, for it began on the evening of the day of atonement. The *joy of jubilee* followed up the ceasing from all other joy. But, as this feast occurred only once in every fifty years, it is not taken in here among the annual feasts, but is delayed to a separate place. See chapter xxv.

THE FEAST OF TABERNACLES

Ver. 33–36. *And the Lord spake unto Moses, saying, Speak unto the children of Israel, saying, The fifteenth day of this seventh month shall be the feast of tabernacles for seven days unto the Lord. On the first day shall be an holy convocation; ye shall do no servile work therein. Seven days ye shall offer an offering made by fire unto the Lord; on the eighth day shall be an holy convocation unto you, and ye shall offer an offering made by fire unto the Lord: it is a solemn assembly; and ye shall do no servile work therein.*

These verses do not fully describe the feast of tabernacles, but only shew its place among the other feasts. It is peculiarly marked; for this notice of it is given as

if to sound the note of preparation; then, verses 37, 38
declare that when this feast shall be over, all the feasts of
the year are over. It is like the manner of annunciation
in Rev. x. 7 : "In the days of the seventh angel . . . .
the mystery of God shall be finished"—thus raising high
our expectations of it, ere it is itself formally declared.
And hence it is, probably, that verses 37, 38 come in
here.

> Ver. 37, 38. *These are the feasts of the Lord, which ye shall*
> *proclaim to be holy convocations, to offer an offering made by*
> *fire unto the Lord, a burnt-offering, and a meat-offering, a*
> *sacrifice, and drink-offerings, every thing upon his day:*
> *beside the sabbaths of the Lord, and beside your gifts,* and*
> *beside all your vows, and beside all your free-will offerings,*
> *which ye give unto the Lord.*

Is it not an instance of the love of the Holy Spirit
that he should so frame the language and manner of a
passage as to call special attention to what is most joyful ? He dilates on scenes that are peculiarly gladsome
throughout all the prophets, *e.g.* Isa. xxxv. and lx., Rev.
xxi. And so here; for ver. 37, 38 shut up the passage,
finishing the enumeration of facts, and giving a general
review, saying, "These are your feasts, and these include
the offering made by fire (אִשֶּׁה), and the whole burnt-
offering (עֹלָה), and the bread-offering (מִנְחָה), and any
bloody sacrifice (זֶבַח), drink-offerings too, and every day's
provision, and Sabbaths, with all the occasional gifts,
vows, and free-will offerings." Immediately after this the
pen of the ready writer returns to the feast of tabernacles.
"*Surely,*" says he (using אַךְ, a word used in stating strong
convictions, or things that have good reason in their

---

* מַתָּנוֹת, " presents" of such things as Exod. xxxv. 5-9 mentions—different
from קָרְבָּן, which refers chiefly to offerings that were sacrificial.

favour, as Ps. lxxiii. 1)—"*Surely* ye shall keep the feast of tabernacles" (ver. 39).   He seems to hasten back to that scene of joy and glory, and, now that all other things are despatched, to dwell leisurely upon this alone.

> Ver. 39–43. *Also (surely) in the fifteenth day of the seventh month, when ye have gathered in the fruit of the land, ye shall keep a feast unto the Lord seven days: on the first day shall be a sabbath, and on the eighth day shall be a sabbath. And ye shall take you on the first day the boughs of goodly trees, branches of palm-trees, and the boughs of thick trees, and willows of the brook; and ye shall rejoice before the Lord your God seven days. And ye shall keep it a feast unto the Lord seven days in the year. It shall be a statute for ever in your generations; ye shall celebrate it in the seventh month. Ye shall dwell in booths seven days; all that are Israelites born shall dwell in booths; that your generations may know that I made the children of Israel to dwell in booths, when I brought them out of the land of Egypt; I am the Lord your God.*

As it was said of the day of atonement, that "a man had never seen sorrow who never saw the sorrow of that day;"[*] so, on the contrary, it was said of the feast of tabernacles, and especially of its last day, that "he who never saw the rejoicing of drawing water, never saw rejoicing in his life." It fell at the time of vintage, and when all kinds of increase were gathered in. It was, however, apt to be a rainy month: it was not in itself the best suited for dwelling in booths. Hence, the Jews say that this season of the year was fixed upon as being on this very account the better fitted to shew that they acted from regard to a Divine command.[†] Had it been in spring-time, it might have been thought the suggestion of natural feeling.

---

[*] " Rightly to feel sin is the torture of tortures."—*Luther.*
[†] *See* Patrick, *ad loc.*

One object of it was to keep in memory Israel's·dwelling in tents in the desert, while their God dwelt among them in the pillar-cloud. They were to realise these past times in their imagination, and have a vivid view of the scene, viz. *their God spreading his covering over the tents of Israel*, while as yet Israel wandered from place to place (2 Sam. vii. 6), *journeying with them*. In this manner it was a most fitting type of the yet better dwelling among men of the same God, in the latter days, when "His Tabernacle shall be with men" (Rev. xxi. 3), and *the Lamb* shall lead them to living fountains of water.

During the seven days, they dwelt in booths. They made booths out of the various trees wherewith their land abounded; they did not only carry the boughs in their hands, they also formed them into tents or booths. For so Nehemiah (viii. 15, 16) states very plainly, adding, "to make booths, *as it is written*," that is, according to the original intention of the command. From Neh. viii. 15, 16, we infer that "the courts of the Lord's house" were the heart of the scene.

Imagine the scene thus presented to the view. It is an image of paradise restored—the New Earth in its luxuriance during the reign of righteousness, and peace, and joy. "*Every goodly tree*" * furnishes its boughs for the occasion. The *palm*—so especially used in after days as a token of triumph, and a symbol of Judah's land—the *palm* is first mentioned. Besides, it is the tree that had oftenest sheltered them in the wilderness, as at Elim, being one of those that grow even in the sandy deserts. Then, the "branches of *thick* trees," or,

---

* The Jews limit this to the *citron;* but this is a mere tradition of men. The words mean any tree whatsoever that was attractive and goodly. Jahn says, " Any noble tree, such as the palm, or the malum Punicum." So Rosenmüller.

" of *bushy* thick-twisted trees," such as the myrtle—thus plucking some boughs from the lower thickets, as well as from the lofty palms.   In Neh. viii. 15, the *myrtle* is noticed by name.   Next, "the *willow*" from the river-side, hanging its boughs over the brooks of water, as if to shade them, for Israel's sake, from the scorching heat.   There were also "*the olive and the pine*" (Neh. viii. 15), the former representing the species that served for Israel's domestic uses, and the latter those that supplied public necessities ; the one yielding its berries, the other its massy beams.   All these, and any other such,* were used on this joyful occasion.   The booths so formed exhibited the scene of a world clad in rich, luxuriant verdure—men dwelling in peace, and sending up songs of praise amid every token of fresh and lively joy.   Some have fancied that they can discern more still, as they gaze on these booths of every bough : they think they see the love of the God of Jeshurun pictured forth, as being noble and lofty in its bearing, like the *pine* or *cedar ;* fragrant and sweet as the *myrtle ;* triumphant over all obstacles, like the *palm ;* full of richness, like the *olive ;* while, like the *willow* of the brook, it bends over the children of men, and over his own Israel above all, in lowly condescension.   But, at all events, this is implied in the scene taken as a whole.   For here is Eden restored, a fit abode for Him who shall dwell among them.

The eighth day was reckoned the great day of the feast, as is said in John vii. 37.   It was the day when the *ingathering of the vintage*, and all other fruits (Exod. xxiii. 16), was completed.   It thus combined in it the "joy of harvest" and the "shouting of them that tread the wine-press," with the gladness peculiar to the feast

---

* " Any of the fine trees then in bloom," says Rosenmüller.

itself. But the *Jews,* not satisfied with all this, added the ceremony of drawing water from the pool of Siloam, to represent the water out of the smitten rock in the desert; and in pouring out this pitcher of water in the Temple, so great used to be the joy, that it became a proverb, " He who never saw the rejoicing of drawing water, never saw rejoicing in all his life." But this addition to the feast betrays, it would seem, a sad truth concerning Israel. They rested in the type and shadow, and sought their full joy from the mere feast and its gladsome ceremonies, instead of looking through these rites to the future. Hence they were disappointed; they were not fully satiated with joy; they felt an emptiness left, even after all the ceremonies of this day of joy. Attempting, therefore, to make the shadow more substantial, they invented the *drawing of water,* to see if thus they might get more to complete their longing. Poor Israel! This feast is but a type; it is not thy heaven. The true Feast of Tabernacles is kept when the Son of the Blessed, who dwelt in the pillar-cloud, shall dwell as *Immanuel* among us. And Jesus intimated this when, at the very moment in which the water was poured forth, and Israel were vainly trying to expel all sadness from their spirit, he lifted up his voice, and said, " If any man thirst, let him come to me, and drink" (John vii. 37).

So natural to a Jew was the connexion between joy and this feast, that Peter, on the hill of transfiguration, no sooner felt the strange, surpassing joy of the scene, than he seems to fancy, " This is the day of the Feast of Tabernacles." He fancies himself and his two brethren to be already dwelling under booths or tabernacles, when lo! their joy is increased by the presence of three strangers who have come up among them—the Master,

and Moses, and Elijah.   He proposes to detain these, by
twining booths for them also (Mark ix. 5), and so retain
the exquisite joy which their presence caused; for his cup
was running over.   In all this we see, probably, a dim
hint of the truth, viz. that the coming of Jesus shall
indeed be the true time of the Feast of Tabernacles, and
his presence the true source of that day's overwhelming
bliss.   Peter spoke confusedly; but his confused words are
recorded, because in his very confusion he was led to utter
more than he really knew or meant.   It is when the
Lord shall come in his glory, and his kingdom has been
set up by him in power (Mark viii. 38 ; ix. 1), that the
antitype of the Feast of Tabernacles shall arrive.   Then
is earth to be clothed with its new-created loveliness
(Isa. xxxv. 1, 2), the very "trees of the wood rejoicing
before the Lord" (Ps. xcvi. 12).   Then shall Jesus give
the thirsty all their desire, and they shall sorrow no
more at all.   "He that sees not the rejoicing of that
day shall never see joy at all."

And the many sacrifices offered during these seven
days (see Num. xxix. 12), all pointing to the *Lamb of
God*, may intimate that *Jesus* shall be the chief object of
delight in all that feast.   It shall still be, "*Master*, it is
good to be here."   Outward glory shall be like the case
of a telescope, all intended to direct and fix the eye on
the Master himself.   "Lo! this is our God; we have
waited for him."   The decrease of the sacrifices (one a
day), as the week went on (Num. xxix.), may indicate
that there will be always less and less need to point the
redeemed to Jesus as the sum and centre of all; they
will be so entirely satisfied of his being so—so completely
bent over to entire oneness of feeling with him.   It will
become their only nature—the only thing natural to them

—to find Jesus their all in all. Oh, what are men who are "without Christ" in this world!

The close of this season is called, in ver. 36, "a solemn assembly." This is the eighth day, already mentioned above; but we notice it here again. The word is peculiar, עֲצֶרֶת, "day of restraint," or rather, a day of closing and shutting up. It is applied to the close of the Feast of Unleavened Bread (Deut. xvi. 8), and perhaps ought always to be thus understood, viz. as denoting *a solemn close.** On the eighth day, Israel returned to their houses, and rejoiced there. And some suppose the final state, *after the days of Christ's kingdom*, may be hinted at here—"the ages to come"—the undescribed, unknown, but unutterably blessed eternity after the Thousand Years.

THE CONCLUSION OF THIS SUBJECT

Ver. 44. *And Moses declared unto the children of Israel the feasts of the Lord.*

The Lord thus testifies that Moses was faithful to the letter in all he was commanded to do; and leaves us with an example before our eyes of true adherence to the revealed will of our God. If we would at length enter into these happy scenes, let us be as Moses was in his generation. Let us follow the Lord fully. "O that thou hadst hearkened to my commandments! then had thy peace been as a river, and thy righteousness as the waves of the sea."

---

* Joel i. 14 signifies, "Hold the most solemn assembly you can, like the closing day in any of your feasts." Josephus uses " ἀσαρθα"—a word formed from this, to denote the close of the Feast of Pentecost.

CHAPTER XXIV

Duty of Priests when out of Public View in the Holy Place

" That thou mayest know how thou oughtest to behave thyself in the house of God, which is the church of the living God."—1 Tim. iii. 15

DUTY OF PRIESTS IN REGARD TO THE GOLDEN CANDLESTICK

> Ver. 1–4. *And the Lord spake unto Moses, saying, Command the children of Israel, that they bring unto thee pure oil-olive beaten for the light, to cause the lamps to burn continually. Without the veil of the testimony, in the tabernacle of the congregation, shall Aaron order it from the evening unto the morning before the Lord continually: it shall be a statute for ever in your generations. He shall order the lamps upon the pure candlestick before the Lord continually.*

HERE are some directions referring neither to the priest's public duty, nor yet to his domestic, but to his official duties when withdrawn from the sight of men in the Holy Place—what may be called his *private official duties.*

The people are to bring the oil. Asher must send up to the holy place the produce of his olive-trees, and every Israelite must learn to feel an interest in the unseen work of the sanctuary. And not only must they bring it— they must bring it " pure," clear and unmixed, and " beaten," prepared with care. By thus prescribing to the people the duty of bringing to the priests the oil for the lamps well prepared, they were made to feel that they, as much as the priests, had an interest in the transactions of the Holy Place. It was equivalent to a declaration that the seven-lamped candlestick burnt there for them. And so it did. That golden candlestick, with its seven lamps at the end of the seven branches, was a type of God's Church standing in Christ (He is the shaft of gold), and supplied by the Spirit with light and life ; or, to put the same truth in a different form, it was Christ holding up his Church (the seven branches), while the Holy Spirit was the indwelling light and life of each. Each Israelite had, therefore, a special interest in these lamps.

They burned "*continually*" (תָּמִיד), that is, from day to day, like the "*continual burnt-offering*," or daily sacrifice.* The lamps were kindled every morning at break of day, and burned till evening. At evening they were trimmed again, and burned on till the dawn of day. Hence we find, in 1 Sam. iii. 3,† it was *set in order* at sunset, that it might burn till the oil was exhausted ; and when they found it gone out *in the morning*, they *set it in order* again for the day, and it burnt till evening. It was allowed to go out for want of oil and trimming, in order to teach our need of and dependence upon the Holy Spirit for every moment's light and life, and upon the Priest's care—even the watchful care of Jesus.

---

* It has been remarked, that 2 Sam. ix. 7, 13, is an instance that explains the true force of תָּמִיד. Mephibosheth ate bread at David's table "*continually.*" Hence some explain 1 Thess. v. 17, as nothing more than "Pray at stated times, without allowing interruption." But that passage includes much more, viz. a frame of mind which never feels indisposed for prayer.

† In *The Tabernacle of Moses*, by the Rev. W. Mudge (a very excellent and refreshing work), this passage is quoted as proving the spread of corruption in Eli's days. But it is not so, if our view is right ; and Witsius (*De Mysterio Tabern.*) maintains the view we have given.

"*Order them from evening till morning,*" points to a yet more special point.   They burned during night, *until* near the dawn, as a type of the Church giving light, but getting very dim as the daybreak approaches.   Perhaps the burning during day might signify the need of another light than the blaze of nature, even when at its noon.

The candlestick stood "*pure*" (*i. e.* its golden shaft and branches kept ever free from what might dim their brightness), in the Holy Place, on the outside of the veil that hung between to divide this place from the *Holiest of all*, where stood "*the testimony.*"*

Let us turn aside for a time to view more leisurely this great sight.   We on earth are interested in it; for it stands not in *the holiest of all*, which is heaven, but in *the holy* place, which represents spiritual or heavenly things enjoyed on earth.   True, it speaks primarily to Israel; for his is the one candlestick with its seven branches, giving light in a dark world.   But since his day, this same figure or type has been used by Jesus—our High Priest after the order of Melchisedec—to represent his scattered churches among the Gentiles (see Rev. i. 20). What, then, did Israel see in the golden candlestick and its lamps ?

Did they not, first of all, see, as it were, *the true vine* spreading out its many *branches ?*   They saw seven branches proceeding from one stem or shaft, each branch adorned with "knots and flowers."   The massy shaft upheld the whole—the *sevenfold*, or complete, array of branches.   Next, whether or not they knew it, it is

---

* הָעֵדֻת.   Is this word specially a name for *the ark*, wherein *the law* was deposited, and which so testified to the law's demands, and magnified it, by the blood sprinkled above?   Out of that closed ark, when so sprinkled, a voice was ever proclaiming the Lawgiver's holy, holy, holy name, in accents of love.   And this is *the testimony* needed by a sinner.

revealed now (Rev. iv. 8) that the *seven lamps* of fire were typical of the *sevenfold Spirit of God.*

How beautiful the truth exhibited here! *Christ is the golden candlestick.* He bears up all the branches; every Church and every member would give way, and fall with a crash to the dust, if he were to withdraw his upholding strength. Flowers, light, oil, are first in him, and belong to his Church because it stands on him. Were Christ to sink—had he sunk in Gethsemane—then all would have sunk! *Enoch's* three hundred years' walk with God, *Moses'* forty days and nights' communion, *Abraham's* sacrifice of Isaac—all the graces, holiness, beautiful walk, of all the saints in Old Testament times would have availed nothing had they not been on the *golden shaft.* To him, therefore, we ever sing, " *To him that is able to keep you from falling*" (Jude 24).

The olive-oil feeding the flame of every lamp is the Holy Spirit. In 1 John ii. 27, " *the anointing*" is the work of the Holy Spirit; and in Rev. iii. 1, Christ is represented as giving the Holy Spirit, who is *the oil,* to each candle-stick. All *light* was from the pure oil; all grace is from the Spirit; and Christ pours the Spirit into his own, as the priest poured oil into the lamps, "from morning to evening, continually." Without oil, the wick of the lamp would be extinguished in noisome fumes, after a short blaze; without the Holy Spirit, the Church, and every member of the Church, would sink into darkness like that of the world around them, and their profession would only leave behind most offensive remembrances. Thus, then, is Jesus giving out the Holy Spirit to his Churches.

The priest, setting the lamps in order daily, represents Christ causing his people daily to receive and give forth light and life. In the midst of a dark world, believers are

set up as lights (see Phil. ii. 15 ; Matt. v. 16).   They
should be as the Baptist, "burning and shining lights."
They should be representatives of Christ himself, who
"shone as the light in darkness."   And they must shine
—1. Not *by natural gifts, but by grace.*   There must be
a supply of beaten oil, pressed out of Israel's olive-trees;
not merely talent, or natural fervour and benevolence.
2. *Clearly.*   There were golden snuffers for these lamps,
and the use of them was committed to the priest who
went in to set things in order.   Believers must have
their gifts and graces stirred up, so that there be no dull-
ness, indecision, languor.   When you feel a little pride
stealing in, or love of praise, or fondness for comforts, or
earthly cares, go then, believer, to the priest ; let him
dress the lamp.   3. *Constantly.*   Every day in succession
shine as before ; *never* hide the light.   If there be
a place where it is not duty to speak, yet there is no
place where it is not duty to think and feel for God.
4. *Calmly;* for the light of these lamps did not sputter as
it burned.   The oil was pure.   Believers must have the
lamb-like spirit of Jesus, putting away all admixture of
human temper ; not reproving with the heat of human
passion, not harshly upbraiding the obstinate sinner, not
impatient or hasty or fierce even when enormous wickedness and deceit appear.   A calm light generally shines
full.   5. *In the face of the world.*   Cast your light fair on
the world's sins, that they may see them.   Point out
their ungodliness, their lawlessness, their unbelief.   Reprove their acts of Sabbath-profanation.   Check them
when they swear in your presence.   Bear your testimony
where the truth is denied in your presence.   Never be
afraid of dazzling the world with too much light ; but
plainly shew them that they are wholly sinful, wholly

ruined, wholly helpless; and speak of a present, immediate, free, full pardon in the Saviour. 6. So as *to shew
the golden table and the golden altar.* The light of the
candlestick did so. Was not this pointing the eye to
Christ, *who died, and who is risen?* The bread on the
table is Christ, who gave his life for us; the golden altar
and its incense is Jesus exalted and accepted. Here is
full salvation. 7. As if *you alone were responsible for
the enlightening of the dark world.* The candlestick was
the only light; so is the Church. And let every member feel responsibility. Perhaps if *you* shine not, some
soul shall be left for ever in darkness. If one light-house
on the sea-shore were obscured, how many ships might be
lost in consequence! especially if formerly that light-house
used to direct to the haven. Oh, then, how many may
perish if you backslide, and shine not as before! This is
our time for shining. When Jesus comes, his light will
dim ours; we shall shine with him, but our privilege of
bringing others to the truth shall be ended. When the
sun rises, the vessel needs no more the help of the
beacon-light.

Lord, give us the light that shineth in the dark world,
and make us shine ourselves till the day dawn and the
Daystar arise, whose beams shall gladden and sanctify
our hearts to the full!*

DUTY OF PRIESTS IN REGARD TO THE GOLDEN TABLE

Ver. 5–9. *And thou shalt take fine flour, and bake twelve cakes*

* In 2 Pet. i. 19, there may be a reference to the candlestick that shone in
the holy place. As it continued to be used until the Lord Jesus came, and a
Church of living souls had received his healing beams into their hearts, so shall
his *word of prophecy* continue to light the steps of his Church until their Lord
come again and substitute *himself* for *the word.* The force of " In your hearts"
may be this: " Until those hearts of yours, which at present receive the word
that tells of him, shall be shone upon by himself."

*thereof: two tenth-deals shall be in one cake. And thou
shalt set them in two rows, six on a row, upon the pure table
before the Lord. And thou shalt put pure frankincense upon
each row, that it may be on the bread for a memorial, even
an offering made by fire unto the Lord. Every sabbath he
shall set it in order before the Lord continually, being taken
from the children of Israel by an everlasting covenant. And
it shall be Aaron's and his sons': and they shall eat it in the
holy place: for it is most holy unto him of the offerings of the
Lord made by fire by a perpetual statute.*

The name appropriated to these loaves was לֶחֶם הַפָּנִים,
"shew-bread," or *the bread of presence;** that is, bread
fit to be, or honoured to be, set in the presence of the
King of Jeshurun.   1. It was set before God in the holy
place, just as the incense on the golden altar was offered
to God.   It was thus a type of *Jesus*, on whom the
Father's delight was placed with infinite complacency, so
that he might be said to be the food of heaven, He on
whom God feasted with delight.   And thus was represented the truth, "God gave his only-begotten Son." It
has been beautifully said, "Every sigh of Jesus was a
crumb of imperishable bread to us" (Mudge). 2. *These
loaves stood on a pure, golden table*, or a table made of
Shittim-wood, overlaid with gold.   Now, these materials
were the very materials of the ark, exhibiting views of
Christ's person, viz. his humanity in humiliation, expressed by the Shittim-wood, and his humanity glorified,

---

* The article ה in this connexion defines *the bread*, according to that rule of
Hebrew grammar which says, "that when a compound idea, represented by one
noun following another in the genitive, is to be expressed definitely, it is done
by prefixing the article to the noun in the genitive." It is not "bread of *the*
presence," but "*the* presence-bread." So Isa. lxiii. 9, is simply, "His *presence-angel*." No doubt "*presence-bread*," and "*presence-angel*," were
similar to Esther i. 14; 2 Kings xxv. 19, who would be called by the name
"*presence-men*," *q. d.* fit to stand, and honoured to be, in presence of the
king.

expressed by gold, shining like New Jerusalem streets.
Is not this to teach that the food of our souls is the Son
of man from heaven, his person presenting his finished
work to us in its complete adaptation to our souls?
3. The *twelve* loaves exhibit this truth, that for each
name on his breastplate the high priest has a full supply.
And hence, not one of these shall perish. At the same
time, the supply for each was superabundant ; it was two
tenth-deals, two omers. Now, that was double the quantity needed for one individual's wants. When manna
fell, two omers sufficed for two persons. It may teach
that there is a sufficiency in Jesus so great, that far more
souls than ever come could be supplied out of his abundance. Yes, sinner, you may not know that your name
is on his breastplate ; but this you do know, that there
is plenty on his table to satisfy you, and a welcome
withal to you when you go to take it. You will cease to
crave sooner far than He will cease to give. The blame
of your perishing will never lie on the insufficiency of
the provision. And, inasmuch as all this was managed
by *a priest*—inasmuch as it was the priest's duty to see
that these loaves were ever there in their place—inasmuch as no hand but a priest's must touch that bread,
does it not seem to say, that this provision is all for
sinners; not for the holy and righteous, but for perishing
sinners ? 4. *It was renewed weekly.* Thus it never
moulded. It was fresh at all times. For so is the
Antitype, ever fresh to us, as truly as in apostolic days.
He never waxes old ; this food never moulds. You may
get the same joy in believing on him, the same peace, the
same assurance, that were found in apostolic days ; and
may be moved with the same love and zeal and holiness,
by feeding on the same primitive food. 5. And yet

more : it will be on the morning of *the Sabbath,* the seventh thousand year of earth, that He shall be set gloriously before his people in fresh fulness.

They were set in two rows (not piled up) on the table. This was the most convenient position ; and the priest standing before them would appear one who had full occupation for both his hands—a busy, ever-busy priest, opening his hand liberally to supply the hungry through all the tribes of Israel.* Besides all this, Dr Owen's idea seems true, that in reference to the curse of the ground, Israel was taught how *their food* would be *blessed.*†

The *frankincense* (ver. 7) on the top of each row was similar in use to what is said in chap. ii. 15, 16. It denoted acceptance, and that this bread was well-pleasing to the Lord; and when burnt at the week's end, instead of the loaves, it was in order that Aaron's sons might feast on the loaves themselves. And this *feeding on the loaves* (ver. 9) while the *frankincense* ascended in sweet fragrance, seems to shadow forth Christ interceding for us at the very moment we are enjoying fellowship with him. Eaten in the courts of the sanctuary ("the holy place," as chap. vi. 16) by those who had a right of constant access, it exhibited God's children enjoying fellowship and access to their God, keeping their eye all the time on the memorial presented in their behalf.

These loaves were to be " taken *from the children of*

---

* In 2 Chron. iv. 19, Solomon is said to have made " the golden altar; the tables (הַשֻּׁלְחָנוֹת) also, whereon the shew-bread was." There were ten tables, and the Hebrew words are literally rendered, " And on them (viz. these tables) the shew-bread"—probably ten tables, each with twelve loaves. This vast increase of material in Solomon's temple is remarkable throughout; four cherubim, ten lavers, ten candlesticks, all pointing to the amazing enlargement of vision and of fruition in the days of the Prince of peace.

† On the Epistle to the Hebrews.

Israel" (ver. 8). The people were to supply them, just as ver. 2 commanded regarding the *olive-oil* for the lamps. Israel must feel that all this is done for their sakes.

And last of all, "the everlasting covenant" (ver. 8) and "perpetual statute" (ver. 9) throw a fence around to prevent neglect. As regularly as the Sabbath came on, the prepared loaves must be on the table. We must not put other food before the Lord's people. Ministers dare not change it. What mean those who set before God's people a supply of eloquence, intellect, argument, or of history, or of speculation on the truth? Even if the table have on it an array of duties, row upon row of graces and virtues, yet if Christ, the life, and the food of life, be not there, the "everlasting covenant" is broken, the "perpetual statute" annulled.

AN EVENT THAT SOLEMNLY CONFIRMED THE AUTHORITY OF THE LAWS BOTH TO ISRAELITES AND TO STRANGERS AMONG THEM, 10—16

> Ver. 10–16. *And the son of an Israelitish woman, whose father was an Egyptian, went out among the children of Israel; and this son of the Israelitish woman and a man of Israel strove together in the camp; and the Israelitish woman's son blasphemed* * *the name of the Lord, and cursed. And they brought him unto Moses;. (and his mother's name was Shelomith, the daughter of Dibri, of the tribe of Dan;) and they put him in ward, that the mind of the Lord might be shewed them. And the Lord spake unto Moses, saying, Bring forth him that hath cursed without the camp, and let all that heard him lay their hands upon his head, and let all the congregation stone him. And thou shalt speak unto the children of Israel, saying, Whosoever curseth his God shall bear his sin. And he that blasphemeth the name of the Lord, he shall surely be put to death, and all the congregation shall certainly stone him: as well the*

---

* Or, more correctly, "he uttered the name of the Lord, and then cursed him" (Hengstenberg, *on Pentateuch*, Dissert. iii. ; Rosenm., &c.)

stranger, as he that is born in the land, when he blasphemeth the name of the Lord, shall be put to death.

In ver. 10, we should probably understand the words thus : " son of an Egyptian who was among the children of Israel," that is, who was a proselyte in the midst of Israel.

In ver. 11, "*the name*" stands alone,* without the words " of Jehovah," though in ver. 16 this addition is inserted. The expression, "*The Name,*" beyond all doubt means Jehovah; and there may be a reference to this very passage in the New Testament passages where we find the Lord Jesus mentioned thus, in order to shew his high exaltation : " He hath given him a name that is above every name," ὄνομα τὸ ὑπὲρ πᾶν ὄνομα (Phil. ii. 9). If the Jews in Paul's day were in the habit (as they are now) of not uttering the word "*Jehovah*," but of substituting instead "Adonai," or the phrase used here, " the name," this clause would then have double significance to a Jew. The argument in Heb. i. may have a tacit reference to the event before us. At all events, the passage before us is itself a remarkable instance of deep reverence for the Lord's name; for what else can account for the peculiar phrase, "*the name*," except that the Holy Spirit here taught Moses to utter with awe a name which men could learn to pronounce so rashly. Hence, "*Jehovah*" is omitted twice, and " *the name* " stands alone. The solemn manner in which Exod. iii. 14, 15 records this title, gave origin to this special reverence, and suggested the expression, " *The Name.*" †

It seems as if this occurrence had taken place while

* The Septuagint here have τὸ ὄνομα κατηράσατο; and ver. 16, " ὀνομάζων τὸ ὄνομα Κυρίου."

† In Exod. iii. 15, " *memorial*" differs from the " *name;*" for " memorial" always contains a reference to *the acts* of God, *e. g.* his being the God who kept

Moses was within the tabernacle conversing with God. It is as if the people had come to the door of the tabernacle in quest of him, that he might hear the sad event, and go in and ask counsel of the God with whom he was conversing. The introduction of it into this record of ceremonial rites is not without a meaning. It was an event fitted by its results to confirm the authority of Jehovah over Israel. *Providence* was seen co-operating with *revelation* for this end. Occasion was taken from this occurrence to exhibit some precepts that drew an outward fence round the pavilion of the Great King.

And the *grace* of God shone forth amid this dark cloud. For lo! he is dealing with a camp wherein such corruption springs up, and yet he goes on still with his revelations of love. That straw on the surface shewed how the current ran. But the Lord was acting in pure grace amid a camp of sin.

The fact of the lad being the son of a Jewish mother and of an Egyptian father afforded occasion to shew that the law applied equally and impartially to the Jew and to the stranger. And his being the son of a well-known woman, *Shelomith* (whose name might have suggested *peacefulness* to her son), daughter of Dibri, made the judgment passed on him appear the more impartial.

Moses went to the Lord, while the blasphemer lay in ward. The sentence is calm and deliberate. The Lord commands that he be stoned. Every witness lays his hands on the blasphemer's head, as if to say, " Thy blood be on thyself;" and he is hurried beyond the camp, that is, beyond the place of blessing to the scene of curse—to

Abraham, Isaac, and Jacob. Whereas " *I am*" refers to past, present, and future *nature*. So Hengstenberg, on Psalm xxx. 4, thinks that "*memorial*" is his historically manifested properties, his character exhibited in acts.

where the sin-offering used to be burnt, probably. There he dies an awful death; and by his death leaves these warnings (ver. 15, 16) for all Israel. Even thus the sinner who despises "*the name* that is above every name." shall perish. The swearer, the blasphemer, the rash and irreverent, the quarrelsome and passionate, they who sin grievously under the provocation of injury, or under the ignorance and stupefaction of strong drink, belong to the class before us. So also do all those who despise and lightly esteem "that name" of Jesus. And, lo! every hand is put on their head, pointing to the fact that they themselves are to blame for their ruin! Even thus the unbelieving man perishes under the awful certainty that he is most justly doomed. Amid the crush of the shower of stones, the blasphemer's conscience louder far proclaimed to him that he deserved this doom; and, amid the flashing flames of the day of God, and the weeping and wailing and gnashing of teeth, the unbelieving man who rejected "the only name given under heaven whereby we must be saved" (Acts iv. 12) shall hear the thunder of his own accusing conscience, "The Lord is righteous, and I am self-destroyed."

Ver. 17–22. *And he that killeth any man shall surely be put to death. And he that killeth a beast shall make it good; beast for beast. And if a man cause a blemish in his neighbour; as he hath done, so shall it be done to him; breach for breach, eye for eye, tooth for tooth; as he hath caused a blemish in a man, so shall it be done to him again. And he that killeth a beast, he shall restore it: and he that killeth a man, he shall be put to death. Ye shall have one manner of law, as well for the stranger as for one of your own country: for I am the Lord your God.*

The quarrel of Shelomith's son is still in view; and even it gives occasion to a statement of the Lord's mind.

The first table requires reverence to the Lord ; this has been enjoined. The second table requires kindness to our fellow-men; this is enjoined in ver. 17–21. Murder, however men may allege the excuse of passion or of drunkenness, or the like, shall be punished by death; and lesser injuries by corresponding penalties. In the case of killing a beast (ver. 21), the crime is not to be so judged, though in that case, too, the man must make restitution ; but so precious in God's sight is the life of man, that *death* must ever be the penalty of murder. Stranger or fellow-countryman, the rule must apply alike to both.

We see, 1. *The Lord's righteousness.* His rule of equity and recompence is exhibited in judging the affairs of men. Men are taught his stern justice. 2. *The Lord's grace to men.* He draws a fence round their lives, for their souls' sake. As he was jealous for his own name, so is he for their safety. "Who is a God like unto thee !"

Moses is now appointed to decide such quarrels by fixed rules. How differently would he feel at this time from what he did when too hastily he put himself forward in the quarrel between the Israelite and the Egyptian, and next day between the two men of Israel. Then he would have recompensed "breach for breach, tooth for tooth." But to do so at that time was sinful in him; for he was not invested with authority; he was only giving vent to the natural feelings of righteous indignation at the sight of injustice perpetrated. Now, however, he acts as magistrate and "king in Jeshurun ;" and when he enjoins "*tooth for tooth, eye for eye,*" it is not done as the scribes enjoined (Matt. v. 38) ; it is not done by way of private revenge, but as representative of the Holy One of Israel.

Ver. 23. *And Moses spake to the children of Israel, that they*

should bring forth him that had cursed out of the camp, and
stone him with stones: and the children of Israel did as the
Lord commanded Moses.

Moses came back from meeting with the Lord. He
told the people that the Lord commanded the guilty man
to be led forth out of the camp—away from the place
where blessing fell like dew, and over which the Pillar
hovered, and where Jehovah dwelt, to a spot beyond the
circle of the blessing, and there be stoned. Behold the
wretched blasphemer led forth ! His head covered, after
he has cast his last look on the happy tents of Israel and
his weeping, widowed mother ; his hands bound, his lips
quivering, his steps slow and heavy ! A silent group
attend him, and multitudes gaze afar off. The sentence
and the principles of it have been just uttered by Moses
in the name of God : and, with the conviction of his own
desert plain even to himself, the man is struck to the
earth and crushed to death. "Without the camp" he
lies, a spectacle to angels and to men.

Now, of what does that mangled and marred form emphatically speak to one that passes by? It speaks of the
curse of an injured God.   Each wound, left by the pon-
derous mass that some witness cast upon his shivering
body, was an external representation of the infinite curse
that cleaves to the condemned soul.   And hence it is that
when we see Jesus, "wounded and bruised," "his visage
so marred more than any man, and his form more than the
sons of men," we therein see the marks of the curse having
really fallen on him—the curse which our sins wreathed
around him. The Father lays his hand on his holy head,
as if pointing him out as guilty—but only *guilty in our
guilt*—and every overwhelming curse is showered upon
his head.   "Surely he hath borne our griefs and carried

our sorrows!" Never man spake like that man, and yet he seems visited with the same marks of tremendous wrath as this son of Shelomith.

The wrath is equally real in both cases, while the reason is very different in either case. The mangled body of Shelomith's son declared that the wrath due to him was poured out, and in exhausting its terrors had swept life away. Even so, the dead body of our Surety, all bruised and torn, declared to Joseph and Nicodemus, as they wrapt it in the fine linen and spices, that the curse had fallen and had spent its fury on him. Well might they have sung as they bore his body, his pale body, to the new-hewn tomb without the gate, " Christ has redeemed us from the curse of the law, being made a curse for us!"

CHAPTER XXV

𝕮𝖍𝖊 𝕾𝖆𝖇𝖇𝖆𝖙𝖎𝖈 𝖄𝖊𝖆𝖗, 𝖆𝖓𝖉 𝖙𝖍𝖊 𝖄𝖊𝖆𝖗 𝖔𝖋 𝕵𝖚𝖇𝖎𝖑𝖊𝖊— 𝕸𝖎𝖑𝖑𝖊𝖓𝖓𝖎𝖆𝖑 𝕿𝖎𝖒𝖊𝖘

" There remaineth, therefore, a rest to the people of God."—Heb. iv. 9.
" The year of my redeemed is come."—Isa. lxiii. 4

Ver. 1–7. *And the Lord spake unto Moses in mount Sinai,* saying, Speak unto the children of Israel, and say unto them,
When ye come into the land which I give you, then shall the
land keep a sabbath unto the Lord. Six years thou shalt sow
thy field, and six years thou shalt prune thy vineyard, and
gather in the fruit thereof; but in the seventh year shall be a
sabbath of rest unto the land, a sabbath for the Lord: thou
shalt neither sow thy field, nor prune thy vineyard. That
which groweth of its own accord of thy harvest thou shalt not
reap, neither gather the grapes of thy vine undressed: for it is
a year of rest unto the land. And the sabbath of the land shall
be meat for you; for thee, and for thy servant, and for thy
maid, and for thy hired servant, and for the stranger that
sojourneth with thee, and for thy cattle, and for the beasts that
are in thy land, shall all the increase thereof be meat.*

As soon as they should be settled in the Promised Land,
this ordinance must be kept. As each *Sabbath-day* was
a type of the coming rest to creation after its 6000
years of woe, and as each *year's seventh month* brought
round a type of the same in the feast of tabernacles, so

---

* *" In,"* that is, while still at the same region as when the preceding precepts were given; for Israel was a year there. Numbers x. 11, 12, says they
did not remove till the second month of the second year after leaving Egypt.

each *seventh year* also.   There is a yearning in the heart
of God towards this happy time.   Jesus himself is he who
says in the Song, " Till the day break and the shadows
flee away, I will get me to the mountain of myrrh and to
the hill of frankincense" (Song, iv. 6); and these repeated
types, at every new period of time, days, months, and
years, intimate the same desire.   O how should we long
for that day of God—for what Paul calls, in 2 Thess. i. 7,
" *rest with us,* when the Lord Jesus shall be revealed from
heaven ! "

They were to keep it " *to the Lord,*" even as the Sabbath-day.   He delighted to see in that year a type of
creation's rest ; and they were to spend that year of com-
parative leisure in serving him more entirely.

When it is said, " Six years thou shalt sow," there is a
precept as well as permission given.   Till the seventh
year comes we *must* work and toil; the sweat must hang
on our brow, the testimony and effect of the Fall.   But
the seventh year wipes that away.   " There shall be no
more curse," was thus suggested to every keeper of the
Sabbatic year.   No work on that year (ver. 4), no *reaping* even of what grew of itself ; they might pluck the
few grapes that grew on " the undressed vine "* (ver. 5),
and the handfuls found springing up in the corn fields of
themselves.   This they might do just as need required.
But there was to be none of the toil of harvest or of vintage: " *the Sabbath of the land,*" that is (chap. xxiii. 38),
what the Sabbath of the land furnishes and presents, shall
be sufficient.

---

* נָזִיר, the vine, in the undressed state of a Nazarite whose locks grew unre-
strained.   As Propertius (ii. 15) speaks of the *coma* of the vine (Rosenmüller).
Or, it may be from נָזַר directly, *q.d.* the vine in the state of *consecration* to God,
which implied that no human hand pruned it.   *Patrick* remarks that olive-
yards, and such like, were included under these rules (Exod. xxiii. 10).

It was during this year also that every Israelite remitted debts due to him by his brother Israelite, and every Hebrew slave might leave his servitude (Exod. xxi., &c.), at least, if this to him were the seventh year of his bondage. There must be a full picture of rest. For this is the type of what the earth shall be under Christ, the Prince of Peace. Of Him it is said, " His rest shall be glorious" (Isa. xi. 10); and of that final rest it is written, " There remaineth a rest for the people of God" ($\sigma\alpha\beta\beta\alpha\tau\iota\sigma\mu\grave{o}s$, Heb. iv. 9), a time combining in itself all that was prefigured by the *seventh day*, and in the *seventh month*, and during the *seventh year*. Walk through Israel's land at such a time, and, lo! every one sits under his vine and under his fig-tree in peace. No sound of the oxen treading out the corn, no shouting from the vineyard; a strange stillness over all the land, while its summer-days are as bright as ever, and its people as happy as a nation on earth could be found. Amid this rest—which in a nation of agriculturists would be nearly equivalent to universal cessation from toil—how continually do the godly sing the praises of Jehovah! The whole year round, they use their leisure for God. " His servants serve him." They rest not from this ; and so they make this outward rest more truly a type of the heavenly. No sweat upon their brow (as if anticipating those days in Ezek. xliv. 18) from tilling the ground; and yet, what with last year's plentiful and superabundant supply (ver. 20), and what with the supplement yielded by this year's self-produce, each man has sufficiency. " So giveth he his beloved sleep"— and they rest in his love. And the beasts of the field rest ; " creation itself" seems to share in this liberty of the sons of God, anticipating its season of deliverance from corruption (Rom. viii. 21).

The very soil on which their harvests grew was improved by this rest, as if to shadow forth the time when it should no more yield less than it did in Paradise. And, besides all this, no man appropriated to himself anything that the land then produced; all was common, to the rich, to the poor, to the Hebrew, to the stranger—a token of the restoration of mutual love. Rest on the ground, among the beasts of the field, in the dwellings of men, with praise and worship unceasingly ascending from harp and psaltery and gracious lips, while every man partook of earth's produce as freely as his neighbour, in token of established good-will—was not all this a scene of true, real peace? Might not Israel say, "Let the heavens rejoice, and let the earth be glad ; let the sea roar, and the fulness thereof. Let the field be joyful, and all that is therein; then shall all the trees of the wood rejoice before the Lord" (Ps. xcvi. 11, 12).

So much did God love these blessed shadows of the rest to come, that Israel's neglect of them is reckoned one of the causes of their being carried away to Babylon. Shall not, then, the neglect of any among us to realise that "rest that remaineth," be also displeasing to the Lord? It is true, their neglect arose rather from present eagerness about the world, than from dislike of the season of rest ; but, from whatever cause, the duty was left undone—the type was neglected. A true longing for *the rest* would have helped much to free them from worldly attractions, and their contentedness with present scenes shewed at least that they were not over fond of the future. Is it not so still ? There is little of the pilgrim spirit in those who never long for "the rest that remaineth." There is too little weariness of sin—little of Brainerd's cry, " *O that my soul were holy as He is holy! O that it were pure*

*as Christ is pure, and perfect as my Father in heaven is
perfect! These are the sweetest commands in God's book,
comprising all others. And shall I break them? Must I
break them? Am I under a necessity of it as long as I
live in the world? O my soul! woe, woe is me, that I am
a sinner!"* There is much groaning under human misery,
but there is little groaning under a sense of deep dishon-
our done to God. There is, too, now and then, a longing
to be at rest ourselves; but rarely do you find souls who
are groaning in sympathy with all creation. A Jeremiah
may be found, weeping, not for himself, but for "the slain
of the daughter of his people;" but where shall we find
a heart so large as Paul describes: "Not they only, but
ourselves also, who have the first-fruits of the Spirit,
even we ourselves groan within ourselves," through excessive longing for a world's deliverance? O to hear earth's
hills and valleys ringing with hallelujahs that come from
souls reposing with true Sabbatic rest on their God, while
all creation listens in Sabbatic peace and serenity! One
of our own poets has sung of this expected time, when
the praise of Him who giveth rest to the weary, and who
then himself enters fully on his glorious rest, shall be the
daily employment of nations in every land.

> "The time of rest, the promised Sabbath comes!
> 　　*　　*　　*　　*　　*　　*
> Rivers of gladness water all the earth,
> And clothe all climes with beauty.   The reproach
> Of barrenness is past.   The fruitful field
> Laughs with abundance; and the land, once lean,
> Or fertile only in its own disgrace,
> Exults to see its thistly curse repeal'd.
> The various seasons woven into one,
> And that one season an eternal spring,
> The garden feels no blight; and needs no fence,
> For there is none to covet—all are full.

The lion, and the leopard, and the bear
Graze with the fearless flocks. .   .   .   .   .
One song employs all nations; and all cry,
'Worthy the Lamb, for he was slain for us!'
The dwellers in the vales and on the rocks
Shout to each other, and the mountain-tops
From distant mountains catch the flying joy;
Till, nation after nation taught the strain,
Earth rolls the rapturous Hosanna round."—COWPER.

THE YEAR OF JUBILEE

Ver. 8–13. And thou shalt number seven sabbaths of years unto thee, seven times seven years; and the space of the seven sabbaths of years shall be unto thee forty and nine years. Then shalt thou cause the trumpet of the jubilee to sound, on the tenth day of the seventh month; in the day of atonement shall ye make the trumpet sound throughout all your land. And ye shall hallow the fiftieth year, and proclaim liberty throughout all the land unto all the inhabitants thereof: it shall be a jubilee unto you; and ye shall return every man unto his possession, and ye shall return every man unto his family. A jubilee shall that fiftieth year be unto you; ye shall not sow, neither reap that which groweth of itself in it, nor gather the grapes in it of thy vine undressed. For it is the jubilee; it shall be holy unto you: ye shall eat the increase thereof out of the field. In the year of this jubilee ye shall return every man unto his possession.

Like the striking of a clock from the turret of some cathedral, announcing that the season of labour for the day is closed, so sounded the notes of *the silver trumpet* from the sanctuary, announcing that a year of cessation from all toil was come, and a year of redemption from all burdens. It is this that Isaiah seems to mean when, in chap. xxvii. 13, he speaks of "*the great trumpet being blown,*" and instantly Israel, in all lands, hear and flow together.

This year was a most peculiar time. The very name

(יוֹבֵל), " Jobel," seems invented for the occasion, and is
used onward, from this time, whenever the trumpets were
to sound joyfully. It is probable that the word is derived
from the root הוֹבִיל (Hiphil of יָבַל), meaning *" to restore,*
or *bring back;"** because on this day the silver trumpet
proclaimed release and restoration throughout all Israel.

Does *the Jubilee* represent the *preaching of the gospel?*
Some argue that it does, because Isa. lxi. 1, 2, as used
by Jesus at Nazareth, seems to be clothed in the language
of the Jubilee. The true answer to this is, that *Jesus
was the High Priest who blew the jubilee trumpet throughout all the land of Israel, when he proclaimed, " The
kingdom of heaven is at hand !"* That kingdom which he
preached brought in its train " the opening of the prison
door to the bound, deliverance to the captive," as well as
"glad tidings to the poor." But then Jesus seems to
have intended to proclaim, at that time, only that *the
rights and privileges of the jubilee year should belong to
all his true Israel.* The true time of the actual jubilee
was not yet come ; for the Day of Atonement was not
past, nor had the high priest gone in within the veil with
his sacrifice, far less come forth from the veil. It is clear,
therefore, that our Lord's ministry was not the fulfilment
of this type, but only the prelude of it ; as if the high
priest of Israel had, on the morning of the Day of Atonement, proclaimed to all the worshippers, that whoever
was of the seed of Israel should, at the close of the day,
hear the glad sound of entire deliverance, and enter on a

---

* Some Jewish commentators derive it from the supposed Arabic signification,
" a ram," as if meant "rams' horns." But even they are evidently only throwing
out conjectures. So are those who derive it from *Jubal,* the inventor of musical
instruments. The Septuagint have " ἄφεσις," and Josephus has " ἐλευθερία,"
both pointing to the sense of "restoring." Some think that " *the times of the
restitution of all things,*" ἀποκατάστασις, refers to this very word (Acts
iii. 21).

year of rest. Christ's first coming gives *the earnest* of those blessings which his second coming shall give in full. Just as a Sabbath, truly enjoyed, gives us at present that rest and refreshing of soul which we shall yet have also in body amid a universe at rest.[*]

The proper fulfilment of the type is found by the references in Isa. xxvii. 13, "*the great trumpet blown*" for Israel's restoration; and Isa. lxiii. 4, "*the year of my redeemed*" (גְאוּלַי)—those to whom I acted the kinsman's part (גּוֹאֵל). There may be reference to it, also, in Zech. ix. 12, where the blood of the covenant is assigned as the reason why these "*prisoners of hope*"[†] are to be set free; and where, in ver. 14, we hear "the blowing of the trumpet." The time of fulfilment is thus indicated to be the time of Israel's final restoration, and the time of the Lord's glorious Appearing.

This year of *Jubilee* typified the same as the *Sabbatical year*, in some degree (see ver. 11, 12, compared with ver. 4, 5); but it did so with great enlargement. It exhibits some of the *joy*, and the *causes of the joy*, of that millennial time (ver. 10, 13), while the Sabbatical year shewed merely the entire rest and peace that should prevail. Thus we find these different types advancing upon one another, just as you draw out a telescope farther and farther, till you find the proper focus for gazing on the as yet dimly perceived features of the scene. The *seventh day* exhibits a type of millennial peace; the seventh year, yet more; and now the seventh year of sevens is fuller than all the rest.

---

[*] The jubilee which Christ's first coming brings us is redemption from the guilt of sin and its dominion. The jubilee which his second coming brings is redemption from all the bitter consequences of sin, and from sin's existence.

[†] הַתִּקְוָה, expecting and looking forward to the day of deliverance with the ἀποκαραδοκία of creation (Rom. viii. 19).

The Jubilee (ver. 9) always began on the evening of the Day of Atonement. There was first given to the people a full display of the way of pardon, by all the ceremonies of that day; nay, this had been done year after year, on seven times seven occasions, ere this glorious Jubilee was proclaimed. They were taught, and we by them are taught, that the full atonement of Jesus— his blood shed and sprinkled on the mercy-seat, his entering in himself, accepted and interceding, and his coming forth " without sin unto salvation "—is the foundation and groundwork of all other blessings. No external blessing can be ours, in that millennial day, unless previously we have been accepted in the Beloved—forgiven, sanctified, made heirs with Christ. Is it thus with thee, O brother ? Can Christ, the Redeemer, the גּוֹאֵל, say of thee this day, " Thou art one of my redeemed, one of גְּאוּלַי ?" For only thus canst thou hope that he will have thee on his heart and in his eye on the day he cries, " *The year of my redeemed is come !* "

In their returning to their possessions (ver. 10, 13), we see a picture of human happiness in one of its most natural and intelligible forms. You see parents rejoicing for their children's sake, and children for their own, in being once more allowed to sit under their vine and fig-tree, and pluck the flowers and fruit of a region so sweet, and balmy, and abundant. You seem to see their happy countenances, and eyes bright with joy ; and the holy look toward heaven of the man of faith and prayer, who thanks the Lord for all. They forget the past in the joy of the present. Past losses are made up. Nor is one solitary individual forgotten (ver. 13) ; every man (אִישׁ) has his portion. This is the picture, to the eye, of that

glorious season when, "in the Regeneration,* every one
(πᾶς ὅστις) that has forsaken houses, or brethren, or
sisters, or father, or mother, or wife, or children, or
lands," for Christ's sake, shall inherit everlasting life
(Matt. xix. 29). There shall be a mansion for each; and
each shall stand "*in his lot,*" or assigned portion, "at the
end of the days" (Dan. xii. 13), when the Lord Jesus
fulfils what is written of him as the bringer back of
Eden, the restorer of Paradise, the reverser of the Fall,
" causing to inherit the desolate heritages, and restoring
the earth" (Isa. xlix. 8).

> Ver. 14–17. *And if thou sell ought unto thy neighbour, or buyest
> ought of thy neighbour's hand, ye shall not oppress one an-
> other. According to the number of years after the jubilee thou
> shalt buy of thy neighbour, and according unto the number of
> years of the fruits he shall sell unto thee. According to the mul-
> titude of years thou shalt increase the price thereof, and accord-
> ing to the fewness of years thou shalt diminish the price of it:
> for according to the number of the years of the fruits doth he
> sell unto thee. Ye shall not therefore oppress one another; but
> thou shalt fear thy God: for I am the Lord your God.*

Here are some of the abuses to which this glorious
ordinance might be perverted by ungodly men. The selfishness of men has, in every age, and under every form
of truth, discovered itself as now. An ungodly, self-seek-
ing Jew said in his heart, " I might make some gain of
this Jubilee; let me see how wisely I may calculate my
circumstances in reference to it. I have a garden at Engedi, which I might let at a high price. The purchaser
will perhaps not remember that the Jubilee is near, and
so I shall let out my garden to him at a rate which a few

---

* The word is "παλιγγένεσια," which, it is remarkable, Josephus uses to
express the restoration of one to his native country, after the exile to Babylon;
and which is also used of the renewal of earth after the deluge, and of the
restoration of Job to his former prosperity.—(Bretschneider's *Lex*).

years' possession of the garden would more than refund. He will probably have this in view when he accepts my terms ; but it is now just a year to the Jubilee, and so I shall get this large rent in the meantime, and my garden also in the course of a year." In this way, the worldly Israelite turned grace into licentiousness, " supposing that gain was godliness." *

Or if he did not overreach his neighbour in this manner, the ungodly Israelite sometimes tried to do it by another mode equally deceitful. He cunningly *included* in his estimate of the valued worth of an estate the seven Sabbatical years, although during these years no fruit was gathered ; and thus a bargain made immediately after the jubilee, which reckoned on the increase of *forty-nine* years yet to run, was really a defrauding the purchaser of seven whole years of fruit. This is meant by saying (ver. 15, 16), that only " the *years of the fruits,*" *i.e.* the productive years, and not the Sabbatical ones, are to be counted in such bargains.

It is thus that men abuse the doctrines of grace, deceiving their fellow-creatures and injuring their own souls. One man uses the Lord's table as a means of establishing his character in the sight of the world. Another asks baptism for his children from the same motive. Some adopt the doctrines of free grace as their tenets, in order to be able to sin on without abandoning the hope of running to the Ark whenever the first drops of the deluge fall. It is the doctrines of Christ's first coming that men so abuse now ; whereas it was, in the case before us, the doctrine or type of his second, that Israel abused to pur-

* 1 Tim. vi. 5. Our version does not here give the real sense; for the position of the article proves that " gain" is the predicate: " *Godliness is gain,*" " πορισμὸν εἶναι τὴν εὐσέβειαν." Such men think that *godliness* is just a system to be upheld for the sake of *worldly ends.*

poses of gain, forgetting the spiritual glory of the days of jubilee, and that " every man that hath this hope in Him (*i. e.* in Christ), purifieth himself even as he is pure."

Ver. 18–22. *Wherefore ye shall do my statutes, and keep my judgments, and do them; and ye shall dwell in the land in safety. And the land shall yield her fruit, and ye shall eat your fill, and dwell therein in safety. And if ye shall say, What shall we eat the seventh year? behold, we shall not sow, nor gather in your increase: then I will command my blessing upon you in the sixth year, and it shall bring forth fruit for three years. And ye shall sow the eighth year, and eat yet of old fruit * until the ninth year; until her fruits come in ye shall eat of the old store.*

Unbelief steps in, arising from human reason. The godly will not abuse the glorious ordinances of the *Sabbatic year* and *the jubilee;* but they may be tempted to unbelief. They may be ready to say, " What shall we eat?" Hence, our most gracious God anticipates such risings of distrust. Suspicion, and doubt, and fear, on the part of his own people are always most grievous to him ; and, therefore, he seeks to prevent them. How truly he knows our frame, our tendency to distrustful anxieties, is manifest in the words, " If ye say, What shall we eat?" It was this Jesus also, dwelling among us in flesh, perceived too plainly when he said, " Seek not ye what ye shall eat, or· what ye shall drink, neither be ye of doubtful mind" (Luke xii. 29). The Lord pledges his providence in their behalf ; and surely this should be enough for every believing man ; even as now also he says, " Your heavenly Father knoweth that ye have need of these things." Yet how often still is a man overcome by the fear of losing employment, place, support, friends, if he adhere to the Lord's cause ! How many fall before these

* תְּבִיאָה יָשָׁן, " produce," viz. old store.

temptations still! Oh, we little credit the Lord's faithfulness! How abundant is the promised provision, reach-
ing over the three years of which they were in doubt
even until the new fruits came in. May we not leave
in his hands all our difficulties as to the *manner* of future
provision, and his mode of operation?

The blessing of the Lord, not their industry, or skill,
or foresight, was to be the source of all their safety and
plenty. Nothing else is in sight, to sustain faith, but the
assurance given that the Lord is able and willing—his
heart full of love to them, his holy arm full of strength
for them. It was thus that Israel was kept looking to
Jehovah himself amid the luxuriance of their land—even
as when we gaze on the endless glories of the infinitely
varied clouds of a summer's sunset, we cannot fail all the
time to feel that every crimson tint and every flush of
beauty is dependent on the far more glorious sun. And,
when the jubilee came round with its many joys, all Israel
must have felt that the nether springs were fed directly
from the upper springs—the gladness of their happy
tribes was the immediate effect of the love of their God
and King.

> Ver. 23–28. *The land shall not be sold for ever:* * *for the land is
> mine; for ye are strangers and sojourners with me. And in all
> the land of your possession ye shall grant a redemption for the
> land. If thy brother be waxen poor, and hath sold away some
> of his possession, and if any of his kin come to redeem it, then
> shall he redeem that which his brother sold. And if the man
> have none to redeem it, and himself be able to redeem it; then
> let him count the years of the sale thereof, and restore the over-
> plus unto the man to whom he sold it, that he may return unto
> his possession. But if he be not able to restore it to him, then
> that which is sold shall remain in the hand of him that hath*

---

* לִצְמִיתֻת "*for extinction;*" so as to disappear from the page of history, like
(Job vi. 17) a brook that sinks into the sand.

*bought it until the year of jubilee: and in the jubilee it shall
go out, and he shall return unto his possession.*

Here appears God's intention to preserve Israel's land
for them, as well as them for it. The Lord, in allusion to
Egyptian affairs, says, " *The land is mine.*" The land in
Egypt was properly the king's; and all others were his
tenants,* since the days of Joseph (Gen. xlvii. 13–26).
On the other hand, Israel's land belonged to Jehovah;
and the people were his guests, or tenants, "sojourners
with him." On this account, no man had a right to sell
any portion of it "for ever." The Lord wished each
tribe, and each family of a tribe, to retain its original
possessions for the sake of—(1.) preserving genealogies
unmixed, till Messiah came; (2.) preventing the covetous
and ambitious from " adding field to field; " (3.) cherishing family associations with places, as thereby domestic
feelings and the ties of kindred are strengthened.

Hence, " a right of redemption" belonged to every one
whose portion of land had been sold for a time—a right
to redeem it whenever he was able. If the man afterwards grew rich, recovering from poverty, and was able to
pay the value of the income for the years still remaining
till the jubilee ("the overplus," ver. 27), he might at once
enter again on possession. If not able " to restore the
overplus" (ver. 28), still his portion of land shall be his
at the jubilee. Thus, for example, if Elimelech's land
(Ruth iv. 3, 4) had actually been alienated, still it would
have returned to Naomi's family at the jubilee. But if
some Boaz slip in—if the poor Jew have a relative—
" *any of his kin*"— (הַקָּרֹב אֵלָיו גֹּאֲלוֹ)—able and willing
to pay the price and restore him back his possession, this

---

* Except the priests, who received their support from the king, also, as part
of the Government (see Hengstenberg's *Egypt.*)

kinsman shall have the liberty to do so. The expression,
" If any of his kin *come to* redeem it," implies the necessity for *willingness* on the friend's part; and it points at
the same time very naturally onward to Him who is so
often spoken of as " *coming* to redeem" us. " The *Re-*
deemer shall come to Zion," says Isaiah (lix. 20), using
the name *Goel.* Himself said in eternity, "Lo, I come!"
The shout, the hosanna-shout, is yet to be raised when he
comes again to redeem *earth itself* and not its people
only : " Blessed is *He that cometh* "—the kinsman, the
Goel, that cometh to restore our possession. And Job's
hope becomes fruition, " I know that my *Redeemer* (גֹּאֲלִי)
liveth, and shall stand on the earth at the latter day"
(Job xix. 25).

Our Saviour needed to be our " *kinsman,*" in order to
possess a right to offer the price of redemption. Hence,
he took our very nature, and was "bone of our bone, and
flesh of our flesh" (Eph. v. 30). " Forasmuch as the
children are partakers of flesh and blood, he also himself
likewise took part of the same" (Heb. ii. 14). And by
becoming thus related to us, he has the right, which he
will enforce, of redeeming not only the persons of his own,
but the very earth on which they dwell. They are from
all " kindreds and tongues and people; " and so he shall
claim a right to entire possession of the earth; and Satan
shall be driven forth from his long-usurped throne. How
joyful for us to traverse the 'plains, or stand on the hills,
or trace the winding rivers of this earth, and to remember
that " *the Redeemer* " of this decayed inheritance is living
now, and soon to come again; and that he is one who has
all the affections, as well as ties, of relationship ! How
glorious our prospect—how sure our redemption, body,
soul, and spirit, as well as inheritance, when our Re-

deemer is such an one as would become our kinsman in very love to us! He loved "the children;" and since they had flesh and blood, lo! therefore, he must out of love insist on taking the same! And it is done. He is born of Mary's substance, yet continuing holy, harmless, undefiled.* He is feeble, and needs to be swaddled in swaddling clothes, and to lean on a mother's breast; and now so evidently and truly is God manifest in flesh, that Luther could write—

> "There is no God but He,
> Who lay upon his mother's knee
> And suck'd the Virgin's breasts."

"He increased in wisdom and stature, and in favour with God." His human faculties expand; and even as a lily, while it grows and unfolds its leaves, receives more and more of the sunshine into its bosom, so he receives more and more of the favour of his Father, has fuller manifestations of his Father's love poured into him, according as his faculties expand and enlarge. He lives on the creatures, not on angelic food. He takes for his food the bread that disciples bring him from Sychar, or the barley loaves and small fishes of the lake that the young man of Galilee happens to have in his basket; or plucks a fig from the tree, and is refreshed by a piece of a honeycomb. He drinks the wine of the grape at Cana, and pure water from the well of Jacob. If no food from earth is at hand, he hungers; if heat beats on him, he grows weary and thirsty. He is glad of a pillow whereon to place his head on board the ship, and is revived by the sound slumber of a few hours. And his *human soul* puts forth its powers upon the objects upon which *man* ought

---

* "Nam illa quæ Deceptor intulit, et homo deceptus admisit, nullum habuere in salvatore vestigium."—*Leo's Epistle*, quoted by Marcus Dodds on *Incarnat.*

to exercise his mind and feeling.   His soul lives by faith
—upheld by the Father's testimony.   For, hearken: " The
Lord God will help me; therefore shall I not be confounded: *therefore* have I set my face like a flint, and *I
know that I shall* not be ashamed " (Isa. l. 7) ; or, again,
when sense says, " I have laboured in vain, I have spent
my strength for nought and in vain," faith responds,
" Yet surely my judgment is with the Lord, and my
work with my God" (Isa. xlix. 4).   And *hope*, too, enlivened his dark sorrow: " For the joy that was set before
him, he endured the cross" (Heb. xiii. 3); even from
his birth it shed its cheerful rays over his marred countenance : " Thou didst make me hope when I was on my
mother's breasts" (Ps. xxii. 9).   He sang : " Thou art my
hope, O Lord God; thou art my *trust* from my youth "
(Ps. lxxii. 5).   And after the fear, and sore amazement,
and heaviness of Gethsemane, and that expression of
most affectionate human feeling toward his mother in
the very hour of infinite woe (John xix. 26), his assured
faith, reposing on his Father's bosom of love even in
the hour of darkness, shone forth with a brightness that
casts into the shade all other acts of faith ever manifested on this earth—" Father, into thy hands I commend
my spirit !"

Truly he is our *kinsman !* Nay, like one who is nearest
of kin; for his feelings are most vehement toward us. He
will not, like the nearest friend of Naomi (Ruth iv. 4–6),
refuse to redeem either our persons or our inheritance,
for he has all Boaz's desire toward us, in thousand-fold
strength, with the undoubted *right* to appear for us.   Nay,
Rev. v. 5–7 declares, that not only has he already, by his
blood, paid the price for our persons * as the Lamb slain,

* The redemption of our *persons* is referred to afterwards (ver. 48), but of

but has also claimed the right to enter for us on possession of the inheritance. He took the *seven-sealed* book;
thereby claiming to be *heir* of the property (Jer. xxxii.
8–11), and all heaven rejoiced, and the Father acknowledged his claim. Already, then, by hope may we anti-
cipate our return to our lost estate. We may, like the
Church above, use our harps to praise Him who cometh to
put us in possession; and we may, like them also, hold
up our *vials of prayer*—that is, all our prayers ever sent
up in faith, which now are filling those vials mentioned
in Rev. v. 8. For these prayers are turned by our Priest
into sweet incense, and shall not fail to be acknowledged
by him then; and we shall sing with the Psalmist, " Our
prayers are ended!" (Ps. lxxii. 20), since every desire of
our heart shall then be satisfied. Meanwhile, he " puts
our tears into his bottle " (Ps. lvi. 8), and we wait for his
Appearing.

> Ver. 29–34. *And if a man sell a dwelling-house in a walled city,
> then he may redeem it within a whole year after it is sold:
> within a full year may he redeem it. And if it be not redeemed
> within the space of a full year, then the house that is in the
> walled city shall be established for ever to him that bought it,
> throughout his generations: it shall not go out in the jubilee.
> But the houses of the villages, which have no walls round about
> them, shall be counted as the fields of the country; they may be
> redeemed, and they shall go out in the jubilee. Notwithstand-
> ing, the cities of the Levites, and the houses of the cities of their
> possession, may the Levites redeem at any time. And if a
> man purchase of the Levites, then the house that was sold, and
> the city of his possession, shall go out in the year of jubilee:
> for the houses of the cities of the Levites are their possession
> among the children of Israel. But the field of the suburbs of
> their cities may not be sold; for it is their perpetual possession.*

course only in connexion with the redemption of the land. For the redemption
of our souls has been detailed throughout this book.

It is *the land,* and God's allotment of the land, that is to continue; not man's work in it. Even as it is the earth itself that is to abide for ever as the theatre of redemption, and not man's works on it, which are to be burnt up. Hence, houses in towns might be perpetually alienated, these being the invention of men. And while the type was kept entire in regard to *the land,* this rule enabled proselytes and strangers to take up permanent abode in Israel.

Next (ver. 31); the villages being properly the country, built as they were amid the olive, and fig, and pomegranate, and palm, with the vine entwining its boughs by the sides of their houses, must fall under the rule of redemption, and must never be alienated. And thus, while the type in regard to *the land* is preserved entire here also, there is a provision against the tyranny of the princes, who might have tried from their baronial residences to subject the people of a poor village to their domination.

But as to the Levites' possessions (ver. 32-34), these must never be alienated; for they are the Lord's gift to them. Hence, even their *walled cities* may be redeemed; for these are properly the Lord's provision for them, not man's provision for himself. Also, ver. 33 ought to be rendered more literally thus: "And should any one *redeem* (יִגְאַל) from the Levites, then the house that was sold, and the city of his possession, shall go out in the year of jubilee." That is, if one not of the tribe of Levi, but a relative and kinsman by marriage, probably, *redeem* one of these houses of the Levites: in other words, if he buy the house on account of his relationship, and to give the use of it to his friend, yet still it shall in no way be removed from the tribe of Levi. It must return as a

Levitical possession to the Levite himself at the time of the jubilee. So jealously does the Lord guard his gifts to his people. "They are without repentance."

Ver. 35–46. *And if thy brother be waxen poor, and fallen in decay* with thee, then thou shalt relieve him; yea, though he be a stranger, or a sojourner: that he may live with thee. Take thou no usury of him, or increase: but fear thy God; that thy brother may live with thee. Thou shalt not give him thy money upon usury, nor lend him thy victuals for increase. I am the Lord your· God, which brought you forth out of the land of Egypt, to give you the land of Canaan, and to be your God. And if thy brother that dwelleth by thee be waxen poor, and be sold unto thee; thou shalt not compel him to serve as a bondservant: but as an hired servant, and as a sojourner, he shall be with thee, and shall serve thee unto the year of jubilee: and then shall he depart from thee, both he and his children with him, and shall return unto his own family, and unto the possession of his fathers shall he return. For they are my servants, which I brought forth out of the land of Egypt: they shall not be sold as bondmen. Thou shalt not rule over him with rigour, but shalt fear thy God. Both thy bondmen and thy bondmaids, which thou shalt have, shall be of the heathen that are round about you; of them shall ye buy bondmen and bondmaids. Moreover, of the children of the strangers that do sojourn among you, of them shall ye buy, and of their families that are with you, which they begat in your land; and they shall be your possession: and ye shall take them as an inheritance for your children after you, to inherit † them for a possession; they shall be your bondmen for ever: but over your brethren the children of Israel ye shall not rule one over another with rigour.*

Here begins a statement of our duties in prospect of "That Blessed Hope." The glorious prospect of jubilee is not to supersede present duty. Nay, rather, like Matt. xxv. 34, 35, it enforces present duty by exhibiting to us

---

* "If his hand be tottering," literally.

† See Isaiah xiv. 2, using the same Hebrew expression, with reference to other circumstances.

what is the mind of God, and what his feelings would be in our situation.

You are not to say, " Let me leave my poor brother as he is; he will soon get relief better than I could give ; for the jubilee is coming on." No, saith the Lord, you in the meantime must do what is in your power to help him, even though he be no relative of yours, nor acquaintance, but a mere sojourner. Let him " live with thee," *i. e.* live prosperously, or lead what may be called *a life*. Be generous to him. You must not relieve him in the hope of recompence (except that at the resurrection of the just, Luke xiv. 14); no *usury* for the loan, far less any " *increase*" (or interest on his very victuals) must be ever thought of. " Fear thy God;" do all from holy love and regard to his will. " I brought you from Egypt;" let redemption open your heart to others. " *I gave thee Canaan;*" and may I not ask thee to give of its produce to the poor ? " *I am thy God;*" and so thou hadst all things in me, and art never poor. How easily may you part with all things, since I am your God! See Acts ii. 43, to the end, for a New Testament proof that redeemed men estimate fully all these arguments, and are easily led to obey.

Further : an Israelite must shew his brotherly feelings if (ver. 39–41) one of his countrymen be reduced so low in poverty as to be sold for debt, like the widow's two sons, 2 Kings iv. 1. He must treat him as only a hired servant, and even in that case detain him no longer than the jubilee. The reason is very precious (ver. 42): "for they are *my servants.*" The Lord will not leave any of his purchased ones to the cruelty of others. Woe to those who use a believer harshly! They touch the " apple of his eye." Have the workers of iniquity no knowledge ?

Why persecute ye *Jesus?* "The year of his redeemed" is near.

Once more : an Israelite may have slaves and bond-maids from the heathen, and these he may retain as slaves for ever. In this there lies a type. It is not that Moses, or the Lord speaking by Moses, sanctions slavery. He gives no right to one man over another's person, except where there is sin and crime to be punished, as in the case of criminals. But here the Lord wished to punish the Canaanites and other heathen nations, because of their heathenism; and of course the Lord has a right so to do. His decree, therefore, is this: that *heathens* shall be exposed to bondage, and Israel shall take them as their slaves. *Slavery* here is evidently altogether another thing from modern slavery; for—1. It proceeds on the Lord's permission and command. 2. It is the consequence of sin in the enslaved. And while it is a penalty paid by rebellious ones who cleaved to idols, it is so overruled as to exhibit in type the future exaltation of the sons of God in the time of the jubilee of earth. It shews " the liberty of the sons of God" (Rom. viii. 21), and their dominion. Israel, in those days, shall have " strangers to feed their flocks, and sons of the alien to be their ploughmen and their vine-dressers" (Isa. lxi. 5); and the risen, glorified saints shall " execute vengeance on the heathen, and punishments upon the people" (Ps. cxlix. 7); and all men shall know that the Lord has loved them, when "they have power over the nations" (Rev. ii. 26).

Ver. 47–55. *And if a sojourner or stranger wax rich by thee, and thy brother that dwelleth by him wax poor, and sell himself unto the stranger or sojourner by thee, or to the stock of the stranger's family: after that he is sold he may be redeemed again; one of his brethren may redeem him : either his uncle, or his uncle's son, may redeem him, or any that is nigh of kin unto him of his family may redeem him; or, if he be able, he may redeem himself. And he shall reckon with him that bought him, from the year that he was sold to him, unto the year of jubilee: and the price of his sale shall be according unto the number of years, according to the time of an hired servant shall it be with him. If there be yet many years behind, according unto them he shall give again the price of his redemption out of the money that he was bought for. And if there remain but few years unto the year of jubilee, then he shall count with him, and according unto his years shall he give him again the price of his redemption. And as a yearly hired servant shall he be with him: and the other shall not rule with rigour over him in thy sight. And if he be not redeemed in these years, then he shall go out in the year of jubilee, both he, and his children with him. For unto me the children of Israel are servants; they are my servants, whom I brought forth out of the land of Egypt: I am the Lord your God.*

Here is comfort for all Israel in hope of the jubilee.

The case is supposed of a rich foreigner purchasing for his bondman one of the poor of Israel who had fallen into decay. The Lord states the case, and shews his desire that this Israelite should not so continue. It is the duty of friends to redeem them (ver. 48, 49). At all events, no stranger shall hold him in bondage beyond the jubilee.

Here is the Lord's determination to exalt his peculiar people, saving them from all oppressors, even when they have, through their own sins, fallen into decay. The times of the Gentiles shall end; and Israel shall " return and come to Zion with songs and everlasting joy upon their heads." But here, also, is the Lord's determination regarding Christ's own, whom he redeems, to deliver them from external oppression and sorrow. The whole family of God shall be freed from weeping and sorrow ; for their Redeemer is mighty.

God's Israel have no room left for despair. All is bright hope for the future, if there is not present joy (ver. 54); for the jubilee is near. Each believer must, meanwhile, wipe away the other's tears and bear his brother's burdens (ver. 48); while all fix an eager eye on the coming Day of God—"the year of the redeemed."

> " Make haste, my beloved, and be thou like to a roe,
>   Or to a young hart, upon the mountains of spices."
>
> Song, viii. 14.

We may here stay a little to observe the fact, that in the description of millennial days given in this chapter, the *negative* nature of the blessedness is chiefly insisted on; that is, that there shall be no toil, no hard labour, no regrets for lost possessions, no bondage, no oppression, no poverty, no want.

Now, somewhat of the actual blessedness of these times is spoken of under the typical history of Israel in chap. xxvi. But, distinct from historical types, we conjecture that the *positive* nature of the blessedness of these days is reserved for description in the types exhibited by *Solomon's temple*. It appears that *the Tabernacle worship* was intended chiefly to exhibit Christ's person and his work, in dying, rising, ascending, interceding. *The Temple*,* besides exhibiting the same, adds *Christ coming again and reigning*.

Let us glance at the difference. The ark, from the days of Moses till it was fixed on Mount Zion by David, represents Christ, weary, wandering among men, until he ascended to his Father's right hand. The ark, removed from its rest on Zion to the magnificent temple, represents Christ leaving the Father's right hand to take his

---

* See 1 Kings vi., vii., and 2 Chron. iii., iv.

abode in the new earth—his temple and kingdom—when
he appears as Solomon, "Prince of Peace." And then
in that temple every type receives some expansion, or
some change to a more splendid shape—all done by
express Divine direction, as we find declared in 2 Chron.
iii. 3, and other places. The *brazen altar* was greatly
enlarged. Instead of *one laver*, there were ten. Instead
of one *candlestick*, there were ten ; and also there were
ten *tables* for the shew-bread, as we saw above. The
golden altar he made of cedar, and covered it with gold
(1 Kings vi. 20). He made two additional *cherubim*, very
large and beautiful, and put figures of cherubim on the
great veil. Besides all this, there were added to this
temple *two pillars*, of finest workmanship, and *the sea*
of brass with its *ten bases* that wheeled along the temple
floor, conveying the water easily to any spot (see
p. 146). Many chambers, too, were built and occupied,
all around the courts ; and the floor of The Holy and
Most Holy was of pure gold, like the streets of New
Jerusalem.

The temple was finished in the seventh year, and in
the seventh month, at harvest-time—the time of joy.
Is there not here a shadowing forth of millennial fulness
of glory ? Is not the scene different in many respects
from that of the tabernacle ? 1. *These tall palm-like*
pillars, with their rich and various ornaments. Do not
the names "*Jachin* and Boaz" declare that *Jehovah's*
strength shall establish this place for ever (compare Ps.
lxxxvii. 1, 5) ? And are they not placed in these
courts as trophies of victory ? They may be reckoned to
be trophies erected to shew that all war is ended, and
the *Prince of Peace* is triumphant. 2. *That gold*, shining
everywhere, and *these precious stones*, and *these harps*

and psalteries, made of the algum-trees, such as were never seen before in the land of Judah. Is not this an indication of New Jerusalem times? "For brass he has brought gold, and for iron silver" (Isa. lx. 17). And these instruments of music send forth bursts of joy, such as are heard only from Zion's "harpers, harping with their harps" (Rev. xiv. 2). 3. *Yonder sea of brass*, full to the brim, standing on oxen that look north, and south, and east, and west; its full water, clear and pure, laving a border that is set with lilies. Is this not the emblem of the *Holy Spirit*, shewing Christ to north, south, east, and west, filling the earth "as the waters cover the sea" (Isa. xi. 9)? Here are flowers and oxen; and the ten bases that stand by are bordered with lions, oxen, palm-trees, and *cherubim*. Is this not an emblem of redeemed men, amid the trees of Eden restored, with lions and oxen in harmonious fellowship at their feet, as Isa. xi. 6–8 foretells? 4. *These cherubim* on the walls, and on *the great veil*. Is this not the type of the redeemed Church dwelling in the Lord's presence, revelling, so to speak, in the mysteries of God? There were, it appears, *cherubim* on the veil on its inward side, to indicate redeemed men freely entering into the Holiest of all.* 5. *These chambers all around*. The "many mansions" are here. 6. *These ten candlesticks, ten lavers, ten shew-bread tables, ten tables* for the slain sacrifices. All these

---

* We fully agree with those who consider the *cherubim* everywhere to be symbols of the *redeemed Church*. They stand on the ark, *i.e.* Christ; their feet touching the blood sprinkled; while the glory of God is over them, and they see it reflected in the golden mercy-seat, as they bend under the glory. See Candlish on *Genesis*, and Fairbairn's *Typology*. So again; there were *cherubim on the veil* (Exod. xxvi. 31; 2 Chron. iii. 14); and the veil represented Christ's body (Heb. x. 20), to typify, "He that sanctifieth, and they who are sanctified, are all of one." And when the veil was rent, the *cherubim were rent*, thereby shewing that when Christ died, all he stood for also died (2 Cor. v. 14). They were "crucified with Christ."

intimate that in those days of millennial glory, much that
is new shall be discovered ; tenfold light shall be cast
on many a truth.   Yet still, the present truths are the
elements of all the discoveries to be made then.   Truth
revealed now shall then be opened more fully on the
view ; grace given now shall then be given in far, far
richer measure.   O blessed times! with "the Greater
than Solomon" in the midst "telling plainly of the
Father" (John xvi. 25), and declaring to his redeemed,
"Thou art all fair ; there is no spot in thee.   Thou hast
ravished my heart, my sister, my spouse."   Who shall be
able to stand under the weight of such bliss!   The Queen
of Sheba represents something of the overwhelming
effects ; not one remnant of self-complacency left, not
one thought of self at all, except in the form of shame
and abasement.

"Come quickly, Lord Jesus!"   Prepare these eyes for
seeing the King in his beauty—these ears for hearing the
sound of blessed voices and golden harps—these feet for
the golden streets—these hands for the palms of victory
—this brow (often wet with the sweat of the curse) for
the crown of righteousness—and, above all, this heart for
loving thee, who lovedst me and gavest thyself for me!
In that day, "the tongue of the stammerers shall be
ready to speak plainly," while with all the saints they
ever speak of the King on whom they gaze, and into
whose image they are changed.   And only then shall
every faculty find itself satisfied always, and yet ever
bewildered in the blessed attempt to understand the
"breadth and length, and depth and height; and to
know the love of Christ, that passeth knowledge."
Hallelujah !

CHAPTER XXVI

Israel's Temporal Blessings, in contrast to the Curse

" But seek ye first the kingdom of God, and his righteousness, and all these things shall be added unto you."—Matt. vi. 33

RICH promises of temporal blessing to Israel form the solemn conclusion to the full declaration made throughout this book of their duty and privileges in things spiritual. He that is so gracious in blessing the soul is not sparing in his kindness to the body. And while all here is spoken *nationally*, yet do we not recognise Him who said these things *at the foot of Sinai*, speaking in the same kind tone on the *mountain in Galilee*, when to every disciple he promises, "Seek first the kingdom of God, and his righteousness, and all these things shall be added unto you?" O Israel, our Redeemer is your Jehovah! The same heart yearns, the same lips move, at Sinai, and in Galilee. O that thou hadst hearkened to his commandments! *"then had thy peace been as a river"*—like thine own river Jordan, ever flowing, often overflowing—*"and thy righteousness like the waves of the sea."* Like thy great Western Sea with all its waves, able to cover over all thy sins, such would have been the righteousness that he would have given thee (Isa. xlviii. 18). And then all other things would have followed.

" *Thy seed had been as the sand*"—numerous as the
countless sands of that wide Mediterranean Sea—"and
the offspring of thy bowels like the gravel thereof"—filling
thy happy land ; while "thy *name should not have been
cut off, nor destroyed from before him.*" O Israel, return,
return! He earnestly remembers thee still.

> Ver 1, 2.   *Ye shall make you no idols* (אֱלִילִים) *nor graven image,
> neither rear you up a standing image, neither shall ye set
> up any image of stone in your land, to bow down unto it :
> for I am the Lord your God.   Ye shall keep my sabbaths,
> and reverence my sanctuary : I am the Lord.*

The Lord alone must be worshipped (ver. 1), and he
must be worshipped as he requires (ver. 2).   The Lord
seeks our whole heart, our unaverted eye, our entire soul.
" *No idols,*" says he ; any objects that sit on the throne
of our heart, whether of silver and gold, or of flesh and
blood, or of earth's common objects, like houses and
lands, riches and honour, all these are אֱלִילִים, "things
of nought"—utterly despicable in his view.   " Graven
images," and " standing images" (or pillars like obelisks),
and "images of stone" (or " *stones of imagery,*" such as
Ezekiel (viii. 8) describes)—all these are wholly abominable to the Lord.   Set up no rival, none that approaches near ; not even father or mother, wife or
child.   And in order to cherish this state of soul, his
Sabbaths must be kept and his *sanctuary* reverenced ;
the sinner must employ himself, amid holy scenes and at
holy times, in bathing his soul in the love of God.   If
any one neglects *the time* set apart by God for this end
—"*the Sabbath*"—how can such a one ever expect to
feel steeped in the holy awe and love that is due to the
Lord ?   When a man goes to the region of the Alps, he
requires time to see the relative magnitude of objects ;

he does not at one glance see their immense height and
sublime elevation. It is often days ere he arrive at a
proper estimate, because he is now in a new and
unfamiliar region. So it is with Divine realities; you
must spend time, continuously and uninterruptedly,
in order to have your soul truly affected. In like
manner, also, *the sanctuary* must be frequented. It is
the Lord's ordinance. Would you have refrained from
taking the fruit of the forbidden tree, as a test of obedience, who will not reverence the sanctuary? Where is
your childlike submission of will? Nay, where is your
love to your Father, if you go not to the spot where he
meets with his own so specially?

All declension and decay may be said to be begun
wherever we see these two ordinances despised—the
Sabbath and the *sanctuary*. They are the *outward* fence
around the *inward love* commanded by ver. 1.

THE BLESSING HELD OUT

Ver. 3–6. *If ye walk in my statutes, and keep my commandments,
and do them; then I will give you rain in due season, and
the land shall yield her increase, and the trees of the field
shall yield their fruit. And your threshing shall reach unto
the vintage, and the vintage shall reach unto the sowing-time;
and ye shall eat your bread to the full, and dwell in your land
safely. And I will give peace in the land, and ye shall lie
down, and none shall make you afraid; and I will rid evil
beasts out of the land, neither shall the sword go through your
land.*

The Lord made Israel "*Jeshurun*," *i.e.* the prosperous
one, blessing him with all temporal things whenever
Israel sought the spiritual. It was a scene like the
unfallen age.*

Israel was offered the privilege of being, even in

---

* Such as Hesiod (Ἐργα κ. ἡμερ. 115) fancies to have been in the golden age.

respect of *temporal blessings*, a type of *Eden restored*. As their ceremonies and institutions were to the world a type of all the *spiritual* blessings which Jesus brings, so the very aspect of their land might have been the type of the *external* blessings which Jesus brings at his second coming to the earth.

In Solomon's days, these blessings were probably realised more fully than at any period of Israel's history. His were the times of peace, so peculiarly typical of Messiah's reign in the latter day.

Think of the blessings spread out to their view here. The sky above their land, pure and sapphire-blue at other times, sends down needful rains at the proper season with such regularity, that in ver. 4 the Hebrew calls them "*your rains*" (גִּשְׁמֵיכֶם). Would they not learn, by every such shower, lessons like the following?—"*Every good gift and every perfect gift is from above*, and cometh down from the Father of lights" (James i. 17). Their *soil* scarcely feels what barrenness means; "it yields its increase" for man and beast—even as, when the curse is repealed, we shall sing yet more fully than they, "Let all the people praise thee; then shall the earth yield her increase" (Ps. lxvii. 6). The *trees* that shade their dwellings, or stand thick in their orchards, give abundant fruit; figs, dates, pomegranates, grapes, are poured into their lap as the season returns. Their *corn fields* yield so plentifully, that scarcely can the husbandman finish his labours here before the vintage calls for his care; and he has not ceased the cares of vintage when sowing-time arrives.

Israel had, at least in Solomon's days, a shadow of

Ἄφνειοι μήλοισι, φίλοι μακάρεσσι θέοισι. Indeed, Israel's land answers well to the poetic descriptions of that time, "flowing with milk and honey:"

"Flumina jam lactis jam flumina nectaris ibant,
Flavaque de viridi stillabant ilice mella."—OVID, *Met.* i. 111.

what is coming on—"Behold, the days come, saith the
Lord, that the ploughman shall overtake the reaper, and
the treader of grapes him that soweth seed; and the
mountains shall drop sweet wine, and all the hills shall
melt" (Amos ix. 13).

And lo! Israel enjoys the very fulness of bread that
Sodom had in her best days; and this fulness is a blessing, not a curse, to Israel. There is safety, too; for no
foe appears, neither is there disquiet in the land. No
civil broils, no domestic quarrels, no heartburnings. No
robbers in the land disturb them by day or night; no fear
on any side. How like the time when men "shall beat
their swords into ploughshares, and their spears into
pruning-hooks!" (Isa. ii. 4.) O house of Jacob! come ye,
and walk in the light of the Lord, and this shall be yours
again. And "*evil beasts*" shall cease; the great proof of
the land returning to something of an Eden-state, where
man had full dominion over the beasts of the field; and
"*no sword*" passes through, for this is the land of the
Prince of Peace.

Surely Israel's land in such days as Solomon's, was
intended to be typical of the earth's millennial rest!

> Ver. 7–10. *And ye shall chase your enemies, and they shall fall
> before you by the sword. And five of you shall chase an hun-
> dred, and an hundred of you shall put ten thousand to flight:
> and your enemies shall fall before you by the sword. For I will
> have respect unto you, and make you fruitful, and multiply you,
> and establish my covenant with you. And ye shall eat old
> store, and bring forth the old because of the new.*

If foes invade your land, they shall be driven back,
and so easily driven back, that five shall put a hundred
to flight, and a hundred defeat a whole host of ten
thousand. By stating the foes' defeat in this form, we
are led to understand that the Lord would bless their

united and harmonious efforts, so that *five united* would
be equal to twenty of the foe, and *ten* to a thousand.
They act together—none stands aloof from the other ; *
and in this they resemble believers asking "with one
accord" (Acts iv. 24), and obtaining, in return, such a
blessing that the place is shaken with the Lord's presence.
And in millennial days, what foe shall stand before men
who are "as the angel of the Lord ? " (Zech. xii. 8.) All
this shall be secured to them—fertility, numerous popu-
lation, plentiful produce, so that last year's store shall
not be nearly exhausted before this year's is at the barn-
door, seeking to be lodged in the granary.   Even Egypt,
in the seven years of plenty, could scarcely be more
abundant.   But it is free grace that bestows these blessings : "*I will establish my covenant with you;*" the Lord
engages to give on his own generous terms—terms which
we may judge of by this fact, which is also stated here,
that his covenant itself is the outflowing of free love: "*I
will have respect unto you.*"   Israel's streams of blessing
in Solomon's days, as well as the floods of blessing yet to
be poured out in coming days, are all free and spontaneous, unmerited gifts from the Lord's love. O what
has not that love imparted! and yet how unweariedly
that love yearns to impart still more and more!

Ver. 11–13. *And I will set my tabernacle among you, and my
soul shall not abhor you.   And I will walk among you, and
will be your God, and ye shall be my people.   I am the Lord
your God, which brought you forth out of the land of Egypt,
that ye should not be their bondmen; and I have broken the
bands of your yoke, and made you go upright.*

* Joshua (xxiii. 10) says, " One man of you shall chase a thousand ;" and
Deut. xxxii. 30, " How should one chase a thousand, and two put ten thousand
to flight?" There is no inconsistency ; but here the victory is represented as
given to a cluster, or compact band, in order to exhibit the brotherly union of
those days.

The type here reaches its highest point. "Behold, the tabernacle of God is with men, and he will dwell with them, and they shall be his people, and God himself shall be with them, and be their God" (Rev. xxi. 3). Solomon's temple in all its glory, and Solomon himself there in all his wisdom, formed but a type of the Prince of Peace when he shall fulfil that portion of the prophetic word. But, O happy Israel! who is like unto thee? Thou hadst the foretastes of these precious things. Thy God dwelt, by his cloud of glory, among thy tribes, and was felt to be present throughout all thy borders. And there yet await thee, O Jeshurun! happier days than all, when thou returnest to the Lord ; for then the antitype of all these shadows shall be with thee. The *Lord Jesus*, on the transfiguration-hill, was found, at the close, alone (Mark ix. 7, 8), shining with the light inaccessible. And, at that moment, the bright cloud, which was no other than the cloud that rested over Israel's mercy-seat, was seen hanging over him and pointing toward his person, while the voice of the Father cried, " This is my Beloved Son, in whom I am well pleased!" Jesus, then, is the antitype of the mercy-seat that was in Israel's tabernacle; and in him, therefore, shall the glory of God be manifested in that day when Ezekiel's words are fulfilled, "*My tabernacle shall be with them*" (Ezek. xxxvii. 27); and when the Lamb in the midst of the throne shall lead his own to the living fountains of water, then, too, shall he wipe all tears from their eyes, and be known as *their God;* even as in type he freed Israel from bondage, and made them walk "*upright*," *i.e.* not as dejected, burdened men, hanging their heads through sorrow of heart, but as freemen, walking cheerfully and confidently in their own land.

But why is that clause inserted, "*And my soul shall not abhor them?*" It seems thrown in on purpose to remind Israel, that though they are thus favoured, they deserved it not. This store of blessing is all free grace. These highly favoured ones were once "cast out in the open field, to *the loathing of their persons.*" For, as if to explain this clause, Ezekiel (chap. xvi. 5) uses the words that are used here, saying of them that they were thrown out, like unburied carcases, on the surface of the ground, "in a state that might make one loathe them" (בְּגֹעַל נַפְשֵׁךְ); though the king, in wondrous grace, chose to love them, saying, "My soul shall not loathe thee" (לֹא תִגְעַל). His redeemed can never forget whence they were taken, and yet they can never doubt of the security of their state now; He that had mercy on them can never more forsake them. His spontaneous love is their everlasting assurance of security, shining as it did to them through the tabernacle-veil — the veil of the Redeemer's flesh.

THE BLESSING REJECTED

Ver. 14, 15. *But if ye will not hearken unto me, and will not do all these commandments; and if ye shall despise my statutes, or if your soul abhor my judgments, so that ye will not do all my commandments, but that ye break my covenant: I also will do this unto you.*

The curses, or judgments, that follow, are effects of despising the blessing. They do not seem intended to exhibit hell *in all its aspects*, but only that misery which arises from *rejecting the offers of grace.* Israel needed to be warned of this danger in special, for it was to characterise their history. The judgments mentioned here did not fall on heathen nations. There are woes that none shall ever feel except men that might have been blessed beyond their fellows. Israel, who might have had such continuance of unchanging love to their souls, and such millennial-like blessings to their land, suffer punishment beyond other men. They have become the most emphatic warning that can be given to sinners, to beware of despising offered grace. And now the offer has come to thee, sinner—the offer, through Christ's work, of present salvation and future glory in his kingdom. Thou must accept, and be blessed above other men; or thine only alternative is, thou must, in rejecting it, be unspeakably more cursed than all besides.

THE CURSE UPON REJECTERS OF THE BLESSING

Ver. 16, 17. *I will also do this unto you; I will even appoint over you terror, consumption, and the burning ague, that shall consume the eyes, and cause sorrow of heart:* * *and ye shall sow your seed in vain, for your enemies shall eat it. And I will set my face against you, and ye shall be slain before your enemies: they that hate you shall reign over you; and ye shall flee when none pursueth you.* [A stroke upon their *persons.*]

God's majesty cannot suffer wrong. We cannot slight his proffered gifts without exposing our souls to the severest rebukes of his anger. The majesty of his love is wronged by the indifference of the sinner, as well as by the obstinate rebellion of the sinner. Israel was made to feel this. "*Terror,*" instead of calm, serene peace; "*consumption and ague,*" instead of health and strength, once characteristic of the people of the God of Jeshurun; blasted hopes and labours, defeated armies, foreign governors in their cities, and their own heart sinking in hopelessness. The Lord did this in the days of *the Judges;* and though it be only the weakness of Israel, and their many disasters, that are recorded, yet I think

* The form מְדִיבַת is for מְדִאִיבֹת.

we may certainly conclude that these diseases—this "*consumption and burning ague,*" and this "*terror*"— were secretly at work, bringing down the people's strength and courage. When the prophet tells Eli, from the Lord, "The man of thine, whom I shall not cut off from mine altar, *shall be to consume thine eyes and grieve thy heart*" (1 Sam. ii. 33), he is using language which Israel no doubt understood as a reference to the passage before us. What is meant by (Ps. lxxviii. 63) "*The fire* consumed their young men?" May these plagues be meant in part? And again, after the first captivity, did not the many diseases in our Lord's time correspond to the "*diseases of Egypt*" in Deut. xxviii. 60 ?*

The Lord appointed these judgments. The word is הִפְקַדְתִּי, the same as in Ps. cix. 6, "Set thou a wicked man over him," and the same as in Isaiah lxii. 6, "I have set watchmen over thy walls, O Jerusalem." The word means, that a charge is given to these instruments to execute a certain purpose; they are appointed to the office of seeing to this being done. In our Lord's time these plagues surely had begun? So many diseases in so healthy a land? And The Physician came, offering to turn back the begun calamity, and shewing his power.

Ver. 18–20. *And if ye will not yet, for all this, hearken unto me, then I will punish you seven times more for your sins. And I will break the pride of your power; and I will make your heaven as iron, and your earth as brass. And your strength shall be spent in vain* [shall end in being in vain?]: *for your land shall not yield her increase, neither shall the trees of the land yield their fruits.* [A stroke on their *possessions.*]

* It might be inquired, also, if "*the evil angels*" sent on the Egyptians, Ps. lxxviii. 49, may not have been the same as the devils that possessed the demoniacs.

From this let sinners carefully observe, that offers of kindness rejected, after warning has been given of the fatal consequences, shall be followed by severer strokes of wrath than would have come on them before. Every offer of grace, especially if accompanied by warning as to the fatal consequences of rejection, brings sevenfold guilt on the rejecter.

"*The pride of your power*," may mean the luxuriance of their land, in which they boasted; or if it mean their power as a mighty people, then the *bringing it down* refers to the effects of famine upon the resources of their kingdom. "Their strength is spent in vain," when, as in Ahab's days, their heaven over them yields no rain, but is as iron.

Some have ascribed the present sterility of Palestine to want of cultivation. But this verse proves that there is *a curse* besides. It is here declared that "*the land shall not yield her increase*," even if tilled. Nor shall "*the trees of the land yield their fruits*," even if cultivated; so that it is not only because not carefully attended to that the palm does not now grow luxuriantly there, and the vines. There is a secret curse fallen on that land that rejected mercy and despised warning.

Ver. 21, 22. *And if ye walk contrary** unto me, and will not hearken unto me; I will bring seven times more plagues upon you, according to your sins. I will also send wild beasts among you, which shall rob you of your children, and destroy your cattle, and make you few in number; and your highways shall be desolate.* [A stroke upon their *children and cattle*.]

---

* קְרִי is for בְּקְרִי, as it occurs ver. 24, and literally it would be rendered, "And if your way of walking with me be ' *contra me*,' " " in opposition to my will " (see Rosenmüller). Originally קְרִי would be a noun, *q. d.* If your walk be a " going counter to," or meeting of me face to face.

New calamities come, because of new provocations. So, unbelieving soul, every new offer pressed home on thee by warnings, and yet rejected, adds to thy condemnation, and draws out another arrow from the Lord's quiver!

Instead of man's original lordship over the creatures, lo! the beasts of the field rise up against rebellious man. This strange foe advances to their dwellings; and the cattle grazing before their door, and their little children playing on the grass, are devoured before their eyes by this new assailant. The *cockatrice*, and serpents that will not be charmed (Jer. viii. 17), bite their little ones, destroying the type that Israel's land presented of the time when "the weaned child should put his hand on the cockatrice' den" (Isa. xi. 8). The leopard watches his opportunity; the evening wolf ravages the flock; and the bear tears what he finds within his reach; the lion springs on his prey.

It must have appeared singular that in a land so fully peopled as Palestine was in the days of the kings, there should be so often notices of wild beasts roaming among them—bears from the forests of Bethel (2 Kings ii. 24), and lions on the highway between Bethel and Judah (1 Kings xiii. 24). But it is evident that their existence in so densely a peopled land was somewhat miraculous; it was by Divine appointment. It was to keep Israel in mind of this passage of the law; and whenever wild beasts multiplied, they were to see herein a proof that they had advanced far onward in rebellion, this being the third stage of the Lord's wrath. And hence Judah could read the indignation of the Lord in the *lions of Samaria* (2 Kings xvii. 26), and tremble at the progress of wrath. So Jer. ii. 15 may refer to

this—the roaring and yelling of young lions in the
desolate cities of Samaria.

> Ver. 23–25. *And if ye will not be reformed by me by these things,
> but will walk contrary unto me; then will I also walk
> contrary unto you, and will punish you yet seven times for
> your sins. And I will bring a sword upon you, that shall
> avenge the quarrel of my covenant.*

The *sword* goes through the land! Instead of peace
and safety, the blood of Israel is shed by violent hands.
The *blood* that ratified their covenant with God had
been despised; therefore, lo! their own blood must be
shed to avenge the broken covenant.

> Ver. 25. *And when ye are gathered together within your cities, I
> will send the pestilence among you; and ye shall be delivered
> into the hand of the enemy.*

Pestilence and plague ravage their cities. Thinking
to escape the sword of the invader, they betake themselves to fenced cities, and defy the enemy. But the
Lord scales their walls and leads in his troops, viz. the
pestilence with all its horrors. The raging pestilence
soon weakens the hands of the defenders of their cities,
and opens the gates to the foe. "Know, then, that it is
an evil and a bitter thing to depart from the Lord."

> Ver. 26. *And when I have broken the staff of your bread, ten
> women shall bake your bread in one oven, and they shall
> deliver you your bread again by weight: and ye shall eat, and
> not be satisfied.*

Famine follows pestilence! So scarce is food now,
that instead of each family having its own oven, one
oven suffices for ten families, and the quantity given to
each is scrupulously weighed, and none receive enough to
satisfy their hunger. When *Judah* felt these horrors of
famine in the siege of Jerusalem by the Babylonians

(Jer. xxxviii. 9), they might know assuredly that the Lord's arrows were coming fast from his quiver.

Ver. 27–33. *And if ye will not for all this hearken unto me, but walk contrary unto me; then I will walk contrary unto you also in fury; and I, even I, will chastise you seven times for your sins. And ye shall eat the flesh of your sons, and the flesh of your daughters shall ye eat. And I will destroy your high places, and cut down your images, and cast your carcases upon the carcases of your idols, and my soul shall abhor you. And I will make your cities waste, and bring your sanctuaries unto desolation, and I will not smell the savour of your sweet odours. And I will bring the land into desolation; and your enemies which dwell therein shall be astonished at it. And I will scatter you among the heathen, and will draw out a sword after you; and your land shall be desolate, and your cities waste.*

" Behold ! their house is left unto them desolate!"

He is an awfully holy and an infallibly true God! He did do all that is threatened here. And as assuredly as he did these things, so shall he assuredly kindle the flames of an unquenchable fire for the unbelieving and often-warned man. Gospel-hearer, this picture of the Lord's strict truth looks with terrible frown on you. For this shall be thy doom. "*I, even I, shall chastise seven times!*" Oh! this is the work of a long-suffering God. "I will walk contrary to you *in fury!*"*

This is the wrath of the Lamb! Israel felt this fury. In the siege of Jerusalem by the Babylonians, of which the siege of Samaria in former days was a feeble prototype, mothers ate their children, according to Lam. iv. 10 ; and in their final siege by Titus, the same scene of horrid and terrific despair was exhibited. It

---

* The Hebrew is peculiar, בַּחֲמַת־קֶרִי, " in the fury of opposition," or contrariety. See קֶרִי, note, page 468.

seems a type of what shall take place in hell—all natural ties for ever broken; and nearest relations reproaching and accusing and tormenting each other, finding no other food but to upbraid others with their ruin.

The lightning of God's wrath struck down their high places and idolatrous images; not a vestige of these can be found by any traveller. As for the worshippers, they perished with the "carcases," or broken images of their gods—a type of hell again! For there the sinner's idols shall be seen to be for ever ruined and destroyed; and yet the sinner's memory rolls over and over upon past scenes that only cause him torment.

Their cities lie waste at this day, and their "sanctuaries," *i.e.* their temple with its courts, and there are no sweet-smelling offerings presented to the Lord in Judah's land. No one can discover more than the mere foundations of ancient edifices, and few even of these. *Jerusalem's* walls and temple exist only in fragments of foundation-stones; *Bethel* is a field overspread with demolished walls; *Samaria's* foundations, and a few of her shattered columns, are all that remain to her of former glory. No one has found *Tirzah*. Hundreds of ruined towns can be discovered by the name still lingering over the ruins, but by that alone. *Shiloh* is now *Seilwan*, and presents no dwelling or town, but only a few ruins. *Lebonah*, now *Khan Leban*, has a well for watering flocks at noon, and two or three dwellings near. *Kirjath-jearim*, now *Karieh*, is a beautiful village, but its pomegranates and olives shade no more than a dozen dwellings. *Beersheba* has its well still, and plentiful water, but is no more a city. *Jericho*, now *Riha*, has some mud houses near the spring that Elisha sweetened; and this is all that remains of the city of palm-trees.

Libnah and *Lachish* and *Maresha*, famous in the wars
of Judah, are not to be found even in name. *Hazor*,
famous as a northern citadel, has only lately been found
by Dr Keith, bearing the name, but possessing no more
than a few remnants of an ancient fortress. *Capernaum*,
Bethsaida, and *Chorazin*, are not truly ascertained.
Sarepta is a little village called Sarfand, on a hill-side,
overlooking the sea-shore, whereon its stately mansions
once were built. *Zebulon*, now *Abilene*, is but a village;.
and *Cana* a very small one. Even peopled cities that
do remain boast of few thousands; *Jerusalem* has its
twenty thousand; *Hebron*, its ten; *Sychar*, its ten—and
this, or such-like, is all that the cities of Judah and of
Israel yield! "*True* and righteous are thy judgments,"
O Lord God of Israel!

The land is desolate. The plains of Jezreel and
Sharon lie nearly untilled. Every traveller wonders at
large spaces of rich soil left to lie fallow. Enemies
occupy their inheritance, and destroy it—yet once "the
kings of the earth would not have believed that the
adversary should have entered into the gate of Jerusalem" (Lam. iv. 12).

And poor Israel wanders over every country and
kingdom on the face of the earth—"scattered and
peeled." And while the Lord still pities them, he
"abhors them" (ver. 30) for their sin, as "in the day
when they were cast out in the open field," though he
still loveth the nation for their father's sake (ver. 44).
On that open field they are cast again, to the loathing
of their person! Who is there that knows not this to
be the fate of Israel? Not a word has fallen to the
ground.

Ver. 34–39. *Then shall the land enjoy her sabbaths, as long as* *it lieth desolate, and ye be in your enemies' land; even then shall the land rest, and enjoy*her sabbaths. As long as it lieth desolate it shall rest; because it did not rest in your sabbaths, when ye dwelt upon it. And upon them that are left alive of you I will send a faintness into their hearts in the lands of their enemies; and the sound of a shaken leaf shall chase them; and they shall flee, as fleeing from a sword; and they shall fall when none pursueth. And they shall fall one upon another, as it were before a sword, when none pursueth: and ye shall have no power to stand before your enemies. And ye shall perish among the heathen, and the land of your enemies shall eat you up. And they that are left of you shall pine away in their iniquity in your enemies' lands; and also in the iniquities of their fathers shall they pine away with them.*

So full and obviously are verses 34, 35 fulfilled, that Dr Keith quotes Bowring's *Report of the Commercial Statistics of Syria in* 1840, which says, "Regions of the highest fertility remain fallow."

Some adopt Houbigant's view that the Jews had never kept the Sabbatic year from the days of *Saul* till the captivity, a space of four hundred and ninety years, giving *seventy* Sabbatic years. But there is no authority for this singular assertion regarding the neglect of the Jews; nay, 2 Kings xix. 26 and Jer. xxxiv. 17 are sufficient to shew that these seasons were observed.

The sin of Israel lay in their *manner* of keeping Sabbath-days and Sabbath-years. Their God was not honoured; they did not give spiritual service. They also turned the observance of the seasons appointed into times of pleasure—riding in their chariots, probably, and giving themselves to amusements. But the reference chiefly is to cases of such neglect occurring, not to the

---

* Heb. תִּרְצֶה, "atone for;" in Hiphil, according to Gesenius. She shall pay the Sabbaths she owes. The Talmud uses it in this sense. It is, *q.d.* to please a creditor.

continuance of it so long a time as seventy years.   Nay,
their land lies desolate still for that same sin.   Men
shall suffer if they keep not God's way.   Your land
"shall atone for her Sabbaths" (Gesenius).*   Alas! our
land seems near its day of doom!   Incessant movement,
of men over its breadth and length!   Where is *the rest?*
But so it shall be as the time draws near wherein *the
Sabbath* of earth shall arrive, when the disturbers of its
rest are brought to silence.

The unwarlike, timid, feeble state of the Jews in
every land fulfils verses 36, 37.   The word מֹרֶךְ implies
timidity and softness of spirit, unable to bear up against
trouble, and shewing a cowardice under their oppressions
very different from the mighty warriors of Israel in the
days of their fathers.   Easily alarmed, and so alarmed
that, like men in hasty flight, "they fall on one another."
The Jews never can resist, and never try to resist, their
foes: they suffer and complain, and their cries spread
over the earth.

History tells (as ver. 38) how many have perished in
the enemies' land, and how miserably they have spent
their days, degraded and oppressed.   Their own sin and
their fathers' has been broken Sabbaths, and the rejection of the Saviour, the Lord of the Sabbath.   For is
there not a hint given us of this in the "iniquities of
their fathers?"   Is not the cry, *"His blood be on us
and on our children"* included here?   O how like the.
comfortless, heart-sickening, hopeless state of the lost are
these poor Israelites, "without God, and without hope,"
because "without Christ!"   Shall it always be thus?
"Turn their captivity, O Lord, like the streams of the
south!"

* The Septuagint uses the expression " εὐδοκήσει ἡ γῆ τα σαββατα;" as if
the land were resting with delight over the Sabbatic stillness.

And let us Gentiles fear sin even when only *imputed*. "Our father" Adam's sin lies on us; besides the sins of our fathers in this land. "Lord, wash me thoroughly" (Ps. li. 2).

ISRAEL'S RESTORATION

Ver. 40. *If they shall confess their iniquity, and the iniquity o} their fathers, with their trespass which they trespassed against me.*

Hear, O Israel! Does this not call thee to consider thy unbelief? Is there nothing calling thee to "look on Him whom thy fathers pierced?" What are "thy *fathers' sins?*"

Ver. 40–45. *And that also they have walked contrary unto me; and that I also have walked contrary unto them, and have brought them into the land of their enemies; if* then their uncircumcised hearts be humbled, and they then accept of the punishment of their iniquity: then will I remember my covenant with Jacob, and also my covenant with Isaac, and also my covenant with Abraham will I remember; and I will remember the land. The land also shall be left of them, and shall enjoy her sabbaths, while she lieth desolate without them: and they shall accept of the punishment of their iniquity; because, even because they despised my judgments, and because their soul abhorred my statutes. And yet for all that, when they be in the land of their enemies, I will not cast them away, neither will I abhor them, to destroy them utterly, and to break my covenant with them: for I am the Lord their God. But I will for their sakes remember the covenant of their ancestors, whom I brought forth out of the land of Egypt in the sight of the heathen, that I might be their God: I am the Lord.*

"*I am Jehovah;*" therefore, he remembers his covenant with Abraham. As he *manifested* that name on

---

* In Heb. אך, which Rosenmüller, from the Arabic, proposes to render "donec usque dum." But why not understand it thus: "If they shall confess their iniquity (ver. 40, 41), *or if* their uncircumcised heart be humbled"—whenever this confession with the mouth is heard, or this humbling of the heart is seen.

the first exodus (Exod. vi. 3), though for a long time before he had shewn only his *all-sufficiency,** so shall he manifest it by his acts at the final exodus of Israel from all the lands of their dispersion.

Here we have, so to speak, a permanent fact, or truth, on which to rest the proof of Israel's restoration to their own land.   It is this: the covenant with their fathers contained a grant of the land; and the God of Israel is *Jehovah.* Whenever Israel serves the Lord, Israel obtains all that that grant contains.   If they confess, then, lo! they must return home also.   Israel's repentance and Israel's restoration to their old estates go together.   When, as in Micah vii. 9, the Jews confess and accept, or admit as righteous, what they suffer, then their restoration is at hand.   It is true, they may return *before* they repent ; but the *land* is not theirs *until* they repent. And I think this is the meaning of Ezekiel xxxvi. 37. " I shall yet FOR THIS be inquired of by the house of Israel, to do it for them." It is Israel's prayer to the Lord, when repentant, to settle them in their land and restore to the land its fruitfulness.   See the whole chapter.

Ver. 42 is very remarkable in the Hebrew. It is literally, " I will remember my covenant, Jacob," &c. There is no " *with.*"   May God not be speaking here to these patriarchs whose God He is at this moment, and saying, " I will remember my covenant, O Jacob, made with thee! and my covenant, O Isaac, with thee; and I will remember my covenant, O Abraham, with thee, and *the land* wherein thou wast a stranger?"   The land, too, wherein his own Son was a Man of Sorrows—can that land ever be forgotten ? The cross was there ; shall not the throne be there too ?

* The name אֵל שַׁדַּי.

Ver. 43 repeats the cause why there ever was deso-
ation at all, and tells how long it is to continue. In
ver. 44, the first words, וְאַף גַּם זֹאת, "Yet for all that,"
should rather be, "Yea, moreover, I shall do this"
(Rosenmüller). This is the renewed declaration of the
Lord's determination to restore them ; and hence, some
of the German Jews who are fond of conceit, mark this
word אַף, as "*The golden Aff.*"

All is done in free love. It is *covenant-mercy.* "Salvation to Him that sitteth on the throne, and to the
Lamb!"

> Ver. 46. *These are the statutes, and judgments, and laws, which the
> Lord made between him and the children of Israel in mount
> Sinai, by the hand of Moses.*

He seeth the end from the beginning. He knew the
kind of people whom he had chosen. For see, at the foot
of Sinai, he speaks in this prophetic strain, warning them
of what he sees coming on. He knew their hearts ; he
did not choose them for their worthiness ; he manifested
grace in them. From *Sinai* he looks down the stream of
ages, and sees their sin, and yet goes forward to manifest
his love and make them the objects. "There is none like
the God of Jeshurun."

CHAPTER XXVII

Entire Devotion to God, induced by the Foregoing Views of his Character

" Ye are not your own, for ye are bought with a price; therefore glorify God in your body, and in your spirit, which are God's."—1 Cor. vi. 19, 20

Ver. 1, 2. *And the Lord spake unto Moses, saying, Speak unto the children of Israel, and say unto them,—*

THE connexion of this concluding chapter with all the preceding has been considered a difficulty with many. But most obviously the connexion is that of *feeling*. No wonder God takes up the subject of self-dedication and the devoting of all that a man has; for might not any one expect that the preceding views given of God's mind and heart would be constraining? We find in Scripture, that the link of connexion between one narrative and another often lies in the *feelings* understood to be produced in the reader of the story, or feelings likely to arise. Thus, in Mark xi. 25, *" When ye stand praying, forgive, if ye have ought against any,"* is suddenly introduced; but on being examined, the reason turns out to be, that a feeling of ill-will to others is one of the hindrances to the prayer of faith which our Lord was anxious to lead them to. So, also, the feast of Levi to

Christ, and the question of John's disciples and the
Pharisees about fasting, is placed by two Evangelists
just after Levi's conversion, though Matthew shews that
it occurred at the time Jairus came. The link of connexion is this, viz. Christ exhibited as a Saviour for
sinners, apart from all ceremonial observances, led the
mind to go out in the direction of occurrences that
bore upon that point.

In this chapter, after the Lord has unfolded his system of truth, the impression left on every true worshipper is supposed to be, " What shall I render unto the
Lord for all his benefits?" As Paul, after unfolding the
way of life and righteousness in the first eleven chapters
of Romans, begins at chap. xii. 1 to address his readers,
" I beseech you, therefore, brethren, by the mercies of
God, that ye present your bodies a living sacrifice, holy,
acceptable unto God, which is your reasonable service."
For true has it ever been, that " the grace of God that
bringeth salvation" is grace that " *teaches us*" to deny
ungodliness, and to be a peculiar people (Titus ii. 12).
Indeed, we might almost venture to say, that Micah vi. 8
was uttered in this very feeling, and with a view to these
very ordinances—" *He hath shewed thee, O man, what is
good,*" in those sacrifices and ordinances that are full of
grace and truth; and now, if thou askest how the grateful
feelings of thine accepted soul are to be met, lo! here is
provision made for their outpouring: " What does the
Lord require of thee, but to do justly, and to love mercy,
and to walk humbly with thy God?" So far as we do not
give to God this recompence of a life thankfully devoted
to him, we cannot but cry with Ephraim Syrus, " ταλανίζω
τον ἐμον βιον ὁτι ἀχρηστος ὑπαρχει"—" I pronounce my
life wretched, because it is unprofitable."

Ver. 2–8. *When a man shall make a singular vow,* the persons shall be for the Lord by thy estimation.† And thy estimation shall be of the male from twenty years old even unto sixty years old, even thy estimation shall be fifty shekels of silver, after the shekel of the sanctuary. And if it be a female, then thy estimation shall be thirty shekels. And if it be from five years old even unto twenty years old, then thy estimation shall be of the male twenty shekels, and for the female ten shekels. And if it be from a month old even unto five years old, then thy estimation shall be of the male five shekels of silver, and for the female thy estimation shall be three shekels of silver. And if it be from sixty years old and above, if it be a male, then thy estimation shall be fifteen shekels, and for the female ten shekels. But if he be poorer than thy estimation, then he shall present himself before the priest, and the priest shall value him; according to his ability that vowed shall the priest value him.*

All agree that the meaning of "*making a singular vow*" is vowing something extraordinary, singling out something very valuable, and setting it apart for God.‡ To vow that a child, or a youth, or a person in mature years, should be the Lord's, this surely was a vow beyond ordinary.

"*By thy estimation.*" Michaëlis thinks that Moses is the person meant, who as civil magistrate determined the amount; but it rather seems to mean, "according as it shall be estimated, or valued, among you." The community of Israel had their general rules on such subjects, and these are to be taken by Moses or by the priest (ver. 13).

The rate is the same for persons of all ranks. "To the

---

* "Consecrate something vowed," הִפְלָא.

† The word for "estimation" is עֵרֶךְ. It is interesting to notice, that from the same root comes אִישׁ עֶרְכִּי, "mine equal"—a man estimated as I myself. See Ps. lv. 15, Christ's words concerning Judas.

‡ It is the same word as used in Ps. iv. 3, where the Lord is said to *set apart* the godly one. And observe, that the consequence of being set apart is *protection;* "*The Lord will hear when I call.*" As the priest would run to preserve any dedicated vessel from being broken, or spoilt, so here.

poor the gospel is preached." The great and wealthy
have no place here above the poor; all stand as sinners
to be redeemed by the same blood, and bound by the
same cords of love.

Bush remarks, "The rules of mortality are the principles on which these rates are graduated." Hence,
those in the prime of life are first noticed; and of these
the males, being capable of most service, are rated
highest. It appears to me clear that *Jephtha's* daughter
(Judg. xi. 30) may come under this rule. Her father
vowed to *dedicate to the Lord* (ver. 31) when he should
return victorious—thinking, probably, of some of his
domestic comforts and luxuries—"whatsoever cometh
from the doors of my house." *Jephtha's* daughter, like
young Samuel, was simply set apart personally to the
Lord; and the clause, "*I will offer it as a burnt-offering*," should be understood, as many have rendered it,
"I will offer also *to him* * a burnt-offering," as if to say,
I will load his altar with many gifts of thanksgiving.
Hengstenberg (*Egypt, and Books of Moses*) supports
the opinion that there was an institution of holy women
in the tabernacle, who, like Anna the prophetess, spent
their time in prayer and fasting. At all events, Exod.
xxxviii. 8, and 1 Sam. ii. 22, ought to be rendered,
"The women who *ministered* at the gate of the tabernacle," the word being צָבָא ; just as in Numb. iv. 23,
35, 43, when speaking of the Levites. The Midianites,
Numb. xxxi. 40, were women (ver. 35), and were set
apart for *the Lord*.

---

* Several critics have pointed out similar instances of the suffix so used.
Thus, Judg. i. 15, נְתַתָּנִי, "Thou hast given *to me*." Isa. xlii. 16; Jer. xx. 7;
Ezek. xxix. 3; Micah v. 4. The principle laid down in ver. 11, would of itself
be sufficient to prevent the sacrifice of Jephtha's daughter. In Romaine's works,
there is a view given of the matter, substantially the same as this, which states
the reasons against the sacrifice at great length.

There seems to me a mistake generally fallen into here by commentators. They suppose that these *shekels of money* were paid in order to free the offerers from the obligation of devoting *the person*. Now, surely the whole chapter is speaking of things truly devoted to God, and cases of exchange and substitution are referred to in ver. 10, 13, 15. As for *persons devoted*, there was no substitution allowed. The mistake has arisen from supposing that this amount of money was ransom-money; whereas it was *an addition* to the offering of the person, not a *substitution*. If a person is really to be dedicated to the Lord, then let him give this external, visible declaration of it. Let him bring these shekels of money, according to his age, in token of his having given up the world and devoted himself to God. Hence, *Jephtha's* daughter could not be redeemed; she is *the Lord's*, and there is no alienation of his property.

What do we learn from this? Let us remember how it is written that the price of a slave, gored to death, is, in Exod. xxi. 32, reckoned at thirty shekels; and how, in Zech. x. 12, the same price is weighed for the prophet in his typical character; and then in Matt. xxvi. 15, paid for Jesus. If such was the manner of *making over* a slave to another, have we not here the manner of *making over* persons to *the Lord?* But the Lord gives no price for them. True; because the Lord is not the gainer. It is a privilege to be taken into the Lord's service; and the man is therefore represented here as buying his admission into the Lord's service. It is all to shew how precious is the Lord's service! Men often sacrifice a large sum in order to get a servant to do their work; but lo! it is reversed here. We might well sacrifice all we have in order to be permitted to serve the Lord.

Oh, it is no common blessedness to be allowed to stand in thy presence and worship thee, Lord God Almighty!

> Ver. 9–13. *And if it be a beast, whereof men bring an offering unto the Lord, all that any man giveth of such unto the Lord shall be holy. He shall not alter it, nor change it,* a good for a bad, or a bad for a good: and if he shall at all change beast for beast, then it and the exchange thereof shall be holy. And if it be any unclean beast, of which they do not offer a sacrifice unto the Lord, then he shall present the beast before the priest; and the priest shall value it, whether it be good or bad: as thou valuest it, who art the priest, so shall it be. But if he will at all redeem it, then he shall add a fifth part thereof unto thy estimation.*

When Jephtha's heart was full of gratitude in anticipation of the answer to his prayer, he devoted whatever should meet him as he rode home victorious ; so another man in his review of his flocks and herds observes the remarkable kindness of the Lord to him therein, and upon this devotes one of his flock and of his herd to the Lord. That beast is "holy to the Lord" ever after. He may have fixed upon a favourite animal in the heat of the moment, the best ewe in his flock, but, if so, he must not "*change nor alter*"—*i. e.* neither substitute for it a ram, nor resort to the expedient of giving a greater offering, such as an ox. His original purpose is to stand. If at the time he devoted *the best*, then he will see what the impulse of true gratitude ought still to lead him to ; and if he devoted an inferior animal, he may perhaps look back calmly now and see his sinful grudging toward God. If, however, the man were (ver. 10) to draw back from his first purpose and substitute another, still, in the case of clean animals, the Lord will claim the one originally

---

* *i. e.* not *substitute* another for it, nor make any *alteration*.

devoted. He will follow the original ewe, as well as the ram put in its place, with his eye, and write on both, " Holy to the Lord." The Lord would have us increase in gratitude, never decline; he would teach us to regret nothing that we give to God, but count it all joy. Nay, he teaches us that the more than ordinary excited feelings of our hearts at particular seasons are, after all, the most just and fit for the benefits rendered. Our highest feelings are never wrong in their intensity, when God is the object; it is our cooler and lower moods, our more calculating and grudging frames.

If a grateful man happened to devote one of his camels or asses, then the *value* of that must be offered; for the animal cannot be sacrificed (ver. 12). And the man is not himself to judge of the value; but the estimate is to be made by the priest—" As thou, O priest, valuest it," thou who actest for thy God, and not for thyself. The matter is now in God's hands, not any more in man's.

If, however, it turned out to be a favourite horse or camel, the man might wish to retract. The value he set on these was rather more than he would like to state to the priest, who took all into consideration in estimating the greatness of the gift. Or, because anxious to keep his silver and gold, he might propose substituting another animal—one that was of the clean sort. He might do so. But in such cases, the animal he substituted must be taken with this addition, a fifth part of the value of the original gift. This retraction and wish to alter shews some coldness in the man—it indicates decline from his former state of high feeling and true gratitude. As he walked amid his possessions with his friend last evening, his heart swelled with thankful joy at the sight

of God's love—but this morning, that intense feeling has
decayed, and he rather grieves that he vowed so precious an object. This is decline; and therefore it is
treated somewhat like a trespass. In all the trespass
offerings, one-fifth was given as a mulct, or fine, in addition to the restitution made. So in this case. And thus
the Lord teaches again that he abhors any going back.
He observes, and he hates, any failure in former zeal
and love.

> Ver. 14, 15. *And when a man shall sanctify his house to be holy
> unto the Lord, then the priest shall estimate it, whether it be
> good or bad: as the priest shall estimate it, so shall it stand.
> And if he that sanctified it will redeem his house, then he shall
> add the fifth part of the money of thy estimation unto it, and it
> shall be his.*

The "*sanctifying*" is the same as setting apart by a
vow. The case is supposed of an Israelite whose heart
is full of gratitude for family mercies, or perhaps who
has escaped perils and returned to the quiet enjoyment
of his vine and fig-tree. Sitting in the bosom of his
family, feeling security and peace, he is prompted to
cry, " What shall I render unto the Lord for all his
benefits?" Under this impulse, he devotes the house to
the Lord.

If his gratitude cool, then, as in ver. 13, there is notice
of this taken, and provision made accordingly.

> Ver. 16–21. *And if a man shall sanctify unto the Lord some
> part of a field of his possession, then thy estimation shall be
> according to the seed thereof: an homer of barley seed shall be
> valued at fifty shekels of silver. If he sanctify his field from
> the year of jubilee, according to thy estimation it shall stand.
> But if he sanctify his field after the jubilee, then the priest
> shall reckon unto him the money according to the years that
> remain, even unto the year of the jubilee, and it shall be abated*

from thy estimation. And if he that sanctified the field will in any wise redeem it, then he shall add the fifth part of the money of thy estimation unto it, and it shall be assured to him. And if he will not redeem the field, or if he have sold the field to another man, it shall not be redeemed any more. But the field, when it goeth out in the jubilee, shall be holy unto the Lord, as a field devoted; the possession thereof shall be the priest's.

The fields of some Boaz are waving their crops under an evening breeze, in the cool of the day; luxuriance is smiling around from every heavy ear on its stalk. The possessor feels that the Lord has "dropt down fatness." Looking up to the All-sufficient One, who has freely bestowed all, he vows that one of these fields shall be the Lord's, or some portion of one of them shall be so set apart. And he must select the portion out of his patrimony—his "*possession*," or lot, descended to him from his fathers.

What required (ver. 16) an homer of barley-seed to sow it, was to be valued at fifty shekels of silver. This was to be the standard measure; so that a man could easily see the extent of his own gratitude, and be able to test himself lest he should vow away some inferior portion of the soil. And to prevent a man secretly reflecting on the time of the Jubilee, and so appearing to make a very liberal vow, while in fact the nearness of the Jubilee might be rendering it very small, the priest is to consider this element of value also. On the other hand (ver. 18), the land is not to be under-valued, if a man have so large and wide a heart, and gratitude so warm, as to devote a field to the Lord from the time of one Jubilee on to the next. The Lord does not overlook differences in men's views and purposes: "Thou, most upright, dost weigh the path of the just" (Isa.

xxvi. 7). The widow's mite and Mary's ointment are precious in his sight; and so are David's and Solomon's munificent gifts.

But, as in a former case, gratitude might cool, after the moment (ver. 19); and hence permission is given to redeem the field under the penalty of paying one-fifth, as in the trespass-offering, to shew that the person has sinned in thus retracting. His highest feelings were right; this abatement is sinful. Just as running the race at full speed is the proper state of one seeking the prize; anything that sinks below full speed is a fault (1 Cor. ix. 24).

If left unredeemed, according to his vow, it shall be the Lord's for ever. If the unredeemed field be sold* by the priest to another, the original possessor cannot at a future time claim any right to redeem it. He must not have liberty to reverse the acts and feelings of former years. What we do for the Lord must be done in the foresight of all the consequences; and it well befits us to give up anything of ours to the Lord for ever. Our dealings with God are dealings for eternity. There should be no temporising on our part in his matters. He gives "*eternal redemption,*" "*everlasting consolation.*"

> Ver. 22–24. *And if a man sanctify unto the Lord a field which he hath bought, which is not of the fields of his possession; then the priest shall reckon unto him the worth of thy estimation, even unto the year of the jubilee: and he shall give thine estimation in that day, as a holy thing unto the Lord. In the year of the jubilee the field shall return unto him of whom it was bought, even to him to whom the possession of the land did belong.*

This relates to the cases of tenants, not of possessors.

* The construction seems to warrant this sense: "*If he do not redeem the field, and if he* (*i. e.* the person who is now its owner, viz. the priest) *sell it to another.*"

A man who had bought a field until the Jubilee could
not alienate it for ever ; it was only one who had patrimony that could do this. We must give the Lord what
is our own ; not what is borrowed. Willing self-denial
is taught us by such acts ; we give the Lord something
that we feel the value of, and the loss of which would
grieve us, were not the Lord to be the receiver. Whatever goes to the Lord is given to us.

Ver. 25. *And all thy estimations shall be according to the shekel
of the sanctuary : twenty gerahs shall be the shekel.*

The law of the sanctuary is to regulate all. Full
weight is sought for ; but neither superfluity nor abatement. God loves a perfect balance and a just weight.
We do not know whether or not there was a standard
measure kept in the sanctuary; but it is very probable
there was. Some, indeed, render the words, "*shekel
of holiness,*" *i. e.* a true shekel ; still it is every way
likely that the other is the true meaning, even if this
rendering be right. There was probably a standard
measure kept in the sanctuary, by which all other
weights and measures were regulated. Here would be
a type to Israel of the Lord's justice. Here, in the
sanctuary of Jehovah, they found, on the one hand, the
regulating measure of all dealings in business between
man and man; and, on the other, the principles of just
dealing between God and man. Would not this standard measure be felt to be a type of the Lord's original
attribute of righteousness ? He it is that judges ; He it
is that fixes what is right and what is wrong ; He it is to
whom all Israel must come to have thought and action
weighed. May not 1 Sam ii. 3 refer to this ? Hannah's
eye had rested on this standard measure, and so she
sings, " By him actions are weighed."

Who shall stand before this holy God? He perceives what is wanting the moment he has adjusted his balances. He detects the want of faith in Cain at the altar; of true godly zeal in Jehu's heart; of love in Ephesus; of life in Sardis; of oil in the five virgins; of the wedding garment in the speechless guest. He judges according to the real weight—not the apparent. He judges " according as *the work* has been," not according as *the show* has been (1 Cor. v. 10; Rev. xx. 12; xxii. 12).

> Ver. 26–29. *Only the firstling of the beasts, which should be the Lord's firstling, no man shall sanctify it: whether it be ox or sheep, it is the Lord's. And if it be of an unclean beast, then he shall redeem it according to thine estimation, and shall add a fifth part of it thereto: or if it be not redeemed, then it shall be sold according to thy estimation. Notwithstanding no devoted thing that a man shall devote unto the Lord, of all that he hath, both of man and beast, and of the field of his possession, shall be sold or redeemed: every devoted thing is most holy unto the Lord. None devoted, which shall be devoted of men, shall be redeemed; but shall surely be put to death.*

Here are two opposite cases—one wherein there is a prohibition against devoting the thing to the Lord at all; the other wherein there is a prohibition against going back in the slightest degree from the full devotion.

Firstlings were already the Lord's; therefore, it would be mockery to devote them again—specially, the firstlings of all clean beasts. The firstlings of unclean beasts, however, were so far in a different position—they were the Lord's, but yet they could not be offered on his altar. Hence, they might be vowed away, but on the understanding that they were to be redeemed. Since they were not to be offered up as sacrifices, they were redeemed at their birth; and now again being vowed away to the Lord, they are again redeemed; a price is given for them. But a *fifth* is added thereto, to shew that there was something of the nature of a trespass in the man fixing upon that unclean firstling. It was like attempting to make the double use of one thing. We must not so do with God. True love and gratitude will always pour out new streams and full streams.

On the other hand, *"a thing devoted,"* that is, a thing that was more than vowed and set apart, a thing that was חֵרֶם, doomed—devoted to destruction—must in no case be redeemed. The beast, at Sinai, that touched the mountain would be חֵרֶם, doomed. The fields of Gilboa, wet with the blood of Saul and Jonathan, were devoted, or doomed, by David (2 Sam. i. 21). Ahab was told by the Lord that Benhadad was doomed.* Such were the Canaanites, also; such was Jericho in special (Jos. vi. 17), with all its spoil, and hence the awful aggravation of Achan's sin. He was attempting to appropriate what the Lord had demanded for the flames of his wrath; he sought to pull out of the fire the things which God had put on that fire to be fuel to its flame. Hence, also, Saul's sin as to Agag, whom the Lord doomed to utter ruin;† he sought to pull Agag from hell, or at least from under the sword of Divine justice that was drawn against the man here.

In all cases of this kind, it is *the Lord* who devotes,‡ not man. The case of Samuel's mother, and of Jephtha's—the one devoting a son, the other a daughter—

---

* אִישׁ חֶרְמִי (1 Kings xx. 42).

† 1 Sam. xv. 3, the word וְהַחֲרַמְתֶּם.

‡ It is quite a mistake to render ver. 29, "devoted BY men;" it is "from among men" לְן הָאָדָם. The Septuagint has it rightly: "ἀπὸ τῶν ἀνθρώπων," not "ὑπο." It is like Rev. xiv. 4, "redeemed *from among* men;" of course *by* the Lord.

are not at all of the kind meant here. This concluding instance is most solemn—the Lord exercising his sovereignty in fixing upon whom he will and what he will, out of a fallen and already cursed earth, to bear the stroke of wrath in sight of all men. The case of the *fields of Gilboa* is not against this view, as if it were an instance of curse inflicted by man instead of by the Lord; for David spoke by the Spirit of the Lord.

How awful the truth contained!. "What will you do in the day of visitation? To whom will ye flee for help?" O Agag! it is too late to speak of mercy; the Lord has pronounced thy doom. There is no reversion —no redemption—no alteration—no change—no possibility of paying a commutation-price now. You are devoted! All is over for ever. *"None doomed shall be redeemed!"* You provoked the Lord to anger, and this is your latter end. See Matt. xvi. 26, "What shall a man give in exchange for his soul?"

> Ver. 30–33. *And all the tithe of the land, whether of the seed* of the land, or of the fruit of the tree, is the Lord's: it is holy unto the Lord. And if a man will at all redeem ought of his tithes, he shall add thereto the fifth part thereof. And concerning the tithe of the herd, or of the flock, even of whatsoever passeth under the rod, the tenth shall be holy unto the Lord. He shall not search whether it be good or bad, neither shall he change it: and if he change it at all, then both it and the change thereof shall be holy; it shall not be redeemed.*

What Abraham gave to Melchisedec, and Jacob vowed at Bethel, has ever appeared most natural for men to set aside for the Lord regularly—*the tenth of all.* Among the Israelites, there were several kinds of tithe, and yet all were cheerfully paid; the tenth for the Lord, paid to the

---

* Such as corn—whatever is used in the shape of seed; unlike the juicy pomegranate, and fig, and grape.

Levites (Num. xviii. 21), and the next tenth, consecrated and feasted on at Jerusalem, or given away to the poor (Deut. xii. 6, and xxviii. 29).

Seed or *fruit* might be redeemed; and there might be good reasons for a man wishing to redeem this part of the tithe. He might require corn to sow his field, or be in need of the seed of dates or pomegranates to replenish his orchard ; therefore, permission is given to redeem these, though still with the addition of a fifth, in order to shew that the Lord is jealous, and marks anything that might be a retraction, on the man's part, of what was due to the Lord. He may redeem this tithe, but it is done *cum notâ*. As to the tithe of herd and flock, this is not allowed. The owner, or the Levite whose office it was to tithe, held a rod in his hand and touched every tenth animal as it happened to come forward (Jer. xxxiii. 13). Whatever passed under the rod, good or bad, was tithed and taken, inalienably. The Lord does not seek a good animal, where the rod, in numbering, lighted on a bad, as the tenth passed by ; neither does he admit of the substitution of an inferior animal, if the rod has lighted on the best in the whole flock. He seeks just what is his due, teaching us strict and holy disregard of bye-ends and selfish interests.

And thus this book—this Pictorial Gospel of the Old Testament—ends with stating God's claims on us, and his expectation of our service and willing devotedness. As the first believers at Pentecost, rejoicing in pardon and the love of God, counted nothing dear to them, nor said that aught they possessed was their own, so ought we to live. We must sit loose from earth; and true love to our Redeemer will set us loose. This giving up of our possessions, at God's call, teaches us to live a pilgrim

life, and that is an Abrahamic life—nay, it is the life of
faith, in opposition to sight.

The whole of this concluding chapter has been leading
us to the idea of giving to the Lord all we have. It has
been making us familiar with the idea, and by example
inculcating the practice of unreserved devotedness. God
should be all in all to us; he is אֵל־שַׁדַּי, "God all-
sufficient." Let us part even with common, lawful
comforts, and try if He alone be not better than all.
Like the child with the stalk of grapes, who picked one
grape after another from the cluster, and held it out to
her father, till, as affection waxed warm and self faded,
she gaily flung the whole into her father's bosom, and
smiled in his face with triumphant delight; so let us do,
until, loosened from every comfort, and independent of
the help of broken cisterns, we can say, "I am not my
own. Whom have I in heaven but thee? and there is
none upon earth whom I desire besides. Thou art to
me, as thou wert to David at the gates of death—'all
my salvation and all my desire.'" After so much love
on God's part to us, displayed in rich variety of type
and shadow, shall we count any sacrifice hard? Could
not even a heathen say of his ideal virtue—

> "Serpens, sitis, ardor, arenæ,
> Dulcia virtuti."—(Lucan, B. ix.)

Ver. 34. *These are the commandments, which the Lord commanded
Moses, for the children of Israel in mount Sinai.*

At or near Sinai. The sultry heat of that day when
the fiery law was given prepared the people to welcome
these showers of grace that soon after fell. Lord, make
us enjoy these showers, even if there be need of such a
day of heat and fear ere it come. Let every drop from
these blessed clouds wet the soil of our hearts. Thou

who art known in Israel as the giver of plenteous
showers to refresh thy weary heritage, cause these that
fell around Sinai, as we have seen in all this book—these
that shewed so much of the variety of thy love—these
that brought such tidings of thy Son—oh, cause these to
water our weary, parched souls, until we see Him who
is "Rivers of Water."

Thus have we come to the close of our pleasant undertaking. We have traversed the tabernacle courts, inquiring into *"its meats and drinks, and divers washings
and carnal ordinances, imposed on them until the time of
reformation"* (Heb. ix. 10). Had we looked on them
apart from what they signified, we must have grown
weary ere we had well begun. But searching into their
meaning,* we have found that these *"carnal ordinances,"*
i. e. these ceremonies that consisted in the use of earthly
and material things, are all fragrant with gospel truth.
And we plainly see why the Lord should have *"imposed
them,"* *i. e.* enjoined them, and made it incumbent on
Israel to observe them. He saw in each of them some
picture or foreshadowing of the coming Redeemer. The
"time of reformation" has come; *i. e.* the time when a
better mode of teaching the same truth has been brought
in, types being now displaced by the antitypes, shadows
by the substance. But while this "reformation," or
better mode of teaching truth, has come, we still look
back and study, with profit and delight, the symbols of
the old economy that pictured forth the coming of
"better things." I still retain a vivid remembrance of

---

* Not, however, altogether as Jerome would have had us do, when he says,
" *Leviticus liber*, a quo singula sacrificia, immo singulæ pæne syllabæ, et vestes
Aaron, et totus ordo Leviticus, spirant cælestia sacramenta.—*Epist. ad Paul-
inum.*

the impression made on me many years ago, in the
divinity class of Dr Chalmers, when that remarkable man
of God referred to this subject.   He was remarking how,
oftentimes, Christians advancing in years feel a growing
relish for the types, and prophecies, and sketches of
character, and pieces of picturesque history in which the
Old Testament abounds.   They see them pervaded with
New Testament principle and truth.   "There is," he
said, "in this employment, somewhat even of the charm
and delight of poetry.   It is a regaling, as well as satisfactory exercise.   Very pleasant as were the songs of
Zion to good Bishop Horne, as every morning roused him
to his task, and the silence of evening invited him to
pursue it; very pleasant to many a humble Christian are
the things which God hath spoken at sundry times, and
in divers manners, to the fathers by the prophets.   It is
as if the delights of imagination were superadded to the
delights of piety, when the doctrines of the New are
expressed in the drapery of the Old economy.   And if
there be any aged Christian who has leisure to pursue
the employment, we promise him not a different, but the
same gospel, seen through a veil of ever-brightening
transparency, and heightened by time and youthful
remembrances.   Thus the decaying lights of age have
often been revived again; and, in the solace of the
perusal, such men have experienced that these things ·
were written not alone for the generations that then
lived, but for our admonition, on whom the ends of the
world have come."

INDEX OF PRINCIPAL SUBJECTS

TEXTS OF SCRIPTURE

QUOTED AND REFERRED TO